Masteri … ng

Microsoft® Word 2002 Introductory Course

The Future Is Now…

Our Napier & Judd series, *Mastering and Using Microsoft Word 2002 Introductory Course*, is the most comprehensive, instructional tool designed for the user who wants to master and use the application software. This expertly written product provides all the instruction necessary to become certified as a Microsoft Office User Specialist (MOUS) Core user of Word.

Mastering and Using Microsoft Word 2002 Introductory Course
- **Student Text** — **0-619-05817-X**
- **IRK (Instructor's Resource Kit)** — **0-619-05807-2**
- **Review Pack** — **0-619-05806-4**

The Instructor's Resource Kit (CD-ROM) includes lesson plans, SCANS correlations, scheduling charts, PowerPoint presentations, and much more!

Mastering and Using Microsoft Access 2002 Introductory Course
- **Student Text** — **0-619-05811-0**
- **IRK (Instructor's Resource Kit)** — **0-619-05807-2**
- **Review Pack** — **0-619-05806-4**

Mastering and Using Microsoft Excel 2002 Introductory Course
- **Student Text** — **0-619-05829-3**
- **IRK (Instructor's Resource Kit)** — **0-619-05807-2**
- **Review Pack** — **0-619-05806-4**

Mastering and Using Microsoft PowerPoint 2002 Introductory Course
- **Student Text** — **0-619-05823-4**
- **IRK (Instructor's Resource Kit)** — **0-619-05807-2**
- **Review Pack** — **0-619-05806-4**

Mastering and Using Microsoft Office XP Introductory Course
- **Student Text** — **0-619-05805-6**
- **IRK (Instructor's Resource Kit)** — **0-619-05807-2**
- **Activities Workbook (softcover, perfect bound)** — **0-619-05877-3**
- **Review Pack** — **0-619-05806-4**

COURSE TECHNOLOGY™
THOMSON LEARNING

For more information about these Course Technology products and others:
Join us On the Internet at www.course.com/masteringandusing

What's New in Word 2002

Office XP

- Streamlined, flatter look
- Multiple task panes containing command shortcuts
- Ask A Question Box Help tool
- Smart Tags
- AutoCorrect Options
- Revised Office Clipboard
- Paste Options
- Route documents for review with tracked changes via e-mail
- Speech Recognition
- Improved "crash" recovery features
- New Search task pane
- Digital signatures for documents routed over the Internet

Word 2002

- Multiple text selection using the CTRL key
- New task panes to review and apply formatting
- New task panes to apply and create styles
- Select similarly formatted text with shortcut menu
- Revised Mail Merge Wizard
- New table styles
- Revised Track Changes and Compare Documents features
- New drawing tools to create conceptual diagrams
- Native Organization Chart drawing tool
- Revised watermark creation
- New Clear Formatting feature

MICROSOFT®

Word 2002

Introductory Course

Mastering and Using

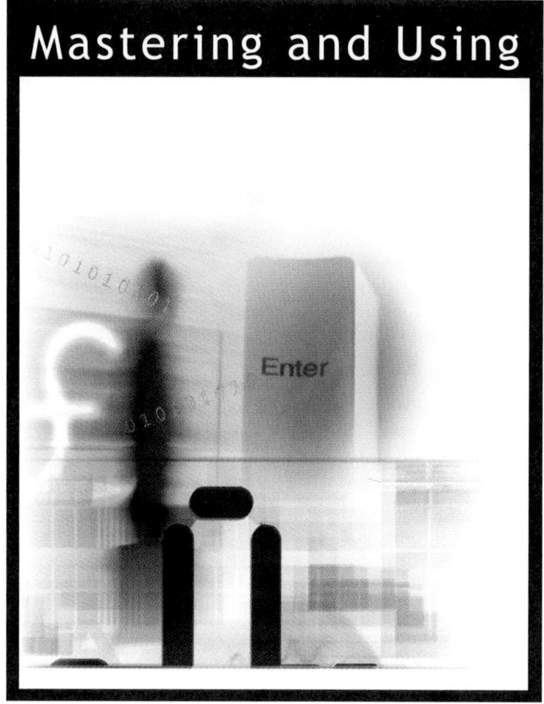

H. Albert Napier

Philip J. Judd

Australia • Canada • Mexico • Singapore • Spain • United Kingdom • United States

Mastering and Using Microsoft® Word 2002 Introductory Course

by H. Albert Napier, Ph.D. & Philip J. Judd

Managing Editor:
Melissa Ramondetta

Development Editor:
Robin M. Romer, Pale Moon Productions

Product Marketing Manager:
Kim Wood

Product Manager:
Robert Gaggin

Editorial Assistant:
Jodi Dreissig

Production Services:
GEX Publishing Services

Copy Editor:
GEX Publishing Services

Cover Design:
Steve Deschene

Compositor:
GEX Publishing Services

Printed in the United States of America

2 3 4 5 6 7 8 9 BM 04 03 02

For more information, contact Course Technology, 25 Thomson Place, Boston, Massachusetts 02210.

Or find us on the World Wide Web at: www.course.com

ISBN 0-619-05817-X

Napier & Judd

In their over 50 years of combined experience, Al Napier and Phil Judd have developed a tested, realistic approach to mastering and using application software. As both academics and corporate trainers, Al and Phil have the unique ability to help students by teaching them the skills necessary to compete in today's complex business world.

H. Albert Napier, Ph.D. is the Director of the Center on the Management of Information Technology and Professor in the Jesse H. Jones Graduate School of Management at Rice University. In addition, Al is a principal of Napier & Judd, Inc., a consulting company and corporate trainer in Houston, Texas, that has trained more than 120,000 people in computer applications.

Philip J. Judd is a former instructor in the Management Department and the Director of the Research and Instructional Computing Service at the University of Houston. Phil now dedicates himself to consulting and corporate training as a principal of Napier & Judd, Inc.

Philip J. Judd

H. Albert Napier, Ph.D.

Preface

At Course Technology, we believe that technology will change the way people teach and learn. Today millions of people are using personal computers in their everyday lives—both as tools at work and for recreational activities. As a result, the personal computer has revolutionized the ways in which people interact with each other. The *Mastering and Using* series combines the following distinguishing features to allow people to do amazing things with their personal computers.

Distinguishing Features

All the textbooks in the Mastering and Using series share several key pedagogical features:

Case Project Approach. In their more than 20 years of business and corporate training and teaching experience, Napier & Judd have found that students are more enthusiastic about learning a software application if they can see its real-world relevance. The textbook provides bountiful business-based profiles, exercises, and projects. It also emphasizes the skills most in demand by employers.

Comprehensive and Easy to Use. There is thorough coverage of new features. The narrative is clear and concise. Each unit or chapter thoroughly instructs on the concepts that underlie the skills and procedures. The text explains not just the *how*, but the *why*.

Step-by-Step Instructions and Screen Illustrations. All examples in this text include step-by-step instructions that explain how to complete the specific task. Full-color screen illustrations are used extensively to provide students with a realistic picture of the software application feature.

Extensive Tips and Tricks. The authors have placed informational boxes in the margin of the text. These boxes of information provide students with the following helpful tips:

- *Quick Tip*. Extra information provides shortcuts on how to perform common business-related functions.
- *Caution Tip*. This additional information explains how a mistake occurs and provides tips on how to avoid making similar mistakes in the future.
- *Menu Tip*. Additional explanation on how to use menu commands to perform application tasks.
- *Mouse Tip*. Further instructions on how to use the mouse to perform application tasks.
- *Task Pane Tip*. Additional information on using task pane shortcuts.
- *Internet Tip*. This information incorporates the power of the Internet to help students use the Internet as they progress through the text.
- *Design Tip*. Hints for better presentation designs (found in the PowerPoint chapters).

End-of-Chapter Materials. Each book in the *Mastering and Using* series places a heavy emphasis on providing students with the opportunity to practice and reinforce the skills they are learning through extensive exercises. Each chapter has a summary, commands review, concepts review, skills review, and case projects so that the student can master the material by doing. For more information on each of the end-of-chapter elements, see page ix of the How to Use This Book section in this preface.

Appendices. *Mastering and Using* series contains three appendices to further help students prepare to be successful in the classroom or in the workplace. Appendix A teaches students to work with Windows 2000. Appendix B illustrates how to format letters; how to insert a mailing notation; how to format envelopes (referencing the U.S. Postal Service documents); how to format interoffice memorandums; and how to key a formal outline. It also lists popular style guides and describes proofreader's marks. Appendix C describes the new Office XP speech recognition features.

Microsoft Office User Specialist (MOUS) Certification.

What does this logo mean? It means this courseware has been approved by the Microsoft® Office User Specialist Program to be among the finest available for learning Microsoft

Office XP, Microsoft Word 2002, Microsoft Excel 2002, Microsoft PowerPoint® 2002, and Microsoft Access 2002. It also means that upon completion of this courseware, you may be prepared to become a Microsoft Office User Specialist.

What is a Microsoft Office User Specialist? A Microsoft Office User Specialist is an individual who has certified his or her skills in one or more of the Microsoft Office desktop applications of Microsoft Word, Microsoft Excel, Microsoft PowerPoint®, Microsoft Outlook® or Microsoft Access, or in Microsoft Project. The Microsoft Office User Specialist Program typically offers certification exams at the "Core" and "Expert" skill levels. The Microsoft Office User Specialist Program is the only Microsoft approved program in the world for certifying proficiency in Microsoft Office desktop applications and Microsoft Project. This certification can be a valuable asset in any job search or career advancement.

More Information: To learn more about becoming a Microsoft Office User Specialist, visit *www.mous.net*. To purchase a Microsoft Office User Specialist certification exam, visit *www.DesktopIQ.com*.

SCANS. In 1992, the U.S. Department of Labor and Education formed the Secretary's Commission on Achieving Necessary Skills, or SCANS, to study the kinds of competencies and skills that workers must have to succeed in today's marketplace. The results of the study were published in a document entitled *What Work Requires of Schools: A SCANS Report for America 2000.* The in-chapter and end-of-chapter exercises in this book are designed to meet the criteria outlined in the SCANS report and thus help prepare students to be successful in today's workplace.

Instructional Support

All books in the *Mastering and Using* series are supplemented with an ***Instructor's Resource Kit.*** This is a CD-ROM that contains lesson plans with teaching materials and preparation suggestions, along with tips for implementing instruction and assessment ideas; a suggested syllabus; and SCANS workplace know how. The CD also contains:

- Career Worksheets
- Evaluation Guidelines
- Hands-on Solutions
- Individual Learning Strategies
- Internet Behavior Contract
- Lesson Plans
- Portfolio Guidelines
- PowerPoint Presentations
- Solution Files
- Student Data Files
- Teacher Training Notes
- Test Questions
- Transparency Graphics Files

ExamView® This textbook is accompanied by ExamView, a powerful testing software package that allows instructors to create and administer printed, computer (LAN-based), and Internet exams. ExamView includes hundreds of questions that correspond to the topics covered in this text, enabling students to generate detailed study guides that include page references for further review. The computer-based and Internet testing components allow students to take exams at their computers, and also save the instructor time by grading each exam automatically.

MyCourse.com. MyCourse.com is an online syllabus builder and course-enhancement tool. Hosted by Course Technology, MyCourse.com is designed to reinforce what you already are teaching. It also adds value to your course by providing content that corresponds with your text. MyCourse.com is flexible: choose how you want to organize the material, by date or by class session; or don't do anything at all, and the material is automatically organized by chapter. Add your own materials, including hyperlinks, assignments, announcements, and course content. If you're using more than one textbook, you can even build a course that includes all your Course Technology texts—in one easy-to-use site! Start building your own course today...just go to *www.mycourse.com/instructor*.

Student Support

Data Disk. To use this book, students must have the Data Disk. Data Files needed to complete exercises in the text are contained on the Review Pack CD-ROM. These files can be copied to a hard drive or posted to a network drive.

*The availability of Microsoft Office User Specialist certification exams varies by application, application version and language. Visit *www.mous.net* for exam availability.

How to Use This Book

Word 2002

Quick Start for Word

Chapter Overview

This chapter gives you a quick overview of creating, editing, printing, saving, and closing a document. To learn these skills, you create a new document, save and close it, then you open an existing document, revise the text, and save the document with both the same and a different name. This chapter also shows you how to view formatting marks and Smart Tags, zoom the document window, and move the insertion point. In addition, you learn to identify the components of the Word window and create a folder on your hard drive to store your documents. You use these basic skills every time you create or edit a document in Word.

LEARNING OBJECTIVES

- Identify the components of the Word window
- Compose a simple document
- Edit a document
- Save a document
- Preview and print a document
- Close a document
- Locate and open an existing document
- Create a new document
- Close the Word application

Case profile

Today is your first day as a new employee at Worldwide Exotic Foods, Inc., one of the world's fastest growing distributors of specialty food items. The company's mission is to provide customers with an unusual selection of meats, cheeses, pastries, fruits, and vegetables from around the world. You report to Chris Lofton, the Word Processing Department manager, to complete an introduction to the Word 2002 word processing application.

chapter one

Learning Objectives — A quick reference of the major topics learned in the chapter

Case profile — Realistic scenarios that show the real-world application of the material being covered

Chapter Overview — A concise summary of what will be learned in the chapter

Clear step-by-step directions explain how to complete the specific task

Caution Tip — This additional information explains how a mistake occurs and provides tips on how to avoid making similar mistakes in the future

Task Pane Tip — Additional information about using task pane shortcuts

Quick Tip — Extra information provides shortcuts on how to perform common business-related functions

Internet Tip — Information to help students incorporate the power of the Internet as they progress through the text

Mouse Tip — Further instructions on how to use the mouse to perform application tasks

Design Tip — Hints for better presentation designs (found in only the PowerPoint chapters)

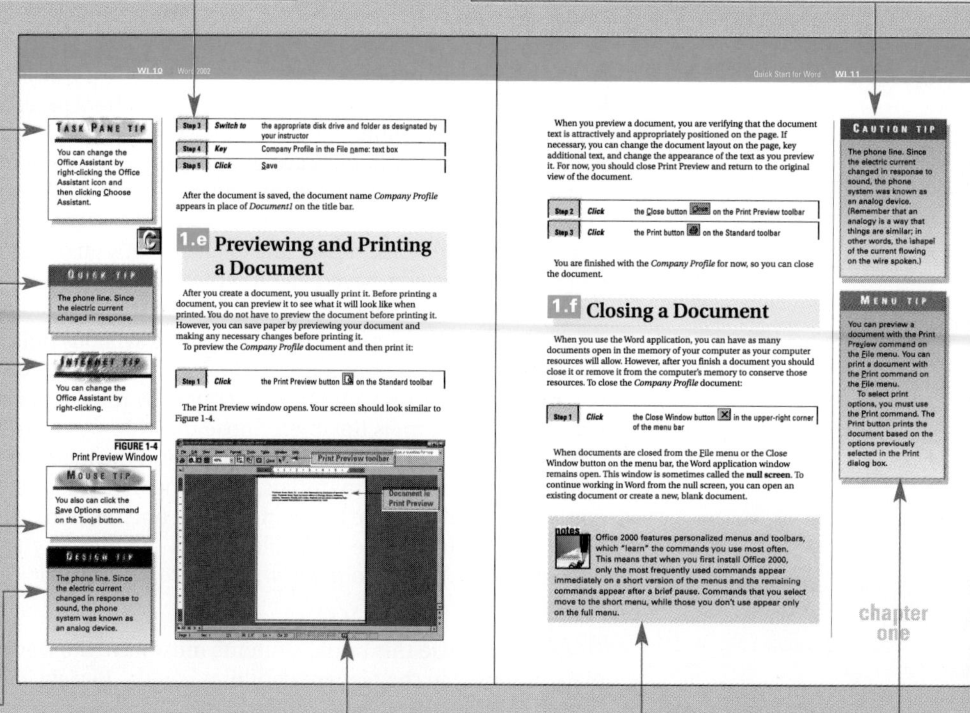

WI 10 Word 2002

TASK PANE TIP

You can change the Office Assistant by right-clicking the Office Assistant icon and then clicking Choose Assistant.

Step 3	Switch to	the appropriate disk drive and folder as designated by your instructor
Step 4	Key	Company Profile in the File name: text box
Step 5	Click	Save

After the document is saved, the document name *Company Profile* appears in place of *Document1* on the title bar.

1.e Previewing and Printing a Document

After you create a document, you usually print it. Before printing a document, you can preview it to see what it will look like when printed. You do not have to preview the document before printing it. However, you can save paper by previewing your document and making any necessary changes before printing it.

To preview the *Company Profile* document and then print it:

Step 1	Click	the Print Preview button on the Standard toolbar

The Print Preview window opens. Your screen should look similar to Figure 1-4.

QUICK TIP

The phone line. Since the electric current changed in response.

INTERNET TIP

You can change the Office Assistant by right-clicking.

FIGURE 1-4 Print Preview Window

MOUSE TIP

You also can click the Save Options command on the Tools button.

DESIGN TIP

The phone line. Since the electric current changed in response to sound, the phone system was known as an analog device.

Quick Start for Word WI 11

When you preview a document, you are verifying that the document text is attractively and appropriately positioned on the page. If necessary, you can change the document layout on the page, key additional text, and change the appearance of the text as you preview it. For now, you should close Print Preview and return to the original view of the document.

Step 2	Click	the Close button on the Print Preview toolbar
Step 3	Click	the Print button on the Standard toolbar

You are finished with the *Company Profile* for now, so you can close the document.

1.f Closing a Document

When you use the Word application, you can have as many documents open in the memory of your computer as your computer resources will allow. However, after you finish a document you should close it or remove it from the computer's memory to conserve those resources. To close the *Company Profile* document:

Step 1	Click	the Close Window button in the upper-right corner of the menu bar

When documents are closed from the File menu or the Close Window button on the menu bar, the Word application window remains open. This window is sometimes called the **null screen**. To continue working in Word from the null screen, you can open an existing document or create a new, blank document.

notes

Office 2000 features personalized menus and toolbars, which "learn" the commands you use most often. This means that when you first install Office 2000, only the most frequently used commands appear immediately on a short version of the menus and the remaining commands appear after a brief pause. Commands that you select move to the short menu, while those you don't use appear only on the full menu.

CAUTION TIP

The phone line. Since the electric current changed in response to sound, the phone system was known as an analog device. (Remember that an analogy is a way that things are similar; in other words, the ishapel of the current flowing on the wire spoken.)

MENU TIP

You can preview a document with the Print Preview command on the File menu. You can print a document with the Print command on the File menu.

To select print options, you must use the Print command. The Print button prints the document based on the options previously selected in the Print dialog box.

chapter one

Full-color screen illustrations provide a realistic picture to the student

Notes — These boxes provide necessary information to assist you in completing the activities

Menu Tip — Additional explanation on how to use menu commands to perform application tasks

End-of-Chapter Material

Concepts Review — Multiple choice and true or false questions help assess how well the student has learned the chapter material

Summary

- The block format is commonly used for business correspondence.
- Word has preset top, bottom, left, and right margins that you can change in the Page Setup dialog box.
- The date and time can be inserted in a document as text or as a field that automatically updates to the current system date when the document is printed.
- You can select characters, words, or groups of words with the mouse or keyboard.
- Selected text can be cut, copied, and pasted using menu commands, a shortcut menu, toolbar buttons, and the Office Clipboard task pane.
- You can collect up to 24 cut or copied selections and then paste them individually or all at one time using the Office Clipboard task pane.
- You can repeat or undo your last action.
- Word has several ways you can view your document, including: Normal view, Print Layout view, and Full Screen view. Use Normal view to key, edit, and format text. Use Print Layout to view and work with margins, headers and footers, columns, graphics, and drawing objects. Use Full Screen view to see more lines of text on the page.

Summary — Reviews key topics discussed in the chapter

Commands Review

Action	Menu Bar	Shortcut Menu	Toolbar	Task Pane	Keyboard
Set margins	File, Page Setup				ALT + F, U
Insert date	Insert, Date and Time				ALT + I, T
Update a selected date field		Right-click, then click Update Field			ALT + SHIFT + D F9
Cut, Copy, Paste	Edit, Cut or Copy or Paste	Right-click, then click Cut or Copy, or Paste		Click an item or Paste All in the Office Clipboard task pane	ALT + E, T or C or P CTRL + C (copy) CTRL + X (cut) CTRL + V (paste)
Turn on or off Overtype			Double-click the OVR mode indicator		INSERT
Undo or Redo actions	Edit, Undo Edit, Redo				ALT + E, U ALT + E, R CTRL + Z CTRL + Y
Repeat actions	Edit, Repeat				ALT+ E, R CTRL + Y
Cancel an action					ESC
Change editing views	View, Normal, Web Layout, Print Layout, Outline, Full Screen				ALT + V, N or W or P or O or U ALT + CTRL + P ALT + CTRL + O ALT + CTRL + N

Commands Review — Provides a quick reference and reinforcement tool on multiple methods for performing actions discussed in the chapter

Concepts Review

Circle the correct answer.

1. You can remove text by selecting the text and pressing the:
[a] EXT key.
[b] ALT + PAGEUP keys.
[c] CTRL key.
[d] DELETE key.

2. You cannot add a date to a document by:
[a] keying the date manually.
[b] inserting a date field that updates automatically.
[c] inserting the date as text.
[d] pressing the Insert key.

3. The selection bar is:
[a] located below the status bar.
[b] used to open other Office applications.
[c] used to select text in different ways.
[d] used to set left and right margins.

4. When you use the block format for a business letter, the:
[a] date and complimentary closing are centered on their respective lines.
[b] letter address is positioned below the salutation.
[c] letter components all begin at the left margin.
[d] letter components all begin at the right margin.

5. Margins refer to the:
[a] distance from the center of the page to the edge of the page.
[b] distance from the top, bottom, left, and right edges of the page to the text.
[c] number of lines you can have on a page.
[d] size of the text on a page.

6. By default, Word is in the:
[a] Overtype mode.
[b] Edit mode.
[c] Online Review mode.
[d] Insert mode.

7. Which of the following is not a selection technique in Word?
[a] pressing the CTRL + SHIFT + END keys to select from the insertion point to the end of the document
[b] double-clicking the selection bar opposite the paragraph you wish to select
[c] double-clicking a word
[d] pressing the ALT key and clicking a word

8. Using the mouse to move or copy text is called:
[a] cut-and-drag.
[b] select-and-cut.
[c] copy-and-cut.
[d] drag-and-drop.

9. Overtype mode allows you to:
[a] select text.
[b] key over existing text.
[c] move text.
[d] copy text.

10. Which of the following is not an editing view?
[a] Full Page view
[b] Full Screen view
[c] Print Layout view
[d] Normal view

Circle **T** if the statement is true or **F** if the statement is false.

T F 1. When you are in the Overtype mode and enter new text, any character you key replaces the character to the right of the insertion point.
T F 2. Word automatically defaults to the Edit mode.
T F 3. Word can undo multiple actions.
T F 4. The mouse and the keyboard can both be used to select text in a document.

chapter two

Skills Review — Hands-on exercises provide the ability to practice the skills just learned in the chapter

Case Projects — Asks the student to synthesize the material learned in the chapter and complete an office assignment

T F 5. The EXT mode indicator appears bolded when you are using the Extend mode feature.
T F 6. You can restore text that has been deleted.
T F 7. You can maximize the number of lines of text displayed on the screen by switching to Full Screen view.
T F 8. Normal view displays your document much like it looks when printed.
T F 9. You can insert the date and the time together in a Word document.
T F 10. The Office Clipboard is a reserved place in the memory of your computer you can use to temporarily store up to 24 items you have cut or copied.

Skills Review

Exercise 1

1. Create the following document. Use the block style with 2-inch top margin and 1-inch left and right margins. Insert the current date in the format of your choice at the top of the document. As you key the text, use the move-ment techniques and insert/delete actions you learned in this chapter to correct any keying errors you make. You revise the document in the next exercise.

> Current date
>
> Ms. Gail Jackson
> Corporate Travel Manager
> International Travel Services
> 1590 W. Convention Street
> Chicago, IL 60605-1590
>
> Dear Ms. Jackson:
>
> Thank you for helping plan business trip to London this winter. I am really looking forward to seeing the sites, as well as taking care of some business. This is my first trip to London, and you were quite courteous in answering my questions.
>
> Yours truly,
>
> Kelly Armstead
> Executive Assistant to B. D. Vickers
>
> ks

2. Save the document as *Travel Letter*. Preview, print, and close the document.

Case Projects

Project 1

B. D. Vickers is traveling on business to Melbourne, Australia in three weeks. Prepare a letter to Mr. David Melville, Reservations Manager at the Excelsior Hotel, 3500 Wayburne Drive, Melbourne, VIC, 30001, Australia, requesting accommodations for a week beginning three weeks from today. Insert the date as text using the Day, Month (in text), Year format. Save, preview, and print the document.

Project 2

Open the document you created in Project 1 and change the accommodation dates to four weeks from today using the Overtype mode. Save the document with a new name, then preview and print it.

Project 3

Kelly Armstead has asked you to find a list of key-board shortcuts you both can use to prepare correspondence. Using the Ask A Question Box, search online Help for a list of keyboard shortcut keys for moving the insertion point in a document and selecting text in a document. Print the lists. With your instructor's permission, use the lists to demon-strate the keyboard shortcuts to a classmate.

Project 4

B. D. Vickers is considering ordering several IntelliMouse pointing devices for the Purchasing Department and has asked you to find out how the devices are used to increase productivity in the department. Using the Help menu resources, including Web resources, search for information on the IntelliMouse pointing device. Create a new document containing at least three paragraphs describing how the Purchasing Department employees can improve their productivity by using the IntelliMouse pointing device. Insert the current date as text using the mm/dd/yy format. Save, preview, and print the document.

Project 5

There have been several power failures because of storms in the area and Kelly is concerned that she may lose documents she is working on if the power fails. She has asked you to find out what options Word has to automatically back up documents as she is working and to automatically recover documents lost during a power failure. Using the Help menu, research what backup and document recovery features Word provides. Create a new document containing at least four paragraphs describing how to set backup procedures and recover lost or damaged documents. Insert the date as a field using the format of your choice. Save, preview, and print the document.

Project 6

B. D. Vickers has extended the business trip discussed in Project 1 and now plans to spend two days in Hong Kong and three days in London before returning. Kelly needs a list of possible accommo-dations in Hong Kong and London and has asked you to search the Web for information on hotels in these cities. She also needs you to review flight schedules and suggest flights from Melbourne to Hong Kong, from Hong Kong to London, and from London to Chicago. Connect to the Internet and search the Web for the information you need. Save at least two URLs as "favorites." Print at least five Web pages. Create a new, blank document and key the title and URL of the pages you printed. Insert the date as text in the format of your choice. Save, preview, and print the document.

chapter two

SCANS icon — Indicates that the exercise or project meets SCANS competencies and prepares the student to be successful in today's workplace

MOUS Certification icon — Indicates that the exercise or project meets Microsoft's certification objectives that prepare the student for the MOUS exam

Internet Case Projects — Allow the student to practice using the World Wide Web

Acknowledgments

We would like to thank and express our appreciation to the many fine individuals who have contributed to the completion of this book.

No book is possible without the motivation and support of an editorial staff. Therefore, we wish to acknowledge with great appreciation the project team at Course Technology: Melissa Ramondetta, managing editor; Robert Gaggin, product manager; and Jodi Dreissig, editorial assistant. Our appreciation also goes to Robin Romer for managing the developmental editing of this series. In addition, we want to acknowledge the team at GEX for their production work, especially Karla Russell, Kendra Neville, Michelle Olson, and Angel Lesiczka.

We are very appreciative of the personnel at Napier & Judd, Inc., who helped to prepare this book. We acknowledge, with great appreciation, the assistance provided by Ollie Rivers and Nancy Onarheim in preparing and checking the many drafts of the Office unit, the Word unit, and the appendices of this book and the Instructor's Manual.

Contents

WORD UNIT — WI 1

Microsoft Office XP

Getting Started with Microsoft Office XP

Chapter Overview

Microsoft Office XP provides the ability to enter, record, analyze, display, and present any type of business information. In this chapter, you learn about the capabilities of Microsoft Office XP, including its computer hardware and operating system requirements and elements common to all its applications. You also learn how to open and close those applications and get Help.

LEARNING OBJECTIVES

- Describe Microsoft Office XP
- Determine hardware and operating system requirements
- Identify common elements of Office applications
- Start Office applications
- Get Help in Office applications
- Close Office applications

chapter one

This book assumes that you have little or no knowledge of Microsoft Office XP but that you have worked with personal computers and are familiar with Microsoft Windows 2000 or Windows 98 operating systems.

1.a What Is Microsoft Office XP?

Microsoft Office XP is a software suite (or package) that contains a combination of software applications you use to create text documents, analyze numbers, create presentations, manage large files of data, and create Web pages.

The **Word 2002** software application provides you with word processing capabilities. **Word processing** is the preparation and production of text documents such as letters, memorandums, and reports. **Excel 2002** is software you use to analyze numbers with worksheets (sometimes called spreadsheets) and charts and to perform other tasks such as sorting data. A **worksheet** is a grid of columns and rows in which you enter labels and data. A **chart** is a visual or graphical representation of worksheet data. With Excel, you can create financial budgets, reports, and a variety of other forms.

PowerPoint 2002 software is used to create a **presentation**, or collection of slides. A **slide** is the presentation output (actual 35mm slides, transparencies, computer screens, or printed pages) that can contain text, charts, graphics, audio, and video. You can use PowerPoint slides to create a slide show on a computer attached to a projector, to broadcast a presentation over the Internet or company intranet, and to create handout materials for a presentation.

Access 2002 provides database management capabilities, enabling you to store and retrieve a large amount of data. A **database** is a collection of related information. A phone book and an address book are common examples of databases you use every day. Other examples of databases include a price list, school registration information, or an inventory. You can query (or search) an Access database to answer specific questions about the stored data. For example, you can determine which customers in a particular state had sales in excess of a particular value during the month of June.

Outlook 2002 is a **personal information manager** that provides tools for sending and receiving e-mail as well as maintaining a calendar, contacts list, journal, electronic notes, and electronic "to do" list. The **FrontPage 2002** application is used to create and manage Web sites.

QUICK TIP

Office contains a variety of new features designed to minimize the impact of system crashes and freezes, such as one-click save in case of a system crash, timed recoveries, a new document recovery task pane, the Hang Manager, and a new corrupt document recovery feature.

notes

For the remainder of this book, Microsoft Office XP may be called Office. Rather than include the words *Microsoft* and *2002* each time the name of an application is used, the text refers to the respective software package as Word, Excel, PowerPoint, Access, or Outlook.

A major advantage of using the Office suite is the ability to share data between the applications. For example, you can include a portion of an Excel worksheet or chart in a Word document, use an outline created in a Word document as the starting point for a PowerPoint presentation, import an Excel worksheet into Access, and merge names and addresses from an Outlook Address Book with a Word letter.

1.b Hardware and Operating System Requirements

You can install Office applications on computers using the Windows 2000, Windows 98, or Windows NT Workstation 4.0 (with Service Pack 6a installed) operating systems. Office XP applications do not run in the Windows 95, Windows 3.x or the Windows NT Workstation 3.5 environments.

You can install Office on a "x86" computer with a Pentium processor, at least 32 MB of RAM for Windows 98 or 64 MB of RAM for Windows 2000, a CD-ROM drive, Super VGA, 256-color video, Microsoft Mouse, Microsoft IntelliMouse, or another pointing device, a 28,800 (or higher) baud modem, and 350 MB of hard disk space. To access certain features you should have a multimedia computer, e-mail software, and a Web browser. For detailed information on installing Office, see the documentation that comes with the software.

QUICK TIP

Speech recognition features enable users to speak the names of toolbar buttons, menus, menu items, alerts, dialog box control buttons, and task pane items. Users can switch between two modes—Dictation and Voice command—using the Language bar. For more information on using the Speech Recognition features, see Appendix C.

1.c Common Elements of Office Applications

Office applications share many technical features that make it easier for Information Technology (IT) Departments in organizations to manage their Office software installations. Additionally, the Office applications share many features that enable users to move seamlessly between applications and learn one way to perform common tasks, such as creating, saving, and printing documents or moving and copying data.

Office applications share many common elements, making it easier for you to work efficiently in any application. A **window** is a rectangular area on your screen in which you view a software application, such as Excel. All the Office application windows have a similar look and arrangement of shortcuts, menus, and toolbars. In addition, they share many features—such as a common dictionary to check spelling in your work, identical menu commands, toolbar buttons, shortcut menus, and keyboard shortcuts to perform tasks such as copying data from one location to another.

notes You learn more about the common elements of the Office applications in later chapters of this unit or in specific application units.

Figure 1-1 shows many of the common elements in the Office application windows.

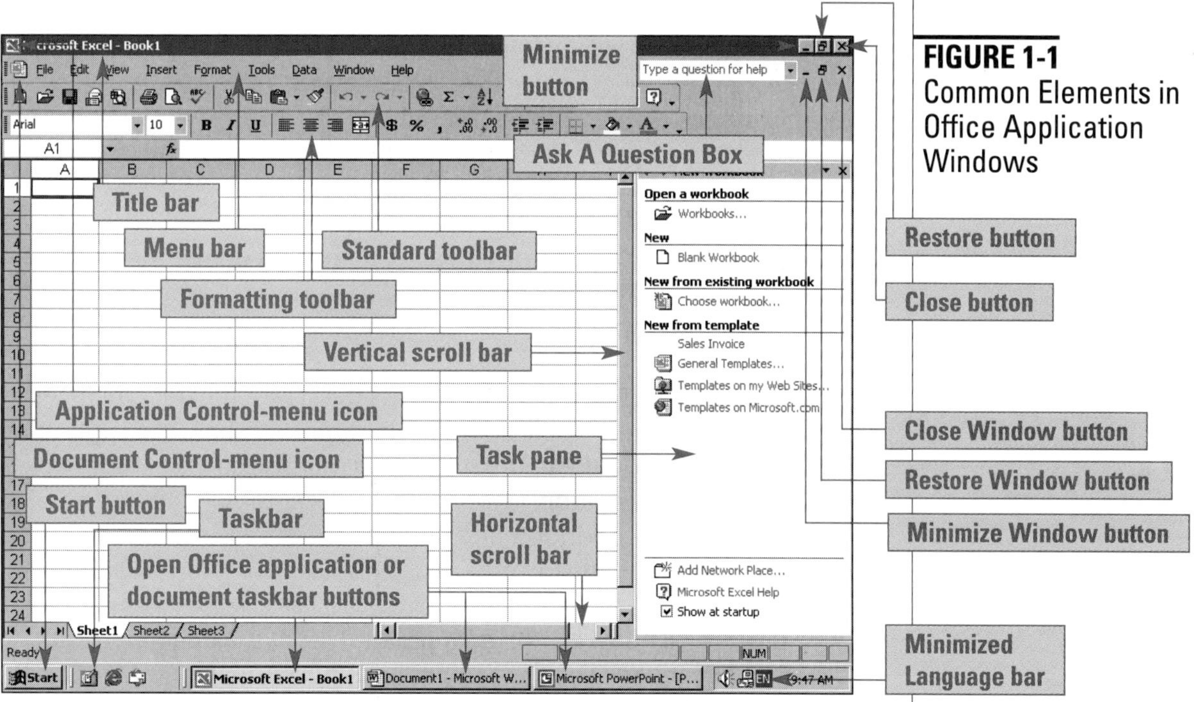

FIGURE 1-1
Common Elements in Office Application Windows

Title Bar

The application **title bar** at the top of the window includes the application Control-menu icon, the application name, the filename of the active document, and the Minimize, Restore (or Maximize), and Close buttons.

The **application Control-menu** icon, located in the upper-left corner of the title bar, displays the Control menu. The Control menu commands manage the application window, and typically include commands such as Restore, Move, Size, Minimize, Maximize, and Close. Commands that are currently available appear in a dark color. You can view the Control menu by clicking the Control-menu icon or by holding down the ALT key and then pressing the SPACEBAR key.

The **Minimize** button, near the right corner of the title bar reduces the application window to a taskbar button. The **Maximize** button, to the right of the Minimize button, enlarges the application window to fill the entire screen viewing area above the taskbar. If the window is already maximized, the Restore button appears in its place. The **Restore** button reduces the application window to a smaller size on your screen. The **Close** button, located in the right corner of the title bar, closes the application and removes it from the computer's memory.

Menu Bar

The **menu bar** is a special toolbar located at the top of the window below the title bar and contains the menus for the application. A **menu** is list of commands. The menus common to Office applications are File, Edit, View, Insert, Format, Tools, Window, and Help. Other menus vary between applications.

The **document Control-menu** icon, located below the application Control-menu icon, contains the Restore, Move, Size, Minimize, Maximize, and Close menu commands for the document window. You can view the document Control menu by clicking the Control-menu icon or by holding down the ALT key and pressing the HYPHEN (-) key.

The **Minimize Window** button reduces the document window to a title-bar icon inside the document area. It appears on the menu bar below the Minimize button in Excel and PowerPoint. (Word documents open in their own application window and use the Minimize button on the title bar.)

The **Maximize Window** button enlarges the size of the document window to cover the entire application display area and share the application title bar. It appears on the title-bar icon of a minimized Excel workbook or PowerPoint presentation. (Word documents automatically open in their own application window and use the Maximize button on the title bar.) If the window is already maximized, the Restore Window button appears in its place.

The **Restore Window** button changes the size of the document window to a smaller sized window inside the application window. It appears in the menu bar to the right of the Minimize Window button in Excel and PowerPoint. (Word documents automatically open in their own application Window and use the Restore button on the title bar.)

The **Close Window** button closes the document and removes it from the memory of the computer. It appears in the menu bar to the right of the Restore Window or Maximize Window button.

Default Toolbars

The **Standard** and **Formatting toolbars**, located one row below the menu bar, contain a set of icons called buttons. The toolbar buttons represent commonly used commands and are mouse shortcuts that enable you to perform tasks quickly. In addition to the Standard and Formatting toolbars, each application has several other toolbars available. You can customize toolbars by adding or removing buttons and commands.

When the mouse pointer rests on a toolbar button, a **ScreenTip** appears, identifying the name of the button. ScreenTips are also provided as part of online Help to describe a toolbar button, a dialog box option, or a menu command.

Scroll Bars

The vertical scroll bar appears on the right side of the document area. The **vertical scroll bar** is used to view various parts of the document by moving or scrolling the document up or down. It includes scroll arrows and a scroll box. The horizontal scroll bar appears near the bottom of the document area. The **horizontal scroll bar** is used to view various parts of the document by moving or scrolling the document left or right. It includes scroll arrows and a scroll box.

Ask A Question Box

The **Ask A Question Box** is a help tool alternative to the Office Assistant that appears on the menu bar of every Office application. The Ask A Question Box is used to quickly key a help question in plain English and then view a list of relevant Help topics.

Task Pane

Office XP includes a **task pane** feature, a pane of shortcuts, which opens on the right side of the application window. The contents of the task pane vary with the application and the activities being performed. For example, task pane shortcuts can be used to create new Office documents, format Word documents or PowerPoint presentations, or perform a Word mail merge. The task pane can be displayed or hidden as desired.

Taskbar

The **taskbar,** located across the bottom of the Windows desktop, includes the Start button and buttons for each open Office document. The **Start button,** located at the left end of the taskbar, displays the Start menu or list of tasks you can perform and applications you can use.

You can switch between documents, close documents and applications, and view other items, such as the system time and printer status, with buttons or icons on the taskbar. If you are using Windows 2000 or Windows 98, other toolbars, such as the Quick Launch toolbar, may also appear on the taskbar.

QUICK TIP

The **Office Assistant** is an interactive, animated graphic that appears in the Office application windows. When you activate the Office Assistant, a balloon-style dialog box opens to display options for searching online Help by topic. The Office Assistant may also automatically offer suggestions when you begin certain tasks. You can customize the Office Assistant by changing the animated graphic image or turning on or off various options. Any customization is shared by all Office applications.

MOUSE TIP

This book uses distinct instructions for mouse operations. **Point** means to place the mouse pointer on the specified command or item. **Click** means to press the left mouse button and then release it. **Right-click** means to press the right mouse button and then release it. **Double-click** means to press the left mouse button twice very rapidly. **Drag** means to press and hold down the left mouse button and then move the mouse on the mouse pad. **Right-drag** means to press and hold down the right mouse button and then move the mouse on the mouse pad. **Scroll** means to use the application scroll bar features or the IntelliMouse scrolling wheel.

1.d Starting Office Applications

You access the Office applications through the Windows desktop. The Windows operating system software is automatically loaded into the memory of your computer when you turn on your computer. After turning on your computer, the Windows desktop appears.

You begin by using the Start button on the taskbar to view the Start menu and open the Excel application. To use the Start button to open the Excel application:

Step 1	*Click*	the Start button Start on the taskbar
Step 2	*Point to*	Programs
Step 3	*Click*	Microsoft Excel on the Programs menu

The Excel software is placed into the memory of your computer and the Excel window opens. Your screen should look similar to Figure 1-1.

notes

You may sometimes use the keyboard to use Office application features. This book lists all keys, such as the TAB key, in uppercase letters. When the keyboard is used to issue a command, this book lists keystrokes as: Press the ENTER key. When you are to press one key and, while holding down that key, to press another key, this book lists the keystrokes as: Press the SHIFT + F7 keys.

You can open and work in more than one Office application at a time. When Office is installed, two additional commands appear on the Start menu: the Open Office Document command and the New Office Document command. You can use these commands to select the type of document on which you want to work rather than first selecting an Office application. To create a new Word document without first opening the application:

Step 1	*Click*	the Start button Start on the taskbar
Step 2	*Click*	New Office Document
Step 3	*Click*	the General tab, if necessary

The New Office Document dialog box on your screen should look similar to Figure 1-2. A **dialog box** is a window that contains options for performing specific tasks.

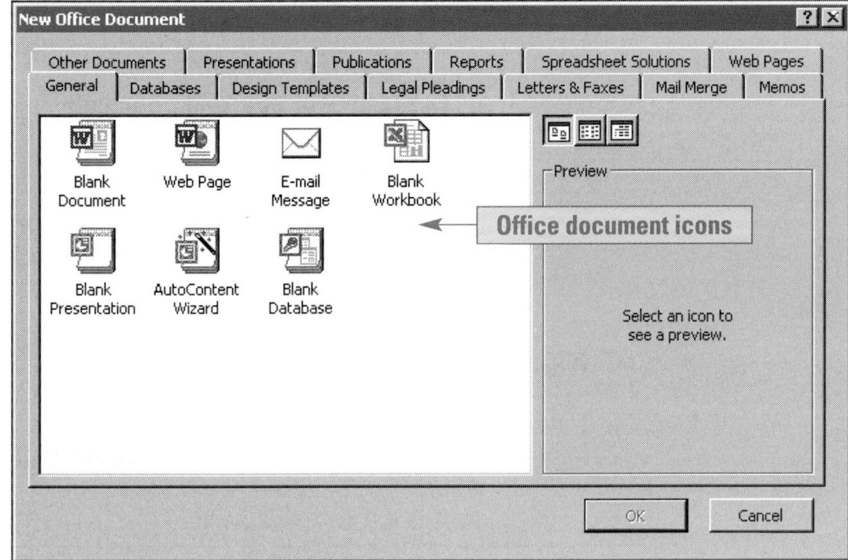

FIGURE 1-2
General Tab in the New Office Document Dialog Box

This dialog box provides options for creating different Office documents. **Icons** (or pictures) represent the Office document options; the number of icons available depends on the Office suite applications you have installed. The icons shown here create a blank Word document, a blank Web page (in Word), an e-mail message (using Outlook or Outlook Express), a blank Excel workbook, a blank PowerPoint presentation, a PowerPoint presentation using the AutoContent Wizard, and a blank Access database. You want to create a blank Word document.

Step 4	***Click***	the Blank Document icon to select it, if necessary
Step 5	***Click***	OK

The Word software is placed in the memory of your computer, the Word application window opens with a blank document. Your screen should look similar to Figure 1-3.

MOUSE TIP

Double-clicking an icon is the same as clicking the icon once to select it and then clicking the OK button.

FIGURE 1-3
Word Application Window

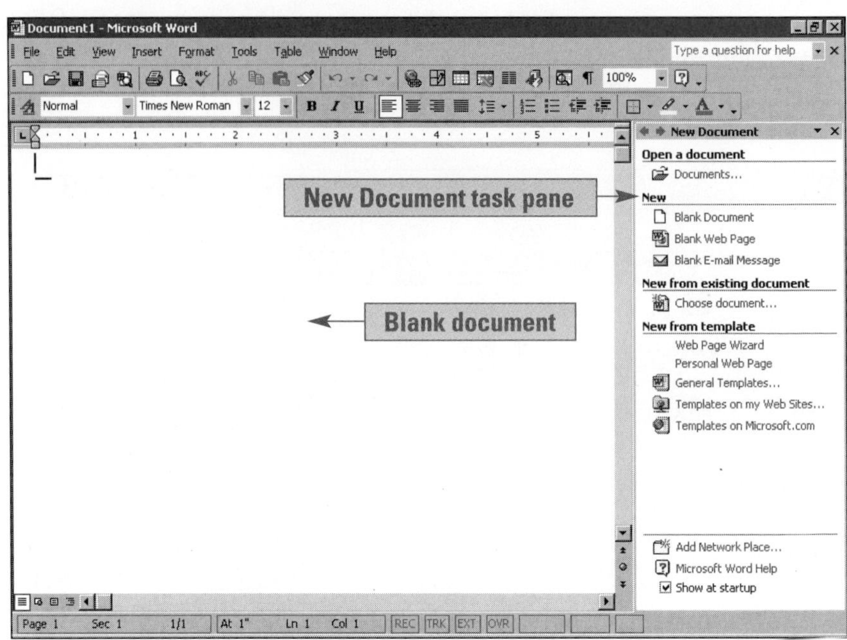

> **MENU TIP**
>
> The task pane containing shortcuts to create new documents or open existing documents opens by default when you launch a Word, Excel, or PowerPoint application. However, if you create or open another document in the same application, the task pane automatically hides. To display it again, click the Task Pane command on the View menu.

Next you open a blank presentation. To open the PowerPoint application:

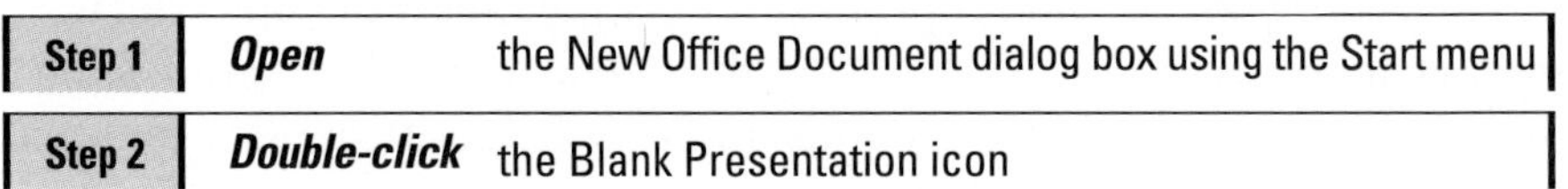

Step 1	***Open***	the New Office Document dialog box using the Start menu
Step 2	***Double-click***	the Blank Presentation icon

Your screen should look similar to Figure 1-4.

FIGURE 1-4
Blank PowerPoint Presentation

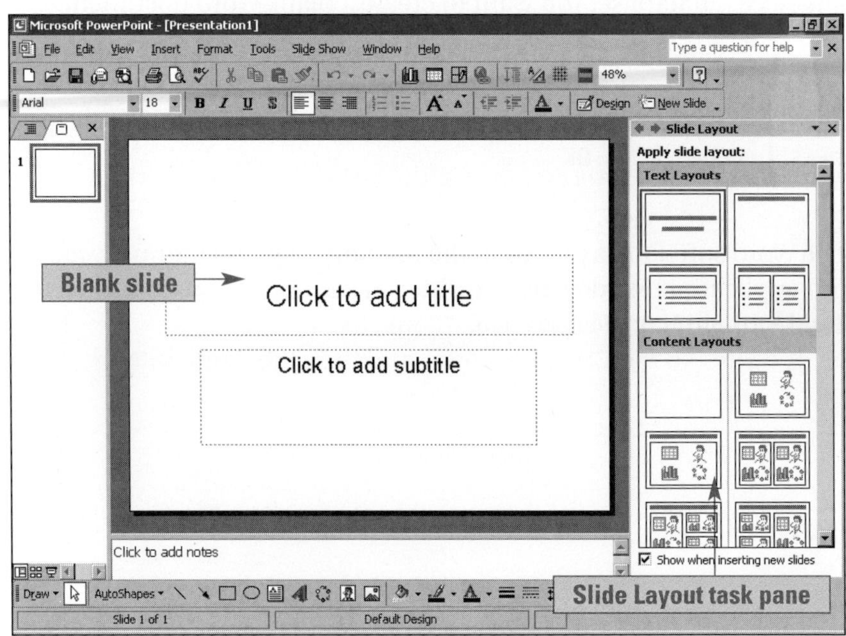

You can also open an Office application by opening an existing Office document from the Start menu. To open an existing Access database:

Step 1	*Click*	the Start button on the taskbar
Step 2	*Click*	Open Office Document
Step 3	*Click*	the Look in: list arrow in the Open Office Document dialog box
Step 4	*Switch to*	the disk drive and folder where the Data Files are stored
Step 5	*Double-click*	*International Sales*

The Access application window and Database window that open on your screen should look similar to Figure 1-5.

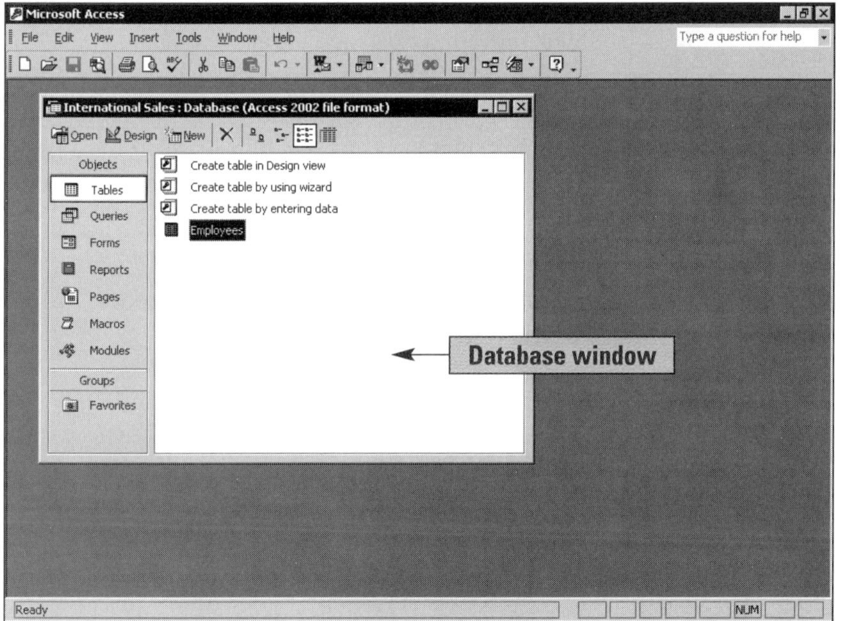

FIGURE 1-5
International Sales Database in Access Window

You can switch between open Office documents by clicking the appropriate taskbar button. If multiple windows are open, the **active window** has a dark blue title bar. All inactive windows have a gray title bar. To switch to the Excel workbook and then the Word document:

Step 1	*Click*	the Excel button on the taskbar
Step 2	*Observe*	that the Excel application window and workbook are now visible
Step 3	*Click*	the Word Document1 button on the taskbar
Step 4	*Observe*	that the Word application window and document are now visible

QUICK TIP

You can have multiple Excel workbooks, PowerPoint presentations, and Word documents open at one time. The number of documents, workbooks, and presentations you can have open at one time is determined by your computer's resources. You can open only one Access database at a time.

1.e Getting Help in Office Applications

You can get help when working in any Office application in several ways. You can use the Help menu, the Help toolbar button, or the F1 key to display the Office Assistant; get context-sensitive help with the What's This command or the SHIFT + F1 keys; or launch your Web browser and get Web-based help from Microsoft. You can also key a help question in the Ask A Question Box on the menu bar.

Using the Ask A Question Box

Suppose you want to find out how to use keyboard shortcuts in Word. To get help for keyboard shortcuts using the Ask A Question Box:

Step 1	***Verify***	that the Word document is the active window
Step 2	***Click***	in the Ask A Question Box
Step 3	***Key***	keyboard shortcuts
Step 4	***Press***	the ENTER key

A list of help topics related to keyboard shortcut keys appears. Your list should look similar to the one shown in Figure 1-6.

FIGURE 1-6
List of Help Topics

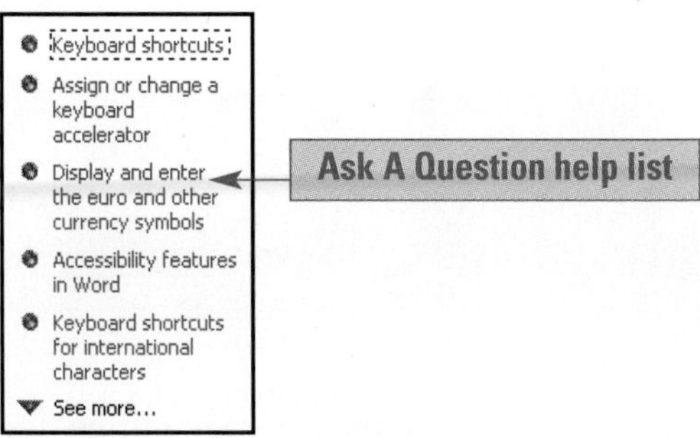

If you want to view the detailed help for any topic, simply click that topic in the list.

Step 5	***Press***	the ESC key
Step 6	***Click***	in the document area to deselect the Ask A Question Box

Using the Help Menu

The Help menu provides commands you can use to view the Office Assistant or Help window, show or hide the Office Assistant, connect to the Microsoft Web site, get context-sensitive help for a menu command or toolbar button, detect and repair font and template files, and view licensing information for the Office application. To review the Help menu commands:

Step 1	*Click*	Help on the menu bar

The Help menu on your screen should look similar to Figure 1-7.

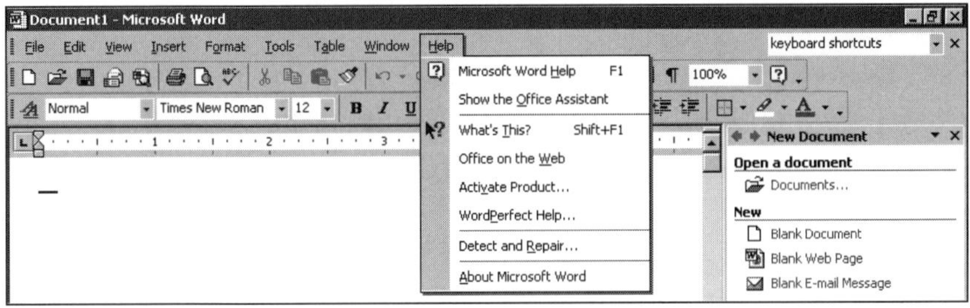

FIGURE 1-7
Help Menu

Step 2	*Observe*	the menu commands
Step 3	*Click*	in the document area outside the menu to close the Help menu

> **QUICK TIP**
>
> You can click the Help button on the title bar in any dialog box to convert the mouse pointer to a What's This help pointer.

Using What's This?

You can get context-sensitive help for a menu command or toolbar button using the What's This? command on the Help menu. This command changes the mouse pointer to a help pointer, a white mouse pointer with a large black question mark. When you click a toolbar button or menu command with the help pointer, a brief ScreenTip help message appears, describing the command or toolbar button. You can quickly change the mouse pointer to a help pointer by pressing the SHIFT + F1 keys.

To view the help pointer and view a ScreenTip help message for a toolbar button:

Step 1	*Press*	the SHIFT + F1 keys
Step 2	*Observe*	the help mouse pointer with the attached question mark
Step 3	*Click*	the Save button on the Standard toolbar
Step 4	*Observe*	the ScreenTip help message describing the Save button

Step 5	*Press*	the ESC key to close the ScreenTip help message

1.f Closing Office Applications

There are many ways to close the Access, Excel, and PowerPoint applications (or the Word application with a single document open) and return to the Windows desktop. You can:

- double-click the application Control-menu icon on the title bar.
- click the application Close button on the title bar.
- right-click the application button on the taskbar to display a shortcut menu and then click the Close command.
- press the ALT + F4 keys.
- click the Exit command on the File menu to close Office applications (no matter how many Word documents are open).

To close the Excel application from the taskbar:

Step 1	*Right-click*	the Excel button on the taskbar
Step 2	*Click*	Close

You can close multiple applications at one time from the taskbar by selecting the application buttons using the CTRL key and then using the shortcut menu. To close the PowerPoint and Access applications at one time:

Step 1	*Press & hold*	the CTRL key
Step 2	*Click*	the PowerPoint button and then the Access button on the taskbar
Step 3	*Release*	the CTRL key and observe that both buttons are selected (pressed in)
Step 4	*Right-click*	the PowerPoint or Access button
Step 5	*Click*	Close

Both applications close, leaving only the Word document open. To close the Word document using the menu:

Step 1	*Verify*	that the Word application window is maximized
Step 2	*Click*	File
Step 3	*Click*	Exit

Summary

- The Word application provides word processing capabilities for the preparation of text documents, such as letters, memorandums, and reports.
- The Excel application provides the ability to analyze numbers in worksheets and for creating financial budgets, reports, charts, and forms.
- The PowerPoint application is used to create presentation slides and audience handouts.
- You use the Access databases to store and retrieve collections of data.
- The Outlook application helps you send and receive e-mail and maintain a calendar, "to do" lists, and the names and addresses of contacts—and perform other information management tasks.
- One major advantage of using the Office suite applications is the ability to integrate the applications by sharing information between them.
- Another advantage of the Office suite applications is that they share a number of common elements such as window features, shortcuts, toolbars, and menu commands.
- You can start the Office suite applications from the Programs submenu on the Start menu and from the Open Office Document or New Office Document commands on the Start menu.
- To close the Office applications, you can double-click the application Control-menu icon, single-click the application Close button on the title bar, right-click the application button on the taskbar, press the ALT + F4 keys, or click the Exit command on the File menu.
- To get help in an Office application, you can click commands on the Help menu, press the F1 key or the SHIFT + F1 keys, or click the Microsoft Help button on the Standard toolbar.

Concepts Review

Circle the correct answer.

1. ScreenTips do not provide:
[a] the name of a button on a toolbar.
[b] help for options in a dialog box.
[c] context-sensitive help for menu commands or toolbar buttons.
[d] access to the Office Assistant.

2. To manage a Web site, you can use:
[a] Outlook.
[b] FrontPage.
[c] Excel.
[d] Publisher.

3. The title bar contains the:
[a] document Control-menu icon.
[b] Close Window button.
[c] Standard toolbar.
[d] application and document name.

4. The Excel application is best used to:
[a] prepare financial reports.
[b] maintain a list of tasks to accomplish.
[c] prepare text documents.
[d] manage Web sites.

5. A major advantage of using Office applications is the ability to:
[a] store mailing lists.
[b] analyze numbers.
[c] share information between applications.
[d] sort data.

6. Word processing is used primarily to:
[a] create presentation slides.
[b] analyze numbers.
[c] prepare text documents.
[d] maintain a calendar and "to do" lists.

7. Right-click means to:
[a] press the left mouse button twice rapidly.
[b] place the mouse pointer on a command or item.
[c] press and hold down the right mouse button and then move the mouse.
[d] press the right mouse button and then release it.

8. You cannot close Office XP applications by:
[a] clicking the Exit command on the File menu.
[b] clicking the Close button on the title bar.
[c] right-clicking the application button on the taskbar and clicking Close.
[d] pressing the SHIFT + F4 keys.

Circle **T** if the statement is true or **F** if the statement is false.

T **F** 1. You use Excel to create newsletters and brochures.

T **F** 2. Word is used to create presentation slides.

T **F** 3. The Office Assistant is an interactive graphic used to get online help in Office applications.

T **F** 4. Access is used to create and format text.

T **F** 5. You can open and work in only one Office application at a time.

T **F** 6. When you open multiple documents in an Office application, each document has its own button on the taskbar.

Skills Review

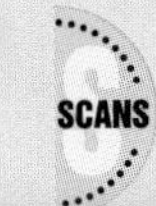

Exercise 1

1. Identify each of the numbered elements of Office application windows in the following figure.

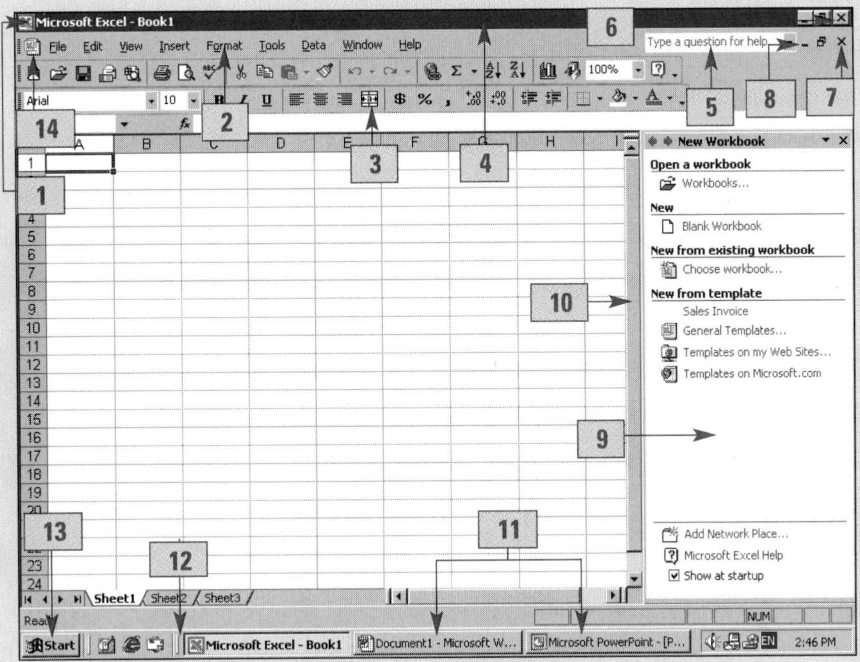

Exercise 2

1. Open the Word application using the Programs command on the Start menu.
2. Close the Word application using the taskbar.

Exercise 3

1. Open the Excel application using the Programs command on the Start menu.
2. Open the PowerPoint application using the Programs command on the Start menu.
3. Open the Access application and the *International Sales* database using the Open Office Document command on the Start menu.
4. Switch to the PowerPoint application using the taskbar button and close it using the Close button on the title bar.
5. Close the Excel and Access applications at the same time using the taskbar.

Exercise 4

1. Create a new, blank Word document using the New Office Document command on the Start menu.
2. Create a new, blank Excel workbook using the New Office Document command on the Start menu.
3. Switch to the Word document using the taskbar and close it using the Close button on the title bar.
4. Close the Excel workbook using the taskbar button.

Exercise 5

1. Open the Word application using the Start menu.
2. Show the Office Assistant, if necessary, with a command on the Help menu.
3. Hide the Office Assistant with a shortcut menu.
4. Show the Office Assistant with the Microsoft Word Help button on the Standard toolbar.
5. Search online Help using the search phrase "key text."
6. Click the "Change typing and editing options" link.
7. Review the Help text and then close the Help window.
8. Show the Office Assistant, and then click the Options command on the Office Assistant shortcut menu.
9. Click the Use the Office Assistant check box to remove the check mark and turn off the Office Assistant.

Exercise 6

1. Write a paragraph that describes the different ways to close the Word application.

Exercise 7

1. Open any Office application and use the Ask A Question Box and the keyword "Office Assistant" to search for online Help for information on using the Office Assistant.
2. Write down the instructions for selecting a different Office Assistant graphic image.

Case Projects

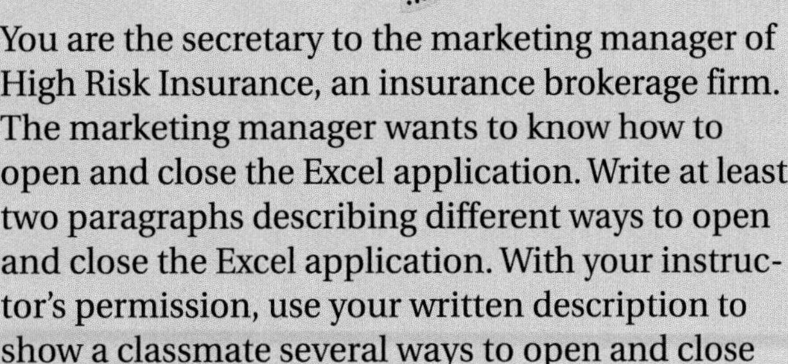

Project 1

You are the secretary to the marketing manager of High Risk Insurance, an insurance brokerage firm. The marketing manager wants to know how to open and close the Excel application. Write at least two paragraphs describing different ways to open and close the Excel application. With your instructor's permission, use your written description to show a classmate several ways to open and close the Excel application.

Project 2

You work in the administrative offices of Alma Public Relations and the information management department just installed Office XP on your computer. Your supervisor asks you to write down and describe some of the Office Assistant options. Display the Office Assistant. Right-click the Office Assistant graphic, click the Options command, and view the Options tab in the Office Assistant dialog box. Click the What's This? or Help button on the dialog box title bar and review each option. Write at least three paragraphs describing five Office Assistant options.

Project 3

As the new office manager at Hot Wheels Messenger Service, you are learning to use the Word 2002 application and want to learn more about some of the buttons on the Word toolbars. Open Word and use the What's This? command on the Help menu to review the ScreenTip help for five toolbar buttons. Write a brief paragraph for each button describing how it is used.

Project 4

You are the administrative assistant to the vice president of operations for Extreme Sports, Inc., a sports equipment retailer with stores in several cities in your state. The vice president wants to save time and money by performing business tasks more efficiently. She asks you to think of different ways to perform common business tasks by sharing information between the Office XP applications. Write at least three paragraphs describing how the company can use Word, Excel, PowerPoint, Access, and Outlook to improve efficiency by combining information.

Working with Menus, Toolbars, and Task Panes

Chapter Overview

Office tries to make your work life easier by learning how you work. The personalized menus and toolbars in each application remember which commands and buttons you use and add and remove them as needed. Office has two new tools—task panes and Smart Tags—that provide shortcuts for performing different activities. In this chapter, you learn how to work with the personalized menus and toolbars and how to use task panes and Smart Tags.

Learning Objectives

- Work with personalized menus and toolbars
- View, hide, dock, and float toolbars
- Work with task panes
- Review Smart Tags

chapter two

2.a Working with Personalized Menus and Toolbars

A **menu** is a list of commands you use to perform tasks in the Office applications. Some of the commands also have an associated image, or icon, which appears to the left of each command in the menu. Most menus are found on the menu bar located below the title bar in the Office applications. A **toolbar** contains a set of icons (the same icons you see on the menus) called "buttons" that you click with the mouse pointer to quickly execute a menu command.

notes

The activities in this chapter assume the personalized menus and toolbars are reset to their default settings. As you learn about menus and toolbars, task panes, and Smart Tags you are asked to select menu commands and toolbar buttons by clicking them with the mouse pointer. You do not learn how to use the menu command or toolbar button, task pane, or Smart Tags to perform detailed tasks in this chapter. Using these features to perform detailed tasks is covered in the individual application chapters.

When you first install Office and then open an Office application, the menus on the menu bar initially show only a basic set of commands and the Standard and Formatting toolbars contain only a basic set of buttons. These short versions of the menus and toolbars are called **personalized menus and toolbars**. As you work in the application, the commands and buttons you use most frequently are stored in the personalized settings. The first time you select a menu command or toolbar button that is not part of the basic set, that command or button is automatically added to your personalized settings and appears on the menu or toolbar. If you do not use a command for a while, it is removed from your personalized settings and no longer appears on the menu or toolbar. To view the personalized menus and toolbars in PowerPoint:

Step 1	*Click*	the New Office Document command on the Start menu
Step 2	*Click*	the General tab in the New Office Document dialog box, if necessary
Step 3	*Double-click*	the Blank Presentation icon
Step 4	*Click*	Tools on the menu bar
Step 5	*Observe*	the short personalized menu containing only the basic commands

The Tools menu on your screen should look similar to Figure 2-1.

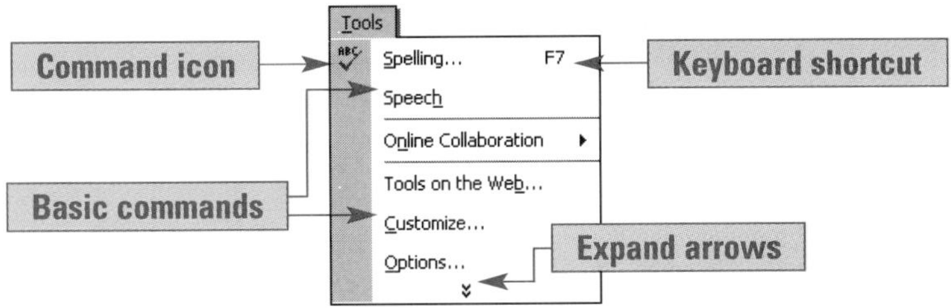

FIGURE 2-1
Personalized Tools Menu

If the command you want to use does not appear on the short personalized menu, you can expand the menu. The fastest way to expand a personalized menu is to double-click the menu command on the menu bar. For example, to quickly expand the Insert menu, you can double-click the Insert command on the menu bar. Another way to expand a menu is to click the Expand arrows that appear at the bottom of the personalized menu when it opens. Finally, after opening a menu, you can pause for a few seconds until the menu automatically expands. To expand the Tools menu:

Step 1	***Pause***	until the menu automatically expands *or* click the Expand arrows at the bottom of the menu to expand the menu

The expanded Tools menu on your screen should look similar to Figure 2-2.

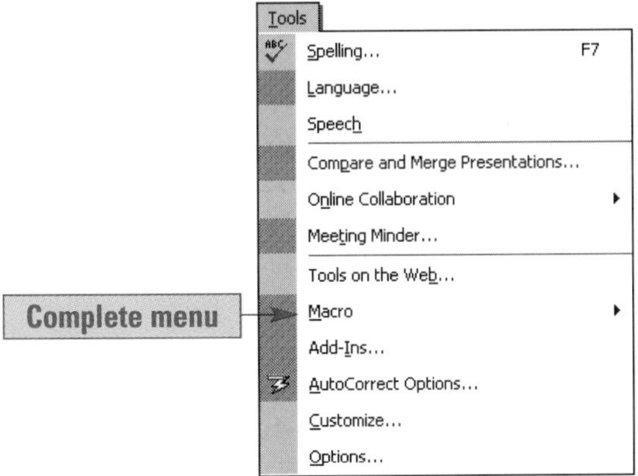

FIGURE 2-2
Expanded Tools Menu

You move a menu command from the expanded menu to the personalized menu simply by selecting it. To add the AutoCorrect Options command to the short personalized Tools menu:

Step 1	***Click***	AutoCorrect Options

Step 2	*Click*	Cancel in the AutoCorrect dialog box to close the dialog box without making any changes
Step 3	*Click*	Tools on the menu bar
Step 4	*Observe*	the updated personalized Tools menu contains the AutoCorrect Options command

The Tools menu on your screen should look similar to Figure 2-3.

FIGURE 2-3
Updated Personalized Tools Menu

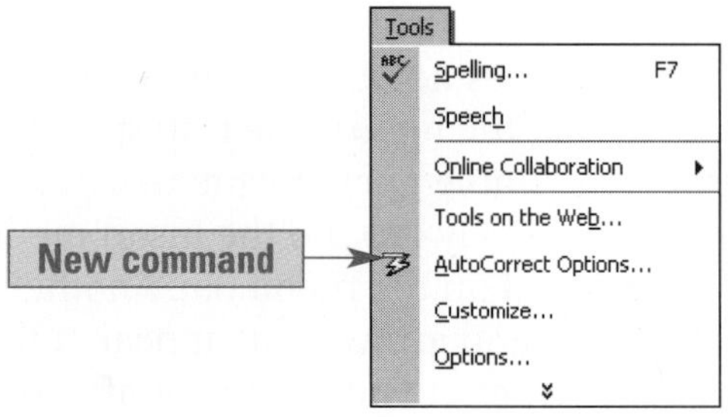

Step 5	*Press*	the ESC key twice to close the menu

The first time you launch most Office applications, the Standard and Formatting toolbars appear on one row below the title bar. In this position, you cannot see all their default buttons. If a toolbar button is not visible, you can resize or reposition one of the toolbars. When the mouse pointer is positioned on a toolbar **move handle** (the gray vertical bar at the left edge of the toolbar), the mouse pointer changes from a white arrow pointer to a **move pointer**, a four-headed black arrow. You can drag the move handle with the move pointer to resize or reposition toolbar. To resize the Formatting toolbar:

Step 1	*Move*	the mouse pointer to the move handle on the Formatting toolbar
Step 2	*Observe*	that the mouse pointer becomes a move pointer

The move pointer on your screen should look similar to Figure 2-4.

FIGURE 2-4
Move Pointer on the Formatting Toolbar Handle

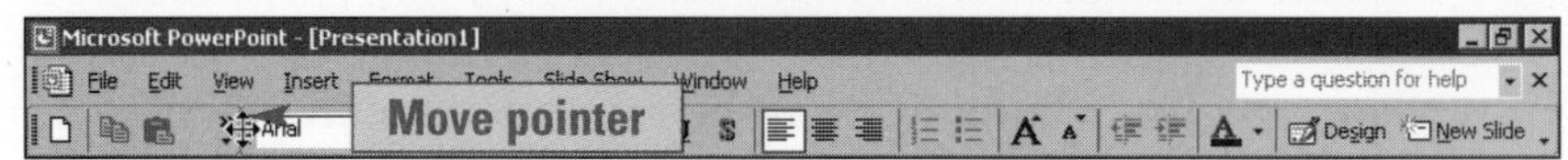

Step 3	*Click & hold*	the left mouse button
Step 4	*Drag*	the Formatting toolbar to the right as far as you can to view the default buttons on the Standard toolbar

Step 5	***Drag***	the Formatting toolbar to the left as far as you can to view the default buttons on the Formatting toolbar
Step 6	***Release***	the mouse button
Step 7	***Observe***	that you now see three buttons on the Standard toolbar

The buttons that don't fit on the displayed area of a toolbar are collected in a Toolbar Options list. The last button on any toolbar, the Toolbar Options button, is used to display the Toolbar Options list. To view the Toolbar Options list:

Step 1	***Click***	the Toolbar Options button list arrow on the Standard toolbar
Step 2	***Observe***	the default buttons that are not visible on the toolbar

The Toolbar Options list on your screen should look similar to Figure 2-5.

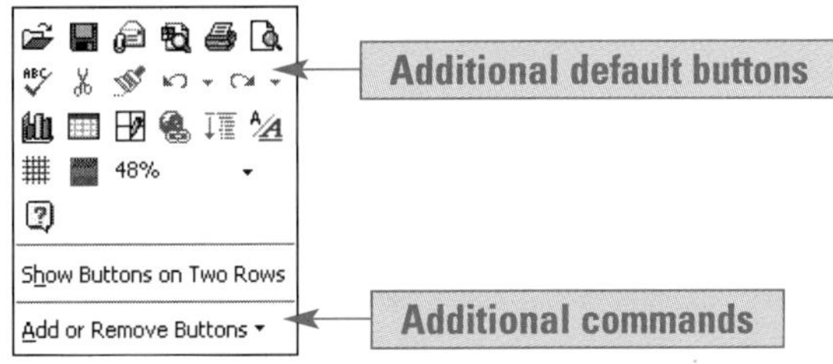

FIGURE 2-5
Toolbar Options List

If you want to display one of the default buttons on a personalized toolbar, you can select it from the Toolbar Options list. To add the Search button to the personalized Standard toolbar:

Step 1	***Click***	the Search button
Step 2	***Observe***	that the Search button is added to the personalized Standard toolbar

When you add another button to the personalized Standard toolbar, one of the other buttons might move out of view. This is because of the limited viewing area of the Standard toolbar in its current position. If you want to view all the menu commands instead of a short personalized menu and all the default toolbar buttons on the Standard and Formatting toolbars, you can change options in the Customize dialog box. To view the Customize dialog box:

Step 1	***Click***	Tools on the menu bar

Step 2	*Click*	Customize
Step 3	*Click*	the Options tab, if necessary

The Customize dialog box on your screen should look similar to Figure 2-6.

FIGURE 2-6
Options Tab in the Customize Dialog Box

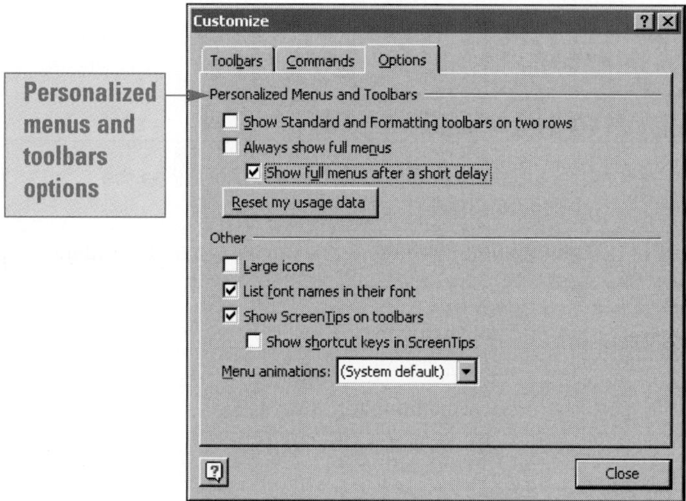

If you reposition the Formatting toolbar below the Standard toolbar, you can view all the default buttons on both toolbars. You can do this by inserting a check mark in the Show Standard and Formatting toolbars on two rows check box. You can insert a check mark in the Always show full menus check box to view the entire set of menu commands for each menu instead of the short personalized menus. If you do not want the short personalized menus to expand automatically when you pause, you can remove the check mark from the Show full menus after a short delay check box. Then, to show the full menu, you have to double-click the menu or click the expand arrows at the bottom of the menu.

You want to show all the Standard and Formatting toolbar buttons and menu commands.

Step 4	*Click*	the Show Standard and Formatting toolbars on two rows check box to insert a check mark
Step 5	*Click*	the Always show full menus check box to insert a check mark
Step 6	*Click*	Close to close the dialog box
Step 7	*Observe*	the repositioned and expanded Standard and Formatting toolbars

Step 8	*Click*	Tools to view the entire set of Tools menu commands
Step 9	*Press*	the ESC key to close the Tools menu

You can return the menus and toolbars to their initial (or **default**) settings in the Customize dialog box. To open the Customize dialog box and reset the default menus and toolbars:

Step 1	*Click*	Tools
Step 2	*Click*	Customize
Step 3	*Click*	the Options tab, if necessary
Step 4	*Remove*	the two check marks you just inserted
Step 5	*Click*	Reset my usage data
Step 6	*Click*	Yes to confirm you want to reset the menus and toolbars to their default settings
Step 7	*Close*	the Customize dialog box
Step 8	*Observe*	that the Tools menu and Standard toolbar are reset to their default settings

MOUSE TIP

You can use a command on the Toolbar Options list to place the Standard and Formatting toolbars that currently appear on one row on two rows. You can also place the Standard and Formatting toolbars that appear in two rows back to one row with a command on the Toolbar Options list.

2.b Viewing, Hiding, Docking, and Floating Toolbars

Office applications have additional toolbars that you can view when you need them. You can also hide toolbars when you are not using them. You can view or hide toolbars by pointing to the Toolbars command on the View menu and clicking a toolbar name or by using a shortcut menu. A **shortcut menu** is a short list of frequently used menu commands. You view a shortcut menu by pointing to an item on the screen and clicking the right mouse button. This is called right-clicking the item. The commands on shortcut menus vary depending on where you right-click, so that you view only the most frequently used commands for a particular task. An easy way to view or hide toolbars is with a shortcut menu.

notes

Although the PowerPoint application is used to illustrate how to customize toolbars, the same techniques are used to customize toolbars and menus in the Word, Excel, and Access applications.

To view the shortcut menu for toolbars:

Step 1	***Right-click***	the menu bar, the Standard toolbar, or the Formatting toolbar
Step 2	***Observe***	the shortcut menu and the check marks next to the names of displayed toolbars

Your shortcut menu should look similar to Figure 2-7.

FIGURE 2-7
Toolbars Shortcut Menu

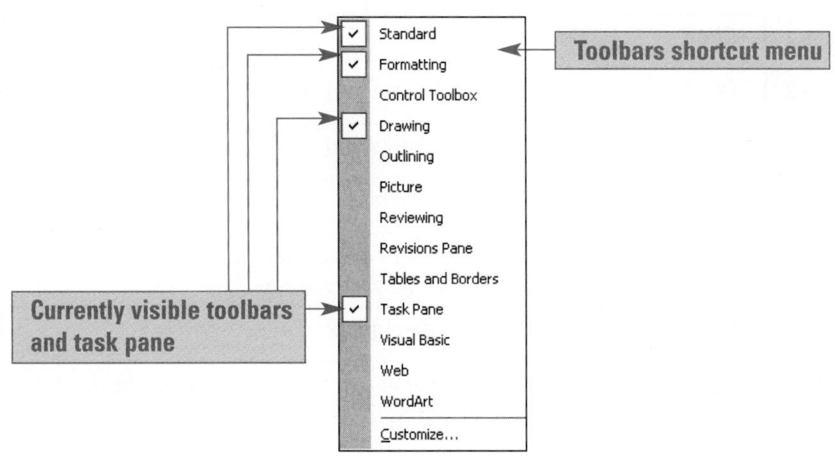

Step 3	***Click***	Tables and Borders in the shortcut menu
Step 4	***Observe***	that the Tables and Borders toolbar appears on your screen

QUICK TIP

Some of the toolbars that appear on the toolbars shortcut menu vary from one Office application to another.

The Tables and Borders toolbar, unless a previous user repositioned it, is visible in its own window near the middle of your screen. When a toolbar is visible in its own window, it is called a **floating toolbar** and you can move and size it with the mouse pointer similar to any window. When a toolbar appears fixed at the screen boundaries, it is called a **docked toolbar**. The menu bar and Standard and Formatting toolbars are examples of docked toolbars because they are fixed below the title bar at the top of the screen. In PowerPoint, the Drawing toolbar is docked at the bottom of the screen above the status bar. You can dock a floating toolbar by dragging its title bar with the mouse pointer to a docking position below the title bar, above the status bar, or at the left and right boundaries of your screen.

To dock the Tables and Borders toolbar below the Standard and Formatting toolbars, if necessary:

Step 1	***Click & hold***	the title bar in the Tables and Borders toolbar window

Step 2	*Observe*	that the mouse pointer becomes a move pointer
Step 3	*Drag*	the toolbar window up slowly until it docks below the Standard and Formatting toolbars
Step 4	*Release*	the mouse button

Similarly, you float a docked toolbar by dragging it away from its docked position toward the middle of the screen. To float the Tables and Borders toolbar, if necessary:

Step 1	*Position*	the mouse pointer on the Tables and Borders toolbar move handle until it becomes a move pointer
Step 2	*Drag*	the Tables and Borders toolbar down toward the middle of the screen until it appears in its own window

When you finish using a toolbar, you can hide it with a shortcut menu. To hide the Tables and Borders toolbar:

Step 1	*Right-click*	the Tables and Borders toolbar
Step 2	*Click*	Tables and Borders to remove the check mark and hide the toolbar

2.c Working with Task Panes

The task pane is a tool with many uses in the Office applications. For example, when you launch Word, Excel, PowerPoint, or Access a new file task pane appears on the right side of the application window. This task pane allows you to create new documents in a variety of ways or open existing documents and replaces the New dialog box found in earlier versions of the Office applications. For example, in the Word application, this task pane is called the New Document task pane and contains hyperlink shortcuts for creating a new document or opening an existing document, creating a blank Web page, sending an e-mail message, choosing an existing document to use as the basis for a new document, and other options. A **hyperlink** is text or a graphic image that you can click to view another page or item. The hyperlink shortcuts in the task pane are colored blue. When you place your mouse pointer on a blue hyperlink shortcut, the mouse pointer changes to a hand with a pointing finger. You can then click the hyperlink shortcut to view the page or option to which the shortcut is linked.

Another way to use a task pane in each of the Office applications is to display the Search task pane and use it to search your local computer

MOUSE TIP

You can dock a floating toolbar by double-clicking its title bar. The toolbar returns to its previously docked position.

You can close a floating toolbar by clicking the Close button on the toolbar's title bar.

QUICK TIP

In Excel, the new file task pane is called the New Workbook task pane; in PowerPoint, it is called the New Presentation task pane; in Access, it is called the New File task pane.

Each Office application also contains specific task panes: for example—you can format text in a Word document, copy and paste data in an Excel worksheet, and apply an attractive design and animation scheme to a PowerPoint presentation—all from special task panes.

system and network for files based on specific criteria such as keywords in the file text, the file's location, the file type, and the file's name. You can also search for Outlook items using the Search task pane.

To view a blank Word document and the Search task pane:

Step 1	*Start*	the Word application using the Start menu
Step 2	*Click*	File on the menu bar
Step 3	*Click*	Search

The Basic Search task pane is now visible. Your screen should look similar to Figure 2-8.

FIGURE 2-8
Basic Search Task Pane in Word

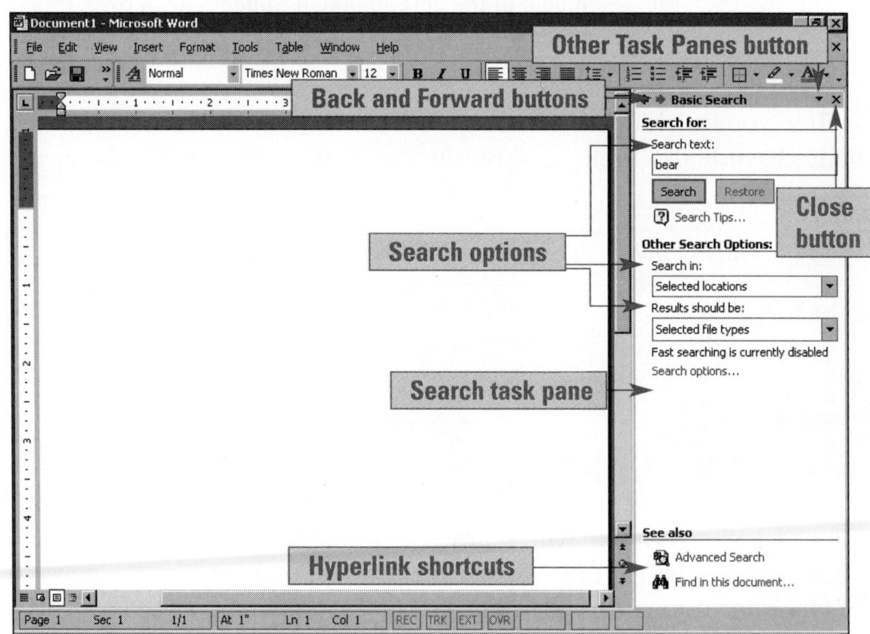

MOUSE TIP

You also can view the Search task pane by clicking the Search button on the Standard toolbar.

When you have multiple task panes open, you can use the Back and Forward buttons on the task pane title bar to switch between the task panes. To switch from the Basic Search task pane to the New Document task pane:

Step 1	*Click*	the Back button in the Basic Search task pane to view the New Document task pane
Step 2	*Click*	the Forward button in the New Document task pane to view the Basic Search task pane

You can key text in the Search text: text box to look for files containing specific text. You can use the Search in: list to select the locations in which to search, and use the Results should be: list to select the file types to search for. If your search criteria are more complex, you can click the Advanced Search link to view the Advanced Search task pane, where you can set additional search criteria such as file attributes called **properties**, or use operators such as "and" to set multiple criteria or "or" to set exclusive criteria.

A task pane appears docked on the right side of the application window by default. You can "float" the task pane in the application window or dock it on the left side of the application window, as you prefer. Like docking a floating toolbar, when you double-click a task pane title bar, it returns to its last docked or floating position. To float the docked task pane:

Step 1	***Double-click***	the Basic Search task pane title bar
Step 2	***Observe***	the task pane's new position, floating in the application window

Your screen should look similar to Figure 2-9.

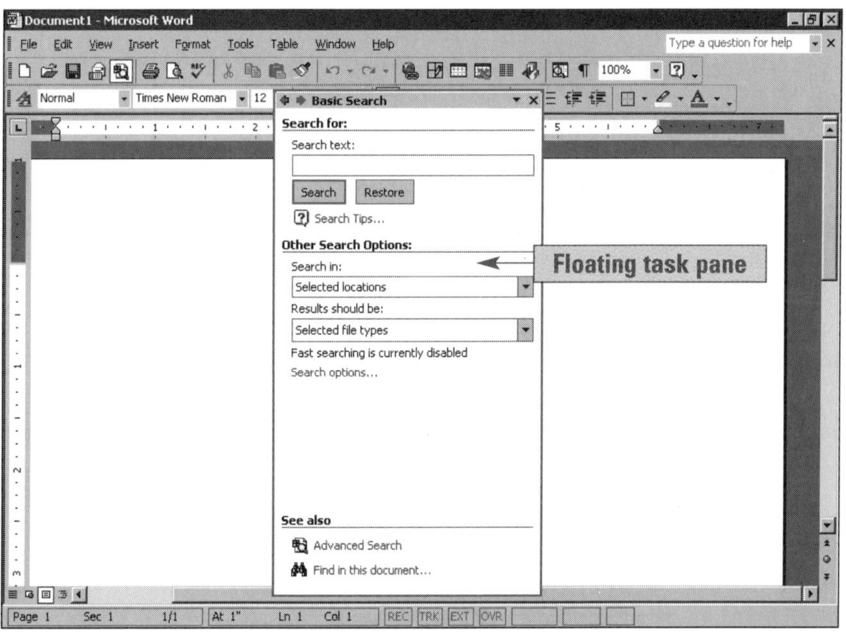

FIGURE 2-9
Floating Task Pane

Step 3	***Double-click***	the Basic Search task pane title bar
Step 4	***Observe***	that the Basic Search task pane returns to its previous docked position

TASK PANE TIP

You can click the Other Task Panes list arrow on the task pane title bar to view a list of different task panes available in the application. Then, you can click one of the task panes in the list to open it. Additionally, some task panes appear automatically as you perform certain activities in an application.

You can also display the last previous visible task pane by using the Task Pane command on the View menu.

MOUSE TIP

You can float a docked task pane by dragging the task pane away from its docked position using the mouse and the task pane title bar. Conversely, you can dock a floating task pane by dragging the task pane to the left or right side of the screen.

You can size a floating task pane by dragging the pane's top, bottom, left, or right borders with the mouse pointer.

You can close the current task pane by clicking the Close button on the task pane title bar. When you close the current task pane, all open task panes are also closed. For example, you currently have the New Document task pane and the Basic Search task pane open. When you close the Basic Search task pane, both task panes are closed. You can view the New Document task pane again with a menu command or toolbar button. To close the Basic Search and New Document task panes and then reopen the New Document task pane:

Step 1	*Click*	the Close button on the Basic Search task pane title bar
Step 2	*Observe*	that neither the Basic Search nor the New Document task pane is visible
Step 3	*Click*	File on the menu bar
Step 4	*Click*	New

The New Document task pane opens at the right side of the application window.

> **QUICK TIP**
>
> The **Office Shortcut Bar** is a toolbar that you can open and position on your Windows desktop to provide shortcuts to Office applications and tasks. The Office Shortcut Bar can contain buttons for the New Office Document and Open Office Document commands you see on the Start menu, shortcut buttons to create various Outlook items, and buttons to open Office applications installed on your computer. You can access the Office Shortcut Bar with the Microsoft Office Tools command on the Programs menu.

2.d Reviewing Smart Tags

Smart Tags are labels used to identify data as a specific type of data. You can use Smart Tags to perform an action in an open Office application instead of opening another application to perform that task. For example, a person's name is one kind of data that can be recognized and labeled with a Smart Tag. Suppose you key a person's name in a Word document and then want to create a contact item for that person in your Outlook Contacts folder. You can use a Smart Tag to create the contact item from Word without opening Outlook.

Smart Tags are represented by an action button and a purple dotted line underneath the text. The Smart Tag options are found in the AutoCorrect dialog box. To view the Smart Tag options in the Word application:

Step 1	*Click*	Tools on the menu bar
Step 2	*Click*	AutoCorrect Options
Step 3	*Click*	the Smart Tags tab in the AutoCorrect dialog box

The AutoCorrect dialog box on your screen should look similar to Figure 2-10.

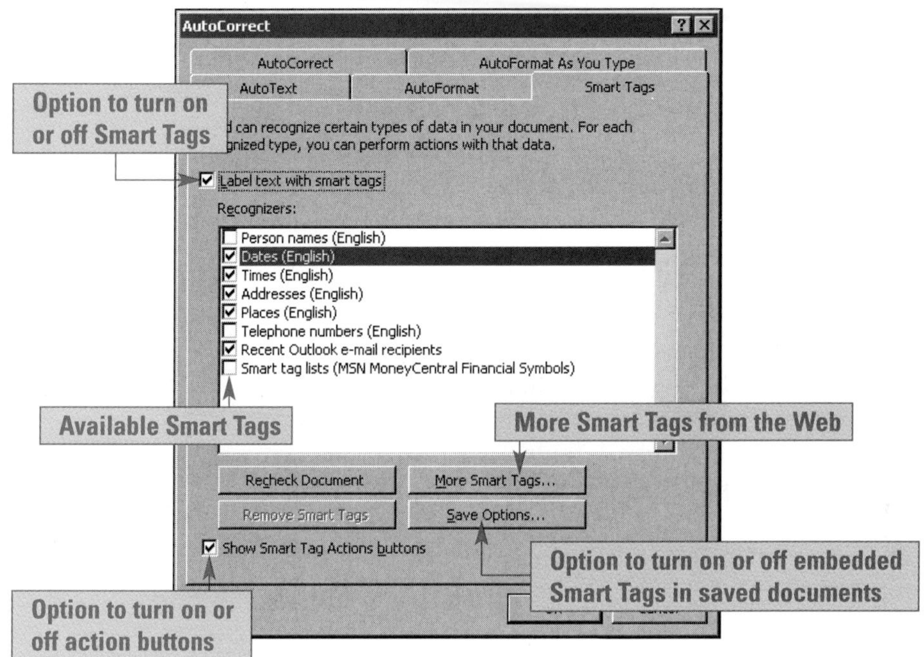

FIGURE 2-10
Smart Tags Tab in the AutoCorrect Dialog Box

You can turn on or off the Smart Tag feature with the Label text with smart tags check box. You can use the Show Smart Tag Actions buttons check box to turn on or off the Smart Tag action buttons. By default, Smart Tags are embedded in a document when it is saved. You can turn off this feature with the Save Options button. You can also remove the Smart Tags or recheck the document using the Remove Smart Tags or Recheck Document buttons. The use of specific Smart Tags and action buttons is covered in more detail in later chapters.

Step 4	***Click***	the Cancel button to close the AutoCorrect dialog box without making any changes
Step 5	***Click***	the Close button [X] on the title bar to close Word
Step 6	***Close***	the PowerPoint application

QUICK TIP

A limited number of Smart Tags are installed with the Office applications. You can access more Smart Tags from the Microsoft Web site by clicking the More Smart Tags button in the Smart Tags tab of the AutoCorrect dialog box.

Summary

- The first time you launch an Office application after installing Office, you see personalized menus that contain basic commands. As you use different commands, they are automatically added to the personalized menu. Commands that are not used for some time are removed from the personalized menus.
- The first time you launch an Office application after installing Office, the Standard and Formatting toolbars share a single row below the menu bar. You can reposition the Formatting toolbar to view more or fewer toolbar buttons. The remaining default toolbar buttons that are not visible on the toolbars can be added from the Toolbar Options list. You can turn off or reset the personalized menus and toolbars in the Options tab of the Customize dialog box.
- You can hide or view toolbars as you need them by using a shortcut menu. Toolbars can be docked at the top, bottom, or side of the screen, or they can be floating on screen in their own window.
- You can open task panes that contain shortcuts to perform various activities; these task panes can be docked at the left or right side of the application window, or they can be floating in the application window. Two examples of a task pane are the New Document and Basic Search task panes.
- Smart Tags are labels that identify text or data as a certain type and provide shortcuts to taking certain actions with the text or data.

Commands Review

Action	Menu Bar	Shortcut Menu	Toolbar	Task Pane	Keyboard
Display or hide toolbars	View, Toolbars	Right-click a toolbar, click the desired toolbar to add or remove the check mark	[X] on the toolbar title bar		ALT + V, T
View the New Document task pane	File, New				ALT + F, N
View the Search task pane	File, Search				ALT + F, H
View the last visible task pane	View, Task Pane	Right-click a toolbar, click Task Pane			ALT + V, K
View the available Smart Tag options	Tools, AutoCorrect Options, Smart Tags tab				ALT + T, A

Concepts Review

Circle the correct answer.

1. A menu is:
- [a] a set of icons.
- [b] a list of commands.
- [c] impossible to customize.
- [d] never personalized.

2. A toolbar is:
- [a] a list of commands.
- [b] always floating on your screen.
- [c] a set of icons.
- [d] never docked on your screen.

3. Which of the following is not an option in the Options tab in the Customize dialog box?
- [a] turning on or off ScreenTips for toolbar buttons
- [b] turning on or off Large icons for toolbar buttons
- [c] adding animation to menus
- [d] docking all toolbars

4. Right-clicking an item on screen displays:
- [a] the Right-Click toolbar.
- [b] animated menus.
- [c] expanded menus.
- [d] a shortcut menu.

5. Double-clicking the menu name on the menu bar:
- [a] resets your usage data.
- [b] floats the menu bar.
- [c] turns off the personalized menus.
- [d] expands a personalized menu.

6. A Smart Tag is:
- [a] a personalized menu.
- [b] displayed by double-clicking an item on your screen.
- [c] automatically expanded when you pause briefly.
- [d] a label used to identify text or data items for shortcut actions.

7. To view all the default buttons on both the Standard and Formatting toolbars at once, you should:
- [a] view the toolbar with a shortcut menu.
- [b] add the View All button to the toolbar.
- [c] reposition the Formatting toolbar on another row below the Standard toolbar.
- [d] drag the Formatting toolbar to the left.

8. The Advanced Search task pane cannot be viewed by clicking a:
- [a] command on a shortcut menu.
- [b] command on the File menu.
- [c] button on the Standard toolbar.
- [d] link on the Basic Search task pane.

Circle **T** if the statement is true or **F** if the statement is false.

T F 1. The Standard and Formatting toolbars must remain on the same row.

T F 2. When updating docked personalized toolbars, some buttons may be automatically removed from view to make room for the new buttons.

T F 3. One way to use a Smart Tag is to create an Outlook contact from a name in a Word document.

T F 4. You cannot add animation to menus.

T F 5. A floating toolbar window can be resized and repositioned using techniques that are similar to those used for any other window.

T F 6. When you open an Office application, the Search task pane is docked at the right side of the application window.

T F 7. You cannot use keyboard shortcuts to run commands in Office applications.

T F 8. You cannot turn off the personalized menus and toolbars options.

Skills Review

Exercise 1

1. Open the Word application.
2. Open the Options tab in the Customize dialog box and reset the usage data; show the Standard and Formatting toolbars on one row, and show full menus after a short delay.
3. If necessary, drag the Formatting toolbar to the right until you can see approximately half of the Standard and half of the Formatting toolbar.
4. Add the Show/Hide button to the personalized Standard toolbar using the Toolbar Options list.
5. Add the Font Color button to the personalized Formatting toolbar using the Toolbar Options list.
6. Open the Customize dialog box and reset your usage data in the Options tab.
7. Close the Word application and click No if asked whether you want to save changes to the blank Word document.

Exercise 2

1. Open the Excel application.
2. Open the Options tab in the Customize dialog box and reset the usage data; show the Standard and Formatting toolbars on one row, and show full menus after a short delay.
3. View the personalized Tools menu.
4. Add the AutoCorrect Options command to the personalized Tools menu.
5. Reset your usage data.
6. Close the Excel application.

Exercise 3

1. Open the PowerPoint application.
2. Display the Basic Search task pane using a menu command.
3. Display the advanced search options.
4. Close the Advanced Search task pane.
5. Close the PowerPoint application.

Exercise 4

1. Open an Office application and verify that the New Document, New Presentation, or New Workbook task pane is docked at the right side of the application window.
2. Float the task pane by dragging it to the center of the application window.
3. Drag the left border of the floating task pane to resize it.
4. Double-click the task pane title bar to dock it in its previous position.
5. Close the task pane.
6. Open the Basic Search task pane using the Search button on the Standard toolbar.
7. Open the New Document task pane using the File menu.
8. Switch between task panes using the Back and Forward buttons on the task pane title bar.
9. Close the task pane.
10. Close the application.

Exercise 5

1. Open the Excel application.
2. View the Drawing, Picture, and WordArt toolbars using a shortcut menu.
3. Dock the Picture toolbar below the Standard and Formatting toolbars.
4. Dock the WordArt toolbar at the left boundary of the screen.
5. Close the Excel application from the taskbar.
6. Open the Excel with the New Office Document on the Start menu. (*Hint:* Use the Blank Workbook icon.)
7. Float the WordArt toolbar.
8. Float the Picture toolbar.
9. Hide the WordArt, Picture, and Drawing toolbars using a shortcut menu.
10. Close the Excel application.

Exercise 6

1. Open the Word application.
2. Turn off the personalized menus and toolbars.
3. Open the Options tab in the Customize dialog box and change the toolbar buttons to large icons and add random animation to the menus.
4. Observe the toolbar buttons and the menu animation.
5. Turn off the large buttons and remove the menu animation.
6. Turn on the personalized menus and toolbars and reset your usage data.
7. Close the Word application.

Case Projects

SCANS

Project 1

As secretary to the placement director for the XYZ Employment Agency, you have been using an earlier version of Word—Word 97. After you install Office XP, you decide you want the Word menus and toolbars to appear on two rows the way they did in the Word 97 application. Use the Ask A Question Box to search for help on "personalized menus." Review the Help topics and write down all the ways to make the personalized menus and toolbars appear on two rows.

Project 2

You are the administrative assistant to the controller of the Plush Pets, Inc., a stuffed toy manufacturing company. The controller recently installed Excel 2002. She is confused about how to use the task panes and asks for your help. Use the Ask A Question Box to search for help on "task panes." Review the topics and write down an explanation of how task panes are used. Give at least three examples of task panes.

Project 3

As administrative assistant to the art director of MediaWiz Advertising, Inc. you just installed PowerPoint 2002. Now you decide you would rather view the complete Standard and Formatting toolbars rather than the personalized toolbars and want to learn a quick way to do this. Use the Ask A Question Box to search for help on "show all buttons." Review the topic and write down the instructions for showing all buttons using the mouse pointer. Open an Office application and use the mouse method to show the complete Standard and Formatting toolbars. Turn the personalized toolbars back on from the Customize dialog box.

Introduction to the Internet and the World Wide Web

Chapter Overview

Millions of people use the Internet to shop for goods and services, listen to music, view artwork, conduct research, get stock quotes, keep up to date with current events, and send e-mail. More and more people are using the Internet at work and at home to view and download multimedia computer files that contain graphics, sound, video, and text. In this chapter, you learn about the Internet, how to connect to the Internet, how to use the Internet Explorer Web browser, and how to access pages on the World Wide Web.

Learning Objectives

- Describe the Internet
- Connect to the Internet
- Use Internet Explorer
- Use directories and search engines

chapter three

3.a What Is the Internet?

To understand the Internet, you must understand networks. A **network** is simply a group of two or more computers linked by cable or telephone lines. The linked computers also include a special computer called a **server** that is used to store files and programs that everyone on the network can use. In addition to the shared files and programs, networks enable users to share equipment, such as a common network printer.

The **Internet** is a worldwide public network of private networks, where users view and transfer information between computers. For example, an Internet user in California can retrieve (or **download**) files from a computer in Canada quickly and easily. In the same way, an Internet user in Australia can send (or **upload**) files to another Internet user in England. The Internet is not a single organization, but rather a cooperative effort by multiple organizations managing a variety of different kinds of computers.

You find a wide variety of services on the Internet. You can communicate with others via e-mail, electronic bulletin boards called newsgroups, real-time online chat, and online telephony. You can also download files from servers to your computer and search the World Wide Web for information. In this chapter, you learn about using a Web browser and accessing pages on the World Wide Web. Your instructor may provide additional information on other Internet services.

QUICK TIP

Large commercial enterprises, colleges, universities, and government institutions may already have a network that is part of the Internet through which users can connect to the Internet. Many public library systems also provide free Internet access.

There are several commercial networks that are separate from the Internet. These commercial networks provide users with features such as online newspapers and magazines, chat groups, access to investment activities, computer games, and special-interest bulletin boards as well as Internet access. Popular commercial networks include America Online and the Microsoft Network.

USENET is another network that is separate from but closely connected to the Internet. A **newsgroup** is an Internet discussion group whose members use e-mail to exchange articles of interest on specific topics. The **USENET** network is a collection of computers that maintain and exchange newsgroup articles.

3.b Connecting to the Internet

To connect to the Internet you need some physical communication medium connected to your computer, such as network cable or a modem. You also need a special communication program called a Web browser program (such as Microsoft Internet Explorer) that allows your computer to communicate with computers on the Internet. The Web browser allows you to access Internet resources such as Web pages.

After setting up your computer hardware (the network cable or modem) and installing the Internet Explorer Web browser, you must make arrangements to connect to a computer on the Internet. The computer you connect to is called a **host**. Usually, you connect to a host computer via a commercial Internet Service Provider, such as America Online or another company who sells access to the Internet. An **Internet Service Provider (ISP)** maintains the host computer, provides a gateway or entrance to the Internet, and provides an electronic "mail box" with facilities for sending and receiving e-mail. Commercial ISPs usually charge a flat monthly fee for unlimited access to the Internet and e-mail services.

3.c Using Internet Explorer

A **Web browser** is a software application that helps you access Internet resources, including Web pages stored on computers called Web servers. A **Web page** is a document that contains hyperlinks (often called links) to other pages; it can also contain audio and video clips.

notes

The activities in this chapter assume you are using the Internet Explorer Web browser version 5.0 or higher. If you are using an earlier version of Internet Explorer or a different Web browser, your instructor may modify the following activities.

To open the Internet Explorer Web browser:

Step 1	*Connect*	to your ISP, if necessary
Step 2	*Double-click*	the Internet Explorer icon on the desktop to open the Web browser

When the Web browser opens, a Web page, called a **start page** or **home page**, loads automatically. The start page used by the Internet Explorer Web browser can be the Microsoft default start page, a blank page, or any designated Web page. Figure 3-1 shows the home page for the publisher of this book as the start page.

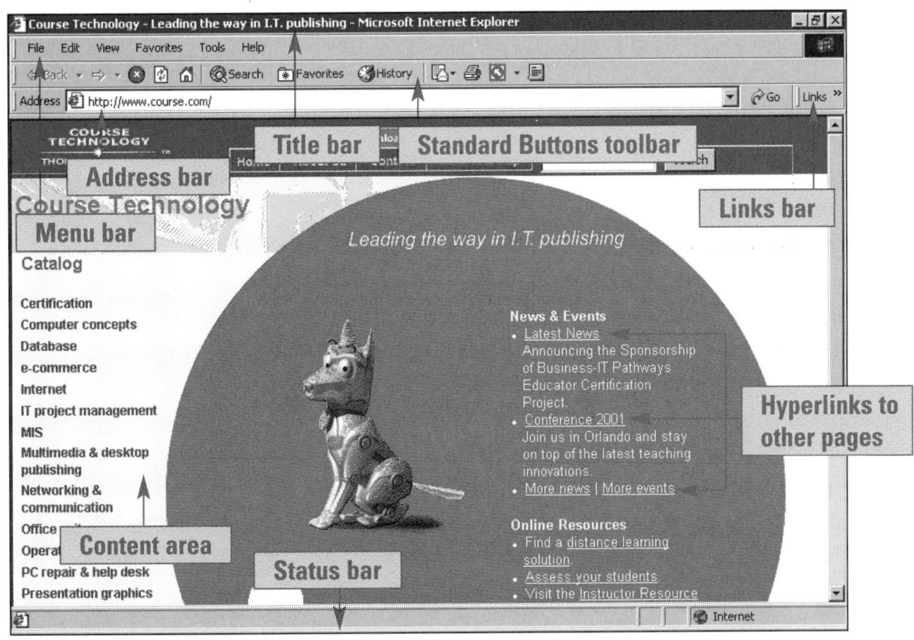

FIGURE 3-1
Internet Explorer Web Browser

CAUTION TIP

During peak day and evening hours, millions of people are connecting to the Internet, and you may have difficulty connecting to your host computer or to other sites on the Internet.

QUICK TIP

Challenges to using the Internet include the amount of available information, communication speed, the dynamic environment, lack of presentation standards, and privacy/security issues. Evaluate the source and author of information from the Internet and confirm business-critical information from another source.

chapter three

MENU TIP

You can create a favorite by clicking the Favorites command on the menu bar and then clicking Add to Favorites, by right-clicking the background (not a link) on the current Web page and clicking Add to Favorites, or by right-clicking a link on the current Web page and clicking Add to Favorites.

MOUSE TIP

You can click the Stop button on the Standard Buttons toolbar to stop downloading a Web page.

QUICK TIP

Another way to load a favorite is to use the Favorites button on the toolbar to open the Favorites list in the Explorer bar. The **Explorer bar** is a pane that opens at the left side of the Web browser screen.

The **title bar** contains the Internet Explorer Web browser Control-menu icon and application name, the title of the current Web page, and the Internet Explorer Web browser Minimize, Restore, and Close buttons. The **menu bar** contains the menu commands you can use to perform specific tasks when viewing the Internet Explorer Web browser window—such as opening a file from your hard disk or printing the current Web page. The **Standard toolbar** contains buttons that provide shortcuts to frequently performed tasks. The **Address bar** contains a text box in which you key the path and filename of the Web page you want to load and a drop-down list of recently loaded Web pages and files. You can click the Go button to load the Web page after keying the page's address in the Address Bar. The **Links bar** is a customizable bar to which you can add shortcuts Web pages you load frequently. The **status bar** displays information about the current Web page. The security zone indicator on the right side of the status bar identifies the security zone you have assigned to the current Web page.

As a Web page loads, the progress bar illustrates the progress of the downloading process. When you place the mouse pointer on a link in the current Web page, its URL appears in the left side of the status bar. The **content area** contains the current Web page. Vertical and horizontal scroll bars appear as necessary so that you can scroll to view the entire Web page after it is loaded.

Loading a Web Page

Loading a Web page means that the Web browser sends a message requesting a copy of the Web page to the Web server where the Web page is stored. The Web server responds by sending a copy of the Web page to your computer. In order to load a Web page, you must either know or find the page's **URL** (Uniform Resource Locator)—the path and filename of the page that is the Web page's address. One way to find the URL for a Web page is to use a search engine or directory. If you are looking for a particular company's Web page, you might find its URL in one of the company's advertisements or on its letterhead and business card. Examples of URLs based on an organization's name are:

Course Technology	*www.course.com*
National Public Radio	*www.npr.org*
The White House	*www.whitehouse.gov*

You can try to "guess" the URL based on the organization's name and top-level domain. For example, a good guess for the U.S. House of Representatives Web page is *www.house.gov.*

You can key a URL directly in the Address bar by first selecting all or part of the current URL and keying the new URL to replace the selection. Internet Explorer adds the "http://" portion of the URL

for you. To select the contents of the Address bar and key the URL for the U.S. House of Representatives:

Step 1	*Click*	the contents of the Address bar
Step 2	*Key*	www.house.gov
Step 3	*Click*	the Go button or press the ENTER key
Step 4	*Observe*	that the home page of the U.S. House of Representatives' Web site opens in your Web browser

Creating Favorites

Web pages are constantly being updated with new information. If you like a certain Web page or find a Web page contains useful information and plan to revisit it, you may want to save a shortcut to the page's URL in the Favorites folder. Such shortcuts are simply called **favorites**. Suppose you want to load the U.S. House of Representatives home page frequently. You can create a favorite that saves the URL in a file on your hard disk. Then at any time, you can quickly load this Web page by clicking it in a list of favorites maintained on the Favorites menu.

The URLs you choose to save as favorites are stored in the Favorites folder on your hard disk. You can specify a new or different subfolder within the Favorites folder and you can change the name of the Web page as it appears in your list of favorites in the Add Favorite dialog box. To create a favorite for the U.S. House of Representatives Web page:

Step 1	*Click*	Favorites
Step 2	*Click*	Add to Favorites
Step 3	*Click*	OK
Step 4	*Click*	the Home button to return to the default start page

One way to load a Web page from a favorite is to click the name of the favorite in the list of favorites on the Favorites menu. To load the U.S. House of Representatives home page from the Favorites menu:

Step 1	*Click*	Favorites
Step 2	*Click*	the United States House of Representatives favorite to load the page

CAUTION TIP

Any Web page you load is stored in the Temporary Internet Files folder on your hard disk. Whenever you reload the Web page, Internet Explorer compares the stored page to the current Web page either each time you start the browser or each time you load the page. If the Web page on the server has been changed, a fresh Web page is downloaded. If not, the Web page is retrieved from the Temporary Internet File folder and you do not have to wait for the page to download. To view and change the Temporary Internet File folder options (and other options that control how Internet Explorer works), click the Internet Options command on the Tools menu.

MENU TIP

You can remove a favorite by displaying the Favorites menu, right-clicking the desired favorite shortcut, and then clicking the Delete command on the shortcut menu. You can also open the Organize Favorites dialog box with the Organize Favorites command on the Favorites menu and select and delete a favorite shortcut.

Step 3	*Click*	the Home button to return to the default start page

The Back and Forward buttons allow you to review recently loaded Web pages without keying the URL or using the Favorites list. To reload the U.S. House of Representatives home page from the Back button list:

Step 1	*Click*	the Back button list arrow on the toolbar
Step 2	*Click*	United States House of Representatives

3.d Using Directories and Search Engines

Because the Web is so large, you often need to take advantage of special search tools, called search engines and directories, to find the information you need. To use some of the Web's numerous search engines and directories, you can click the Search button on the Standard toolbar to open the Search list in the Explorer bar. To view the Search list:

Step 1	*Click*	the Search button on the Standard toolbar
Step 2	*Observe*	the search list options

MOUSE TIP

The Links bar provides shortcuts to various Web pages at the Microsoft Web site. You can also add shortcuts to your favorite Web pages by dragging the URL icon from the Address bar to the Links bar. You can reposition the toolbar, the Address bar, and the Links bar by dragging each one to a new location below the title bar.

Search engines maintain an index of keywords used in Web pages that you can search. Search engine indexes are updated automatically by software called **spiders** (or **robots**). Spiders follow links between pages throughout the entire Web, adding any new Web pages to the search engine's index. You should use a search engine when you want to find specific Web pages. Some of the most popular search engines include AltaVista, HotBot, and Northern Light.

Directories use a subject-type format similar to a library card catalog. A directory provides a list of links to broad general categories of Web sites such as "Entertainment" or "Business." When you click these links, a subcategory list of links appears. For example, if you click the Entertainment link, you might then see "Movies," "Television," and "Video Games" links. To find links to Web sites containing information about "Movies," you would click the "Movies" link. Unlike a search engine, whose index is updated automatically, Web sites are added to directories only when an individual or a company asks that a particular Web site be included. Some directories also provide review comments and ratings for the Web sites in their index. Most directories also provide an internal search engine that can only be used to search the directory's index, not the entire Web. You use a directory when you are looking for information on broad general topics. Popular directories include Yahoo and Magellan Internet Guide.

To search for Web pages containing "movie guides":

Step 1	***Key***	movie guides in the Find a Web page containing text box
Step 2	***Click***	the Search button or press the ENTER key
Step 3	***Observe***	the search results (a list of Web pages in the search list)

The search results list consists of Web page titles displayed as hyperlinks. You can click any hyperlink to load that page from the list. To close the Explorer bar and search list:

Step 1	***Click***	the Search button Search on the Standard toolbar
Step 2	***Close***	Internet Explorer

The Web's many search tools are all constructed differently. That means you get varying results when using several search engines or directories to search for information on the same topic. Also, search tools operate according to varying rules. For example, some search engines allow only a simple search on one keyword. Others allow you to refine your search by finding phrases keyed within quotation marks, by indicating proper names, or by using special operators such as "and," "or," and "not" to include or exclude search words. To save time, always begin by clicking the search tool's online Help link. Study the directions for using that particular search engine or directory, and then proceed with your search.

QUICK TIP

You can reload pages from the History folder, which stores the Web pages you load for a specific period of time. You set the number of days to store pages on the General tab in the Options dialog box. The default number of days to store pages in the History folder is 20 days. Click the History button on the toolbar to open the History list in the Explorer bar.

CAUTION TIP

After you find the desired information, "let the user beware!" Because the Web is largely unregulated, anyone can put anything on a Web page. Evaluate carefully the credibility of all the information you find. Try to find out something about the author and his or her credentials. Many college or university library Web sites have good tips on how to evaluate online information.

Summary

- A network is a group of two or more computers linked by cable or telephone lines, and the Internet is a worldwide "network of networks."
- The World Wide Web is a subset of the Internet from which you can download files and search for information.
- Other external networks related to the Internet are large commercial networks like America Online, CompuServe, Prodigy, the Microsoft Network and USENET.
- To access the Internet, your computer must have some physical communication medium such as cable or dial-up modem, and a special communication program such as Internet Explorer.
- An Internet Service Provider (or ISP) maintains a host computer on the Internet. In order to connect to the Internet, you need to connect to the host computer.
- You use a Web browser, such as Internet Explorer, to load Web pages. Web pages are connected by hyperlinks that are text or pictures associated with the path to another page.
- Directories and search engines are tools to help you find files and Web sites on the Internet.

Commands Review

Action	Menu Bar	Shortcut Menu	Toolbar	Task Pane	Keyboard
Load a Web page	File, Open		Go		ALT + F, O Key URL in the Address bar and press the ENTER key
Save a favorite	Favorites, Add to Favorites	Right-click hyperlink, click Add to Favorites	Drag URL icon to Links bar or Favorites command		ALT + A, A Ctrl + D
Manage the Standard toolbar, Address bar, and Links bar	View, Toolbars	Right-click the Standard toolbar, click desired command	Drag the Standard toolbar, Address bar, or Links bar to the new location		ALT + V, T
Load the search, history, or favorites list in the Explorer bar	View, Explorer Bar		Search Favorites History		ALT + V, E

Concepts Review

Circle the correct answer.

1. A network is:
[a] the Internet.
[b] two or more computers linked by cable or telephone wire.
[c] two or more computer networks linked by cable or telephone lines.
[d] a computer that stores Web pages.

2. Which of the following is not a challenge to using the Internet?
[a] light usage
[b] dynamic environment
[c] volume of information
[d] security and privacy

3. The Address bar:
[a] is a customizable shortcut bar.
[b] contains the search list.
[c] contains your personal list of favorite URLs.
[d] contains the URL of the Web page in the content area.

4. The content area contains the:
[a] Standard toolbar.
[b] status bar.
[c] list of favorites.
[d] current Web page.

5. You can view a list of recently loaded Web pages in the:
[a] Channel bar.
[b] Explorer bar.
[c] Address bar.
[d] Links bar.

6. Search engines update their indexes of keywords by using software called:
[a] Webcrawler.
[b] HTTP.
[c] HotBot.
[d] spiders.

Circle **T** if the statement is true or **F** if the statement is false.

T F 1. Commercial networks that provide specially formatted features are the same as the Internet.

T F 2. USENET is the name of the military Internet.

T F 3. All search engines use the same rules for locating Web pages.

T F 4. Internet users in Boston or New York can access computer files on computers located in the United States only.

T F 5. Spiders are programs that help you locate pages on the Web.

T F 6. A Web page URL identifies its location (path and filename).

Skills Review

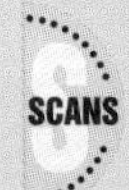

Exercise 1

1. Open the Internet Explorer Web browser.
2. Open the Internet Options dialog box by clicking the Internet Options command on the Tools menu.
3. Review the options on the General tab in the dialog box.
4. Write down the steps to change the default start page to a blank page.
5. Close the dialog box and close the Web browser.

Exercise 2

1. Connect to the Internet and open the Internet Explorer Web browser.
2. Open the search list in the Explorer bar.
3. Search for Web pages about "dog shows."
4. Load one of the Web pages in the search results list.
5. Close the Explorer bar.
6. Print the Web page by clicking the Print command on the File menu and close the Web browser.

Exercise 3

1. Connect to the Internet and open the Internet Explorer Web browser.
2. Load the National Public radio Web page by keying the URL, *www.npr.org*, in the Address bar.
3. Print the Web page by clicking the Print command on the File menu and close the Web browser.

Exercise 4

1. Connect to the Internet and open the Internet Explorer Web browser.
2. Load the AltaVista search engine by keying the URL, *www.altavista.com*, in the Address bar.
3. Save the Web page as a favorite.
4. Search for Web pages about your city.
5. Print at least two Web pages by clicking the Print command on the File menu and close your Web browser.

Exercise 5

1. Connect to the Internet and open the Internet Explorer Web browser.
2. Load the HotBot search engine by keying the URL, *www.hotbot.com*, in the Address bar.
3. Save the Web page as a favorite.
4. Locate the hyperlink text or picture that loads the online Help page. Review the search rules for using HotBot.
5. Print the HotBot Help page by clicking the Print command on the File menu and close your Web browser.

Exercise 6 

1. Connect to the Internet and open the Internet Explorer Web browser.
2. Load the Yahoo directory by keying the URL, *www.yahoo.com*, in the Address bar.
3. Save the Web page as a favorite.
4. Search for Web sites that contain information about restaurants in your city.
5. Print at least two Web pages by clicking the Print command on the File menu and close your Web browser.

Exercise 7 

1. Connect to the Internet and open the Internet Explorer Web browser.
2. View the Links bar by dragging the bar to the left using the mouse pointer.
3. Click each shortcut on the Links bar and review the Web page that loads.
4. Drag the Links bar back to its original position with the mouse pointer.

Exercise 8 

1. Connect to the Internet and open the Internet Explorer Web browser.
2. Click the History button on the Standard toolbar to load the History list in the Explorer bar.
3. Review the History list and click a hyperlink to a page loaded yesterday.
4. Print the page by clicking the Print command on the File menu, close the Explorer bar, and close the Web browser.

Case Projects

Project 1

Your organization recently started browsing the Web with the Internet Explorer Web browser and everyone wants to know how to use the toolbar buttons in the browser. Your supervisor asks you to prepare a fifteen-minute presentation, to be delivered at the next staff meeting, that describes the Internet Explorer Standard Buttons toolbar buttons. Review the Standard Buttons toolbar buttons and practice using them. Write an outline for your presentation that lists each button and describes how it is used.

Project 2 

You are working for a book publisher who is creating a series of books about popular movie actors and actresses from the 1940s and 1950s, including Humphrey Bogart and Tyrone Power. The research director asks you to use the Web to locate a list of movies that the actors starred in. Use the Explorer bar search list and the Yahoo directory search tool to find links to "Entertainment." Click the Entertainment link and close the Explorer bar. Working from the Yahoo Web page, click the Actors and Actresses link. Search for Humphrey Bogart in the Actors and Actresses portion of the database. Link to the Web page that shows the filmography for Humphrey Bogart. Print the Web page that shows all the movies he acted in. Use the History list to return to the Actors and Actresses search page. Search for Tyrone Power, then link to and print his filmography. Close the Internet Explorer Web browser.

Project 3 

You are the new secretary for the Business Women's Forum, a professional association. The association's president asked you to compile a list of Internet resources, which she will distribute at next month's lunch meeting. Connect to the Internet, open Internet Explorer, and search for Web pages containing the keywords "women in business" (including the quotation marks) using the AltaVista search engine. To load the AltaVista search engine key the URL, *www.altavista.com*, in the Address bar. From the search results, click the Web page title link of your choice to load the Web page. Review the new Web page and its links. Create a favorite for that page. Use the Back button list to reload the AltaVista home page and click a different Web page title from the list. Review the Web page and its links. Create a favorite for the Web page. Continue loading and reviewing pages until you have loaded and reviewed at least five pages. Return to the default home page. Use the Go To command on the View menu and the History bar to reload at least three of the pages. Print two of the pages. Delete all the favorites you added in this chapter, and then close Internet Explorer.

Microsoft Word 2002 Introductory

Word 2002

Quick Start for Word

Chapter Overview

This chapter gives you a quick overview of creating, editing, printing, saving, and closing a document. To learn these skills, you create a new document, save and close it, then you open an existing document, revise the text, and save the document with both the same and a different name. This chapter also shows you how to view formatting marks and Smart Tags, zoom the document window, and move the insertion point. In addition, you learn to identify the components of the Word window and create a folder on your hard drive to store your documents. You use these basic skills every time you create or edit a document in Word.

Learning Objectives

- Identify the components of the Word window
- Compose a simple document
- Edit a document
- Save a document
- Preview and print a document
- Close a document
- Locate and open an existing document
- Create a new document
- Close the Word application

Case profile

Today is your first day as a new employee at Worldwide Exotic Foods, Inc., one of the world's fastest growing distributors of specialty food items. The company's mission is to provide customers with an unusual selection of meats, cheeses, pastries, fruits, and vegetables from around the world. You report to Chris Lofton, the Word Processing Department manager, to complete an introduction to the Word 2002 word processing application.

chapter one

notes

This text assumes that you have little or no knowledge of the Word application. However, it is assumed that you have read Office Chapters 1–3 of this book and that you are familiar with Windows 98 or Windows 2000 concepts.

The illustrations in this book were created using Windows 2000. If you are using the Word application installed on Windows 98, you may notice a few minor differences in some figures. These differences do not affect your work in this book.

1.a Identifying the Components of the Word Window

Before you can begin to work with Word, you need to open the application. When you open the application, a new, blank document opens as well. To open the Word application and a new, blank document:

Step 1	*Click*	the Start button Start on the taskbar
Step 2	*Point to*	Programs
Step 3	*Click*	Microsoft Word

When the Word application opens, it contains a blank document with the temporary name *Document1*. Word has many different ways to view a document. The new, blank document is in Print Layout view. However, you want to switch the document to Normal view. Changing document views is discussed in more detail in later chapters. To change the view to Normal view:

Step 1	*Click*	View
Step 2	*Click*	Normal

Your screen should look similar to Figure 1-1, which identifies the specific components of the Word application window.

FIGURE 1-1
Word Application Window with a Blank Document

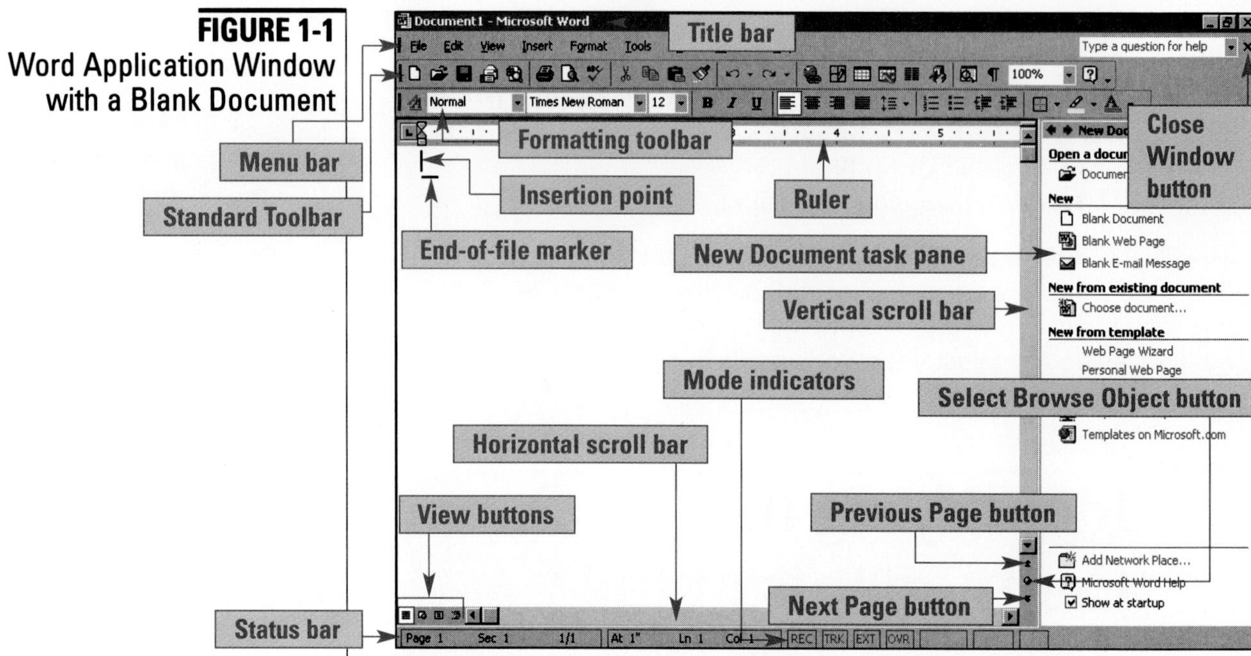

For the activities in this text, you view your documents in Normal view unless otherwise instructed.

QUICK TIP

Office XP features personalized menus, which "learn" the commands you use most often. When you first install Office XP, only the most frequently used commands appear immediately on a short version of the menus and the remaining commands appear after a brief pause. Commands that you select move to the short menu, while those you don't use appear only on the full menu.

Menu Bar

The **menu bar**, located below the title bar, contains nine drop-down menu commands that contain groups of additional, related commands. For example, the File menu contains commands for opening, closing, previewing, and printing files. You can use the mouse or the keyboard to select a command from the menu bar. The activities in this book instruct you to select menu bar commands with the mouse. The Commands Review section at the end of each chapter provides a summary of both mouse and keyboard techniques to select a menu command.

Standard Toolbar

The **Standard toolbar** is located beneath the menu bar and is made up of buttons that represent commonly used commands. For example, the Standard toolbar contains buttons for opening saving, previewing, and printing a file. The Standard toolbar allows you to perform commands quickly by clicking the button that represents that command. You can customize the Standard toolbar (or any other toolbar) by adding or deleting buttons.

Formatting Toolbar

The **Formatting toolbar** is located under the Standard toolbar in Figure 1-1 and is made up of buttons that represent commonly used formats. For example, the Formatting toolbar contains buttons for changing text appearance, such as the font or text alignment.

Ruler

The horizontal **ruler**, located under the Formatting toolbar, provides features you can use to change the tab settings, margins, and indentations in your document.

Insertion Point

The blinking vertical bar in the upper-left corner below the horizontal ruler is the insertion point. The **insertion point** marks the location where text is entered in a document.

End-of-file Marker

The short horizontal line below the insertion point is the **end-of-file marker** that marks the point below which you cannot enter text. This marker moves down as you insert additional lines of text in the document. The end-of-file marker is visible only in Normal view.

Select Browse Object Button

You can use the **Select Browse Object button**, located below the vertical scroll bar, to choose the specific item—such as text, graphics, and tables—you want to use to move or browse through a document.

Previous Page and Next Page Buttons

You use the **Previous Page button** and **Next Page button**, also located below the vertical scroll bar, to move the insertion point to the top of the previous or next page in a multipage document. When you specify a different browse object, the button name changes to include that object, such as Previous Comment or Next Comment. Clicking the buttons moves you to the previous or next browse object specified.

View Buttons

Word has several editing **views**—or ways to look at a document as you edit it. The Normal View, Web Layout View, Print Layout View, and Outline View buttons, located to the left of the horizontal scroll bar, can be used to view and work with your document in a different way. Normal view is the best view for most word-processing tasks, such as keying, editing, and basic formatting. Web Layout view shows how

MOUSE TIP

The Standard and Formatting toolbars appear on the same row when you first install Office XP. In this position, only the most commonly used buttons of each toolbar are visible. All the other default buttons appear on the Toolbar Options drop-down lists. As you use buttons from the Toolbar Options drop-down list, they move to the visible buttons on the toolbar, while the buttons you don't use move into the Toolbar Options drop-down list. If you arrange the Formatting toolbar below the Standard toolbar, all buttons are visible. Unless otherwise noted, the illustrations in this book show the Formatting toolbar positioned below the Standard toolbar.

your document will look if displayed in a Web browser. Print Layout view shows how your document will look when printed on paper. Outline view displays your document in outline format so you can work on its structure and organization.

Status Bar

The **status bar** appears at the bottom of the screen above the taskbar, and provides information about your document and a task in progress. It indicates the current page number (Page 1), the current section of the document (Sec 1), and the current page followed by the number of pages in the document (1/1). In the center of the status bar you see indicators for the current vertical position of the insertion point measured in inches (At 1"), the current line number of the insertion point on that page (Ln 1), and the horizontal position of the insertion point (Col 1).

There may be up to six mode indicators at the right of the status bar. These indicators provide mouse shortcuts to: record a macro (REC), track changes (TRK), extend a text selection (EXT), type over existing text (OVR), check the spelling and grammar in the document (Spelling and Grammar Status), and change the language. (The Language mode indicator may be blank, depending on the language selections during installation; the Spelling and Grammar Status mode indicator is blank unless the document contains text).

Task Pane

The **New Document task pane**, located on the right side of the application window, gives you the capability of quickly creating a new document or opening an existing document. Word includes task panes for viewing the items on the Clipboard, searching for text, inserting clip art, applying styles and formatting to selected text, displaying formatting properties of selected text, for mail merge, and translating text to another language.

1.b Composing a Simple Document

Chris gives you a short paragraph to key. As you key the text, it is visible on the screen and resides in your computer's memory. Word uses a feature called **word wrap** to automatically move words that do not fit on the current line to the next line. As a result, you can key the text without worrying about how much text fits on a line. You do not press the ENTER key at the end of each line. You press the ENTER key only to end a paragraph or to create a blank line.

The paragraph in Step 1 below contains two intentional errors. Key the text exactly as it appears. If you make additional errors, just continue keying the text. You learn two methods of correcting keying errors in the next section. Remember, do not press the ENTER key at the end of each line. To key the text:

Step 1	*Key*	Worldwide Exotic Foods, Inc. is one of the fastest-growing distributors of specialty food items. Worldwide Exotic Foods branch offices in Chicago, Illinois, Melbourne, Australia, Vancouver, Canada, and London, England, and specializes in supplying high-quality and unusual food products too customers around the world.

Next, you correct any keying errors in the paragraph.

1.c Editing a Document

One of the important benefits of using Word is the ability to easily modify a document by inserting, removing, or editing text without having to key the document again. When you position the mouse pointer in a text area, it changes shape to look like a large "I" and is called the **I-beam**. You use the I-beam to position the insertion point in the text area where you want to correct keying errors or add new text. Recall that the insertion point is the blinking vertical bar that indicates where the next keyed character will appear. The text you just entered contains at least two errors. The first error you should correct is a missing word in the second sentence. To insert the word "has:"

Step 1	*Move*	the I-beam before the "b" in the word "branch" in the second sentence
Step 2	*Click*	the mouse button to position the insertion point

CAUTION TIP

Certain words or phrases may have a red or green wavy line underneath. The red line indicates the word is misspelled or not in the Word English-language dictionary or any custom dictionaries being used. The green line indicates a possible grammar error. Chapter 3 discusses the Spelling and Grammar features.

Your screen should look similar to Figure 1-2.

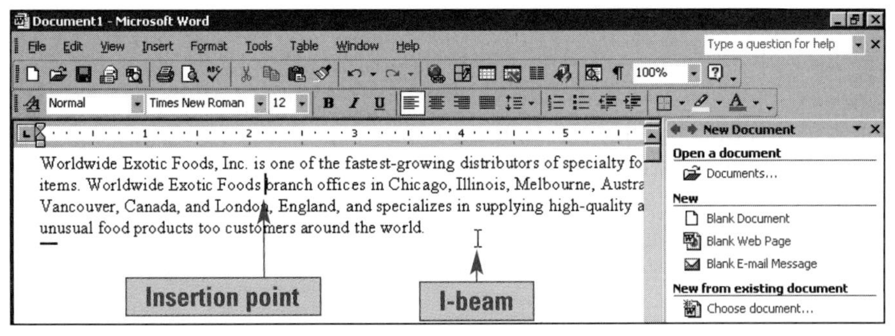

FIGURE 1-2
Repositioned Insertion Point

QUICK TIP

The BACKSPACE and DELETE keys delete individual text characters in your document to the left and right of the insertion point, respectively. You can also use the BACKSPACE or DELETE keys to delete selected text.

You can press the CTRL + BACKSPACE keys to remove the word before the insertion point and the CTRL + DELETE keys to remove the word after the insertion point.

Step 3	*Key*	has
Step 4	*Press*	the SPACEBAR

The second error is an extra letter "o" in the word "too" in the last sentence, which you need to delete. To delete the letter "o":

Step 1	*Move*	the I-beam before the second "o" in the word "too" in the last sentence
Step 2	*Click*	the mouse button to position the insertion point
Step 3	*Press*	the DELETE key
Step 4	*Correct*	any additional errors, if necessary, by repositioning the insertion point and inserting or deleting text

While you are creating or editing a document, every change you make is stored temporarily in your computer's memory. If the power to your computer fails or you turn off the computer, your work is lost. You can prevent such a loss by frequently saving the document to a disk.

1.d Saving a Document

You can save files to a floppy disk, an internal hard disk, or a network server. When you save a file for the first time, it does not matter whether you choose the Save command or the Save As command on the File menu, or click the Save button on the Standard toolbar. Regardless of which method you use, the Save As dialog box opens—providing a way for you to give your document a new name and specify the disk drive and folder location where you want to save the document.

After you have specified the location for saving your document, you key the name of the document in the File name: text box. A filename can have up to 255 characters—including the disk drive reference and path—and can contain letters, numbers, spaces, and some special characters in any combination. Filenames cannot include the following special characters: the forward slash (/), the backward slash (\), the colon (:), the semicolon (;), the pipe symbol (|), the question mark (?), the less than symbol (<), the greater than symbol (>), the asterisk (*), and the quotation mark (").

Using longer descriptive filenames helps you locate specific documents when you need to open and print or edit them. For example, the filename *Letter* won't mean much if you have written many letters, but the filename *Mendez Hire Letter* has meaning even months later.

QUICK TIP

You can use many different keyboard shortcuts when working in Word. For example, you can press the CTRL + S keys for the Save command or press the F12 key for the Save As command. You can locate a complete list of keyboard shortcuts by entering the phrase "keyboard shortcuts" in the Ask A Question Box to search online Help.

Be sure to check with your instructor if you do not know the disk drive and folder in which to save your documents.

To save your document:

Step 1	*Click*	the Save button on the Standard toolbar

The Save As dialog box on your screen should look similar to Figure 1-3.

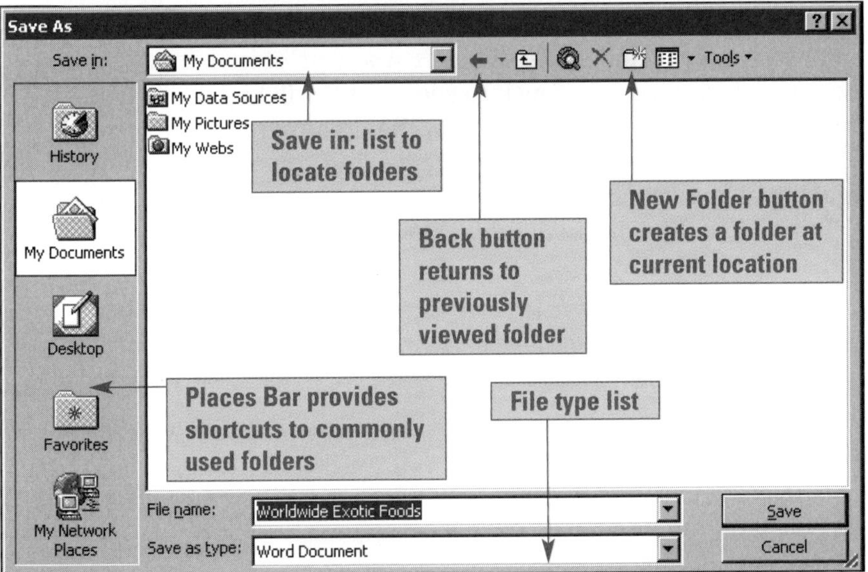

FIGURE 1-3
Save As Dialog Box

You can quickly locate a folder with the Save in: list, move back to the previous viewed folder contents with the Back button, move up one level in the Save in: list, launch the Internet Explorer Web browser and search the Web, delete selected folders or files, create a new folder in the current location, change the viewing options for the folder icons, and change the file type with options in this dialog box. For easier access to commonly used folders, the Save As dialog box also contains a **Places Bar**, which provides shortcuts for opening the My Documents and Favorites folders. You can view any icons on your Windows desktop with the Desktop shortcut in the Places Bar. My Network Places shortcut in the Places Bar allows you to display the computers on your network. The History shortcut on the Places Bar provides access to shortcuts to recently opened folders and files.

Step 2	*Click*	the Save in: list arrow

INTERNET TIP

You can save your documents as HTML documents (Web pages) by clicking the Save As Web Page command on the File menu or by changing the file type to Web Page in the Save As dialog box.

MENU TIP

To view different save options, click the Options command on the Tools menu, and then click the Save tab in the Options dialog box. Other important Options tabs you should review are User Information, Compatibility, and File Locations.

Step 3	*Switch to*	the appropriate disk drive and folder as designated by your instructor
Step 4	*Key*	Company Profile in the File name: text box
Step 5	*Click*	Save

After the document is saved, the document name *Company Profile* appears in place of *Document1* on the title bar.

C

1.e Previewing and Printing a Document

MOUSE TIP

You also can click the Save Options command on the Tools button drop-down list in the Save As dialog box to view only the Save tab in the Options dialog box.

You can resize the Save As dialog box by dragging a dialog box boundary with the mouse pointer.

After you create a document, you usually print it. Before printing a document, you can preview it to see what it will look like when printed. You do not have to preview the document before printing it. However, you can save paper by previewing your document and making any necessary changes before printing it.

To preview the *Company Profile* document and then print it:

Step 1	*Click*	the Print Preview button on the Standard toolbar

The Print Preview window opens. Your screen should look similar to Figure 1-4.

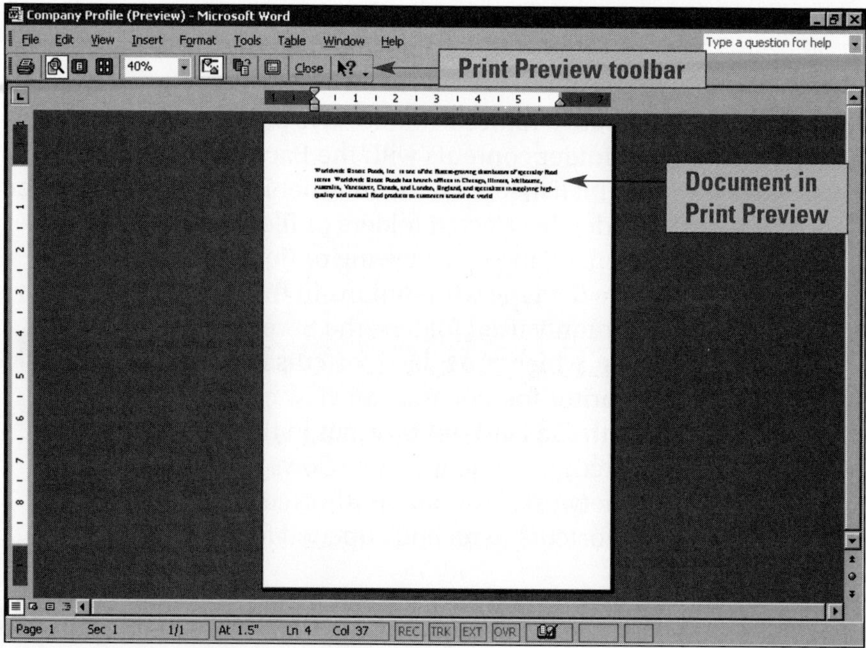

FIGURE 1-4
Print Preview Window

When you preview a document, you are verifying that the document text is attractively and appropriately positioned on the page. If necessary, you can change the document layout on the page, key additional text, and change the appearance of the text as you preview it. For now, you should close Print Preview and return to the original view of the document.

Step 2	*Click*	the Close button on the Print Preview toolbar
Step 3	*Click*	the Print button on the Standard toolbar

You are finished with the *Company Profile* for now, so you can close the document.

1.f Closing a Document

When you use the Word application, you can have as many documents open in the memory of your computer as your computer resources will allow. However, after you finish a document you should close it or remove it from the computer's memory to conserve those resources. To close the *Company Profile* document:

Step 1	*Click*	the Close Window button in the upper-right corner of the menu bar

When documents are closed from the File menu or the Close Window button on the menu bar, the Word application window remains open. This window is sometimes called the **null screen**. To continue working in Word from the null screen, you can open an existing document or create a new, blank document.

1.g Locating and Opening an Existing Document

When you want to edit an existing document, you need to open a copy of it from the disk where it is stored. From inside the Word application, you can open a document in three ways: (1) with the Open command on the File menu, (2) with the Open button on the

QUICK TIP

To customize the Places Bar, select the folder you want to add and then click the Add to "My Places" command on the Tools menu in the Save As or Open dialog box. To reposition a shortcut on the Places Bar or to remove a custom shortcut from the Places Bar simply right-click the shortcut and click the desired command on the shortcut menu.

MENU TIP

You can preview a document with the Print Preview command on the File menu. You can print a document with the Print command on the File menu.

To select print options, you must use the Print command. The Print button prints the document based on the options previously selected in the Print dialog box.

> **QUICK TIP**
>
> Documents saved to an Exchange 2000 Web server can be edited offline when the computer is not connected to the network. To save a document to an Exchange 2000 server, select the My Network Places shortcut in the Save As dialog box and then navigate to the Exchange 2000 server where you want to save the document.

> **MENU TIP**
>
> You can click the Options command on the Tools menu and then view the Security tab to set privacy options for removing personal information such as the author's name from documents when they are saved.

Standard toolbar, or (3) with a shortcut on the New Document task pane. Any of these methods opens the Open dialog box. In this dialog box you first select the disk drive and folder where the document is located. Then you can select the specific document you want from a list of documents available at that location.

Chris asks you to open an existing document that contains several paragraphs so that you can see how to scroll and move the insertion point in a larger document. To open an existing document:

Step 1	*Verify*	that the New Document Task Pane is visible
Step 2	*Click*	the link More Documents in the New Document task pane
Step 3	*Observe*	the Open dialog box, which is similar to the Save As dialog box
Step 4	*Click*	the Look in: list arrow to display a list of locations
Step 5	*Switch to*	the disk drive and folder where the Data Files are stored
Step 6	*Double-click*	*New Expense Guidelines*

The document contains characters you can see as well as characters you cannot see.

Viewing Formatting Marks and Smart Tags

When you create a document Word automatically inserts some characters that you do not see called **formatting marks**. For example, each time you press the ENTER key to create a new line, a paragraph mark character (¶) is inserted in the document. Other formatting marks include tab characters (→) and spaces (·) between words. Sometimes these formatting marks are called **nonprinting characters** because they do not print, but they can be viewed on the screen.

You may want to view the formatting marks to help you edit a document. The Show/Hide button on the Standard toolbar turns on or off the view of formatting marks. To show the formatting marks:

Step 1	*Click*	the Show/Hide button ¶ on the Standard toolbar

Your screen should look similar to Figure 1-5.

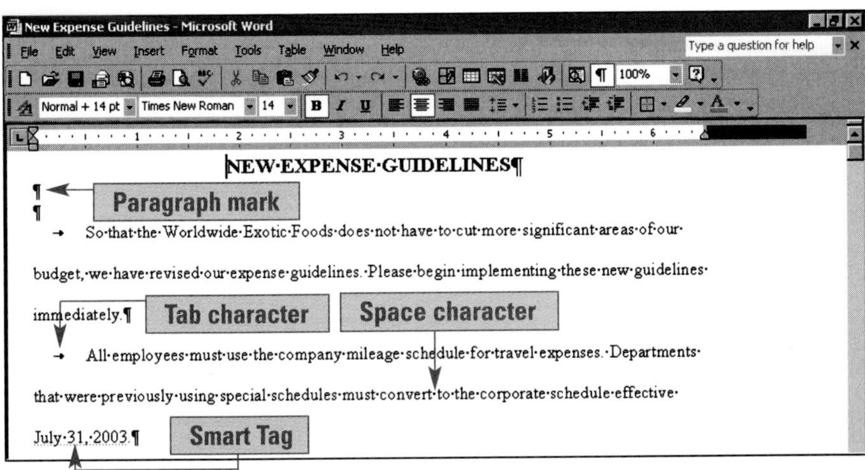

FIGURE 1-5
Formatting Marks and Smart Tags

Paragraph marks appear at the end of each paragraph, the tab character at the beginning of each paragraph, and the space indicators between each word. You won't be formatting this document now, so you can hide the formatting marks. To turn off the view of formatting marks:

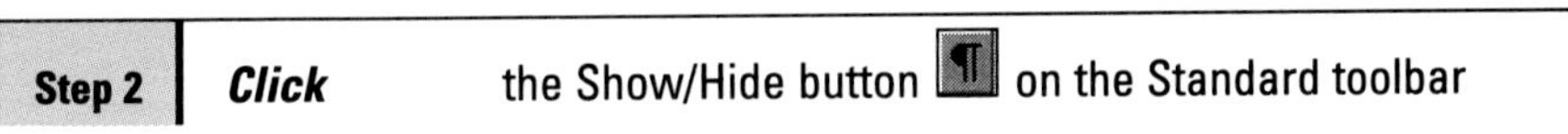

Step 2	*Click*	the Show/Hide button on the Standard toolbar

notes

The illustrations in this text assume the Smart Tag label and button options in the AutoCorrect dialog box are turned on.

Observe the dotted purple line below the text "July 31, 2003" in the second paragraph. This indicates that the underlined text has a Smart Tag. You can display the Smart Tag Actions button and menu options by simply moving the mouse pointer to the Smart Tag text. To observe the Smart Tag Actions button and menu:

Step 1	*Move*	the mouse pointer to the text "July 31, 2003"
Step 2	*Observe*	the Smart Tag Actions button
Step 3	*Move*	the mouse pointer to the Smart Tag Actions button to activate it
Step 4	*Observe*	that the Smart Tag Actions button changes color and a list arrow appears, indicating a drop-down menu is available
Step 5	*Click*	the Smart Tag Actions button list arrow to view the Smart Tag menu

CAUTION TIP

If you edit a document and then try to close it without saving, Word opens a message dialog box prompting you to save your changes.

TASK PANE TIP

The New Document task pane closes when you create a new, blank document from the New button on the Standard toolbar or when you open an existing document. To show the New Document task pane you can click the New command on the File menu or, if the New Document task pane was the last task pane closed, you can click the Task Pane command on the toolbar shortcut menu to redisplay the New Document task pane.

To close any task pane, click the Close button on the task pane title bar.

Your screen should look similar to Figure 1-6. You can remove the Smart Tag, create an Outlook appointment item or schedule a meeting using Outlook, or view the Smart Tag options in the AutoCorrect dialog box with options in this menu. For now, you do not want to take any action using the Smart Tag, so you close the Smart Tag menu.

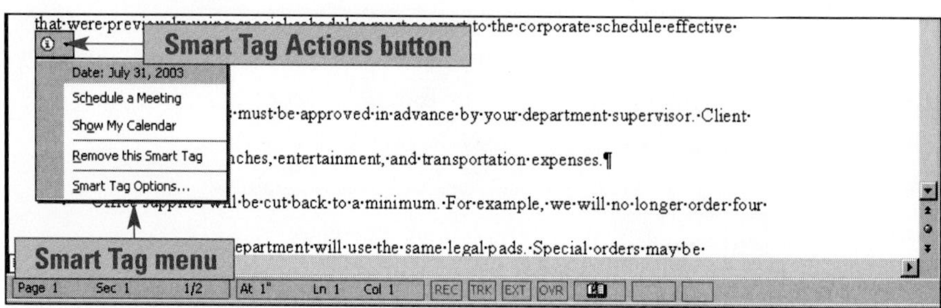

FIGURE 1-6
Smart Tag Menu

QUICK TIP

Word displays Smart Tag labels and action buttons if the Smart Tag labels and action buttons features have been turned on. You can turn the Smart Tag labels and action buttons on or off in the Smart Tag tab of the AutoCorrect dialog box.

Step 6	*Press*	the ESC key or click in the document outside the menu

Whether or not the formatting marks are visible, you can take a closer look at your document.

Zooming the Document Window

When creating a document, you may want to enlarge your document to read the text more easily or look at a miniature view of an entire page to see how the text is arranged on the page. Resizing the view is called **zooming** the document.

You can zoom a document from 10% to 500% of the actual size. You also can resize the view to show the document's entire width by using the Page Width option. To make the text appear larger on the screen, increase the zoom percentage. To make the text appear smaller on the screen, decrease the zoom percentage. Zooming your document changes only the view on the screen; it does not change the size of characters on the printed document. To zoom the *New Expense Guidelines* document:

MENU TIP

You can change the view of your document by clicking the Zoom command on the View menu.

Step 1	*Click*	the Zoom button list arrow 100% on the Standard toolbar
Step 2	*Click*	200%
Step 3	*Observe*	that the Zoom text box indicates 200% and the text is very large
Step 4	*Click*	the Zoom button list arrow 100% on the Standard toolbar
Step 5	*Click*	Page Width to view the entire width of the document

Being able to change the document view is helpful when you are formatting a document. However, when using large zoom percentages or viewing large documents, you might need to scroll to display other parts of your document.

> **QUICK TIP**
>
> You can change the document zoom by keying a value from 10 to 500 in the text area of the Zoom button. Click the Zoom button text area, key a value, and then press the ENTER key.

Using the Scroll Bars

When you want to view different parts of a document without moving the insertion point, use the vertical and horizontal scroll bars. Scrolling changes only that part of the document you see in the document window; it does not change your keying position in the document. The scroll bars appear on the right side and bottom of the window above the status bar. The **vertical scroll bar** enables you to scroll up and down in your document. The **horizontal scroll bar** allows you to scroll left and right in your document. A scroll bar has two scroll arrows. A gray shaded area containing a scroll box separates these scroll arrows. The **scroll box** represents your viewing position in the document. For example, if the vertical scroll box appears in the middle of the vertical scroll bar, you are viewing the middle of your document. (Figure 1-1 also identifies the vertical and horizontal scroll bars.) Table 1-1 summarizes how to view a document using the scroll bars.

TABLE 1-1
Navigating a Document with the Scroll Bars

To Scroll	Do This
Down one line	Click the down scroll arrow
Up one line	Click the up scroll arrow
Down one screen	Click the gray shaded area below the vertical scroll box
Up one screen	Click the gray shaded area above the vertical scroll box
Up or down one page	Click and hold the scroll box on the vertical scroll bar to see the current page number, drag the scroll box to a new page, and release when the ScreenTip shows the page number you want.
End of a document	Drag the vertical scroll box to the bottom of the vertical scroll bar
Beginning of a document	Drag the vertical scroll box to the top of the vertical scroll bar
Right side of document	Click the right scroll arrow
Left side of document	Click the left scroll arrow
Far right side of document	Click the gray shaded area right of the horizontal scroll box
Far left side of document	Click the gray shaded area left of the horizontal scroll box
Beyond the left margin (in Normal view)	SHIFT + Click the left scroll arrow on the horizontal scroll bar
Beyond the right margin (in Normal view)	SHIFT + Click the right scroll arrow on the horizontal scroll bar
To hide the area beyond the left margin (in Normal view)	Click the horizontal scroll box

Moving the Insertion Point

You have already learned how to move the insertion point using the I-beam. You can also use the Next Page, Previous Page, and Select Browse Object buttons to move the insertion point, as explained in Table 1-2. (You must be working in a multipage document to move the insertion point to another page.)

TABLE 1-2
Moving the insertion point

To Move the Insertion Point to	Do This
a new page	Click the Select Browse Object button below the vertical scroll bar and then click the Browse by Page button
the top of the next page	Click the Next Page button below the vertical scroll bar
the top of the previous page	Click the Previous Page button below the vertical scroll bar

You also can use the keyboard to move the insertion point in your document. Table 1-3 summarizes the ways you can do this.

TABLE 1-3
Moving the Insertion Point with the Keyboard

To Move	Press	To Move	Press
Right one character	RIGHT ARROW	**To the top of the next page**	CTRL + PAGE DOWN
Left one character	LEFT ARROW	**To the top of the previous page**	CTRL + PAGE UP
Right one word	CTRL + RIGHT ARROW	**Up one line**	UP ARROW
Left one word	CTRL + LEFT ARROW	**Down one line**	DOWN ARROW
Down one paragraph	CTRL + DOWN ARROW	**Up one screen**	PAGE UP
Up one paragraph	CTRL + UP ARROW	**Down one screen**	PAGE DOWN
Beginning of the line	HOME	**To the beginning of a document**	CTRL + HOME
End of the line	END	**To the end of a document**	CTRL + END
Back to the previous position of the insertion point or to a previous revision	SHIFT + F5	**To go to a specific line or page or section or table or graphic**	F5
To the top of the window	ALT + CTRL + PAGE UP	**To the bottom of the window**	ALT + CTRL + PAGE DOWN

QUICK TIP

If you are using the IntelliMouse pointing device, you can use the scrolling wheel to scroll a document. For more information on using the IntelliMouse pointing device, see online Help.

When instructed to scroll to change the view or move the insertion point to a different location, use one of the methods described in Table 1-1, 1-2, or 1-3.

To move the insertion point:

Step 1	***Practice***	using the mouse and keyboard to move the insertion point in the *New Expense Guidelines* document
Step 2	***Close***	the *New Expense Guidelines* document without saving any changes

Using the Save Command

You can open a copy of an existing document, edit it, and then save it with the same name to update the document on the disk. You want to edit the *Company Profile* document you created earlier. To open the *Company Profile* document:

Step 1	***Click***	the Open button on the Standard toolbar
Step 2	***Switch to***	the appropriate disk drive and folder
Step 3	***Double-click***	*Company Profile*

The file you selected opens in the document window. You edit the document by inserting text. To add an additional paragraph:

Step 1	***Move***	the insertion point to the end of the last sentence
Step 2	***Press***	the ENTER key twice
Step 3	***Key***	Contact us 24 hours a day, seven days a week at our Web site, www.exoticfoods.com.
Step 4	***Press***	the SPACEBAR

Notice that when you press the SPACEBAR after keying the Web site address and period, Word underlines the Web site address *www.exoticfoods.com* and changes the color to blue. This indicates the text is a hyperlink. A **hyperlink** is text or a picture that is associated with the path to another page. For now, you don't want the Web site address text in your document blue and underlined, so you remove the hyperlink formatting by clicking the Undo button on the Standard toolbar or pressing the CTRL + Z shortcut key combination. Then you save the document to update the copy on the disk.

Step 5	***Click***	the Undo button on the Standard toolbar
Step 6	***Click***	the Save button on the Standard toolbar

The copy of the document on disk is updated to include the additional paragraph.

Creating a Folder and Using the Save As Command

Sometimes you may want to keep both the original document and the edited document in different files on the disk. This allows you to keep a backup copy of the original document for later use or reference. To do this, you can save the edited document with a different name. If you want to create a new folder in which to store the modified document, you can create it from Windows Explorer or from inside the Word Save As dialog box.

notes

Check with your instructor, if necessary, for additional instructions on where to create your new folder.

You need to make an additional edit to *Company Profile* by adding the telephone number. This time, after you edit the document you save it to a new location and with a new name so that the document is available both with and without the phone number. To edit the document, create a new folder, and save the document with a new name:

Step 1	*Key*	You may also contact us at (312) 555-1234.
Step 2	*Click*	File
Step 3	*Click*	Save As
Step 4	*Click*	the Create New Folder button in the Save As dialog box
Step 5	*Key*	Completed Files Folder in the Name: text box
Step 6	*Click*	OK to create and open the new folder
Step 7	*Key*	Company Profile Revised in the File name: text box
Step 8	*Click*	Save

You leave this new copy of the document open while you create a new, blank document.

1.h Creating a New Document

From inside the Word application, you can create a new, blank document in two ways: (1) click the New command on the File menu to open the New Document task pane, or (2) click the New Blank Document button on the Standard toolbar. Each document you create in Word is based on a model document called a **template**. When you create a new document using the New Blank Document button on the Standard toolbar, the document is based on the **Normal template**, which is the basic, default Word document model. When you create a document from shortcuts the New Document task pane, you can access a selection of templates for special documents such as letters, memos, and reports.

To create a new, blank document:

Step 1	*Click*	the New Blank Document button on the Standard toolbar

You should have two documents open, *Company Profile Revised* and a blank document. You can switch easily between open Word documents with the Window command on the menu bar or from the taskbar. To switch to the *Company Profile Revised* document:

Step 1	*Click*	the *Company Profile Revised* taskbar button

You are now viewing the *Company Profile Revised* document. You could work in this document, or return to the new, blank document and work in that document. For now, however, you are finished. When you finish using Word, you should exit or close the application and any open documents.

1.i Closing the Word Application

You can close the Word application without first closing the open documents. If you modify open documents and then attempt to close the Word application without first saving the modified documents, a dialog box prompts you to save the changes you have made.

To close the application:

Step 1	*Click*	File
Step 2	*Click*	Exit

The Word application and both open documents close. Because you did not use the blank document, Word did not prompt you to save changes. Also, because you saved the *Company Profile Revised* document after you last modified it, Word closed the document without prompting you to save it.

Task Pane Tip

You can quickly create a new document based on an existing document by clicking the Choose document shortcut on the New Document task pane. This creates a new document containing all the text and formatting of the existing document. You can then modify the document and save it with a new name.

Quick Tip

When you open or create multiple documents, each document opens in its own Word window and has its own button on the taskbar. To close one document when you have multiple documents open, you can click the Close button on the title bar. You can also close a Word document by right-clicking the document's taskbar button and then clicking Close. Be aware, if you have only one document open, this action also closes the Word application.

Summary

- The components of the Word window in Normal view include the title bar, the Standard and Formatting toolbars, the horizontal ruler, the insertion point, the end-of-file marker, the Previous Page and Next Page buttons, the Select Browse Object button, the View buttons, the vertical and horizontal scroll bars and scroll boxes, the status bar, and the New Document task pane.
- Pressing the ENTER key creates a blank line or a new paragraph.
- You can remove text from your document with the DELETE or BACKSPACE key.
- When you create or edit text, changes are temporarily stored in your computer's memory.
- Word wrap is a word processing feature that automatically moves words that do not fit on the current line to the next line.
- To preserve changes to your document, you should save the document frequently.
- Documents must be saved with unique filenames that can be up to 255 characters long, including the disk drive reference and path.
- When you save a document for the first time, you must specify the disk drive and folder where the document will be stored.
- Before printing a document, it is a good practice to preview it to see what it will look like when it is printed.
- You can have as many documents open as your computer's resources allow; however, it is a good practice to close a document when you finish working with it to conserve these resources.
- You can move the insertion point with both the mouse and the keyboard.
- You can view the special formatting marks inserted by Word with the Show/Hide button.
- You can turn on the Smart Tags labels and action buttons in the AutoCorrect dialog box and then view the individual Smart Tag options with the mouse pointer.
- Zooming the document window allows you to increase or decrease the viewing size of the text.
- The vertical and horizontal scroll bars allow you to view different parts of a document without moving the insertion point.
- When all documents are closed, the Word application remains open and you see the null screen.

- To edit an existing document, you can open a copy of the document stored on a disk.
- After opening and editing an existing document, you usually save it again with the same name and in the same location; however, you can save it with a new name or new location.
- You can easily create a new folder for storing documents from the Save As dialog box.
- When you finish using Word, you should close the application.

Commands Review

Action	Menu Bar	Shortcut Menu	Toolbar	Task Pane	Keyboard
Create a new line or end a paragraph					ENTER
Remove a character to the left of the insertion point					BACKSPACE
Remove a character to the right of the insertion point					DELETE
Save a document for the first time or save a document with a new name or to a new location	File, Save As				ALT + F, A F12
Save a document for the first time or save a previously named and saved document	File, Save				ALT + F, S CTRL + S SHIFT + F12 ALT + SHIFT + F2
Preview a document	File, Print Preview				ALT + F, V CTRL + F2
Print a document	File, Print				ALT + F, P CTRL + P CTRL + SHIFT + F12
Close a document	File, Close	Right-click the document taskbar button, click Close	on title bar on menu bar		ALT + F, C CTRL + W CTRL + F4
Open an existing document	File, Open			Open a document link in New Document task pane	ALT + F, O CTRL + O CTRL + F12 ALT + CTRL + F2
Create a new, blank document	File, New			Blank Document link, Choose document link, or New from template links in New Document task pane	ALT + F, N CTRL + N

Action	Menu Bar	Shortcut Menu	Toolbar	Task Pane	Keyboard
Zoom a document	View, Zoom		100%		ALT + V, Z
Show formatting marks	Tools, Options, View tab, All		¶		ALT + T, O, A
Close the Word application	File, Exit	Right-click the application button on the taskbar, click Close	X on menu bar		ALT + F, X ALT + F4

Concepts Review

Circle the correct answer.

1. The Standard toolbar appears in the Word application window below the:
- [a] menu bar.
- [b] status bar.
- [c] Formatting toolbar.
- [d] scroll bar.

2. When you are completely finished working with a document you should:
- [a] edit it.
- [b] hide formatting marks.
- [c] key it.
- [d] save it.

3. Zooming the document window:
- [a] shows the formatting marks.
- [b] allows you to delete text.
- [c] moves text to the bottom of the document.
- [d] increases or decreases the viewing size of text.

4. The insertion point:
- [a] is located under the Standard toolbar and contains shortcut buttons.
- [b] indicates the location where text is keyed in a document.
- [c] provides features for changing margins, tabs, and indentations.
- [d] always appears at the bottom of the screen above the taskbar.

5. To preserve any changes to the document currently visible on your screen, it is a good idea to:
- [a] save the document frequently.
- [b] preview the document.
- [c] move the document to the null screen.
- [d] scroll the document.

6. The Select Browse Object button is located:
- [a] below the Formatting toolbar.
- [b] on the menu bar.
- [c] in the lower-left corner of the Word screen.
- [b] below the vertical scroll bar.

7. To save a document for the first time, you can click the:
- [a] Select Browse Object button.
- [b] New Blank Document button.
- [c] Print button.
- [d] Save button.

8. When you key a document that contains errors, you should:
- [a] close the document.
- [b] preview and print the document.
- [c] save the document.
- [d] edit the document.

9. Which of the following characters can be used in a filename?
- [a] period (.)
- [b] asterisk (*)
- [c] pipe symbol (|)
- [d] question mark (?)

10. If you edit a document and then try to close the Word application, Word:
- [a] automatically saves the changes without a message prompt.
- [b] closes without saving any changes to the document.
- [c] opens a message prompt dialog box asking you to save changes.
- [d] requires you to save the changes to the document.

Circle **T** if the statement is true or **F** if the statement is false.

T F 1. If you are creating or editing a document, any changes you make are stored temporarily in your computer's memory.

T F 2. When using Word, you need to press the ENTER key at the end of each line of text to move the insertion point back to the left margin.

T F 3. When you have finished working on a document, Word automatically saves the document to disk.

T F 4. The Formatting toolbar is located below the ruler and consists of buttons that represent commonly used commands.

T F 5. The Save As dialog box opens the first time you save a document.

T F 6. You can create a new document based on an existing document using a shortcut on the New Document task pane.

T F 7. You can view Smart Tag labels, action buttons, and options when the Smart Tag feature is turned on in the Open dialog box.

T F 8. You can use letters, numbers, and some special characters in a filename.

T F 9. When all documents are closed, the null screen appears.

T F 10. You can move the insertion point to the top of individual pages of a multiple page document with the scroll arrows.

The Skills Review exercises sometimes instruct you to create a document. The text you key is shown in italics. Do not format the text with italics unless specified to do so. Your text may word wrap differently from the text shown. Do not press the ENTER key at the end of a line of text to force it to wrap the same way.

Skills Review

SCANS

Exercise 1

1. Create a new, blank document using the New Blank Document button on the Standard toolbar and key the following text exactly as shown, including the intentional errors. You correct the text in Exercise 2.

Spreadsheet software is a commmon type of computer application software. Other types of applications include word processing, database management, presentation, communication, and Internet browser.

2. Save the document as *Application Software*. Preview, print, and close the document.

Exercise 2 C

1. Open the *Application Software* document you created in Exercise 1 using a shortcut on the New Document task pane.
2. Delete the extra "m" in the word "common" in the first sentence and delete the word "applications" and replace it with the word "software" in the second sentence.
3. Delete the word "Internet" and replace it with the word "Web" in the second sentence.
4. Save the document as *Application Software Revised*. Preview, print, and close the document.

Exercise 3 C

1. Create a new, blank document using a shortcut on the New Document task pane and key the following text exactly as shown, including the intentional errors. You correct the text in Exercise 4.

   Word processing provides an individual with an effective and efficient means of preparing documents. You can create documents and quickly make needed changes prior to printing the document. The software allows your to save the document in a file for later use.
2. Save the document as *Word Processing*. Preview, print, and close the document.

Exercise 4 C

1. Open the *Word Processing* document you created in Exercise 3 using the Open button on the Standard toolbar.
2. Delete the words "and efficient" in the first sentence of the first paragraph.
3. Delete the words "the document" and replace them with the word "them" in the second sentence.
4. Delete the character "r" in the word "your" in the last sentence.
5. Save the document as *Word Processing Revised*. Preview, print, and close the document.

Exercise 5 C

1. Create a new, blank document using a shortcut on the New Document task pane and key the following text exactly as shown, including the intentional errors. You correct the text in Exercise 6.

   The purchasing department will be ordering employee handboooks for the new employees hired during the month of May. Please determine how many handbooks you need and contact Kelly Armstead at ext. 154 by Monday.
2. Save the document as *Employee Handbooks*. Preview, print, and close the document.

Exercise 6 C

1. Open the *Employee Handbooks* document you created in Exercise 5 using a shortcut on the New Document task pane.
2. Delete the extra "o" in "handboooks" in the first sentence.
3. Insert the word "next" before the word "Monday" in the last sentence.
4. Save the document as *Employee Handbooks Revised*. Preview, print, and close the document.

Exercise 7 C

1. Create the following document, making the noted changes.

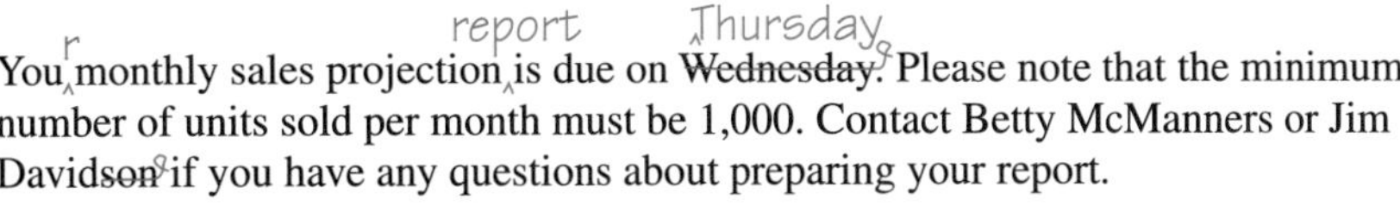
You monthly sales projection is due on Wednesday. Please note that the minimum number of units sold per month must be 1,000. Contact Betty McManners or Jim Davidson if you have any questions about preparing your report.

2. Save the document as *Sales Report.* Preview, print, and close the document.

Exercise 8 

1. Open the *New Expense Guidelines* document located on the Data Disk.
2. Practice using the following keyboard movement techniques to move the insertion point in the document:
   a. Move the insertion point to the end of the document using the CTRL + END keys.
   b. Move the insertion point to the beginning of the document using the CTRL + HOME keys.
   c. Move the insertion point to the word “Foods” in the first line of the first paragraph using the CTRL + RIGHT ARROW keys.
   d. Move the insertion point to the end of the first line of the first paragraph using the END key.
   e. Move the insertion point to the beginning of the first line of the first paragraph using the HOME key.
   f. Move the insertion point to the second paragraph (down one paragraph) using the CTRL + DOWN ARROW keys.
   g. Move the insertion point to the first paragraph (up one paragraph) using the CTRL + UP ARROW keys.
   h. Move the insertion point to the top of the next page using the CTRL + PAGEDOWN keys.
3. Close the document without saving any changes.

Exercise 9 

1. Create a new, blank document using the method of your choice.
2. Key a paragraph of text describing your favorite hobby.
3. Save the document as *My Favorite Hobby.*
4. Preview, print, and close the document.
5. Open *My Favorite Hobby* document you saved in Step 3.
6. Add a second paragraph further describing why you enjoy the hobby.
7. Open the Save As dialog box.
8. Create a new folder named “Hobby” (check with your instructor, if necessary, to select the appropriate location for the new folder).
9. Save the document in the new Hobby folder with the new name *Why I Enjoy My Hobby*. Preview, print, and close the document.

Case Projects

Project 1

Chris Lofton, the Word Processing Department manager at Worldwide Exotic Foods, has asked you to create a new document containing a short paragraph that describes two methods of correcting keying errors, for use in the Word Processing Training Handbook for new employees. Create, save, preview, and print the document.

Project 2

Create a new document for the Word Processing Training Handbook that contains a short paragraph describing the three methods of opening an existing document from inside the Word application. Save, preview, and print the document.

Project 3

If you have not yet done so, read Chapter 1 in the Office Unit in this book to learn more about getting online Help in Office applications. You are working with another new employee at Worldwide Exotic Foods (choose a classmate) to learn how to view, hide, and customize the Office Assistant. Together, review the Office Assistant dialog box options and online Help. Then you and your coworker each create a document and write at least three paragraphs that describe ways to view, hide, and customize the Office Assistant. Save, preview, and print your documents.

Project 4

If you have not yet done so, read Chapter 1 in the Office Unit in this book to learn more about getting online Help in Office applications. Chris asks you to review online Help for several of the buttons on the Standard toolbar and suggests you use the What's This? command on the Help menu to do it. Use the What's This? command on the Help menu to get online Help for three buttons on the Standard toolbar. Create a new document for each button and write one paragraph that describes what the button does and how to use it. Save, preview, and print the documents.

Project 5

If you have not yet done so, read Chapter 3 in the Office Unit in this book to learn about the Internet and the World Wide Web (the Web). Many of your assignments at Worldwide Exotic Foods require using the Web to locate information. Chris asks you to learn how to locate information on the Web by using different search engines and directories. Connect to the Internet and use your Web browser's search feature to load the home page for several search engines. Review each search engine's home page and online Help. Print at least three search engine Help Web pages. Key a brief description of the World Wide Web into a new document. Save, preview, and print the document.

Project 6

Chris asks you to show several new employees how to print multiple documents at one time from the Open dialog box. Using the various tools available on the Help menu, research how to do this. Create a new document with a short paragraph describing how to print multiple documents from the Open dialog box. Save, preview, and print the document. Using your document as a guide, demonstrate to several coworkers how to print multiple documents at one time from the Open dialog box.

Project 7  

Because many of your work assignments at Worldwide Exotic Foods require you to use the Web and your Web browser, Chris wants you to become more familiar with your Web browser's features. Connect to the Internet and load the default home page for your Web browser. Review your Web browser's options to learn how to change the default start page to a page of your choice. With your instructor's permission, change the default start page and close the browser. Open the browser and load the new start page. Reset the option to load the original default start page. Create a new document and key the steps for changing the default start page in your browser. Save, preview, and print the document.

Project 8  

Connect to the Internet and load the home page for a search engine. Use what you learned in Case Project 5 to search for companies on the Web that are similar to Worldwide Exotic Foods. Print at least three Web pages for similar companies. Create a new document and key the names and URLs of the Web pages you found. Save, preview, and print the document.

Creating and Editing a Word Document

Chapter Overview

The basic foundation for every document is creating and editing. This chapter discusses these skills in more detail. You learn to insert dates and text and to select, cut, copy, and delete text. In addition, you learn to set margins and page orientation and use different editing views. With these skills, you can produce finished letters and other documents with minimal rekeying and maximum accuracy.

Learning Objectives

- Create a letter
- Select text
- Cut, copy, and paste text
- Switch between editing views

Case profile

B. D. Vickers, the Administrative Vice President of Worldwide Exotic Foods, requests an assistant in the Purchasing Department and you get the assignment. You work with Kelly Armstead, Vickers' executive assistant, in preparing correspondence for the department. The first letter is a reply to someone inquiring about distribution possibilities for the company.

You should review Appendix B, Formatting Tips for Business Documents, before beginning this chapter.

2.a Creating a Letter

Most organizations follow specific formatting for their letters. A common letter format widely used for both business and personal correspondence is the **block format**. When you create a letter in block format, all the text aligns against the left side of the page. This includes the date, the letter address, the salutation, the body, the complimentary closing, the writer's name, typist's reference initials, and any special letter parts such as an enclosure or subject line. The body of the letter is single-spaced, with a blank line between paragraphs.

Three blank lines separate the date from the letter address information, one blank line separates the letter address information and the salutation, one blank line separates the salutation from the body of the letter, and one blank line separates the body of the letter from the complimentary closing. There are three blank lines between the complimentary closing and the writer's name line. If a typist's reference initials appear below the writer's name, a blank line separates them. If an enclosure or attachment is noted, the word "Enclosure" or "Attachment" appears below the typist's initials with two blank lines separating them. Finally, when keying the letter address information, one space separates the state and the postal code (ZIP+4).

Most companies use special paper for their business correspondence called **letterhead** paper because the organization's name and address are preprinted at the top of each sheet. When you create a business letter, you determine the initial keying position based on the depth of the letterhead information on the paper (most letterheads are between 1 inch and 2 inches deep) and the amount of the letter text. Figure 2-1 illustrates the parts of a block format business letter.

Kelly asks you to create a new letter in the block format. Before you begin keying the text in your letter, you set the appropriate margins and page orientation for the document.

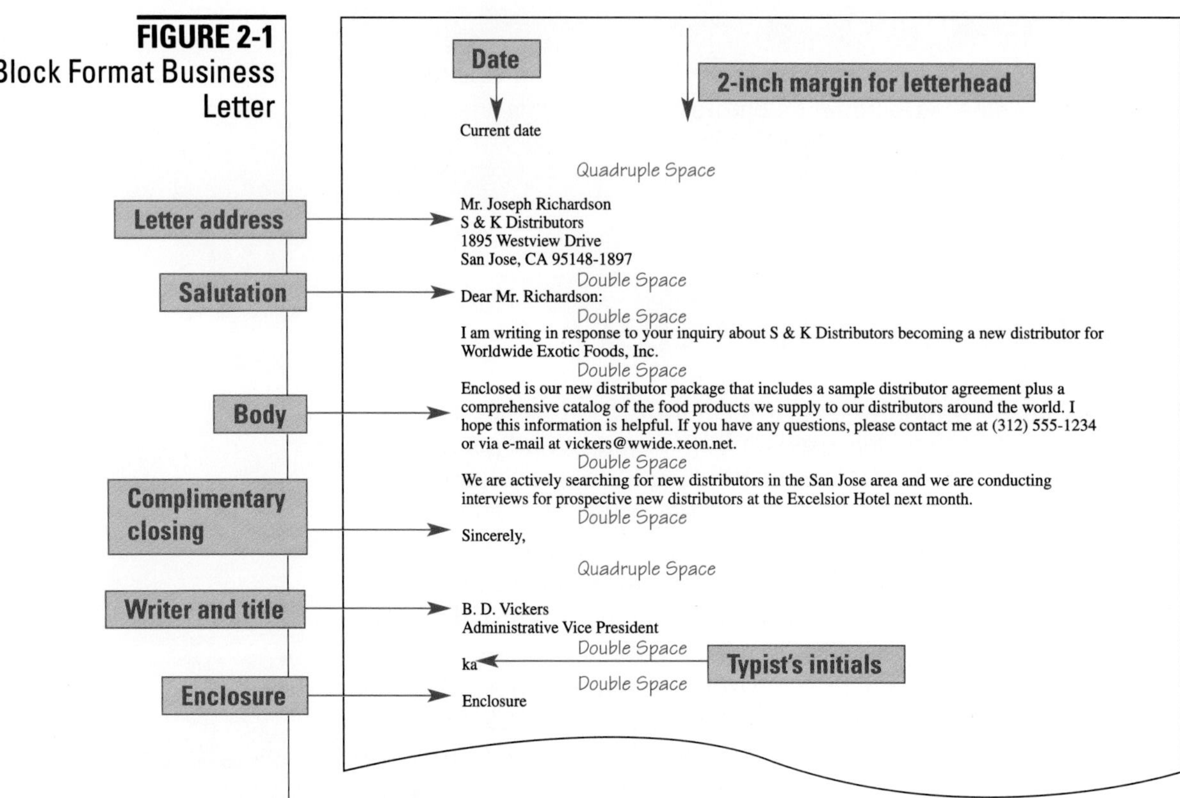

Current date

Mr. Joseph Richardson
S & K Distributors
1895 Westview Drive
San Jose, CA 95148-1897

Dear Mr. Richardson:

I am writing in response to your inquiry about S & K Distributors becoming a new distributor for Worldwide Exotic Foods, Inc.

Enclosed is our new distributor package that includes a sample distributor agreement plus a comprehensive catalog of the food products we supply to our distributors around the world. I hope this information is helpful. If you have any questions, please contact me at (312) 555-1234 or via e-mail at vickers@wwide.xeon.net.

We are actively searching for new distributors in the San Jose area and we are conducting interviews for prospective new distributors at the Excelsior Hotel next month.

Sincerely,

B. D. Vickers
Administrative Vice President

ka

Enclosure

FIGURE 2-1
Block Format Business Letter

Setting Margins

Margins are the distance from the top, bottom, left, and right edges of the page to the text. All text in a document appears within the margins you specify. When printing on letterhead paper, you must consider the depth of the preprinted letterhead when setting top margins and the amount of letter text when setting left and right margins.

You can change the document margins by clicking the Page Setup command on the File menu to open the Page Setup dialog box. Each margin—Top, Bottom, Left, and Right—has a text box that indicates the current margin setting. You can key a new margin size number in the text box. You also can click the up and down arrow buttons at the right side of each text box to increase or decrease the margin setting. The new margins you set affect the entire document by default. However, you can change the document margins from the position of the insertion point or for a section of a document.

You create the letter shown in Figure 2-1 by first creating a new, blank document and setting the appropriate margins and page orientation. Then you key the letter text. Worldwide Exotic Foods uses letterhead paper that requires a 2-inch top margin.

To create a new, blank document and set the margins:

Step 1	*Create*	a new, blank document, if necessary

notes

For the remainder of this text when you are asked to create a new, blank document or open an existing document, you may use the New Blank Document button or the Open button on the Standard toolbar or a New Document task pane link, whichever you prefer.

For the remainder of this text, a task pane may be shown in the illustrations when appropriate.

Step 2	***Click***	File
Step 3	***Click***	Page Setup
Step 4	***Click***	the Margins tab, if necessary

The dialog box on your screen should look similar to Figure 2-2.

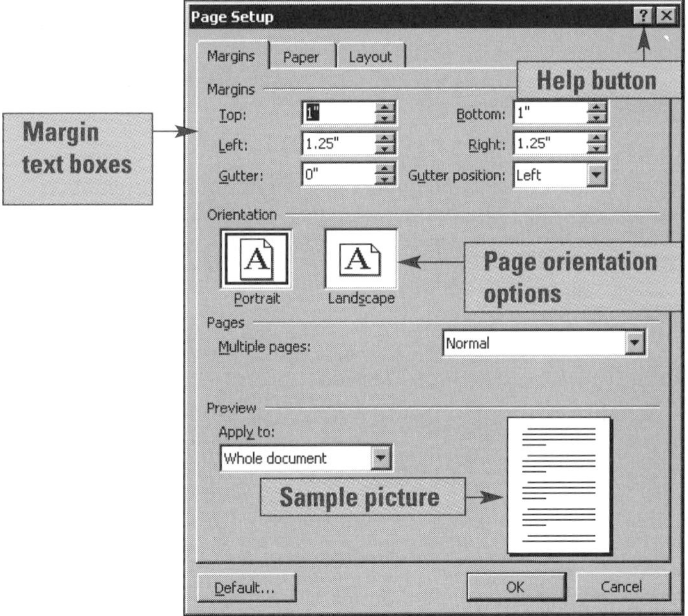

FIGURE 2-2
Page Setup Dialog Box

QUICK TIP

The Multiple pages: list in the Margins tab of the Page Setup dialog box allows you to set special page orientation used for published material such as books or multi-page reports.

You can use the dialog box Help button to review the options on the Margins and other tabs in this dialog box. The blank document already has 1-inch top and bottom margins, and 1.25-inch left and right margins. These **default** margins are preset in the document. You can change the margins as necessary by keying the correct value in each text box. For this letter, you need to change the top margin to 2 inches, and the left and right margins to 1 inch. You can press the TAB key to quickly select the next option in a dialog box.

QUICK TIP

When keying a value for the top, bottom, left, or right margins, it is not necessary to key the inch symbol (").

Step 5	*Key*	2 in the Top: text box
Step 6	*Press*	the TAB key twice
Step 7	*Key*	1 in the Left: text box
Step 8	*Press*	the TAB key
Step 9	*Key*	1 in the Right: text box

Now that you have set the appropriate margins, the next step is to review the page orientation in this same dialog box.

Setting Page Orientation

Page orientation refers to the height and width of a sheet of paper. The default page orientation is **portrait**, which means the paper is taller than it is wide. Most letter documents are printed in portrait orientation. You also can print documents in **landscape** orientation, which means the paper is wider than it is tall. Documents that require more horizontal space such as tabulated reports may be printed in landscape orientation. You can view the current page orientation and change it, if necessary, in the Page Setup dialog box. To view the current page orientation:

Step 1	*Observe*	the Portrait and Landscape options in the Orientation group in the Page Setup dialog box
Step 2	*Observe*	the document preview in the lower-right corner of the dialog box

The default Portrait option is selected and the document preview shows a document that is taller than it is wide. To change the page orientation:

Step 1	*Click*	the Landscape option
Step 2	*Observe*	that the document preview in the lower-right corner of the dialog box is now in landscape orientation

The sample document is now wider than it is tall. Because the standard page orientation for a letter is portrait, you change the page orientation again.

Step 3	*Click*	the Portrait option
Step 4	*Observe*	that the document preview in the lower-right corner of the dialog box returns to portrait orientation

When you change the margins or page orientation you can choose to make those changes for the whole document or for a portion of the document. Because the margins and page orientation are the same for the entire letter, you want the changes to apply to the whole document.

Step 5	***Verify***	that Whole document appears in the Apply to: list
Step 6	***Click***	OK to apply the settings and close the dialog box

After setting the appropriate margins and page orientation, you begin the letter by inserting the current date.

Inserting the Date and Time

Word provides a variety of special options that allow you to insert a date or date and time without keying it. You can insert the date or date and time as text or as a field of information that is automatically updated with the system date. Instead of keying the date manually in the letter, you can have Word insert the date for you. To insert the date:

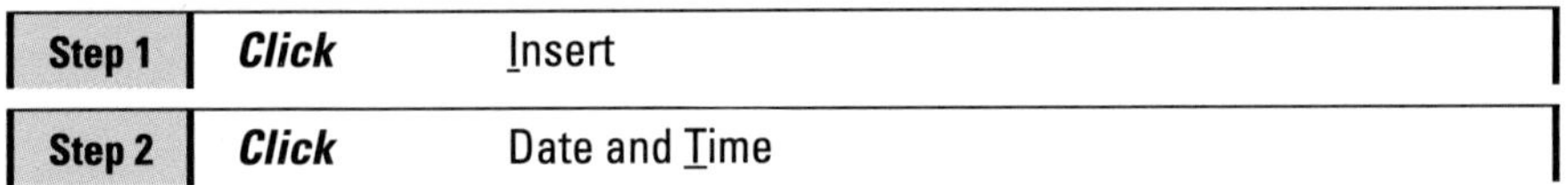

Step 1	***Click***	Insert
Step 2	***Click***	Date and Time

The Date and Time dialog box opens. Except for the dates, the dialog box on your screen should look similar to Figure 2-3.

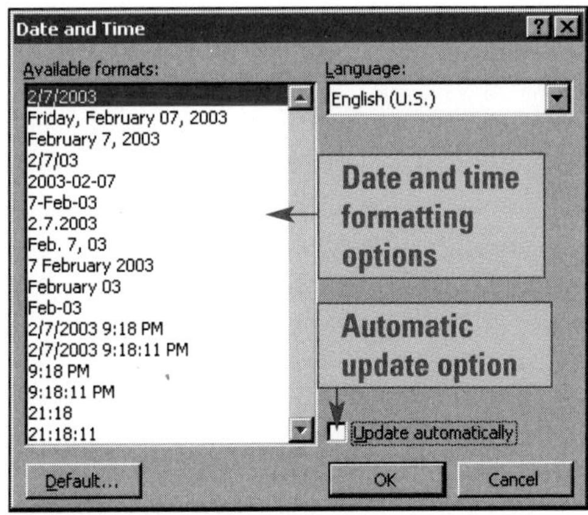

FIGURE 2-3
Date and Time Dialog Box

QUICK TIP

To update a date inserted as a Word date field, select the date and press the F9 key.

You can change the format of the date by selecting a format option in the Date and Time dialog box. The Update automatically check box provides an option to insert the date as text or as a date field, which is updated with the current system date whenever the document is printed. The Default button allows you to set a selected date/time format as the default format for all your Word documents. You use the third date/time format option.

Step 3	***Verify***	that the Update automatically check box is blank
Step 4	***Double-click***	the third date format

After the current date is inserted, you are ready to complete the letter by keying the letter text.

Inserting Text

By default, Word is in **Insert mode**, which enters characters at the position of the insertion point. When you insert text within an existing line of text, the text to the right of the insertion point shifts to make room for the new text. You continue with the letter by inserting the letter address, salutation, body, complimentary closing, typist's initials, and enclosure notation you see in Figure 2-1. To complete and save the letter:

MOUSE TIP

Overtype mode enters new text you key over existing text. In Overtype mode, any character you key replaces the character to the right of the insertion point. To switch between Insert and Overtype modes, double-click the OVR mode indicator on the status bar. The OVR mode indicator appears in boldface type when the Overtype mode is turned on.

Step 1	***Press***	the ENTER key four times
Step 2	***Key***	the remaining letter text as shown in Figure 2-1
Step 3	***Save***	the document as *Richardson Letter* and leave it open

notes

By default, Word capitalizes the first character in the first word of a sentence. When you type your initials, Word automatically capitalizes the first initial. You can manually change it to lowercase by pressing the SPACEBAR and pressing the CTRL + Z keys after you key your initials.

Also, by default, Word changes the color and underlines the path to a Web page or an e-mail address. This allows someone reading the document online to click the e-mail address to open his or her e-mail program. When you press the ENTER key or SPACEBAR after keying an e-mail address, Word changes the e-mail address to a hyperlink. You can remove the hyperlink formatting by clicking the Undo button on the Standard toolbar, by pressing the CTRL + Z keys, or by right-clicking the hyperlink and clicking Remove Hyperlink on the shortcut menu.

When you create a Word document, it is possible to make changes to characters, complete words, or groups of words at the same time by first selecting the text.

2.b Selecting Text

Selecting text is one of the most important word processing techniques. **Selecting** means to highlight one or more characters of text so that you can edit, format, or delete them. Once a character, word, or group of words is selected, Word recognizes the selected text as one unit that you can modify using Word editing features. For example, if you want to underline a group of words for emphasis, you would first select the words and then apply an underline format.

One way to select text is to drag the I-beam mouse pointer across the text. To select text by dragging, click at the beginning of the text, hold down the left mouse button, and move the mouse on the mouse pad in the direction you want to highlight. When the desired text is highlighted, release the mouse button.

The **selection bar** is the vertical area to the far left of the document between the horizontal ruler and the View buttons. When the mouse pointer is in the selection bar, it appears as a right-pointing arrow and you can use it to select text. Figure 2-4 identifies the selection bar and the shape of the mouse pointer when it is in the selection bar.

CAUTION TIP

You should take precautions to back up your work in case of power failure while you are working on a document. You can protect your work by using the AutoRecover feature or the Always create backup copy option. The AutoRecover feature periodically saves a backup copy of a document while you are working on it. The Always create backup copy option saves a backup of your document each time you save it. You can find these options by clicking the Options command on the Tools menu, and then clicking the Save tab in the Options dialog box.

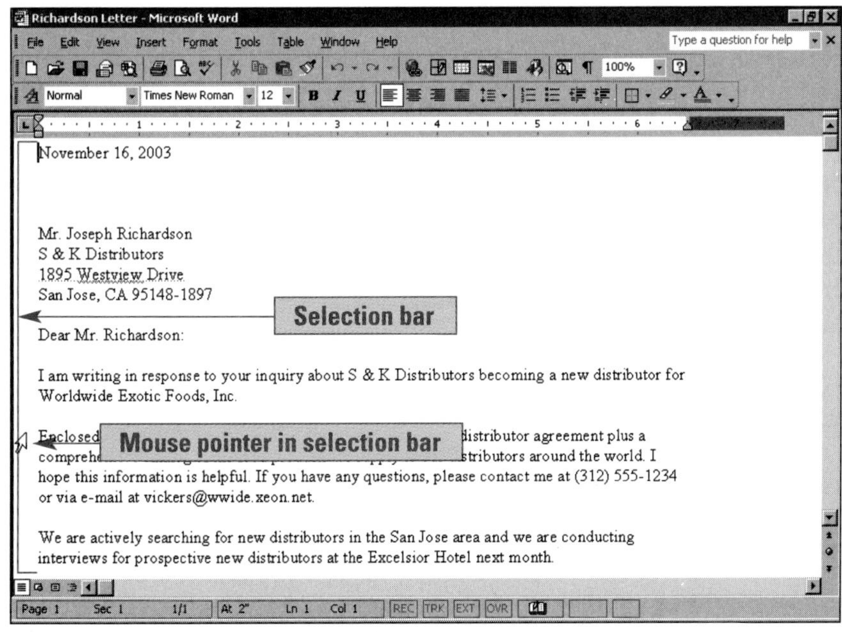

FIGURE 2-4
Selection Bar

chapter two

Word includes many mouse and keyboard shortcuts for selecting text. Table 2-1 lists some frequently used shortcuts.

TABLE 2-1
Keyboard and Mouse Shortcuts for Selecting Text

To Select	Do This
a word and the trailing space	Double-click a word
a sentence and the trailing space	Hold down the CTRL key and click inside the sentence
a line of text	Click in the selection bar next to the line
multiple lines of text	Drag in the selection bar next to the lines
a paragraph	Double-click in the selection bar next to the line or triple-click the paragraph
multiple paragraphs	Drag in the selection bar
the document	Hold down the CTRL key and click in the selection bar, or triple-click in the selection bar
a vertical selection of text	Hold down the ALT key and drag the mouse down and left or right
a variable amount of contiguous text	Place the insertion point at the beginning of the text to be selected, move the I-beam to the end of the text to be selected, hold down the SHIFT key, and click the mouse button
multiple areas of a document	Select the first text, then hold down the CTRL key as you select additional text
the text from the insertion point to the end of the document	Press the CTRL + SHIFT + END keys
the text from the insertion point to the beginning of the document	Press the CTRL + SHIFT + HOME keys

Deselecting text means to remove the highlighting. You can deselect text by clicking anywhere in the document area outside the highlighting, by selecting new text, or by pressing a **pointer-movement key** (UP ARROW, DOWN ARROW, LEFT ARROW, RIGHT ARROW) on the keyboard. To select a paragraph of your document by dragging:

Step 1	***Move***	the I-beam before the "E" in "Enclosed" in the second body paragraph
Step 2	***Drag***	down until you have highlighted the entire paragraph and the following blank line
Step 3	***Press***	the RIGHT ARROW key to deselect the text

To compare the dragging selection technique to using the selection bar:

Step 1	***Move***	the mouse pointer into the selection bar before the "E" in "Enclosed" until the mouse pointer becomes a right-pointing arrow
Step 2	***Double-click***	the selection bar
Step 3	***Click***	outside the selected text to deselect it

To select a variable amount of contiguous text using the SHIFT + Click method:

Step 1	***Click***	in front of the "E" in "Enclosed" to position the insertion point
Step 2	***Press & hold***	the SHIFT key
Step 3	***Move***	the I-beam mouse pointer to the end of the word "questions" in the third line
Step 4	***Click***	the mouse button to select the contiguous text beginning with "Enclosed" and ending with "questions"
Step 5	***Deselect***	the text

To select variable amount of noncontiguous text using the CTRL + Click method:

Step 1	***Select***	the text "Enclosed" in the second paragraph
Step 2	***Press & hold***	the CTRL key
Step 3	***Select***	the text "If you have any questions" in the third line of the second paragraph
Step 4	***Continue***	to hold down the CTRL key
Step 5	***Select***	the text "San Jose" in the first line of the third paragraph
Step 6	***Deselect***	the text

After text is selected, you can perform other tasks with the text—such as deleting it, formatting it, replacing it by keying new text, and copying or moving it to another location.

MOUSE TIP

By default, the automatic word selection feature is turned on. When you begin to drag across a second word, the automatic word selection feature quickly selects the entire word and the trailing space. You can turn off this feature in the When selecting, automatically select entire word check box on the Edit tab in the Options dialog box. To view the Options dialog box, click the Options command on the Tools menu.

QUICK TIP

You can select text by pressing the F8 key (EXT mode) or holding down the SHIFT key and then pressing a pointer-movement key to turn on **Extend mode** at the location of the insertion point. For example, move the insertion point to the beginning of the word, press the F8 key, then press the CTRL + RIGHT ARROW key to highlight the word. To remove a highlighted selection, press the ESC key and then press a pointer-movement key.

2.c Cutting, Copying, and Pasting Text

You can move, or **cut and paste**, text from one location to another in a Word document. You can duplicate, or **copy and paste**, text from one location to another in a Word document. You also can cut and paste or copy and paste text into a different Word document or into another Office application document.

> **QUICK TIP**
>
> The Office Clipboard is separate from the Windows Clipboard. You can collect up to 24 cut or copy selections from different sources, including other Office XP applications and your Web browser, and paste the selections all at once or one at a time from the Office Clipboard. The Windows Clipboard contains just the last item you cut or copied. When you clear all items from the Office Clipboard, the Windows Clipboard is also cleared. For more information on the Office Clipboard and the Windows Clipboard, see online Help.

Cutting and Pasting Using the Office Clipboard Task Pane

You use the Cut command to remove text, the Copy command to duplicate text, and the Paste command to insert the cut or copied text. The Cut and Copy commands collect selected text from your Word document and insert it on the Office Clipboard. The **Office Clipboard** is a reserved place in the memory of your computer that can be used to store text temporarily. The Office Clipboard can hold up to 24 cut or copy actions.

To cut or copy text, you first select the desired text and then click Cut or Copy on the Edit menu or shortcut menu or click the Cut or Copy button on the Standard toolbar. To insert the cut or copied text at a new location in your document, first move the insertion point to the location. Then click the Paste command on the Edit menu or shortcut menu, or click the Paste button on the Standard toolbar. You also can use the Office Clipboard task pane to paste. The Office Clipboard task pane usually appears automatically after you cut or copy a second selection before pasting the first cut or copied selection.

Kelly reviewed the *Richardson Letter* document and wants you to move the third body paragraph to the second body paragraph position. To display the Office Clipboard task pane:

Step 1	***Click***	Edit
Step 2	***Click***	Office Clipboard

> **CAUTION TIP**
>
> Multiple selected noncontiguous areas of a document (selection using the CTRL + Click method) are considered one selected item for cutting, copying, and pasting.

The Office Clipboard is currently empty. The next step is to select the text you want to move. You can use a shortcut menu to quickly place the text to the Office Clipboard. To select and cut text:

Step 1	***Select***	the third paragraph beginning with "We are" and the following blank line

Step 2	*Move*	the mouse pointer to the selected text

notes

Chapter 1 and the previous sections of this chapter provided step-by-step instructions for repositioning the insertion point. From this point forward, you are instructed to move the I-beam or insertion point to the appropriate position. Review Chapter 1 to see the step-by-step process for repositioning the insertion point, if necessary.

Step 3	*Right-click*	the selected text

A shortcut menu for the selected text appears. Your screen should look similar to Figure 2-5.

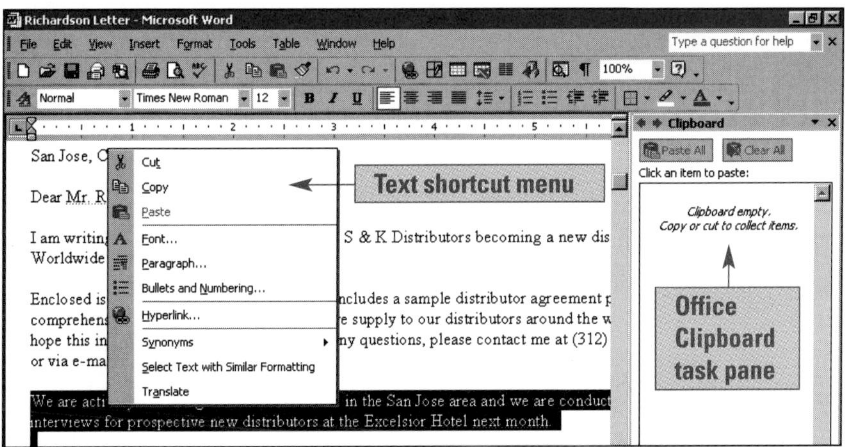

FIGURE 2-5
Text Shortcut Menu

Step 4	*Click*	Cut on the shortcut menu
Step 5	*Observe*	that the third body paragraph no longer appears in the document because it is temporarily stored on the Office Clipboard

TASK PANE TIP

When a task pane is already visible, you can switch to the Office Clipboard task pane with the Other Task Panes button on the task pane title bar.

The Task Pane command on the View menu and the Task Pane command on the toolbar shortcut menu display the last visible task pane. For example, if you open the Office Clipboard task pane and then close it, both the Task Pane command on the View menu and the Task Pane command on the toolbar shortcut menu will redisplay the Office Clipboard task pane.

The Office Clipboard task pane on your screen should look similar to Figure 2-6.

FIGURE 2-6
Text Stored in the Office Clipboard

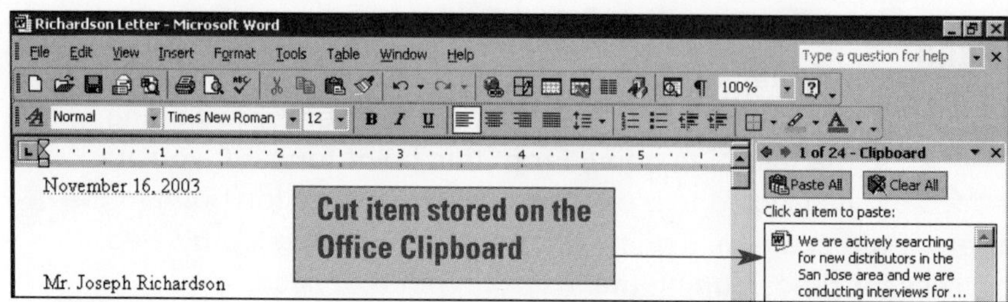

If you have multiple items stored on the Office Clipboard, you can paste all of them at once with the Paste All button. When you move the mouse pointer to an item in the Office Clipboard contents list, the item is selected, a border appears around the item, and a drop-down list arrow appears to the right of the item. To paste an individual item, you can click the item or click the item's drop-down list arrow and click Paste. Once an item is pasted, a dark blue border appears around the item. To paste the individual cut item:

Step 6	***Move***	the insertion point in front of the "E" in "Enclosed" in the second body paragraph
Step 7	***Click***	the individual item in the Click an item to paste: list in the Clipboard task pane
Step 8	***Observe***	that the paragraph is inserted in the new location
Step 9	***Observe***	the dark blue border around the item in the Office Clipboard task pane

After the text is pasted in the document in the new location, the Paste Options Smart Tag icon appears at the end of the pasted paragraph.

QUICK TIP

You can turn on or off the Paste Options feature with an option on the Edit tab in the Options dialog box. To open the Options dialog box, click the Options command on the Tools menu.

Working With Paste Options

The Paste Options Smart Tag feature allows you to control the formatting of the pasted text. You can choose to keep the original formatting, match the destination formatting, keep the text only and remove all formatting, or apply special formatting. Because you are moving text within the same document, you want to keep the original source formatting. To view the Paste Options button menu choices:

Step 1	***Move***	the mouse pointer to the Paste Options icon to activate it
Step 2	***Click***	the Paste Options list arrow to view the menu

Step 3	*Observe*	that the default option is to keep the original source formatting
Step 4	*Press*	the ESC key to close the menu

When you are finished with the Office Clipboard, you can clear it and then close the task pane.

Clearing the Office Clipboard

You can clear the Office Clipboard after you no longer need to paste the items stored there. You can clear all of the items on the Office Clipboard with the Clear All button or you can clear individual items with the Delete command on the individual item's drop-down list.

When the Office Clipboard icon is visible in the taskbar tray, you can right-click it to set Office Clipboard task pane options.

To clear the individual Office Clipboard item:

Step 1	*Move*	the mouse pointer to the item in the Click an item to paste: list in the Clipboard task pane
Step 2	*Click*	the item's list arrow
Step 3	*Click*	Delete
Step 4	*Observe*	that the Office Clipboard is again empty
Step 5	*Close*	the Office Clipboard task pane
Step 6	*Save*	the document as *Revised Richardson Letter*

After reviewing the *Revised Richardson Letter*, Kelly wants to make some additional changes.

Copying and Pasting Using Toolbar Buttons

You do not have to use the Office Clipboard task pane to cut and paste or copy and paste. If you are working with one selection, it may be faster to use the Cut, Copy, and Paste buttons on the Standard toolbar to cut, copy, and paste. Kelly also wants you to copy the letter address and paste it at the end of the document. Before you begin, you add two blank lines at the end of the document. Then you copy the address to the Office Clipboard using the Copy button on the Standard toolbar and paste it using the Paste button.

To copy and paste the address:

Step 1	*Move*	the insertion point to the bottom of the document

TASK PANE TIP

You change how the Office Clipboard task pane is displayed by clicking the Options button in the Office Clipboard task pane. One option allows you to turn on or off the automatic display of this task pane as you cut or copy items. Another option allows you to turn on the Office Clipboard but display an icon in the taskbar tray in the lower-right corner of the screen and then close the Office Clipboard task pane so that you have more area in which to view your document. You can still cut or copy multiple items to the Office Clipboard if you elect to show the taskbar tray icon. When you want to view the Office Clipboard task pane, simply double-click the icon.

> **MENU TIP**
>
> You can cut, copy, and paste selected text with the Cut, Copy, and Paste commands on the Edit menu or a shortcut menu.

Step 2	*Press*	the ENTER key twice to insert two blank lines, if necessary
Step 3	*Select*	the four lines of the letter address
Step 4	*Click*	the Copy button on the Standard toolbar
Step 5	*Move*	the insertion point to the bottom of the document
Step 6	*Click*	the Paste button on the Standard toolbar
Step 7	*Observe*	that the letter address is now in two locations in the document
Step 8	*Save*	the *Revised Richardson Letter* document and close it

Not only can you use menu commands and the Office Clipboard task pane to cut, copy, and paste, you can also use the mouse to move or copy text.

> **QUICK TIP**
>
> When you open the Save As dialog box and then save the current file with the same name as an existing file, Word opens a dialog box that allows you to replace the existing file, save your changes with a different filename, or merge the changes you made into the existing file.

Moving and Copying Text with the Mouse

A shortcut method for moving and copying text is called **drag-and-drop**. This method uses the mouse and does not store any items on the Office Clipboard. To move text using drag-and-drop, first select the text and then drag the selection to its new location. To copy text using drag-and-drop, select the text, press and hold the CTRL key, and then drag the text to its new location, releasing the mouse button before you release the CTRL key.

When you are using the drag-and-drop method, the insertion point changes to a small, dashed, gray vertical line. A small box with a dashed, gray border appears at the base of the mouse pointer. If you are copying text, a small plus sign (+) appears below of the mouse pointer.

You open the *Richardson Letter* from the File menu and move the third body paragraph to the second body paragraph position using the mouse pointer. You can quickly open a recently closed document by clicking the document name on the File menu list of recently closed documents. To use the drag-and-drop method to move text:

Step 1	*Click*	File
Step 2	*Click*	the *Richardson Letter* at the bottom of the File menu
Step 3	*Select*	the paragraph beginning with "We are" and the following blank line
Step 4	*Move*	the mouse pointer to the selected text (the pointer is a left-pointing arrow)
Step 5	*Click & hold*	the left mouse button
Step 6	*Observe*	the dashed line insertion point at the tip of the mouse pointer

Step 7	***Drag***	up until the dashed line insertion point is positioned before the word "E" in "Enclosed" in the second body paragraph
Step 8	***Release***	the mouse button
Step 9	***Deselect***	the text

To copy the letter address to the bottom of the document:

Step 1	***Insert***	two blank lines at the bottom of the document
Step 2	***Select***	the letter address
Step 3	***Move***	the mouse pointer to the selected address text
Step 4	***Press & hold***	the CTRL key
Step 5	***Drag***	the selected text to the bottom of the document
Step 6	***Release***	the mouse button
Step 7	***Release***	the CTRL key
Step 8	***Observe***	the copied address text
Step 9	***Close***	the *Richardson Letter* without saving changes

MOUSE TIP

You can **right-drag** selected text to move or copy it. Select the text you want to move or copy, and then hold down the right mouse button instead of the left mouse button as you drag the text. When you release the mouse button, a shortcut menu containing the Move Here and Copy Here commands appears. Click the appropriate command to paste the selection.

Using Repeat, Undo, and Redo Features

The Repeat, Undo, and Redo features come in handy as you edit documents. The **Repeat** feature allows you to duplicate your last action. The **Undo** feature allows you to reverse a previous action. The **Redo** feature allows you to undo a previously undone action. To repeat the last action, click the Repeat command on the Edit menu or press the CTRL + Y keys. To undo the last action, click the Undo button on the Standard toolbar, click the Undo command on the Edit menu, or press the CTRL + Z keys. To redo the last undone action, click the Redo button on the Standard toolbar. You can undo multiple actions sequentially, beginning with the last action you performed, by clicking the Undo button for each command you want to reverse.

Word has many ways to view a document for editing. The appropriate editing view depends on the kind of editing you are doing.

CAUTION TIP

When copying text with drag-and-drop, do not release the CTRL key until you have first released the mouse button. Releasing the CTRL key first causes Word to move the text instead of copying it.

CAUTION TIP

The Undo and Redo button list arrows on the Standard toolbar provide lists of actions that can be undone or previously undone actions that can be redone. To undo or redo an action, select that action from the Undo or Redo list. Word reverses that action *and any other actions in the list performed after the action you selected.* This means that all the actions listed above the one you select are also reversed.

QUICK TIP

In Print Layout view, the I-beam sometimes appears with a text alignment indicator. This **Click and Type** feature enables you to double-click anywhere in your document in Print Layout view to position the insertion point.

2.d Switching Between Editing Views

You can view documents in several ways for editing: Normal view, Web Layout view, Print Layout view, Full Screen view, Outline view, and Print Preview. The two most commonly used views for entering and editing text are Normal view and Print Layout view. Web Layout view is used to create Web pages, and Outline view is used to create text outlines.

Normal View

Normal view is commonly used for keying, editing, and formatting text. Margins, headers and footers, drawing objects, graphics, and text in column format are not displayed in Normal view. You can switch to Normal view with the Normal command on the View menu or the Normal View button.

Print Layout View

In **Print Layout view**, the document display looks more like the printed page—including headers and footers, columns, graphics, drawing objects, and margins. You also see a vertical ruler in Print Layout view. You can switch to Print Layout view with the Print Layout command on the View menu or with the Print Layout view button. To view a multipage document in Print Layout view:

Step 1	***Open***	the *Vancouver Warehouse Report* located on the Data Disk
Step 2	***Click***	the Print Layout View button to the left of the horizontal scroll bar
Step 3	***Zoom***	the document to Two Pages

Your screen should look similar to Figure 2-7.

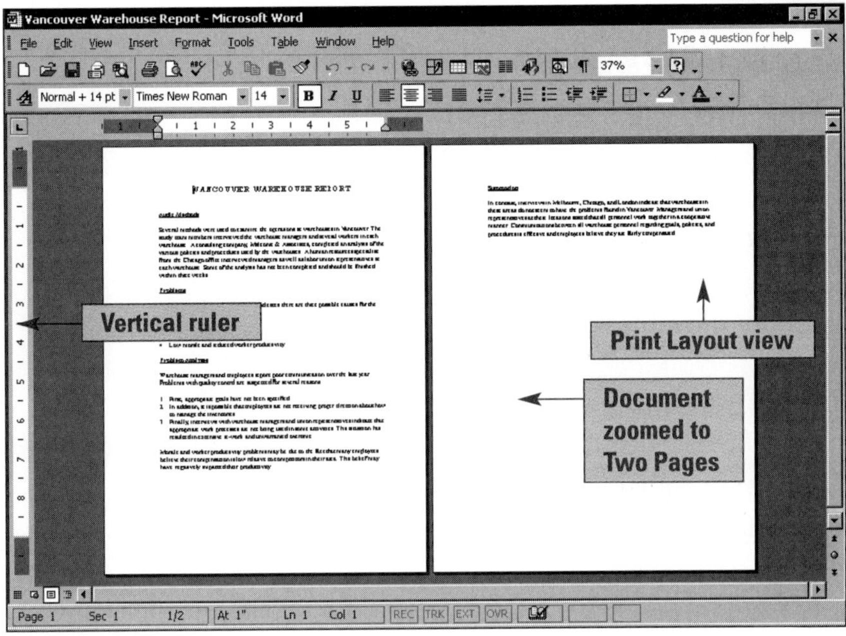

FIGURE 2-7
Print Layout View

Step 4	*Zoom*	the document back to Page Width
Step 5	*Click*	the Normal View button to the left of the horizontal scroll bar
Step 6	*Close*	the *Vancouver Warehouse Report* document without saving changes

MOUSE TIP

You can set margins with the mouse pointer and the horizontal and vertical rulers in Print Layout view. Switch to Print Layout view and point to the margin boundary on the horizontal or vertical ruler. The mouse pointer becomes a black, two-headed move pointer. Drag the boundary to the desired position. If you press and hold the ALT key while dragging, the ruler displays measurements that indicate the margin settings and text area width.

Full Screen View

When you need to maximize the number of text lines you see on your screen, use Full Screen view, which hides the title bar, menu bar, toolbars, scroll bars, status bar, and taskbar. You can switch to Full Screen view with the Full Screen command on the View menu. From Full Screen view, you can switch back to the previous view by clicking the Close Full Screen button on the Full Screen toolbar that appears when in Full Screen view.

Summary

- The block format is commonly used for business correspondence.
- Word has preset top, bottom, left, and right margins that you can change in the Page Setup dialog box.
- The date and time can be inserted in a document as text or as a field that automatically updates to the current system date when the document is printed.
- You can select characters, words, or groups of words with the mouse or keyboard.
- Selected text can be cut, copied, and pasted using menu commands, a shortcut menu, toolbar buttons, and the Office Clipboard task pane.
- You can collect up to 24 cut or copied selections and then paste them individually or all at one time using the Office Clipboard task pane.
- You can repeat or undo your last action.
- Word has several ways you can view your document, including: Normal view, Print Layout view, and Full Screen view. Use Normal view to key, edit, and format text. Use Print Layout to view and work with margins, headers and footers, columns, graphics, and drawing objects. Use Full Screen view to see more lines of text on the page.

Commands Review

Action	Menu Bar	Shortcut Menu	Toolbar	Task Pane	Keyboard
Set margins	File, Page Setup				ALT + F, U
Insert date	Insert, Date and Time				ALT + I, T
Update a selected date field		Right-click, then click Update Field			ALT + SHIFT + D F9
Cut, Copy, Paste	Edit, Cut or Copy or Paste	Right-click, then click Cut or Copy, or Paste		Click an item or Paste All in the Office Clipboard task pane	ALT + E, T or C or P CTRL + C (copy) CTRL + X (cut) CTRL + V (paste)
Turn on or off Overtype			Double-click the OVR mode indicator		INSERT
Undo or Redo actions	Edit, Undo Edit, Redo				ALT + E, U ALT + E, R CTRL + Z CTRL + Y
Repeat actions	Edit, Repeat				ALT+ E, R CTRL + Y
Cancel an action					ESC
Change editing views	View, Normal, Web Layout, Print Layout, Outline, Full Screen				ALT + V, N or W or P or O or U ALT + CTRL + P ALT + CTRL + O ALT + CTRL + N

Concepts Review

Circle the correct answer.

1. You can remove text by selecting the text and pressing the:
[a] EXT key.
[b] ALT + PAGEUP keys.
[c] CTRL key.
[d] DELETE key.

2. You cannot add a date to a document by:
[a] keying the date manually.
[b] inserting a date field that updates automatically.
[c] inserting the date as text.
[d] pressing the Insert key.

3. The selection bar is:
[a] located below the status bar.
[b] used to open other Office applications.
[c] used to select text in different ways.
[d] used to set left and right margins.

4. When you use the block format for a business letter, the:
[a] date and complimentary closing are centered on their respective lines.
[b] letter address is positioned below the salutation.
[c] letter components all begin at the left margin.
[d] letter components all begin at the right margin.

5. Margins refer to the:
[a] distance from the center of the page to the edge of the page.
[b] distance from the top, bottom, left, and right edges of the page to the text.
[c] number of lines you can have on a page.
[d] size of the text on a page.

6. By default, Word is in the:
[a] Overtype mode.
[b] Edit mode.
[c] Online Review mode.
[d] Insert mode.

7. Which of the following is not a selection technique in Word?
[a] pressing the CTRL + SHIFT + END keys to select from the insertion point to the end of the document
[b] double-clicking the selection bar opposite the paragraph you wish to select
[c] double-clicking a word
[d] pressing the ALT key and clicking a word

8. Using the mouse to move or copy text is called:
[a] cut-and-drag.
[b] select-and-cut.
[c] copy-and-cut.
[d] drag-and-drop.

9. Overtype mode allows you to:
[a] select text.
[b] key over existing text.
[c] move text.
[d] copy text.

10. Which of the following is not an editing view?
[a] Full Page view
[b] Full Screen view
[c] Print Layout view
[d] Normal view

Circle **T** if the statement is true or **F** if the statement is false.

T F 1. When you are in the Overtype mode and enter new text, any character you key replaces the character to the right of the insertion point.

T F 2. Word automatically defaults to the Edit mode.

T F 3. Word can undo multiple actions.

T F 4. The mouse and the keyboard can both be used to select text in a document.

T F 5. The EXT mode indicator appears bolded when you are using the Extend mode feature.

T F 6. You can restore text that has been deleted.

T F 7. You can maximize the number of lines of text displayed on the screen by switching to Full Screen view.

T F 8. Normal view displays your document much like it looks when printed.

T F 9. You can insert the date and the time together in a Word document.

T F 10. The Office Clipboard is a reserved place in the memory of your computer you can use to temporarily store up to 24 items you have cut or copied.

Skills Review

Exercise 1

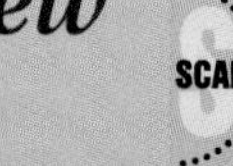

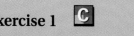

1. Create the following document. Use the block style with 2-inch top margin and 1-inch left and right margins. Insert the current date in the format of your choice at the top of the document. As you key the text, use the movement techniques and insert/delete actions you learned in this chapter to correct any keying errors you make. You revise the document in the next exercise.

Current date

Ms. Gail Jackson
Corporate Travel Manager
International Travel Services
1590 W. Convention Street
Chicago, IL 60605-1590

Dear Ms. Jackson:

Thank you for helping plan business trip to London this winter. I am really looking forward to seeing the sites, as well as taking care of some business. This is my first trip to London, and you were quite courteous in answering my questions.

Yours truly,

Kelly Armstead
Executive Assistant to B. D. Vickers

ka

2. Save the document as *Travel Letter*. Preview, print, and close the document.

Exercise 2

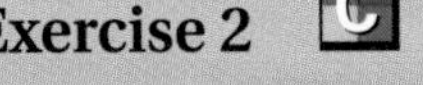

1. Open the *Travel Letter* document you created in Exercise 1 in this chapter.
2. At the end of the street address line, add ", Suite 16A;" in the first sentence, add the word "me" after the word "helping;" in the first sentence, add the word "my" after the word "plan" and delete the word "business;" in the first sentence, delete the word "winter" and replace it with the word "summer."
3. Save the document as *Travel Letter Revised.* Preview, print, and close the document.

Exercise 3

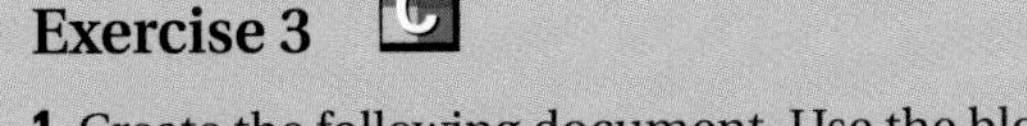

1. Create the following document. Use the block style with 2-inch top margin and 1-inch left and right margins. Insert the date as a field at the top of the document. As you key the letter, use the movement techniques and insert/delete actions to correct any keying errors you make. You revise the document in the next exercise.

Current date

Mr. Taylor Schreier
J & H Electronic Wholesalers
4578 Main Street
Cleveland, OH 78433-6325

Dear Mr. Schreier:

Thank you for inquiry about our holiday basket special offers. I am enclosing our most recent holiday catalog that explains and illustrates our special offers.

Please call our Sales Department at (312) 555-5555 when you are ready to place your order.

Yours truly,

P. L. Brown
Marketing Vice President

pb

Enclosure

2. Save the document as *Schreier Letter*. Preview, print, and close the document.

Exercise 4 

1. Open the *Schreier Letter* document you created in Exercise 3 in this chapter.
2. In the first sentence, add the word "your" after the word "for" and delete the word "about" and replace it with the word "regarding."
3. Using the Overtype mode, replace the text "Yours truly," with the text "Sincerely," in the complimentary closing. Delete any extra characters and then turn off the Overtype mode.
4. Save the document as *Schreier Letter Revised*. Preview, print, and close the document.

Exercise 5 

1. Open the *Employment Application Letter* document located on the Data Disk.
2. Move the second body paragraph to the first body paragraph position using a shortcut menu.
3. Undo the move action.
4. Move the second body paragraph to the first body paragraph position using drag-and-drop.
5. Combine the third body paragraph with the second body paragraph by viewing the formatting marks and deleting the paragraph marks at the end of the second body paragraph and the blank line between the second body paragraph and the third body paragraph. Don't forget to add a space between the two sentences of the revised second body paragraph.
6. Replace the words "Current date" with the current date in the 12 November 2003 format.
7. Save the document as *Employment Application Letter Revised*. Preview, print, and close the document.

Exercise 6 

1. Open the *Business Solicitation Letter* located on the Data Disk.
2. Change the margins to a 2-inch top margin and 1-inch left and right margins.
3. Delete the word "own" in the first sentence of the first body paragraph. Use the Repeat command on the Edit menu to delete the text "explaining and" in the first sentence of the second body paragraph.
4. Replace the words "Current date" with the current date in the format of your choice.
5. Save the document as *Business Solicitation Letter Revised*. Preview, print, and close the document.

Exercise 7 

1. Create the following document. Use the block style with 1.5-inch top margin and 1.25 inch left and right margins. Insert the current date in the format of your choice at the top of the document. As you key the letter, use the movement techniques and insert/delete actions to correct any keying errors you make. You revise the document in the next exercise.

Current date

BCH Software Company
4000 Skywalk Way
Ventura, CA 91015-4657

Dear Sir:

Please send by return mail all of products brochures, technical specifications, and price list for your software related to word processing for IBM PS2/ and IBM-compatible personal computers.

Additionally, please add your mailing list to update us on any future changes in your product line.

Sincerely,

B. D. Vickers
Administrative Vice President

ka

2. Save the document as *BCH Software Letter*. Preview, print, and close the document.

Exercise 8 

1. Open the *BCH Software Letter* document you created in Exercise 7 in this chapter.

2. Edit the document following the proofing notations.

Current date

Mr. James Wilson
BCH Software Company
4000 Skywalk Way
Ventura, CA 91015-4657

Dear ~~Sir:~~ Mr. Wilson

Please send us by return mail all of your products ~~s~~ brochures, technical specifications, and price lists for ~~your~~ software related to ~~word processing~~ accounting for IBM PS2/ and IBM-compatible personal computers.

Additionally, please add us to your mailing list ~~to~~ for updates ~~us~~ on any ~~future~~ changes ~~in~~ to your product line.

Sincerely,

B. D. Vickers
Administrative Vice President

ka

3. Save the document as *BCH Software Letter Revised.* Preview, print, and close the document.

Case Projects

Project 1

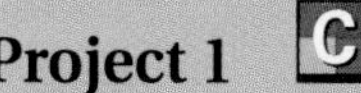

B. D. Vickers is traveling on business to Melbourne, Australia in three weeks. Prepare a letter to Mr. David Melville, Reservations Manager at the Excelsior Hotel, 3500 Wayburne Drive, Melbourne, VIC, 30001, Australia, requesting accommodations for a week beginning three weeks from today. Insert the date as text using the Day, Month (in text), Year format. Save, preview, and print the document.

Project 2

Open the document you created in Project 1 and change the accommodation dates to four weeks from today using the Overtype mode. Save the document with a new name, then preview and print it.

Project 3

Kelly Armstead has asked you to find a list of keyboard shortcuts you both can use to prepare correspondence. Using the Ask A Question Box, search online Help for a list of keyboard shortcut keys for moving the insertion point in a document and selecting text in a document. Print the lists. With your instructor's permission, use the lists to demonstrate the keyboard shortcuts to a classmate.

Project 4

B. D. Vickers is considering ordering several IntelliMouse pointing devices for the Purchasing Department and has asked you to find out how the devices are used to increase productivity in the department. Using the Help menu resources, including Web resources, search for information on the IntelliMouse pointing device. Create a new document containing at least three paragraphs describing how the Purchasing Department employees can improve their productivity by using the IntelliMouse pointing device. Insert the current date as text using the mm/dd/yy format. Save, preview, and print the document.

Project 5

There have been several power failures because of storms in the area and Kelly is concerned that she may lose documents she is working on if the power fails. She has asked you to find out what options Word has to automatically back up documents as she is working and to automatically recover documents lost during a power failure. Using the Help menu, research what backup and document recovery features Word provides. Create a new document containing at least four paragraphs describing how to set backup procedures and recover lost or damaged documents. Insert the date as a field using the format of your choice. Save, preview, and print the document.

Project 6

B. D. Vickers has extended the business trip discussed in Project 1 and now plans to spend two days in Hong Kong and three days in London before returning. Kelly needs a list of possible accommodations in Hong Kong and London and has asked you to search the Web for information on hotels in these cities. She also needs you to review flight schedules and suggest flights from Melbourne to Hong Kong, from Hong Kong to London, and from London to Chicago. Connect to the Internet and search the Web for the information you need. Save at least two URLs as "favorites." Print at least five Web pages. Create a new, blank document and key the title and URL of the pages you printed. Insert the date as text in the format of your choice. Save, preview, and print the document.

Project 7

Open the document of your choice. Practice using various selection techniques to select text. Delete and restore text using the Delete key, Undo command and button, and Repeat command. Close the document without saving any changes.

Project 8

Worldwide Exotic Foods, Inc. participates in a summer internship program for graduating seniors and has a new group of interns starting the program next week. Margie Montez, the program director, has asked you to prepare a ten-minute presentation on creating business letters using Word 2002. You give the presentation next Thursday, at 3 p.m. Create a new document listing the topics you plan to discuss and the order in which you plan to discuss them. Insert the date and time using the format of your choice. Save, preview, and print the document. Ask a classmate to review the document and provide comments and suggestions on the topics and the organization. With your instructor's approval, schedule a time to give your presentation to your class.

Project 9

Kelly has subscribed to an e-mail mailing list and gets Word 2002 user tips every day via e-mail. You also would like to subscribe to this kind of mailing list and want to know more about how to do this. Connect to the Internet and search the Web for information on locating and subscribing to mailing lists. Create a new, blank document that lists titles and URLs for pages that provide mailing list information. Insert the date using the Day (in text), Month (in text) and Date, Year format. Save, preview, and print the document.

Word 2002

Using the Proofing Tools

Chapter Overview

Documents with misspellings and grammar errors indicate sloppiness and inattention to detail—two traits no company wants to convey. Proofing a document before you print it helps to ensure the document is error-free, allowing readers to focus on its content. Word has several tools to help you proof your documents. In this chapter, you learn to use the Spelling and Grammar, Thesaurus, and AutoCorrect proofing tools. You also learn to create and insert AutoText entries and to find and replace text.

Learning Objectives

- Check spelling and grammar in a document
- Use Synonyms and the Thesaurus to replace words
- Use the AutoCorrect tool
- Insert text with the AutoText tool
- Find and replace text

Case profile

Worldwide Exotic Foods requires that all correspondence and documents sent out from the company have accurate spelling and grammar. Kelly Armstead asks you to correct any errors in a letter she keyed before it is printed and mailed.

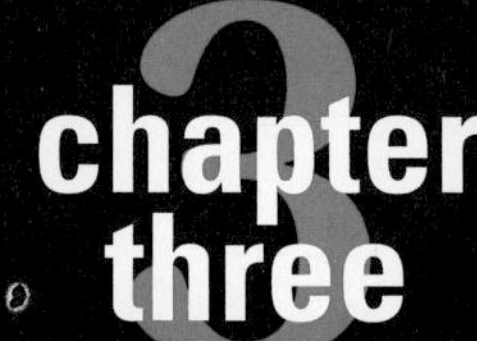

3.a Checking Spelling and Grammar in a Document

Kelly tells you that it is company policy to check the spelling and grammar of any document before you print it. You can check the spelling and grammar in a document with a menu command, a toolbar button, a status bar mode indicator, or a shortcut menu. By default, Word checks the spelling and grammar in your document as you key the text. Using this automatic spelling and grammar tool saves time in editing your document. After you misspell a word or key text that may be grammatically incorrect and then press the SPACEBAR, a wavy red or green line appears below the text. The red line indicates a spelling error and the green line indicates a possible grammar error.

Kelly's letter contains several keying errors. You open the letter and then use the Spelling and Grammar command to correct those errors. To open the letter containing errors:

Step 1	***Open***	the *IAEA Letter* document located on the Data Disk

The wavy red and green lines appear below text that may be misspelled or grammatically incorrect. In this letter the proper names are correct; therefore, you can ignore the wavy red or green lines underneath them if they appear. When necessary, you can add words like proper names to a custom dictionary. *For the activities in this chapter, do not add any words to a custom dictionary.*

There is one grammar error in the letter, indicated by a wavy green line. To correct the grammar error "an" in the second body paragraph:

Step 1	***Right-click***	the word "an"

The Grammar shortcut menu on your screen should look similar to Figure 3-1. The shortcut menu suggestion is to replace the word "an" with "a." You can quickly replace a word by clicking the suggested word in the shortcut menu, or you can display the Grammar dialog box to get more information about the error message. Because this is an obvious error, you can quickly correct it by replacing "an" with "a."

QUICK TIP

You can turn on or off the automatic spelling and grammar checking in the Spelling and Grammar tab of the Options dialog box.

Word can detect text written in many languages other than English when the multiple language features are installed. When you open a document that contains text in other languages or key text in another language, Word uses the spelling and grammar dictionaries, punctuation rules, and sorting rules for that language. For more information on setting up your computer for automatic language detection, see online Help.

MENU TIP

You can right-click a misspelled word or grammar error to correct it. You can also click the Spelling and Grammar command on the Tools menu to correct spelling or grammar errors.

FIGURE 3-1
Grammar Shortcut Menu

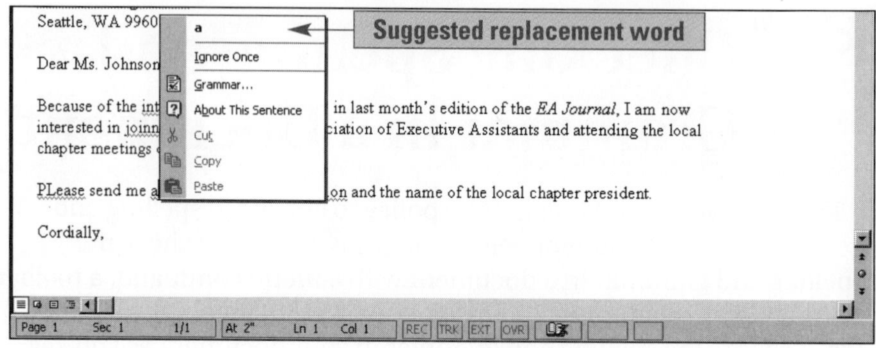

MOUSE TIP

You can click the Spelling and Grammar button on the Standard toolbar or the Spelling and Grammar Status mode indicator on the status bar to correct spelling or grammar errors.

Step 2	*Click*	a on the shortcut menu

Next, you correct the misspellings in the letter. To correct the spelling of the word "intereting" in the first body paragraph:

Step 1	*Right-click*	the word "intereting"

The Spelling shortcut menu on your screen should look similar to Figure 3-2.

FIGURE 3-2
Spelling Shortcut Menu

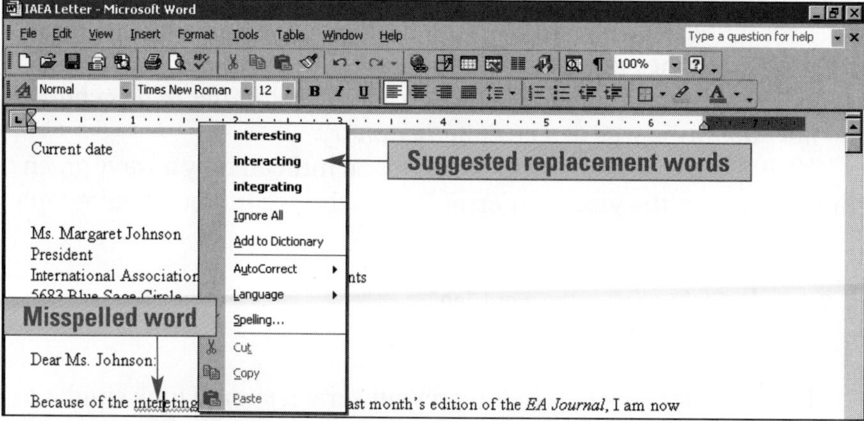

You can click a suggested spelling, ignore the spelling, add the word to a custom dictionary, add the error and suggested replacement word to the AutoCorrect tool, or open the Spelling dialog box. Because the correct spelling is on the shortcut menu, you click it to fix the error.

Step 2	*Click*	interesting on the shortcut menu

You can display the spelling or grammar shortcut menu with the Spelling and Grammar Status mode indicator on the status bar.

To correct the next error, the word "joinng," using the Spelling and Grammar Status mode indicator:

Step 1	***Click***	the word "joinng" to position the insertion point in the word
Step 2	***Double-click***	the Spelling and Grammar Status mode indicator on the status bar
Step 3	***Click***	joining on the shortcut menu

Another way to correct the spelling and grammar is to use the Spelling and Grammar dialog box. The dialog box shows each spelling or grammar error and provides options for you to correct it. To correct the remaining spelling errors using the Spelling and Grammar dialog box:

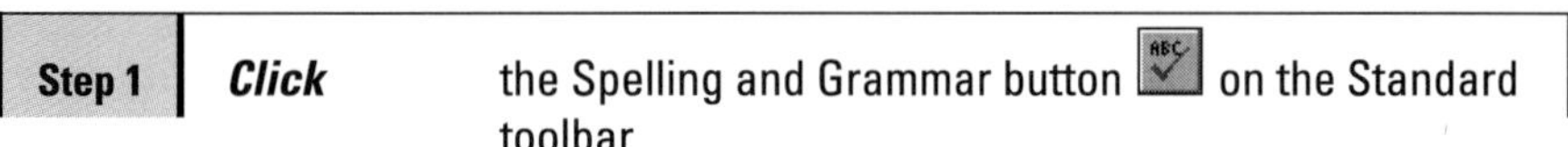

Step 1	***Click***	the Spelling and Grammar button on the Standard toolbar

The Spelling and Grammar dialog box on your screen should look similar to Figure 3-3.

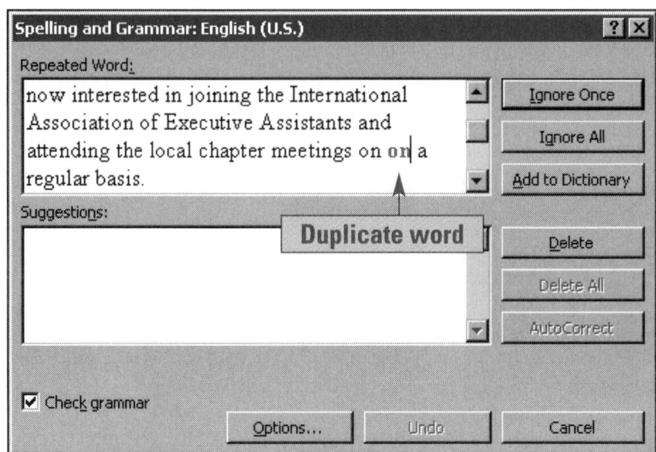

FIGURE 3-3
Spelling and Grammar Dialog Box

MOUSE TIP

You can double-click the Spelling and Grammar Status mode indicator to move to the next misspelled or mistyped word in your document.

The Spelling and Grammar tool detected the duplicate word "on" in the first body paragraph. You want to delete the duplicate word.

Step 2	***Click***	Delete

Word deletes the extra word and moves to the next spelling error. The word "PLease" appears in the dialog box and Word provides a list of

possible corrections in the Suggestions: list. Word highlights the most likely suggested correction—"Please"—for the irregular capitalization.

Step 3	*Click*	Change

The next misspelled word ("appplication") appears in the dialog box and Word suggests the correct spelling "application."

Step 4	*Click*	Change

Word highlights the proper name "Armstead." Because this spelling is correct, you can ignore it and proceed to the next error. You can choose to ignore words that are correct but do not appear in the dictionaries. To ignore the remaining suggested errors:

Step 5	*Click*	Ignore Once until the spelling and grammar checking is complete and a dialog box opens, indicating the spelling and grammar check is complete
Step 6	*Click*	OK
Step 7	*Save*	the document as *IAEA Letter Revised* and leave it open

QUICK TIP

You can create new custom dictionaries and edit or remove existing custom dictionaries in the Custom Dictionaries dialog box. To view this dialog box, click the Spelling & Grammar tab in the Options dialog box and click the Custom Dictionaries button.

In addition to checking the spelling and grammar, you read Kelly's letter and want to find new words to replace certain words in the letter.

C

3.b Using Synonyms and the Thesaurus to Replace Words

The **Thesaurus** enables you to replace a selected word with another word that has the same or a very similar meaning, called a synonym. Kelly suggests that you substitute a different word for the word "article" in the first body paragraph of her letter. You decide to use the text shortcut menu to find an appropriate replacement word. To find a synonym:

Step 1	*Right-click*	the word "article" in the first body paragraph
Step 2	*Point*	to Synonyms

A shortcut menu of replacement words appears along with the Thesaurus command. You decide to replace "article" with "commentary."

Step 3	*Click*	commentary on the shortcut menu
Step 4	*Observe*	that the word "commentary" replaces the word "article"
Step 5	*Save*	the document and leave it open

When you want to look up a variety of possible synonyms, you can use the Thesaurus by selecting a word and opening the Thesaurus dialog box. The Thesaurus subcommand under the Language command on the Tools menu or the Thesaurus subcommand under the Synonyms on the text shortcut menu opens the Thesaurus. In the Thesaurus dialog box you can click the noun, verb, adjective, or adverb form of the selected word and then review a list of synonyms for the word. You can click a word from the list of synonyms and then use it to look up additional synonyms. When you find the replacement word you prefer, you insert it in the document to replace the original selected word.

Another Word proofing tool, AutoCorrect, can automatically correct your keying errors.

3.c Using the AutoCorrect Tool

The **AutoCorrect** tool fixes common errors as you key in the text. For example, if you commonly key "adn" for "and," AutoCorrect corrects the error as soon as you press the SPACEBAR. AutoCorrect also corrects two initial capital letters (DEar), capitalizes the first letter of a sentence, capitalizes the names of days, and corrects errors caused by forgetting to turn off the CAPS LOCK key (aRTICLE). The AutoCorrect tool contains an extensive list of symbols and words that are inserted whenever you type an abbreviation for the symbol or word and then press the SPACEBAR. You can specify certain words as exceptions to this automatic correction.

Marcy Ellison, a purchasing assistant, tells you that the AutoCorrect tool will save you time when you create documents. She suggests you verify that the AutoCorrect tool is turned on. To verify that the AutoCorrect tool is turned on:

QUICK TIP

If AutoCorrect makes a change you do not want, press the CTRL + Z keys or click the Undo button on the Standard toolbar to undo the AutoCorrect action.

Step 1	*Click*	Tools
Step 2	*Click*	AutoCorrect Options
Step 3	*Click*	the AutoCorrect tab, if necessary

The AutoCorrect dialog box on your screen should look similar to Figure 3-4.

FIGURE 3-4
AutoCorrect Dialog Box

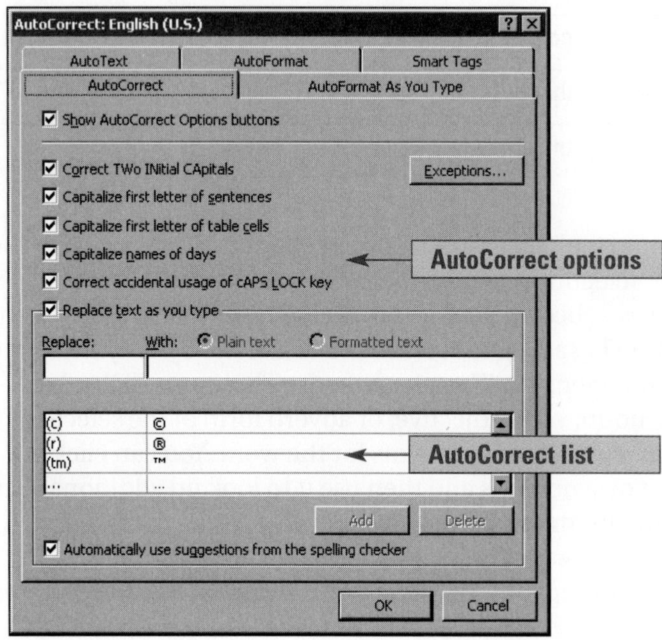

QUICK TIP

AutoCorrect comes with a list of **exceptions**, words or abbreviations that AutoCorrect does not correct automatically. Whenever you key a period (.) in an abbreviation, AutoCorrect may capitalize the next word as if it begins a new sentence. To avoid this, you can set an AutoCorrect exception to ignore capitalization following the period (.) in a specific abbreviation.

If the Automatically add words to list option is turned on in the AutoCorrect Exceptions dialog box, you can backspace over the incorrectly capitalized word and key it again. Word then adds the exception to the list. To keep the AutoCorrect tool from automatically correcting text with mixed upper- and lowercase letters, you can click the INitial CAps tab in the AutoCorrect Exceptions dialog box and add your exception to the list.

Remember that you can use the dialog box Help button to review the all the options on the AutoCorrect tab.

Step 4	*Verify*	that a check mark appears in the Replace text as you type check box
Step 5	*Click*	OK

To test AutoCorrect, you first delete the word "the" before the word "International" in the first body paragraph and then deliberately key the word "teh:"

Step 1	*Select*	the word "the" and following space before the word "International" in the first body paragraph
Step 2	*Press*	the DELETE key
Step 3	*Key*	teh
Step 4	*Verify*	that the word is misspelled
Step 5	*Press*	the SPACEBAR
Step 6	*Observe*	that the word "teh" is automatically corrected to "the" when you press the SPACEBAR

Using AutoCorrect Options

You can control AutoCorrect actions by using the AutoCorrect Options. When you place the mouse pointer over text that has been automatically changed by the AutoCorrect tool, a small blue rectangle appears below the text. If you then move the mouse pointer to the rectangle, the AutoCorrect Options button with a list arrow appears. You click the list arrow to view the AutoCorrect Options menu. To view the AutoCorrect Options button and menu:

Step 1	***Move***	the mouse pointer to the word "the" automatically corrected by the AutoCorrect tool
Step 2	***Observe***	the small blue rectangle
Step 3	***Move***	the mouse pointer to the rectangle
Step 4	***Observe***	the AutoCorrect Options button and list arrow
Step 5	***Click***	the AutoCorrect Options button list arrow to view the menu options

Your screen should look similar to Figure 3-5.

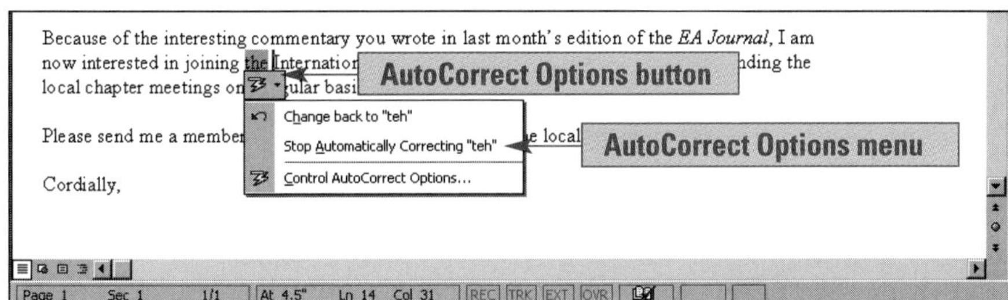

FIGURE 3-5
AutoCorrect Options Menu

You can quickly change text back to the way it was originally keyed, modify the AutoCorrect tool to stop correcting the keyed text, or open the AutoCorrect dialog box and change the AutoCorrect options from this menu. Because you want to maintain the corrected text and continue to automatically correct this particular error in future documents, you can simply close the menu.

Step 6	***Click***	in the document area outside the AutoCorrect Options menu to close it
Step 7	***Save***	the *IAEA Letter Revised* document and close it

Sometimes it is necessary to alter the AutoCorrect tool by adding or removing AutoCorrect items or by setting AutoCorrect exceptions.

Customizing AutoCorrect

You can add and delete items in the AutoCorrect list. You can add not only your own common keying errors or misspelled words, but also words and phrases that you would like to insert whenever you key a certain letter combination and press the SPACEBAR. For example, suppose you want to quickly insert the name of your company into a document by keying an abbreviation and then pressing the SPACEBAR. You can add the name of your company and an abbreviation to the AutoCorrect list. Then, when you key the abbreviation and press the SPACEBAR, the company name is inserted in your document. To add the Worldwide Exotic Foods company name to the AutoCorrect list:

Step 1	*Create*	a new, blank document
Step 2	*Key*	Worldwide Exotic Foods, Inc.
Step 3	*Select*	the text (do not include the paragraph mark at the end of the text)
Step 4	*Click*	Tools
Step 5	*Click*	AutoCorrect Options
Step 6	*Click*	the AutoCorrect tab, if necessary
Step 7	*Observe*	that the company name is already entered in the With: text box

Now add an abbreviation for the company name.

Step 8	*Key*	wef in the Replace: text box
Step 9	*Click*	Add
Step 10	*Observe*	that the company name and abbreviation are added to the AutoCorrect list
Step 11	*Click*	OK
Step 12	*Delete*	the selected company name text

You decide to test the abbreviation you added to the AutoCorrect list. To insert the company name using AutoCorrect:

Step 1	*Key*	wef
Step 2	*Press*	the SPACEBAR
Step 3	*Observe*	the company name is automatically inserted

Adding words you key frequently to the AutoCorrect list is a great timesaver. When you no longer need an AutoCorrect entry, you should delete it. You can delete an AutoCorrect entry by selecting the entry in the AutoCorrect tab in the AutoCorrect dialog box and clicking the Delete button. A quick way to delete an AutoCorrect entry is with the AutoCorrect Options button.

To delete the company name from the AutoCorrect list:

Step 1	*Display*	the AutoCorrect Options button
Step 2	*Click*	AutoCorrect Options list arrow to view the options menu
Step 3	*Click*	Stop Automatically Correcting "wef"
Step 4	*Observe*	that the text is returned to its original "Wef"
Step 5	*Verify*	that the entry is removed from the AutoCorrect list
Step 6	*Delete*	the "Wef" text

If you have a large amount of text you key frequently, you can insert it quickly with AutoText.

QUICK TIP

To maintain a count of the number of words and other statistics related to the current document, you can use the Word Count toolbar. You can display the Word Count toolbar with a command button in the Word Count dialog box, which you open with the Word Count command on the Tools menu. You can also display the Word Count toolbar with the toolbar shortcut menu.

3.d Inserting Text with the AutoText Tool

An **AutoText** entry is a set of stored text that you can insert in your documents. In this way, it is similar to AutoCorrect; however, AutoText is often used for large amounts of preformatted standard text. Word provides standard AutoText entries or you can create custom AutoText entries.

You review the standard AutoText entries that come with Word, and then create a custom AutoText entry for a letter closing.

Inserting Standard AutoText

Word provides standard AutoText entries, such as complimentary closings or mailing instructions for letters. To view the standard AutoText options:

Step 1	*Click*	Insert
Step 2	*Point*	to AutoText

The standard AutoText menu on your screen should look similar to Figure 3-6.

FIGURE 3-6
Standard AutoText Menu

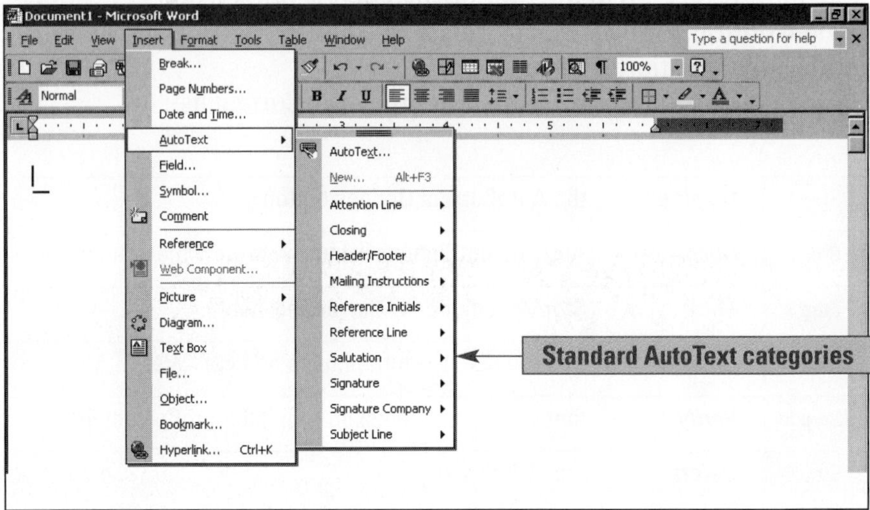

QUICK TIP

You can store AutoText entries in templates other than Normal and share AutoText entries by copying them from one template to another using the Organizer tool in the Templates and Add-ins dialog box, which is opened from the Tools menu. By default, Word saves the AutoText entries to the Normal template without a prompt when you close the application. For more information on storing and sharing AutoText, see online Help.

You can insert the CERTIFIED MAIL mailing instruction in a letter.

Step 3	***Point to***	Mailing Instructions
Step 4	***Click***	CERTIFIED MAIL
Step 5	***Observe***	that the text CERTIFIED MAIL is inserted in the document
Step 6	***Continue***	to explore the standard AutoText entries by inserting an AutoText entry from each AutoText category into the current document and pressing the ENTER key after each insertion
Step 7	***Press***	the ENTER key twice to move the insertion point

In addition to Word standard AutoText, you can create your own custom AutoText entries such as the closing for a letter or standard paragraph text for letters and contracts.

Inserting Custom AutoText

Because you use the same letter closing text for all B. D. Vickers letters, Kelly suggests you create a custom AutoText closing for the letters instead of keying the closing at the end of each letter. To create a custom AutoText entry, first you create and select the text that you want to insert in documents. If you want the text to have a certain format, you must format the text before you select it.

Each AutoText entry must have a unique name. AutoText names can contain spaces and are not case-sensitive. If you name an AutoText entry with uppercase letters, you can insert the entry in the document using lowercase letters. Unless you specify another template, an AutoText entry is saved with the Normal template and is available for all documents created with the Normal template.

You create a custom AutoText complimentary closing for B. D. Vickers that includes the name, your initials, and an Enclosure notation. To create the text for a custom AutoText entry:

Step 1	***Key***	Sincerely,
Step 2	***Press***	the ENTER key four times
Step 3	***Key***	B. D. Vickers
Step 4	***Press***	the ENTER key twice
Step 5	***Key***	your initials and press the SPACEBAR
Step 6	***Press***	the CTRL + Z keys to undo the AutoCorrect capitalization
Step 7	***Press***	the ENTER key twice
Step 8	***Key***	Enclosure

MOUSE TIP

You can view the AutoText toolbar by right-clicking any toolbar and then clicking AutoText.

In order for you and Kelly to be able to use the closing you created for B. D. Vickers as custom AutoText, the AutoText entry must be stored in a way that both of you can access it. By default, AutoText entries are created as global entries in the Normal template. The term *global AutoText entry* means that you can use the entry with all documents based on the Normal template.

After you key the text, and format it if necessary, you can turn it into an AutoText entry. To create the AutoText entry:

Step 1	***Select***	all the lines of text (do not select the paragraph mark following Enclosure)
Step 2	***Click***	Insert
Step 3	***Point to***	AutoText
Step 4	***Click***	AutoText

chapter three

The AutoText tab in the AutoCorrect dialog box on your screen should look similar to Figure 3-7.

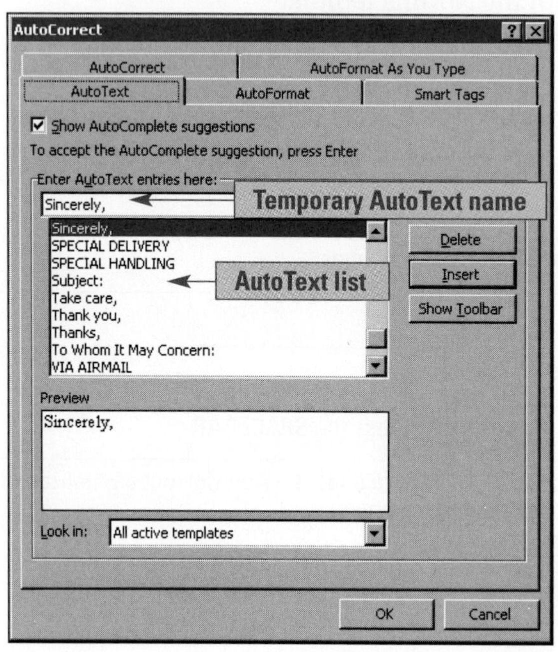

FIGURE 3-7
AutoText Tab in the AutoCorrect Dialog Box

MENU TIP

You can print AutoText entries by clicking the Print command on the File menu and selecting AutoText entries from the Print what: list box in the Print dialog box.

By default, Word inserts text from the first line of the selection as the AutoText name. You change this to a more descriptive, brief, unique name for the AutoText entry that will remind you of its content.

Step 5	***Key***	cl (the first two characters of closing) in the Enter AutoText entries here: text box
Step 6	***Click***	Add
Step 7	***Delete***	the selected text

Now you can insert the closing AutoText entry into your document. You can insert a custom AutoText entry by displaying the AutoText dialog box or by keying the name of the entry and pressing the F3 key. You can also key just enough characters for AutoComplete to identify an AutoText entry's unique name and display an AutoComplete tip, then press the F3 key or the ENTER key.

To insert AutoText using the keyboard:

Step 1	***Key***	cl
Step 2	***Press***	the F3 key
Step 3	***Observe***	that the AutoText closing entry is inserted in the document

AutoText can be modified after it is created to add text or formatting.

Editing AutoText Entries

You can easily edit AutoText entries. You need to include B. D. Vickers' job title in the closing AutoText entry. You can edit an AutoText entry by first changing the text, then selecting the changed text, and then adding new AutoText with the same name. To edit the closing AutoText entry:

Step 1	*Move*	the insertion point after the text "B. D. Vickers" in the closing text
Step 2	*Press*	the ENTER key
Step 3	*Key*	Administrative Vice President
Step 4	*Select*	all the lines of the closing, beginning with Sincerely and ending with Enclosure (do not select the paragraph mark following Enclosure)
Step 5	*Click*	Insert
Step 6	*Point to*	AutoText
Step 7	*Click*	AutoText
Step 8	*Click*	cl in the AutoText list
Step 9	*Click*	Add
Step 10	*Click*	Yes to redefine the AutoText entry with Vickers' title

You test the entry by reinserting the closing AutoText. To test the closing entry AutoText:

Step 1	*Delete*	the closing text you just inserted in the document
Step 2	*Key*	cl
Step 3	*Press*	the F3 key

The redefined AutoText closing entry is inserted in the document.

Deleting AutoText Entries

When you no longer need an AutoText entry, you should delete it. To delete an AutoText entry, open the AutoText dialog box. Then click the AutoText name in the AutoText list box and click the Delete button.

QUICK TIP

By default, AutoText entries are automatically saved with the Normal template so they are available for any document created with the Normal template.

MOUSE TIP

You can open the Go To tab in the Find and Replace dialog box by double-clicking the status bar (not a mode indicator). You can also go to specific components of your document with the Select Browse Object button and the Next and Previous buttons located below the vertical scroll bar.

> **QUICK TIP**
>
> You can turn on or off the display of AutoComplete tips for AutoText and dates in the AutoText tab of the AutoCorrect dialog box.

> **MENU TIP**
>
> When you need to edit text on a specific page, you can go to that page quickly. The Go To feature moves you a specific component of your document, including a page, section, or line. You can go to that component by clicking the Go To command on the Edit menu to open the Go To tab in the Find and Replace dialog box.

To delete the "cl" AutoText entry:

Step 1	*Open*	the AutoText dialog box
Step 2	*Click*	cl in the AutoText list
Step 3	*Click*	Delete
Step 4	*Click*	OK

The **AutoComplete** tool automatically completes the text of the current date, a day of the week, a month, as well as AutoText entries. As you start to key a date, weekday, month name, or AutoText entry, an AutoComplete tip appears above the insertion point. You press the F3 key or the ENTER key to enter the text or continue keying the text to ignore the AutoComplete suggestion. To enter today's date using AutoComplete:

Step 1	*Move*	the insertion point to a blank line in the document
Step 2	*Key*	the first several characters of the current month name until the AutoComplete tip for the current month appears
Step 3	*Press*	the ENTER key to accept the AutoComplete entry for the current month
Step 4	*Press*	the SPACEBAR
Step 5	*Key*	the day of the month until the AutoComplete tip for the current day and year appears
Step 6	*Press*	the ENTER key to accept the AutoComplete entry for the current day and year
Step 7	*Observe*	the completed current date
Step 8	*Close*	the document without saving

3.e Finding and Replacing Text

As you work on existing documents, you may want to move quickly to a certain statement or to each heading in your document. Word can locate a word, a phrase, special characters, or formats each time they occur in a document. You can search for upper- or lowercase text with or without formatting. You can search for whole words or for characters. For example, Word can find the three characters "our" in words such as "hour" or "your" or can find only the whole word "our." Special search operators, such as "?" or "*", enable you to search for text patterns. The

"?" represents any single character. For example, you can use "s?t" to search for three characters beginning with "s" and ending with "t." The "*" represents any series of characters. To search for words ending in "ed" you can use the search pattern "*ed." You can search for words that sound alike but are spelled differently and you can search for all word forms: noun, verb, adjective, or adverb. After Word finds the characters or words, you can edit them manually or replace them with other text automatically.

MENU TIP

You can use the Find command on the Edit menu to locate specific text in your document and the Replace command on the Edit menu to replace specified text with new text.

Finding Text

Kelly asks you to open a document, *Internet Training*, find each instance of the uppercase characters "ISP" as a whole word (so you won't stop at that letter combination in other words), and then bold those characters. To open the document and the Find and Replace dialog box:

Step 1	***Open***	*Internet Training* document located on the Data Disk
Step 2	***Save***	the document as *Internet Training Revised*
Step 3	***Click***	Edit
Step 4	***Click***	Find
Step 5	***Click***	More, if necessary, to expand the dialog box

QUICK TIP

You can select all instances of a word or phrase at once with the Highlight all items found in: check box and list.

The Find and Replace dialog box expands to show the options. The dialog box on your screen should look similar to Figure 3-8.

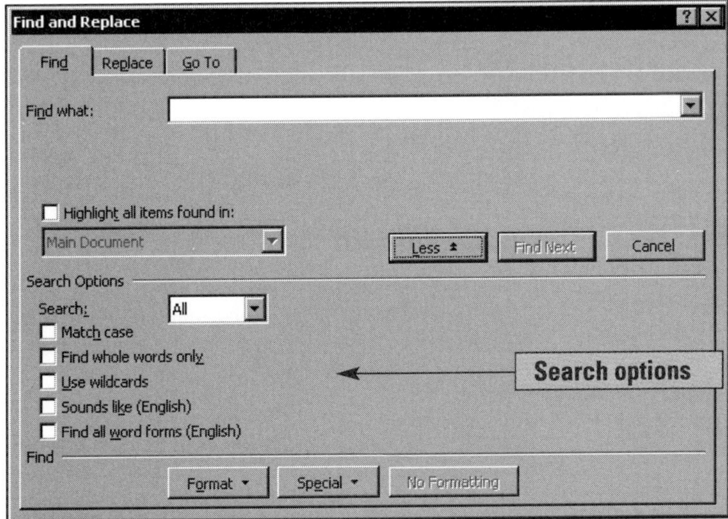

FIGURE 3-8
Find and Replace Dialog Box

Notice that "All" is the default option selected in the Search Options group. This means that Word will search the entire document, regardless

of the position of the insertion point. You can specify that Word find only text with the exact case by turning on the Match case option.

To find the uppercase characters "ISP" as a whole word and bold each instance:

Step 1	*Key*	ISP in the Find what: text box
Step 2	*Click*	the Match case check box to insert a check mark, if necessary
Step 3	*Click*	the Find whole words only check box to insert a check mark, if necessary
Step 4	*Remove*	the check marks from the remaining check boxes, if necessary
Step 5	*Click*	Less to collapse the dialog box
Step 6	*Click*	Find Next

The first instance of the text "ISP" is selected. When the Find and Replace dialog box opens it becomes the active window and the Word application window becomes inactive (the title bar is gray). To edit or delete the selected text you must activate the Word document window. If the Find and Replace dialog box hides the selected text or the toolbar buttons, you can drag it out of the way by its title bar.

Step 7	*Click*	the Word document window to activate the window (the title bar is blue when the window is active)
Step 8	*Click*	the Bold button on the Formatting toolbar

You continue to find and bold each instance of the text "ISP." When all the instances of the text "ISP" are found, Word opens a confirmation dialog box telling you the search is finished.

Step 9	*Click*	Find Next in the Find and Replace dialog box
Step 10	*Click*	the Bold button on the Formatting toolbar to activate the Word window and format the text in one step
Step 11	*Continue*	to find and bold the text "ISP"
Step 12	*Click*	OK to close the confirmation dialog box when it opens
Step 13	*Click*	Cancel to close the Find and Replace dialog box

Kelly instructs you to find each instance of the phrase "electronic mail" in the *Internet Training Revised* document and change it to "e-mail."

MOUSE TIP

You can click the Select Browse Object button below the vertical scroll bar and then click the Find icon to find, replace, or go to a specific location in your document. The Next and Previous buttons become the Next Find/GoTo and Previous Find/GoTo buttons and change color from black (which signifies the default Next or Previous Page) to blue (which signifies an option other than Page). To return the Next and Previous buttons to their default Page option, click the Page icon in the Select Browse Object grid.

CAUTION TIP

Be careful using the Replace All button in the Find and Replace dialog box to replace text in a document with which you are unfamiliar. Replacing all instances of certain characters or words may cause unexpected replacements and create errors in your document.

Replacing Text

Often you want to search for a word, phrase, special character, or format and replace it with a different word, phrase, special character, or format. You can have Word replace the text or formatting automatically without adding it manually each time. To replace the phrase "electronic mail" with the word "e-mail" in the *Internet Training Revised* document:

Step 1	*Click*	Edit
Step 2	*Click*	Replace
Step 3	*Key*	electronic mail in the Find what: text box
Step 4	*Press*	the TAB key to move the insertion point to the next text box
Step 5	*Verify*	that Options: Match Case appears below the Find what: text box (the Find whole words only option automatically turns off when you search for multiple words)
Step 6	*Key*	e-mail in the Replace with: text box
Step 7	*Click*	Find Next and verify that the phrase "electronic mail" is selected
Step 8	*Click*	Replace
Step 9	*Drag*	the dialog box out of the way and scroll to view the selected text, if necessary

The first instance of the phrase "electronic mail" is replaced with the word "e-mail" and Word automatically highlights the next occurrence of the phrase. When Word finds another match, you can replace the phrase by clicking the Replace button. If you want to leave the text unchanged, click the Find Next button to skip that occurrence of the text. If you want to replace every occurrence of the text without reviewing each one, click the Replace All button. When no more matches exist, a confirmation dialog box opens, informing you that Word finished searching the document.

Step 10	*Click*	Replace
Step 11	*Click*	OK to close the confirmation dialog box
Step 12	*Close*	the Find and Replace dialog box
Step 13	*Save*	the document and close it

With find and replace, you can quickly and easily modify any document.

MOUSE TIP

You can close the dialog box and click the Next Find/GoTo or Previous Find/GoTo buttons below the vertical scroll bar to select the next instance of the text or formatting.

QUICK TIP

The Find and Replace dialog box remembers the last search options you set. Always review and turn on or off the search options before each new search. You can also search for and replace formatting as well as text. Always click the No Formatting button to turn off any formatting options set from the previous search before you begin a new search.

Summary

- By default, Word checks the spelling and grammar in your document as you type. A wavy red line indicates a misspelled or mistyped word, and a wavy green line indicates a grammar error.
- When you display the Spelling and Grammar dialog box, you can choose to ignore the selected word, change it to another word, add the word to a custom dictionary, delete the word from the document, or add the word and its correction to the AutoCorrect list.
- The Thesaurus tool and Synonyms command allow you to substitute a word(s) with the same or similar meaning for the word containing the insertion point.
- You can display the Word Count toolbar to view the number of pages, words, characters, and other document statistics for the current document.
- The AutoCorrect tool is turned on by default and allows you to automatically correct commonly misspelled or mistyped words as you type or insert text by keying an abbreviation for the text and then pressing the SPACEBAR.
- The AutoCorrect Options button allows you to manage automatic corrections.
- You can add items to the AutoCorrect list and create exceptions to the AutoCorrect list.
- The AutoText features allow you to insert standard text such as mailing instructions or create and save custom text and then insert it as needed.
- The AutoComplete tool allows you to automatically insert the current month, day of the week, and date by pressing the F3 or ENTER key.
- You can quickly find or find and replace text, formatting, and special characters.

Commands Review

Action	Menu Bar	Shortcut Menu	Toolbar	Task Pane	Keyboard
Turn on or off the AutoCorrect tool	Tools, AutoCorrect Options				ALT + T, A
Check spelling and grammar	Tools, Spelling and Grammar	Right-click a word with a wavy red or green line			ALT + T, S F7 ALT + F7
Substitute words with same or similar meaning	Tools, Language, Thesaurus	Right-click a word, point to Synonyms			ALT + T, L, T
Create, edit, insert, delete custom AutoText entry	Insert, AutoText, AutoText				SHIFT + F7 ALT + I, A, X F3 ENTER ALT + F3
Insert standard AutoText	Insert, AutoText				ALT + I, A
Print AutoText entries	File, Print				ALT + F, P
Find and replace text, formatting, and special characters	Edit, Find or Replace				ALT + E, F or E CTRL + F CTRL + H
Go to a specific page, section, or line	Edit, Go To				ALT + E, G CTRL + G
View document statistics	Tools, Word Count				ALT + T, W

Concepts Review

Circle the correct answer.

1. The AutoCorrect tool:
- [a] provides statistics about your document.
- [b] checks for misspelled words as you key text, and underlines them with a wavy red line.
- [c] checks the grammar in the document.
- [d] corrects Caps Lock errors when you press the SPACEBAR.

2. The Thesaurus tool:
- [a] adds new words to the custom dictionary.
- [b] corrects two initial capitalization.
- [c] checks for misspelled words as you key text.
- [d] allows you to substitute words.

3. The Spelling and Grammar tool does not:
- [a] indicate grammatical errors.
- [b] identify words with capitalization problems.
- [c] show you spelling and grammar errors as you key.
- [d] automatically complete dates.

4. The AutoComplete tool:
- [a] presents a tip with contents you can insert by pressing the ENTER key.
- [b] checks the readability of the document.
- [c] checks the spelling in the document.
- [d] checks the grammar in the document.

5. An AutoText entry:
- [a] must have a unique name.
- [b] cannot be saved for future use.
- [c] cannot be changed once it is created.
- [d] replaces text as soon as you press the SPACEBAR.

6. You can create a new AutoText entry with the:
- [a] F3 key.
- [b] AutoText subcommand on the Insert menu.
- [c] AutoComplete tool and the ENTER key.
- [d] INSERT key.

7. Which Find option allows you to avoid search results that include the individual characters of a word inside other words?
[a] Match case
[b] Find whole words only
[c] Sounds like
[d] Find all word forms

8. You can check the grammar in your document with the:
[a] AutoComplete command.
[b] Thesaurus command.
[c] Synonyms command.
[d] Spelling and Grammar status mode indicator.

9. You can turn on or off the automatic checking of spelling and grammar in the:
[a] AutoCorrect dialog box.
[b] Options dialog box.
[c] Format dialog box.
[d] AutoText dialog box.

10. Which option is not available in the Spelling and Grammar dialog box?
[a] selecting suggested spellings for a word from a list
[b] ignoring the selected word
[c] adding the word to the AutoCorrect list
[d] adding the word to the AutoText list

Circle **T** if the statement is true or **F** if the statement is false.

T F 1. The Spelling and Grammar tool checks the readability of your document.

T F 2. The AutoText tool allows Word to check for spelling errors as you key.

T F 3. The Synonyms command displays words with the same or similar meaning as that of a selected word.

T F 4. You can check the spelling and grammar of your document only with a toolbar button.

T F 5. The Spelling and Grammar tool presents a ScreenTip containing the complete text of the word you are keying.

T F 6. When a word is not found in the dictionaries by the Spelling and Grammar tool, a wavy green line appears underneath it.

T F 7. AutoText names are case-sensitive.

T F 8. You can manage automatic corrections with the AutoCorrect Options button.

T F 9. The AutoCorrect tool automatically corrects commonly misspelled words as they are keyed.

T F 10. You can use the Word Count toolbar to see statistics related to the current document.

Skills Review

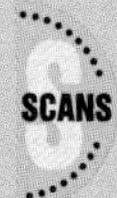

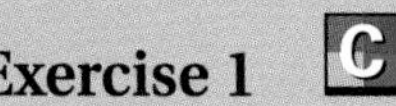

Exercise 1

1. Open the *Vancouver Report With Errors* document located on the Data Disk.
2. Correct the spelling errors using the Spelling and Grammar command on the Tools menu.
3. Save the document as *Vancouver Report Revised*. Preview, print, and close the document.

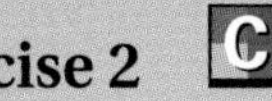

Exercise 2

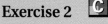

1. Open the *Solicitation Letter With Errors* document located on the Data Disk.
2. Select the text "Current date" and use AutoComplete to replace it with the actual date.
3. Correct the spelling and grammar errors using the Spelling and Grammar Status mode indicator.

4. Use the Synonyms command to choose another word for "growth" in the first body paragraph.
5. Save the document as *Solicitation Letter Revised*. Preview, print, and close the document.

Exercise 3 C

1. Open the *Personal Letter With Errors* document located on the Data Disk.
2. Select the text "Current date" and use AutoComplete to replace it with the actual date.
3. Correct the spelling and grammar errors using the shortcut menus.
4. Use the Thesaurus tool to select another word for "arrangements" in the last paragraph. (*Hint:* Right-click the word, point to Synonyms, and then click Thesaurus.)
5. Replace the text "Student's name" with your name.
6. Save the document as *Personal Letter Revised*. Preview, print, and close the document.

Exercise 4 C

1. Create a new, blank document.
2. Create an AutoText entry to insert a standard complimentary closing for the letters signed by R. F. Williams. Use the "Sincerely yours" closing text. Add your initials and an Attachment line. Name the AutoText entry "Williams Closing."
3. Insert the "Williams Closing" AutoText entry into a new, blank document using the F3 key or the ENTER key.
4. Save the document as *Williams Closing*.
5. Preview and print the document.
6. Edit the "Williams Closing" AutoText entry to include the job title "Vice President Marketing."
7. Save the document as *Williams Closing Revised*. Preview, print, and close the document.

Exercise 5 C

1. Open the *Client Letter* document located on the Data Disk.
2. Select the text "Current date" and use AutoComplete to replace it with the current date.
3. Insert the "Williams Closing" AutoText entry created in Exercise 4 at the bottom of the document. Add any additional blank lines as necessary.
4. Save the document as *Williams Letter*. Preview, print, and close the document.

Exercise 6 C

1. Print all the current AutoText entries.
2. Delete the "Williams Closing" AutoText entry you created in Exercise 4.
3. Close the Word application to update the Normal template.

Exercise 7 C

1. Open the *Application Letter With Errors* document located on the Data Disk.
2. Select the text "Current date" and use AutoComplete to replace it with the actual date.
3. Move the second body paragraph beginning "Per our conversation" to the first body paragraph position.

4. Move the last body paragraph beginning "If you have" and make it the second sentence of the second body paragraph. Delete any extra blank lines, if necessary.
5. Correct the spelling and grammar using the Spelling and Grammar button on the Standard toolbar.
6. Use the Synonyms command to select another word for "department" in the first paragraph.
7. Save the document as *Application Letter Revised.* Preview, print, and close the document.

Exercise 8 

1. Create the document below just as you see it. Use appropriate margins for a letter to be printed on 2-inch letterhead paper. Correct any spelling or grammar errors as you key using the Spelling and Grammar shortcut menus. Use the AutoComplete and standard AutoText features where appropriate to complete the letter, for example, to enter the current date.

Current date

Ms. Lavonia Jackson
Gift Baskets Galore!
1001 Kirby Drive
Houston, TX 77043-1001

Dear Ms. Jackson:

congratulations on starting your own gift shop. I know you will be successful because of the tremendos the growth of the gift basket market.

We would like to order our holiday gifts from your shop and are lookin forward to receiving your holiday catalog as soon as it is available.

Sincerely,

Tom McGregor
Personnel Manager

mj

2. Save the document as *McGregor Letter*. Preview, print, and close the document.

Exercise 9 

1. Open the *British Columbia Report* document located on the Data Disk.
2. Find each occurrence of the text "British Columbia" and replace it with "New York." (*Hint:* Remember to clear any formatting that is set in the dialog box.)
3. Change the left margin to 1 inch.
4. Save the document as *New York Report*. Preview, print, and close the document.

Case Projects

Project 1

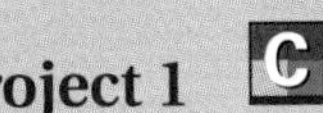

You have been assigned to work in the Legal Department at Worldwide Foods for two weeks. The department manager has asked you to find some way for the three secretaries in the department to save time by using Word to create and proof their documents. Prepare a document describing how the secretaries can use the AutoComplete, AutoText, AutoCorrect, and Find/Replace tools to save time. Include spelling and grammar shortcuts. Use the Spelling and Grammar tool to correct any spelling and grammar errors in your document. Use the AutoCorrect tool to quickly enter symbols and text. Use the Thesaurus tool to replace words with more appropriate or descriptive ones. Use the AutoComplete tool to enter the current date. Save and print the document.

Project 2

As Kelly's assistant, you are often called on to solve user problems with the Word application. You received the following list of problems from the secretaries in the Tax Department about the AutoText and AutoCorrect features:

1. How can I store an AutoCorrect entry without its original formatting?
2. My AutoComplete tips are not displaying when I insert AutoText.
3. How can I share AutoText entries with other secretaries in my department?

Using the Office Assistant or Ask A Question Box, research the answers to these questions. Use the keywords "AutoComplete," "AutoText," and "templates" for your search. Create, save, and print a document that describes how to solve these problems. Use the Spelling and Grammar tool to correct any spelling and grammar errors in your document. Use the AutoCorrect tool to quickly enter symbols and text. Use the Thesaurus tool to replace words with more appropriate or descriptive ones. Use the AutoComplete tool to enter the current date. Discuss your proposed solutions with a classmate.

Project 3

One of the legal secretaries asks for your help creating AutoCorrect exceptions. Using the Office Assistant or Ask A Question Box, research the AutoCorrect exceptions list tool. Create a new document containing a short paragraph describing how to use this tool. Use the Spelling and Grammar tool to correct any spelling and grammar errors in your document. Use the AutoCorrect tool to quickly enter symbols and text. Use the Thesaurus tool to replace words with more appropriate or descriptive ones. Use the AutoComplete tool to enter the current date. Save and print the document. Open the AutoCorrect dialog box and add two items of your choice to the AutoCorrect Exceptions list.

Project 4 

Mark Lee, a human resources consultant, is giving a 30-minute presentation on creating professional resumes at the next meeting of the International Association of Executive Assistants. He asks you to help prepare a list of topics by looking for Web pages that discuss how to create a resume. Connect to the Internet and search the Web for information about writing a resume. Save at least two URLs as "favorites." Print at least two Web pages.

Project 5

Using the research on creating resumes you prepared in Project 4, create, print, and save a document that Mark can use to prepare his presentation. Use the Spelling and Grammar tool to correct any spelling and grammar errors in your document. Use the AutoCorrect tool to quickly enter symbols and text. Use the Thesaurus tool to replace words with more appropriate or descriptive ones. Use the AutoComplete tool to enter the current date.

Project 6

B. D. Vickers has noticed that some letters and reports that contain spelling and grammatical errors are being mailed to clients. He asks you to prepare a document describing how to use the Spelling and Grammar tool, which he will give to all administrative assistants and secretaries during a special luncheon next week. Create a new document containing at least four paragraphs outlining how to use the Spelling and Grammar tool *including* custom/special dictionaries and adding a word to the AutoCorrect list during the spell-checking process as well as how to use the various options in the Spelling and Grammar dialog box. Use the Spelling and Grammar tool to correct any spelling and grammar errors in your document. Use the AutoCorrect tool to quickly enter symbols and text. Use the Thesaurus tool to replace words with more appropriate or descriptive ones. Use the AutoComplete tool to enter the current date. Save, preview, and print the document.

Project 7  

Kelly wants to purchase several reference books for the company library on how to use Microsoft Word. She doesn't have time to check out the local bookstores so she has asked you to look for the books at several online bookstores. Connect to the Internet and search the Web for online bookstores. Load several online bookstore Web pages and search each Web site for books on how to use Microsoft Word. Use the information you gather from the bookstores to prepare a document with a list of books by title. Include the author's name, the price of the book, and the proposed shipping time. Use the Spelling and Grammar tool to correct any spelling and grammar errors in your document. Use the AutoCorrect tool to quickly enter symbols and text. Use the Thesaurus tool to replace words with more appropriate or descriptive ones. Use the AutoComplete tool to enter the current date. Save, preview, and print the document.

Project 8

B. D. Vickers wants to know something about the readability of the documents the administrative staff is preparing and has asked you to find out which tool in Word can provide that information. Using the Office Assistant or Ask A Question Box, research the readability statistics displayed by the Spelling and Grammar tool. Create a new document with at least three paragraphs describing the readability statistics and formulas. Use the Spelling and Grammar tool to correct any spelling and grammar errors in your document. Use the AutoCorrect tool to quickly enter symbols and text. Use the Thesaurus tool to replace words with more appropriate or descriptive ones. Use the AutoComplete tool to enter the current date. Save, preview, and print the document.

Applying Character Formatting

Chapter Overview

The ability to format text provides a word processing application much of its power. The Word formatting features give you the ability to create professional, unique-looking documents. In this chapter, you learn how to change the appearance of text by changing fonts and font styles and by applying character styles and special effects to text characters. You also learn to copy character formats, review and change text formatting using a task pane, and change the case of text. Finally, you learn to highlight text to be read online in a color and to insert symbols and special characters.

Case profile

Because of your successful performance in the Purchasing Department, the Marketing Department has requested you to fill in for Elizabeth Chang, the assistant secretary, who is going on a short holiday. Before she left, Elizabeth left several documents for you to format.

Learning Objectives

- Change fonts and font size
- Apply font styles, character styles, and special character effects
- Change the case of text
- Highlight text in a document
- Insert symbols and special characters

chapter four

4.a Changing Fonts and Font Size

You can change the appearance of a document by changing the shape and size of text characters, by changing the spacing between the characters, and by applying special character effects. Changing the appearance of individual text characters or groups of characters is called **character formatting**. You can apply character formatting to text using menu commands, a shortcut menu, toolbar buttons, and with links or commands in the Reveal Formatting task pane.

One of the first formatting choices you make is the type of font and the font size you want to use in a document. A **font** is a set of printed characters with the same size and appearance. A font has three characteristics: typeface, style, and point (font) size.

1. **Typeface** refers to the design and appearance of printed characters. Here are some examples of different typefaces:

   Times New Roman   Courier New
   Arial   Brush Script MT

2. **Style** refers to bold or italic print. *Italic print is slanted to the right* and **bold print is darker**.
3. **Point (font) size** refers to the height of the printed characters. There are 72 points to an inch; the larger the point size, the larger the characters. Some common point sizes include:

   8 point   10 point   12 point

A font may be **monospaced**, where all characters occupy an identical amount of horizontal space or **proportional**, where different characters occupy various amounts of horizontal space. Courier is an example of a monospaced font and Times New Roman is an example of a proportional font. Most people who use a word processing application to create text documents use proportional fonts.

There are two main categories of proportional fonts: serif and sans serif. A **serif** is a small line extension at the beginning and end of a character to help the reader's eye move across the text. Serif fonts are often used in documents with a large amount of text. A **sans serif** font is one that does not have the small line extensions on its characters (*sans* is the French word for without). Sans serif fonts are often used for paragraph headings and document titles. The Times New Roman font is an example of a serif font and the Arial font is an example of a sans serif font.

MENU TIP

You can select a font from the Font: list box on the Font tab in the Font dialog box. To open the dialog box, click the Font command on the Format menu or right-click selected text and click Font on the shortcut menu.

The default font and font size in Word are the Times New Roman font and 12-point font size. According to Elizabeth's notes, several changes need to be made to the *Library Bulletin* document. First, the document title should be in Arial font and the entire document should be in 11-point font size.

This book assumes that your computer is connected to a Hewlett-Packard LaserJet printer and you use TrueType fonts. If you have a different printer, make the appropriate selections for your printer.

Changing Fonts

To change the font, first select the text to be changed. For example, if you want to change the font for the entire document, select the entire document. Then select the font you want to use. If the document has not been keyed yet, you can select the font before you key the text. That font selection is then used throughout the document. Currently, the entire *Library Bulletin* document is formatted with the Times New Roman, 10-point font. You begin by opening the document and then changing the font of the title text, "INFORMATION SYSTEMS LIBRARY BULLETIN," to the Arial TrueType font. To change the font:

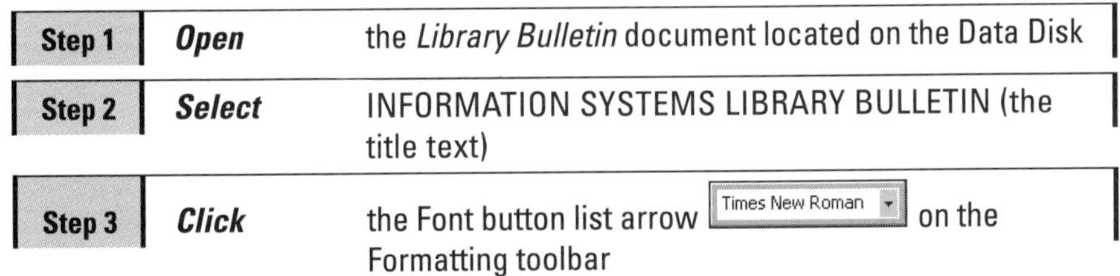

Step 1	***Open***	the *Library Bulletin* document located on the Data Disk
Step 2	***Select***	INFORMATION SYSTEMS LIBRARY BULLETIN (the title text)
Step 3	***Click***	the Font button list arrow [Times New Roman] on the Formatting toolbar

The font list on your screen should look similar to that in Figure 4-1.

QUICK TIP

Word uses the Times New Roman, 12-point size font as the default font for all documents based on the Normal template. You can change the default font for all new documents based on the Normal template with the Default button in the Font dialog box.

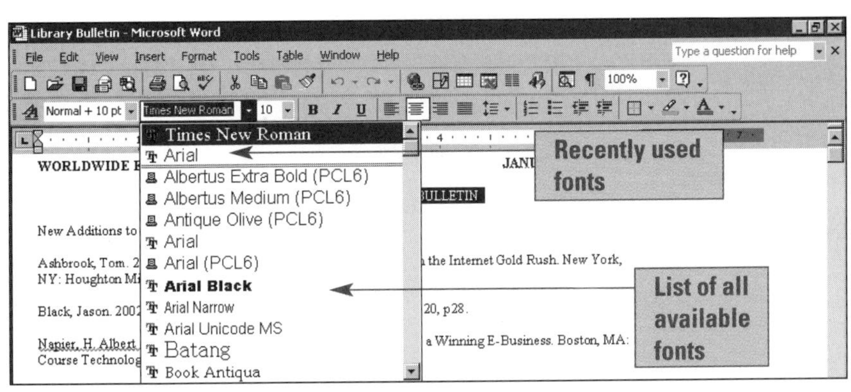

FIGURE 4-1
Font List

Notice that some fonts on the Font list have a symbol to the left of the font name. A "TT" symbol indicates that the font is a **TrueType font** that prints text exactly the way it is displayed on your screen. A printer symbol next to a font indicates that the assigned printer supports the font. A list of the most recently used fonts may appear at the top of the font list, followed by a horizontal double line.

Step 4	***Click***	Arial (scroll to view this option, if necessary)
Step 5	***Deselect***	the text

The document title font is different from the text font, making it distinct. You also can change the font size for your documents.

Changing Font Size

The point (font) size for the text of the entire document is currently 10 point. The *Library Bulletin* document should be in 11 point. To change the point size for the entire document to 11 point:

Step 1	***Select***	the entire document
Step 2	***Click***	the Font Size button list arrow [12] on the Formatting toolbar

The Font Size list on your screen should look similar to the one in Figure 4-2.

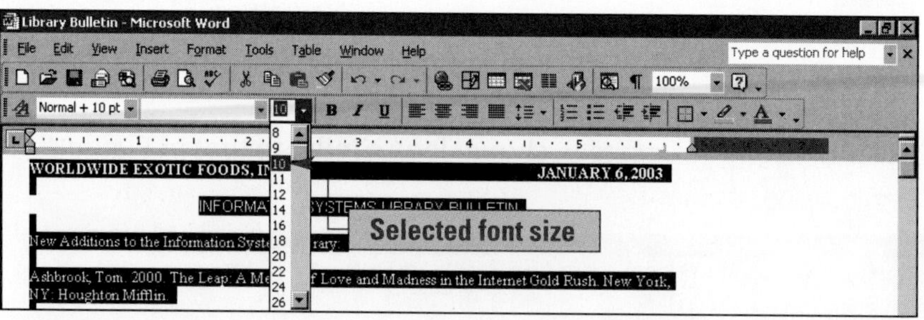

FIGURE 4-2
Font Size List

Step 3	***Click***	11
Step 4	***Deselect***	the text

The entire document changes to 11-point type. Next, you need to add emphasis to certain text by applying font styles, such as bold and italic.

4.b Applying Font Styles, Character Styles, and Special Character Effects

Elizabeth wants certain words emphasized in the *Library Bulletin* document. You can do this by applying the bold or italic font styles to the text.

Applying the Bold Font Style

Applying the **Bold** style makes the selected text darker than other text to attract a reader's attention. When you apply the Bold style, Word makes the text appear darker on the screen as well as on the printed page.

To add the Bold style to the text "New Additions to the Information Systems Library":

Step 1	*Select*	New Additions to the Information Systems Library (do not select the colon)
Step 2	*Click*	the Bold button **B** on the Formatting toolbar
Step 3	*Deselect*	the text, leaving the insertion point in the paragraph

The text appears darker. The Bold button on the Formatting toolbar is outlined with a border, indicating the Bold style is applied. You remove the Bold style by clicking the Bold button again. The first line of the document contains the company name and date formatted with the Bold style. Elizabeth's notes tell you to remove the bold style. To remove the Bold style:

Step 1	*Select*	the first line of the document using the selection bar
Step 2	*Click*	the Bold button **B** on the Formatting toolbar
Step 3	*Deselect*	the text, leaving the insertion point in the first line

QUICK TIP

You can use keyboard shortcuts to apply font styles. For example, press the CTRL + B keys to apply the Bold style to selected text. Use the Ask A Question Box to view and print a complete list of keyboard shortcuts.

MENU TIP

You can apply the font styles to text on the Font tab in the Font dialog box. You can open the Font dialog box by clicking the Font command on the Format menu or shortcut menu.

chapter four

The text is no longer bold and the Bold button on the Formatting toolbar no longer has a border.

Applying the Italic Font Style

Italicizing text allows you to emphasize text by slanting it to the right. You apply and remove italic formatting the same way you do bold formatting—in this case, by selecting the text and applying the italic style. Elizabeth's notes indicate the magazine title in which Jason Black's article appears should be italicized. To italicize the magazine title:

QUICK TIP

You can apply character formatting to a single, complete word by clicking the word to place the insertion point in it, and then applying the format.

Step 1	*Select*	the magazine title "Internet World" in the second item in the list
Step 2	*Click*	the Italic button on the Formatting toolbar
Step 3	*Deselect*	the text, leaving the insertion point in the title

The magazine title is italicized. The Italic button on the Formatting toolbar has a border, indicating that the italic style is applied to the text.

You can remove the italic style by selecting the formatted text and again clicking the Italic button on the Formatting toolbar.

Applying Underline Formatting

Emphasizing text by placing a line below the text is called **underlining**. You can choose to underline selected letters, selected words, or selected words and the spaces between them. Word also provides a variety of underlines you can use to enhance text.

You want to add a thick single line below the title "New Additions to the Information Systems Library." This underline style is not available by clicking the Underline button on the Formatting toolbar, which formats text and the spaces between the text with a thin single line. Instead, you must open the Font dialog box to see a complete list of underline styles.

A quick way to open the Font dialog box is with a shortcut menu. To apply a thick single underline to text:

MENU TIP

You can underline selected text by clicking the Underline Style list arrow on the Font tab in the Font dialog box, and then clicking the underline style of your choice.

Step 1	*Select*	New Additions to the Information Systems Library (do not select the colon)
Step 2	*Right-click*	the selected text
Step 3	*Click*	Font
Step 4	*Click*	the Font tab, if necessary

The Font tab in the Font dialog box on your screen should look similar to Figure 4-3.

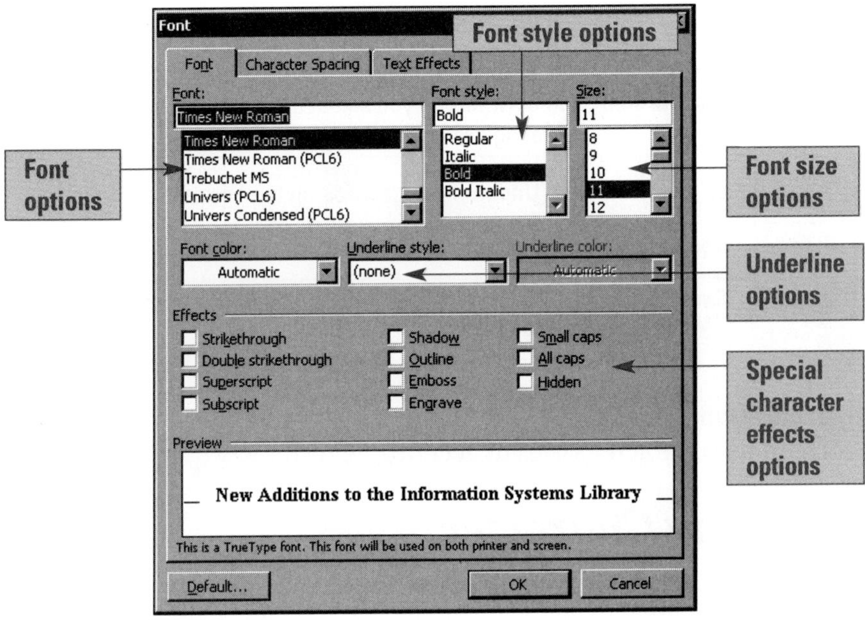

FIGURE 4-3
Font Dialog Box

You can change the font, font style, font size, underlining, underline color, and color of selected text on the Font tab. The Effects group provides options for applying special effects to selected text. The Preview area provides a sample of the formatting options before they are applied to the selected text.

Step 5	***Click***	the Underline style: list arrow
Step 6	***Click***	the thick single line option (the fifth option in the list)
Step 7	***Preview***	the underline formatting in the dialog box
Step 8	***Click***	OK
Step 9	***Deselect***	the text

The text is underlined with a thick single line. The book titles in the first and third items in the list should be underlined. You can add or remove a thin single underline applied to words and spaces with the

Underline button on the Formatting toolbar. To add a thin single underline to both book titles at one time:

Step 1	***Select***	the book title "The Leap: A Memoir of Love and Madness in the Internet Gold Rush"
Step 2	***Press & hold***	the CTRL key as you select the book title "Dot-Commerce: Creating a Winning E-Business"
Step 3	***Click***	the Underline button on the Formatting toolbar
Step 4	***Deselect***	the text
Step 5	***Save***	the document as *Library Bulletin Revised* and leave it open

In addition to using bold, italic, and underlining to emphasize text, you can use character styles to accentuate text.

Applying Character Styles

A **character style** is a collection of character formatting attributes—such as font, font size, and font style—that is given a special name and then applied to selected text by that name. Character styles are applied only to selected text. For example, the Strong character style contains the default Times New Roman font, the default 12-point font size, and the Bold font style. When you want to apply these three formatting attributes to selected text, you can apply all three at once by using the Strong character style.

MENU TIP

You can apply a character style to selected text with the Styles and Formatting command on the Format menu.

MOUSE TIP

You can apply a character style to selected text with the Style button list on the Formatting toolbar.

Elizabeth wants you to apply the Strong character style to the first line of text. You also want to view the nonprinting formatting marks as you format the document. To view the formatting marks and apply the Strong style:

Step 1	***Click***	the Show/Hide button on the Standard toolbar
Step 2	***Select***	the first line of text
Step 3	***Click***	the Styles and Formatting button on the Formatting toolbar

The Styles and Formatting task pane opens. Your screen should look similar to Figure 4-4.

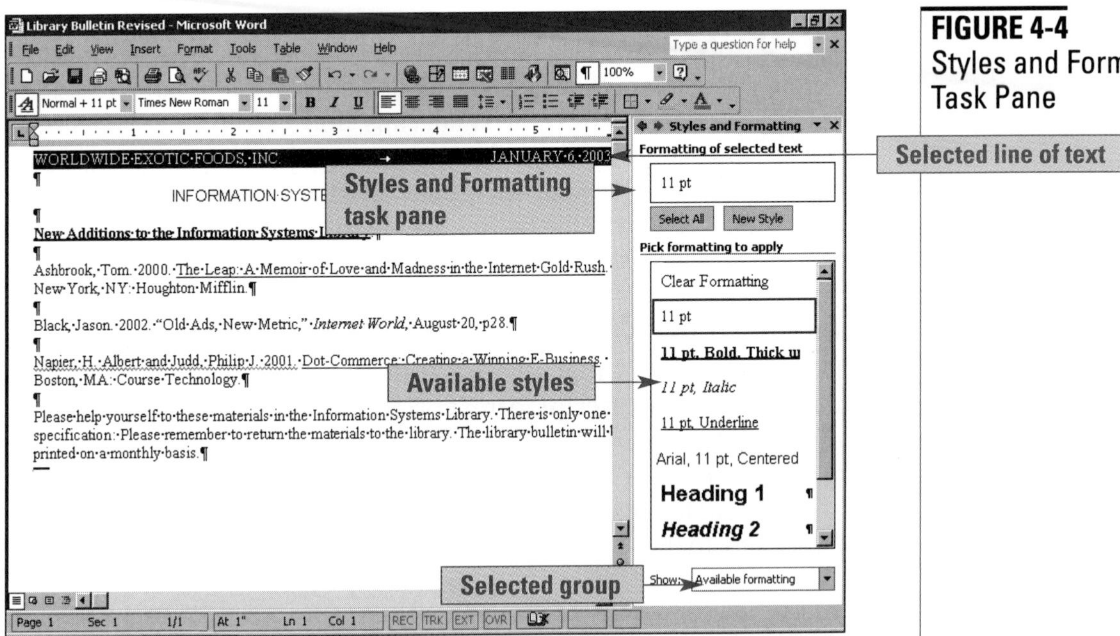

FIGURE 4-4
Styles and Formatting Task Pane

The Formatting of selected text box in the Styles and Formatting task pane shows you the style applied to the currently selected text. The Pick formatting to apply list allows you to select a group of styles to view: all the default available styles for the current document, only the styles currently being used, or a complete list of styles. You select the group of styles to place in the Pick formatting to apply list with the Show: list. To view a complete list of styles:

Step 1	***Click***	the Show: list arrow in the Styles and Formatting task pane
Step 2	***Click***	All styles to view a complete scrollable list of styles
Step 3	***Scroll***	the Pick formatting to apply list to view the Strong character style
Step 4	***Click***	Strong in the Pick formatting to apply list
Step 5	***Deselect***	the text
Step 6	***Observe***	the formatted text
Step 7	***Close***	the Styles and Formatting task pane

In addition to using character styles to format text, you can use special character effects to add emphasis to text.

Applying Special Character Effects

Another way to emphasize text is to add special character effects, such as superscript, subscript, small caps, and strikethrough effects. Elizabeth asks you to add special character effects to specified text in the *Library Bulletin Revised* document. Because you are unfamiliar with special character effects, you decide to experiment by applying and then removing some of the effects.

Applying Superscript and Subscript

The **Superscript** format places text slightly above a line of normal printed text. The **Subscript** format places text slightly below a line of normal printed text. This is ^{superscript}, and this is $_{\text{subscript}}$. You can apply Superscript or Subscript formats to selected text in the Font tab in the Font dialog box. To experiment with the Superscript and Subscript formats:

Step 1	***Move***	the insertion point to the left margin before the "B" in "Black"
Step 2	***Key***	1
Step 3	***Select***	the number 1
Step 4	***Click***	Format
Step 5	***Click***	Font
Step 6	***Click***	the Font tab, if necessary
Step 7	***Click***	the Superscript check box to insert a check mark
Step 8	***Click***	OK
Step 9	***Deselect***	the text
Step 10	***Observe***	the ^{1}Black superscript notation

You apply the Subscript format the same way. To apply the Subscript format:

Step 1	***Move***	the insertion point to the left margin before the "N" in "Napier"
Step 2	***Key***	2
Step 3	***Select***	the number 2
Step 4	***Open***	the Font tab in the Font dialog box
Step 5	***Click***	the Subscript check box to insert a check mark
Step 6	***Click***	OK

Step 7	***Deselect***	the text
Step 8	***Observe***	the $_2$Napier subscript notation
Step 9	***Delete***	the superscript and subscript text
Step 10	***Save***	the document and leave it open

QUICK TIP

You can remove Superscript and Subscript formatting from selected text by removing the check mark from the appropriate check box on the Font tab in the Font dialog box.

Applying Strikethrough

When you edit a document online, you might want to indicate text that should be deleted. One way to do this is to format the text with the **Strikethrough** effect, which draws a line through selected text. To add the Strikethrough effect to the first sentence of the last paragraph:

Step 1	***Select***	the text "in the Information Systems Library"
Step 2	***Open***	the Font tab in the Font dialog box
Step 3	***Click***	the Strikethrough check box to insert a check mark
Step 4	***Click***	OK

MOUSE TIP

You can add Superscript and Subscript buttons to the Formatting toolbar. Click the Toolbar Options list arrow on the Formatting toolbar, point to Add or Remove buttons, point to Formatting to expand the list of buttons, and then click the Superscript or Subscript button to add it to the toolbar.

The selected text now has a line through it, indicating it could be deleted from the document. Because you don't want to delete the text, you remove the Strikethrough.

Step 5	***Click***	the Undo button on the Standard toolbar
Step 6	***Deselect***	the text

Elizabeth indicated that the library name needs to be distinguished from the rest of the text. You decide to apply the Small caps effect.

Applying Small Caps

The **Small caps** effect is a special character effect that displays selected text in all-uppercase characters, where any characters keyed with the SHIFT key pressed display larger than the remaining characters. The Small caps format is appropriate for headings and titles, such as "Information Systems Library." To apply the Small caps effect:

Step 1	***Select***	the text "Information Systems Library" in the first sentence of the last paragraph
Step 2	***Open***	the Font tab in the Font dialog box
Step 3	***Click***	the Small caps check box to insert a check mark

Step 4	*Click*	OK

The text is in all-uppercase characters, with the first character of each word slightly taller than the remaining characters in the word.

Step 5	*Continue*	by applying the Small caps effect to each instance of "Information Systems Library"

The Small caps effect is not visible in the centered title at this time because the text is already in all-uppercase letters.

C

Applying Character Spacing and Animation Effects

Adding extra spacing between text characters in titles adds variety and interest to a document. **Character spacing** is the amount of white space that appears between characters. You can change the character spacing by scaling the characters to a specific percentage, expanding or condensing the characters a specific number of points, or by kerning. **Kerning** adjusts the space between particular pairs of characters, depending on the font.

You want the title of the *Library Bulletin Revised* document to stand out more, so you scale the text. To scale the title text so that it is stretched horizontally to be 120% of its original width:

Step 1	*Select*	INFORMATION SYSTEMS LIBRARY BULLETIN (the title text)
Step 2	*Open*	the Font dialog box
Step 3	*Click*	the Character Spacing tab
Step 4	*Key*	120 in the Scale: text box
Step 5	*Press*	the ENTER key

QUICK TIP

Pressing the ENTER key when working in a dialog box is the same as clicking the selected dialog box button (the button with the dark border). For example, the OK button is the selected button in most dialog boxes. You can press the ENTER key instead of clicking the OK button to accept your option choices and close the dialog box.

The text is "stretched" horizontally to 120% of its original width. Upon her return, Elizabeth plans to attach the *Library Bulletin Revised* document to e-mail messages so recipients can read the document online. She wants you to add animation effects to the *Library Bulletin Revised* document that draw attention to the document's title. To add animation effects:

Step 1	*Verify*	that the title text is still selected
Step 2	*Open*	the Font dialog box

Step 3	***Click***	the Text Effects tab
Step 4	***Click***	Marching Red Ants in the Animations: list box
Step 5	***Click***	OK
Step 6	***Observe***	that a red dashed moving box now appears around the title
Step 7	***Deselect***	the text
Step 8	***Save***	the document and leave it open

The red marching ants will attract immediate attention to the document.

Using the Format Painter

Once you have applied character formatting to text, it's often faster to duplicate that formatting to other text rather than reapplying it each time. Copying formats, rather than recreating them, ensures consistency and saves time. You can copy and paste character formats quickly with the Format Painter button on the Standard toolbar. First place the insertion point in the text that contains the formats to be copied, then click the Format Painter button. When you move the mouse pointer into the typing area, the mouse pointer changes to an I-beam with a paintbrush icon. Drag the Format Painter I-beam across the text you want to format. The Format Painter pastes *all* the formats from the original text.

You want to apply the bold, single underline and font size formats to selected text, and then copy that formatting to unformatted text. To apply multiple character formats:

Step 1	***Select***	the phrase "There is only one specification" in the last paragraph (do not select the colon)
Step 2	***Click***	the Bold button on the Formatting toolbar
Step 3	***Click***	14 in the Font Size button list on the Formatting toolbar
Step 4	***Click***	the Underline button on the Formatting toolbar
Step 5	***Deselect***	the text leaving the insertion point in the formatted text

MENU TIP

You can repeat formatting you just applied to other text by selecting the text and clicking the Repeat command on the Edit menu. If you applied character formats from the Formatting toolbar, only the last formatting option is repeated. If you applied multiple character formats from the Font tab in the Font dialog box, all the formats are repeated.

To copy formats using the Format Painter:

Step 1	*Click*	the Format Painter button on the Formatting toolbar
Step 2	*Observe*	that the mouse pointer is now an I-beam with a paint-brush icon
Step 3	*Drag*	the Format Painter I-beam over the next phrase "Please remember to return the materials to the library" (do not select the period)
Step 4	*Observe*	that when you release the mouse button, the formats are copied to the selected phrase
Step 5	*Save*	the document and leave it open

MOUSE TIP

You can use the Format Painter to paste formats multiple times. Select the text with the formats you want to copy and double-click the Format Painter button. Then select text for formatting throughout your document. Turn off the Format Painter by clicking the Format Painter button again.

When necessary, you can quickly modify the formats of similarly formatted text using a shortcut menu to first select the text.

Selecting Similarly Formatted Text

You just checked your e-mail and find a message from Elizabeth with last-minute instructions for formatting the *Library Bulletin Revised* document. Elizabeth asks you to ignore her note to add a single underline to the two multiformatted phrases in the last paragraph. To select the two similarly formatted phrases:

Step 1	*Right-click*	the phrase "There is only one specification"
Step 2	*Click*	Select Text with Similar Formatting
Step 3	*Observe*	that both phrases are selected
Step 4	*Click*	the Underline button on the Formatting toolbar to remove the underline formatting
Step 5	*Deselect*	the text
Step 6	*Save*	the document and leave it open

QUICK TIP

You can remove character formatting from selected text by pressing the CTRL + SHIFT + Z keys.

C

Using the Reveal Formatting Task Pane

The Reveal Formatting task pane provides a quick summary of the formatting applied to selected text as well as links to formatting dialog boxes in which you can change the selected text's formatting.

You want to review all the character formats you applied in the *Library Bulletin Revised* document. To display the Reveal Formatting task pane:

Step 1	***Move***	the insertion point to the word "bulletin" in the last sentence
Step 2	***Click***	Format
Step 3	***Click***	Reveal Formatting

TASK PANE TIP

When a task pane is already displayed, you can view the Reveal Formatting task pane with the Other Task Panes button on the task pane title bar.

Your screen should look similar to Figure 4-5.

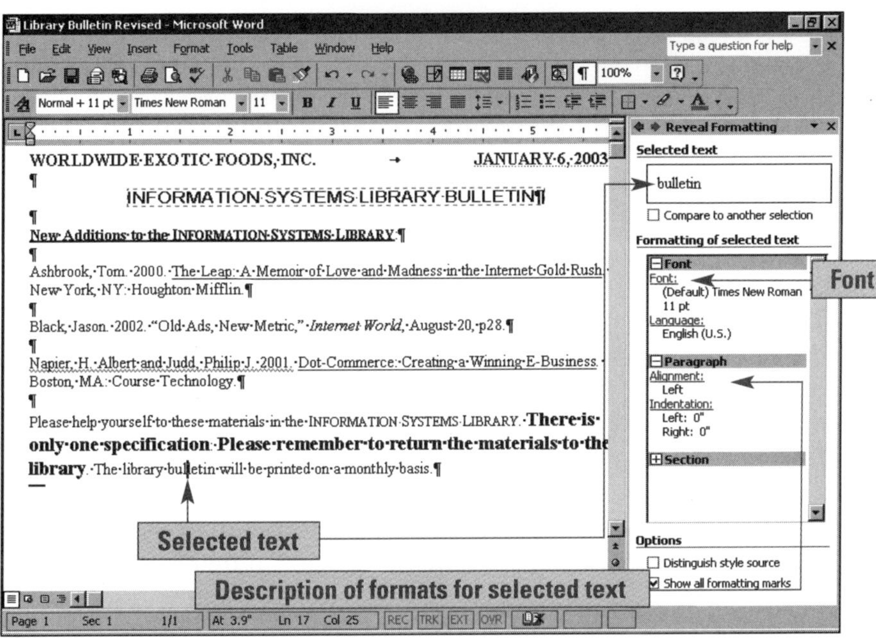

FIGURE 4-5
Reveal Formatting Task Pane

QUICK TIP

You can display the Reveal Formatting task pane by clicking the What's This? command on the Help menu or pressing the SHIFT + F1 keys to change the mouse pointer to a Help pointer and then clicking the desired text to display the Reveal Formatting task pane.

Text you select appears in the Selected text box in the task pane. When you move the mouse pointer to the Selected text box in the task pane, a list arrow appears. You can click this list arrow to view a menu that allows you to select similarly formatted text, format the selected text with the same format as the surrounding text, or clear the formatting.

The Formatting of selected text list box includes links that enable you to open formatting dialog boxes such as the Font dialog box, where you can see a description of the formatting and the formatting applied to selected text. To review some of the text formatting:

Step 1	***Select***	the text "Information Systems Library" in the phrase "New Additions to the Information Systems Library"

TASK PANE TIP

You can turn on or off the view of formatting marks with the Show all formatting marks check box in the Reveal Formatting task pane.

Step 2	*Observe*	the font formatting description in the Formatting of selected text list: (Default) Times New Roman, 11 pt, Bold, Thick underline, English (U.S.), and Small caps effects

You can change any of these formats from the task pane. To remove the Small caps effects:

Step 1	*Click*	the Effects: link in the Formatting of selected text list in the Reveal Formatting task pane
Step 2	*Click*	the Small caps check box to remove the check mark in the Font dialog box
Step 3	*Click*	OK
Step 4	*Close*	the Reveal Formatting task pane
Step 5	*Save*	the document and leave it open

It's easy to switch between uppercase and lowercase letters after you key text.

4.c Changing the Case of Text

Elizabeth wants you to change the case of the title in the *Library Bulletin Revised* document. **Case** refers to the use of capitalized text characters versus noncapitalized text characters. You can change the case of text by first selecting the text you want to change, and then clicking the Change Case command on the Format menu.

The Change Case dialog box contains five case formats:

1. **Sentence** case capitalizes the first word of the selected text.
2. **lowercase** changes all characters of the selected text to lowercase characters.
3. **UPPERCASE** changes all characters of the selected text to uppercase characters.
4. **Title Case** capitalizes the first character of each word in the selected text.
5. **tOGGLE cASE** changes all uppercase characters to lowercase and all lowercase characters to uppercase for the selected text.

To change the case of the title text:

Step 1	*Select*	the title text "INFORMATION SYSTEMS LIBRARY BULLETIN"
Step 2	*Click*	Format
Step 3	*Click*	Change Case

The Change Case dialog box on your screen should look similar to Figure 4-6.

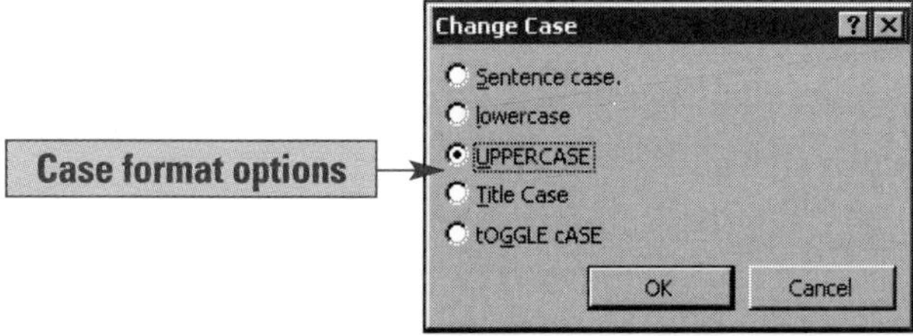

FIGURE 4-6
Change Case Dialog Box

Step 4	***Click***	the Title Case option button
Step 5	***Click***	OK
Step 6	***Deselect***	the text

Notice that you can now see the Small cap formatting you applied earlier to the title.

Step 7	***Click***	the Show/Hide button  on the Standard toolbar to turn off the feature
Step 8	***Save***	the document and close it

One way to draw a reviewer's attention to important text in a document being read online is to highlight the text in a special color.

QUICK TIP

You can turn on or off viewing and printing highlight colors on the View tab in the Options dialog box. Using color to highlight text works best when a document is read on a computer screen. If you print a document with highlighted text, use a light color.

4.d Highlighting Text in a Document

C

Elizabeth wants to draw attention to the text "Warning! Warning! Warning!" in the *Policy #152* document. To do this, she asks you to highlight the text in color. To highlight the text:

Step 1	***Open***	the *Policy #152* document located on the Data Disk
Step 2	***Select***	the text "Warning! Warning! Warning!"
Step 3	***Click***	the Highlight button list arrow on the Formatting toolbar
Step 4	***Click***	Bright Green

Step 5	***Observe***	that the text is highlighted in color
Step 6	***Save***	the document as *Policy #152 With Highlighting* and close it

Another way to enhance text appearance is to insert symbols and special characters into your document.

C

4.e Inserting Symbols and Special Characters

MOUSE TIP

You can select a highlighter color and then drag the mouse pointer over text to apply the color highlighting.

Symbols and special characters can be inserted into a document using the AutoCorrect feature or the Symbol command on the Insert menu. Elizabeth left instructions for you to complete a new Marketing Department training class announcement by inserting the appropriate symbols and special characters.

First, you need to insert the copyright symbol in the document. To insert the copyright symbol using the AutoCorrect feature:

Step 1	***Open***	the *Quality 2003 Training* document located on the Data Disk
Step 2	***Move***	the insertion point to the end of the "Quality 2003 Training" text in the third line
Step 3	***Key***	(c) to insert the copyright symbol using AutoCorrect
Step 4	***Observe***	the inserted copyright symbol

MENU TIP

You can insert symbols by clicking the Symbol command on the Insert menu to open the Symbol dialog box, clicking the desired symbol, and clicking the Insert button.

Special characters such as the en dash (used in inclusive numbers), the nonbreaking space (a fixed space between words that cannot be broken at the right margin), and the em dash (used to insert a break in a thought) as well as the copyright symbol can be inserted from the Special Characters tab in the Symbol dialog box. Elizabeth wants you to replace the hyphen in the first paragraph with an em dash character. To select the hyphen and open the dialog box:

MOUSE TIP

If AutoCorrect incorrectly changes keyed characters to a symbol, click the Undo button on the Standard toolbar to undo the symbol conversion.

Step 1	***Select***	the hyphen following the word "now" in the last sentence of the first body paragraph
Step 2	***Click***	Insert
Step 3	***Click***	Symbol
Step 4	***Click***	the Special Characters tab, if necessary

The Symbol dialog box on your screen should look similar to Figure 4-7.

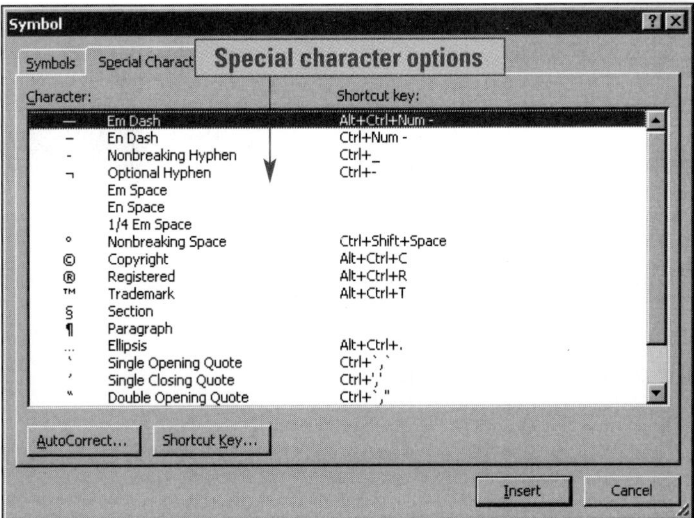

FIGURE 4-7
Symbol Dialog Box

Step 5	***Double-click***	the Em Dash option in the list
Step 6	***Close***	the Symbol dialog box
Step 7	***Observe***	that the em dash replaces the hyphen in the document
Step 8	***Save***	the document as *Quality 2003 With Symbol and Em Dash* and close it

With the Word character formatting features you can make any document look professionally formatted.

QUICK TIP

The **AutoFormat As You Type** feature (in addition to the symbol characters in the AutoCorrect list) automatically formats certain characters as you key them. For example, you can replace ordinals (1st) with superscript (1st), fractions (1/2) with stacked characters (½), and "straight quotes" with “curly quotes.” The automatic formatting is applied when you press the SPACEBAR and is turned on by default.

You can turn off the automatic formatting of characters in the AutoFormat As You Type tab in the AutoCorrect dialog box. The AutoFormat tab in the AutoCorrect dialog box contains options that control how Word automatically formats an entire document. For more information on automatically formatting an entire Word document, see online Help.

Summary

- Character formatting is used to change the appearance of individual text characters or groups of characters.
- A font is a set of printed characters that has the same size and appearance.
- A font has three aspects: typeface, style, and point (font) size.
- In a monospaced font, all characters occupy the same horizontal space.
- In a proportional font, characters occupy different amounts of horizontal space.
- A serif is a small line extension at the beginning of a character that helps guide the reader's eyes across the page. Fonts that do not have a serif are called sans serif fonts.
- The default font in Word is 12-point Times New Roman.
- Bold, italic, and underline formatting can be applied to selected text for emphasis.
- You can use the Styles and Formatting task pane to apply character styles to selected text.
- Superscript or subscript character formats can be applied to selected characters to position the characters slightly above or below the line of normal text.
- You can add animation effects, such as red marching ants, to emphasize text in documents that are to be read online.
- Character formats can be copied to new text using the Format Painter button on the Standard toolbar.
- The Reveal Formatting task pane contains links and commands you can use to select, review, and change character formatting.
- The case of text characters can be changed to Sentence case, lower-case, UPPERCASE, Title Case, or tOGGLE case.
- You can apply colored highlights to emphasize text to read online.
- You can add symbols and special characters to text.
- The AutoFormat As You Type feature automatically formats certain characters such as quote marks, fractions, and ordinals you key when you press the SPACEBAR.

Commands Review

Action	Menu Bar	Shortcut Menu	Toolbar	Task Pane	Keyboard
Change font	Format, Font	Right-click the selected text, click Font	Times New Roman	Click the Font: link in the Reveal Formatting task pane	ALT + O, F CTRL + D CTRL + SHIFT + F, DOWN ARROW
Change font size	Format, Font	Right-click the selected text, click Font	12	Click the Font: link in the Reveal Formatting task pane	ALT + O, F CTRL + SHIFT + P, DOWN ARROW
Apply or remove bold, italic, or underline formatting	Format, Font	Right-click the selected text, click Font	B I U	Click the Font: link in the Reveal Formatting task pane	ALT + O, F CTRL + B, CTRL + I, CTRL + U
Apply a character style	Format, Styles and Formatting		, Normal	Click style in the Pick formatting to apply list in the Styles and Formatting task pane	ALT + O, S
Apply or remove superscript or subscript formatting	Format, Font	Right-click the selected text, click Font		Click the Font: link in the Reveal Formatting task pane	ALT + O, F CTRL + = (sub.) CTRL + SHIFT + + (sup.)
Copy formats					CTRL + SHIFT + C CTRL + SHIFT + V
Remove character formatting					CTRL + SHIFT + Z CTRL + SPACEBAR
Repeat formats	Edit, Repeat				ALT + E, R CTRL + Y
Apply character spacing and text animation effects	Format, Font	Right-click the selected text, click Font			ALT + O, F
Select text with similar formatting		Right-click the selected text, click Select Text with Similar Formatting		Click the Selected text list arrow in the Reveal Formatting task pane and then click Select All Text with Similar Formatting	
View the Reveal Formatting task pane	Format, Reveal Formatting Help, What's This				ALT + O, V ALT + H, T SHIFT + F1
Change case	Format, Change Case				ALT + O, E SHIFT + F3
Add highlighting to text					
Insert symbols and special characters	Insert, Symbol				ALT + I, S

Concepts Review

Circle the correct answer.

1. **Changing the appearance of individual characters or groups of characters is called:**
   [a] paragraph formatting.
   [b] text formatting.
   [c] character formatting.
   [d] page formatting.

2. **Typeface refers to the:**
   [a] horizontal width of the characters.
   [b] height of the characters.
   [c] design and appearance of the characters.
   [d] slant of the characters.

3. **You can copy character formats by:**
   [a] clicking the Bullets button.
   [b] using the Format Painter button.
   [c] clicking the Numbering button.
   [d] pressing the DELETE key.

4. **The character spacing feature that adjusts the space between pairs of characters is called:**
   [a] kelping.
   [b] spacing.
   [c] underlining.
   [d] kerning.

5. **Which of the following task panes provides a link to the Font dialog box?**
   [a] New Document
   [b] Reveal Formatting
   [c] Styles and Formatting
   [d] Clipboard

6. **Which of the following is not a special font effect in the Font dialog box?**
   [a] Emboss
   [b] Engrave
   [c] Hidden
   [d] Bold

7. **Character spacing options are found in the:**
   [a] Font dialog box.
   [b] AutoCorrect dialog box.
   [c] Formatting dialog box.
   [d] AutoText dialog box.

8. **The Underline button on the formatting toolbar applies the following underline style:**
   [a] Dotted.
   [b] Single, words only.
   [c] Single, words and spaces.
   [d] Double wavy.

9. **Italics emphasizes text by:**
   [a] making the text darker.
   [b] slanting the text to the right.
   [c] placing the text above the baseline.
   [d] slanting the text to the left.

10. **Which of the following is not an option for changing the case of text?**
   [a] Uppercase
   [b] Lowercase
   [c] Triple case
   [d] Sentence case

Circle **T** if the statement is true or **F** if the statement is false.

T F 1. The Italic button on the Formatting toolbar allows you to create text that looks and prints darker than the rest of the text.

T F 2. You can easily select similarly formatted text with a shortcut menu.

T F 3. Subscript formatting places text slightly below a line of normal printed text.

T F 4. Superscript formatting places text slightly above a line of normal printed text.

T F 5. The Format Painter button on the Standard toolbar allows you to copy only one format at a time.

T F 6. The three characteristics of fonts are: typeface, weight, and point (font) size.

T F 7. The Reveal Formatting task pane contains a list of special text characters such as the em dash.

T F 8. Sentence case capitalizes each word of selected text.

T F 9. You cannot turn off the automatic formatting of characters.

T F 10. Font style refers to uppercase and lowercase characters.

Skills Review

Exercise 1

1. Open the *Interoffice Meeting Memo* document located on the Data Disk.
2. Replace the text "Current date" with the actual date.
3. Apply the Bold style the text TO, FROM, DATE, and SUBJECT in the memo form headings. (Do not apply bold formatting to the colons. Don't forget to use the CTRL key to select all the text before you apply the formatting.)
4. Apply the Bold style to the day and time for the meeting in the first paragraph.
5. Single underline the number 20 in the third paragraph.
6. Italicize the topic assignments. (Using the CTRL key, select only the topic assignments. Don't select the names.)
7. Select the similarly formatted topic assignment text using the shortcut menu and change the formatting by removing the italic formatting and adding bold formatting to the topic assignment text.
8. Save the document as *Interoffice Meeting Memo Revised*, and then preview, print, and close it.

Exercise 2

1. Open the *Marketing Department Memo* document located on the Data Disk.
2. Replace the text "Current date" with the actual date.
3. Select the TO: heading text (do not select the colon) and open the Reveal Formatting task pane.
4. Using the Select text box list arrow in the task pane, select all text with similar formatting and then turn off the bold formatting style.
5. Select the entire document and change the font to Arial 12 point.
6. Close the Reveal Formatting task pane.
7. Save the document as *Marketing Department Memo Revised*, and then preview, print, and close it.

Exercise 3

1. Open the *Vancouver Sales Report* document located on the Data Disk.
2. Format the title "VANCOUVER BRANCH OFFICE" with the Strong character style using the Styles and Formatting task pane.
3. Apply the Bold style and underline the column titles. (Don't forget to use the CTRL key to select all the column titles before you apply the formatting.)

4. Select all the text except the title and change the font size to 12 point.
5. Save the document as *Vancouver Sales Report Revised,* and then preview, print, and close it.

Exercise 4 C

1. Open the *Commonly Misused Words* document located on the Data Disk.
2. Apply the Bold style to the commonly misused words. (Do not include the example and definition. Don't forget to use the CTRL key to select all the text before you apply the formatting.)
3. Use the shortcut menu to select the similarly formatted definitions text and remove the italic formatting.
4. Save the document as *Commonly Misused Words Revised,* and then preview, print, and close it.

Exercise 5 C

1. Open the *Company Correspondence Memo* document located on the Data Disk.
2. Replace the text "Current date" with the actual date.
3. Change the case of "Memorandum" to all-uppercase.
4. Change the character spacing scale of "MEMORANDUM" to 200%.
5. Apply the Bold style to the text "MEMORANDUM," "TO," "FROM," "DATE," and "SUBJECT." (Do not apply bold formatting to the colons. Don't forget to use the CTRL key to select all the text before you apply the formatting.)
6. Select the text "MEMORANDUM" and change the font to Arial 14 point.
7. Using the CTRL key, select the memo headings using the CTRL key and change the font size to 12 point.
8. Save the document as *Company Correspondence Memo Revised,* and then preview, print, and close it.

Exercise 6 C

1. Open the *Market Research* document located on the Data Disk.
2. Check the spelling and grammar and make the appropriate changes.
3. Insert a superscript number 1 after the word Davidson in the first paragraph.
4. Insert two blank lines at the end of the document and key the following text (including the superscript; do not apply the italic style to the text): [1] *One of the leading market research firms in the country.*
5. Change the case of Vancouver branch in the first paragraph to all-uppercase.
6. Save the document as *Market Research Revised,* and then preview, print, and close it.

Exercise 7 C

1. Open the *Policy #152* document located on the Data Disk.
2. Select the text "Warning! Warning! Warning!" and change the case to uppercase, apply the Bold style, change the font to Arial 24 point, and add the animation effect of your choice.
3. Using the CTRL key, select the text "Only Authorized Personnel" and "May Proceed Beyond This Point," change the case to all-uppercase, and change the font to Arial 14 point bold.
4. Select the remainder of the text and change the font to Arial 12 point.
5. Single-underline only the words in the third sentence beginning "Surveillance."
6. Save the document as *Policy #152 Revised,* and then preview, print, and close it.

Exercise 8 

1. Open the *Business Information Management* document located on the Data Disk.
2. Select the entire document and change the font to Arial 12 point.
3. Select the text "BUSINESS INFORMATION MANAGEMENT", apply the Bold style, and change the font size to 18 point.
4. Apply the Bold style and underline the course number and title "BIM 160," then use the Format Painter to copy the formatting to the remaining course numbers and titles.
5. Underline the last two lines below the BIM 240 line.
6. Save the document as *Business Information Management Revised*, and then preview, print, and close it.

Case Projects

Project 1 

Kelly Armstead asks you to show her the different font effect options available in Word. Open an existing document of your choice. Experiment with the special font effects options in the Font dialog box by selecting text and applying special effects formats and animation effects. Create a new Word document listing, describing, and showing the different effects. Use character formats as appropriate. Save, preview, and print the document. With your instructor's permission, give a printed copy of the document to a classmate and, using the document as your guide, show your classmate how to use the different fonts and animation options.

Project 2

Marcy Wainwright, who works in the Purchasing Department, suggests that you could save time in applying character formatting to text by using keyboard shortcuts. You decide to research which keyboard shortcuts to use to apply character formatting. Using the Ask A Question Box, locate, review, and print a list of keyboard shortcut keys that you can use to apply character formatting. Open the document of your choice and apply different character formatting using keyboard shortcuts. Save, preview, and print the document.

Project 3

You have been assigned to key the text of a new client proposal. Because of the proposal format, you want to use special character spacing for some of the proposal titles but aren't certain what character spacing options are available. Using the Ask A Question Box and other Word Help features, research how to use the character spacing options. Create a new document containing at least two paragraphs describing how you can use these character spacing options in the client proposal. Include some sample titles with special character spacing. Use other character formats in the document as appropriate. Save, preview, and print the document.

Project 4

Albert Navarro, in Human Resources, wants to have a "brown bag" lunch seminar for his staff that includes a short presentation on troubleshooting character formatting in documents. He asked Kelly for help and she assigned the presentation to you. Using the Ask A Question Box, search online Help for tips on how to troubleshoot problems with this topic. Create a new document containing at least two paragraphs that describe possible problems and solutions for applying character formatting. Use character formats in the document as appropriate. Save, preview, and print the document. With your instructor's permission, present your troubleshooting tips to several classmates.

Project 5 

The administrative offices are moving to a new floor in the same building and B. D. Vickers asks you to create a letter announcing the move. The letter should contain the department's new address, phone number, fax number, and e-mail address. Create the letter for B. D. Vickers' signature. Set the appropriate margins, use fictitious data, and apply appropriate character formatting features discussed in this chapter to make the text attractive and easy to read. Use different text effects from the Font dialog box. Use other character formats in the document as appropriate. Save, preview, and print the letter.

Project 6  

Elizabeth left you instructions to create a list of Web sites that are marketing and selling products on the Web. Connect to the Internet, and search the Web for pages that contain information on Web-based marketing and direct sales. Print at least three Web pages. Create a new, blank document and list the title of the Web pages and their URLs. Use character formats in the document as appropriate. Save, preview, and print the document.

Project 7  

Kelly Armstead needs the mailing addresses or e-mail addresses of the senators and congressional representatives from Illinois. You know that this information is available on the Web. Connect to the Internet, and search the Web to locate the home page for the U.S. Senate and U.S. House of Representatives. Follow the links to the names and addresses of the senators and representatives. Print the appropriate pages. Create a new, blank document and key the information you found. Use character formats in the document as appropriate. Save, preview, and print the document.

Project 8 

You want to know more about how to use the Reveal Formatting task pane. Using the Ask A Question Box and other Word Help features, research how to use this task pane. Create a new document describing the Reveal Formatting task pane features and how to use them. Save, preview, and print the document.

Word 2002

Setting and Modifying Tab Stops

Chapter Overview

Some information is more clearly presented in columns and rows than in paragraph text. For example, it's easier to compare monthly expenses when the figures are arranged in columns by month and in rows by item. In this chapter, you learn to organize information attractively on the page in rows and columns, using tab stops and tab formatting marks.

Learning Objectives

- Understand tab stops
- Set left tab stops
- Set center tab stops
- Set decimal tab stops
- Set right tab stops
- Set tab stops with leaders

Case profile

The Accounting Department is overwhelmed with special projects and deadlines. Elizabeth Chang was so pleased with your work in the Marketing Department that she recommended you to Bill Wilson, the accounting manager. Bill wants you to create or modify a summary memo to include with the quarterly sales report.

notes Before beginning the activities in this chapter you should review the Formatting Tips for Business Documents appendix, if you have not already done so.

5.a Understanding Tab Stops

When you need to prepare written communication to someone inside your organization, you can create an interoffice memorandum (or memo) instead of a letter document. Interoffice memorandums generally follow the standard format shown in Figure 5-1. The memorandum should have a 2-inch top margin, 1-inch left and right margins, and the double-spaced heading text TO:, FROM:, DATE:, and SUBJECT: at the beginning of the memorandum, followed by paragraphs that are separated by a blank line. The variable TO:, FROM:, DATE:, and SUBJECT: text that follows each heading should be aligned. You do this with tab stops.

FIGURE 5-1
Standard Interoffice Memorandum

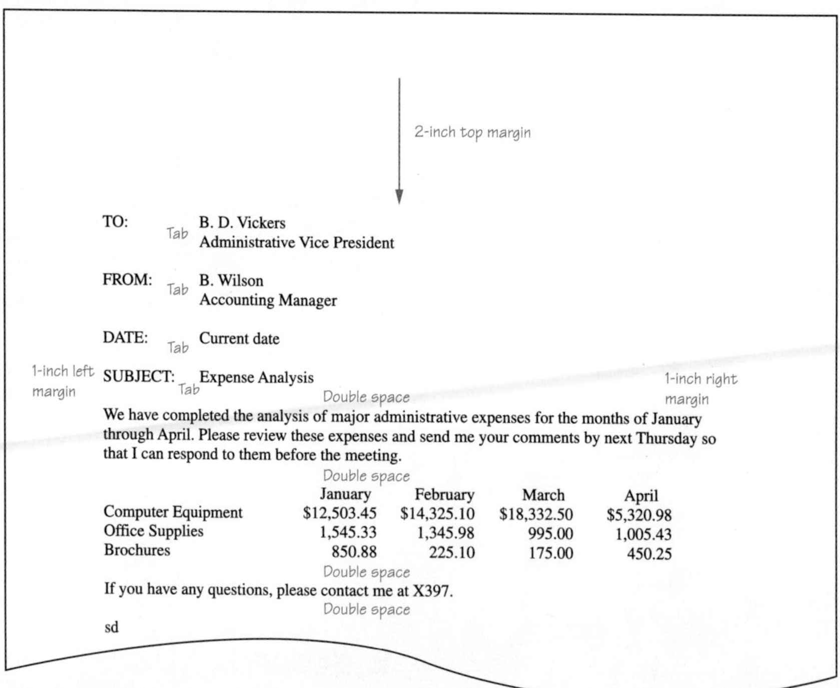

MENU TIP

When Word indents the first line after you press the TAB key, the AutoCorrect Options Smart Tag appears. You can use commands on the AutoCorrect Options drop-down menu to change the indent back to a tab formatting mark or to turn on the feature that automatically sets indents with the TAB and BACKSPACE keys.

After each heading, you insert a **tab formatting mark**, a nonprinting character you key in your document by pressing the TAB key. Each tab formatting mark you insert moves the text to the right of the tab formatting mark to the next tab stop. **Tab stops** are text alignment icons positioned on the horizontal ruler that indicate where text should align. By default, Word documents have tab stops set at every ½ inch. You can also set custom tab stops at any position between the left and right margins for one or more selected paragraphs or the entire document.

Tab stops are part of **paragraph formatting**. This means that only the selected paragraph(s) are affected when you set or modify tabs stops. You must first select the paragraphs for which you want to set custom tab stops. To select a single paragraph, simply move the insertion point into the paragraph. To select multiple paragraphs, use the selection techniques you learned in Chapter 2.

Word has five types of tab stop alignment: Left, Center, Right, Decimal, and Bar. Text is left-aligned at default tab stops and can be left-, center-, right-, or decimal-aligned at custom tab stops. Table 5-1 describes the five tab stop text alignments. For more information on Bar alignment, see online Help.

TABLE 5-1
Tab Stop Alignment Options

Tab Stop	Alignment	Icon
Left	Left-aligns text at the tab stop.	
Center	Centers text over the tab stop.	
Right	Right-aligns text at the tab stop.	
Decimal	Aligns text at the decimal character.	
Bar	Inserts a vertical line at the tab stop and aligns text to the right of the line.	

QUICK TIP

To set custom tab stops that affect all the paragraphs in a new document, set the tab stops before you begin keying the first paragraph. When you press the ENTER key to begin a new paragraph, the tab settings are included in the new paragraph.

Bill Wilson asks you to create an interoffice memo to B. D. Vickers, as shown in Figure 5-1. After you create the memo headings, you insert both the tab stops and the tab formatting marks necessary to align the variable heading text. To create the memo:

Step 1	***Create***	a new, blank document
Step 2	***Set***	a 2-inch top margin, and 1-inch left and right margins
Step 3	***Click***	the Show/Hide button on the Standard toolbar

Your screen should look similar to Figure 5-2.

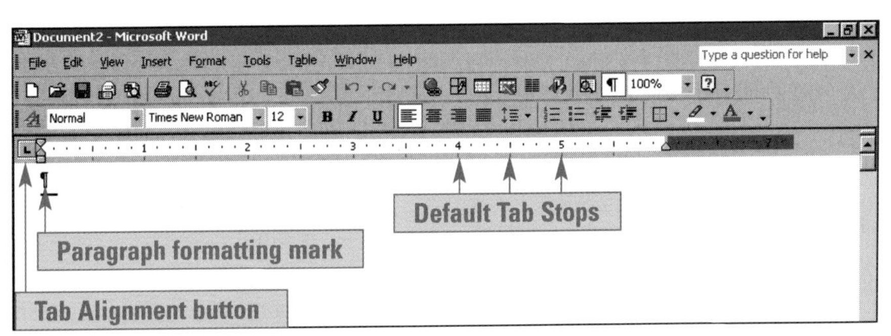

FIGURE 5-2
Formatting Marks, Default Tab Stops, Tab Alignment Button

MENU TIP

You can set custom tab stops with the Tabs command on the Format menu by specifying where each tab formatting mark is inserted on the page, which tab alignment icon is inserted on the horizontal ruler, and whether leader characters are included.

By default, Word sets tab stops every ½-inch on the horizontal ruler. As you key the heading text, you press the TAB key to insert a tab formatting mark, which moves the insertion point to the next default tab stop on the horizontal ruler. Because you displayed the nonprinting characters, you can see the tab formatting marks when you key them. To view the tab formatting marks and create the memo headings:

Step 1	***Observe***	the paragraph formatting mark at the first line
Step 2	***Observe***	the default tab stops set every ½-inch on the horizontal ruler
Step 3	***Observe***	the Tab Alignment button to the left of the horizontal ruler
Step 4	***Key***	TO:
Step 5	***Press***	the TAB key
Step 6	***Observe***	the tab formatting mark
Step 7	***Observe***	that the insertion point moves to the next default tab stop at the ½-inch position on the horizontal ruler

Your screen should look similar to Figure 5-3.

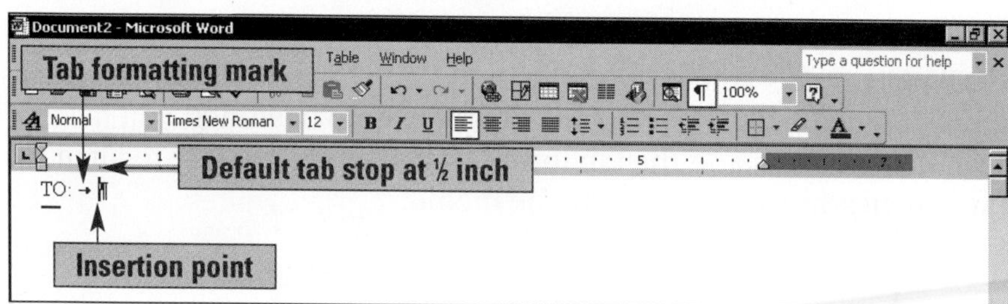

FIGURE 5-3
Insertion Point, Tab Formatting Mark, and Default Tab Stop

MOUSE TIP

You can set the left, center, right, decimal, and bar tab stops by clicking the Tab Alignment button to the left of the horizontal ruler until the appropriate tab alignment icon appears, and then clicking the appropriate position on the horizontal ruler.

Step 8	***Key***	B. D. Vickers
Step 9	***Press***	the ENTER key
Step 10	***Press***	the TAB key
Step 11	***Key***	Administrative Vice President
Step 12	***Press***	the ENTER key twice
Step 13	***Continue***	to key the remaining headings and variable heading text you see in Figure 5-1, inserting one tab formatting mark between each heading and the variable text for that heading
Step 14	***Press***	the ENTER key twice following the SUBJECT: heading and variable text
Step 15	***Save***	the document as *Expense Memorandum* and leave it open

5.b Setting Left Tab Stops

The variable heading text is not properly aligned because each line shifts to the first available default tab stop setting. To properly align the heading text, you need to add a custom left tab stop to the horizontal ruler for all the heading lines. A **left-aligned tab** stop aligns text along the left at the tab stop position. The quickest way to set custom tab stops is to use the mouse, the Tab Alignment button, and the horizontal ruler. Before you set custom tab stops, you must select the appropriate paragraph or paragraphs, then select the appropriate tab alignment icon with the Tab Alignment button, and finally, click the horizontal ruler to insert the tab stop at the appropriate position. When you click the ruler, the tab alignment icon you select from the Tab Alignment button appears on the ruler, and any default tab stops to the left of the custom tab stop disappear from the ruler. To set a custom left tab stop for all the heading lines at one time:

Step 1	*Select*	the text beginning with the "TO:" paragraph and ending with the "SUBJECT:" paragraph
Step 2	*Click*	the Tab Alignment button until the left-aligned tab stop icon appears, if necessary
Step 3	*Move*	the mouse pointer to the 1-inch position on the horizontal ruler
Step 4	*Click*	the horizontal ruler at the 1-inch position
Step 5	*Deselect*	the text, leaving the insertion point in one of the headings

CAUTION TIP

By default, the option to increase and decrease indents when the TAB key and BACKSPACE key are pressed is turned on in the Edit tab of the Options dialog box. If you move the insertion point to the beginning of a line of existing text and press the TAB key, Word moves the First Line Indent marker to the next tab stop on the horizontal ruler. If you press the TAB key *before* you key text, Word inserts a tab formatting mark.

A left-align tab stop icon appears on the horizontal ruler and the variable text in the heading lines aligns at the 1-inch position. Your screen should look similar to Figure 5-4.

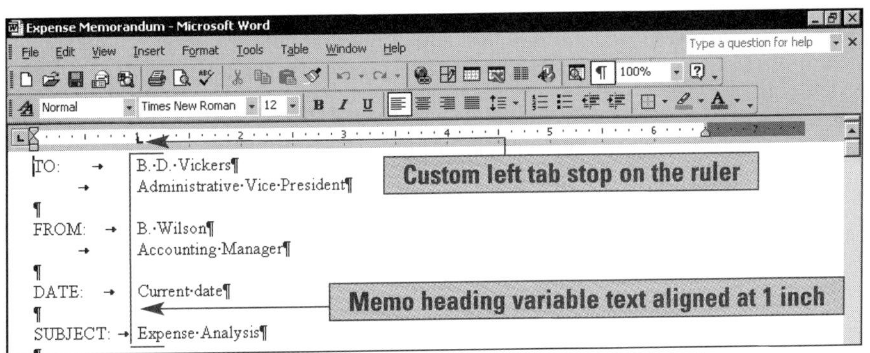

FIGURE 5-4
Custom Left Tab Stop at 1 Inch

You remove tab stops or change the location of tab stops on the horizontal ruler by selecting the appropriate paragraphs and then

QUICK TIP

When you remove custom tab stops, the tab stop settings return to the default settings.

dragging the tab stops with the mouse pointer. To move the custom left tab stop to the 1½-inch position for all the heading paragraphs:

Step 1	***Select***	the heading paragraphs
Step 2	***Position***	the mouse pointer on the left-align tab stop icon at the 1-inch position on the horizontal ruler (the ScreenTip "Left Tab" appears)
Step 3	***Drag***	the left-align tab stop icon to the 1½-inch position on the horizontal ruler

The variable text in each heading paragraph shifts to the 1½-inch position. You remove a tab stop by dragging it completely off the ruler. To remove the custom tab stop at the 1½-inch position:

Step 1	***Verify***	that the heading paragraphs are still selected
Step 2	***Drag***	the tab icon at the 1½-inch position down off the horizontal ruler
Step 3	***Observe***	that the tab stops on the horizontal ruler indicate the ½-inch default settings and the variable heading text is no longer properly aligned

You set custom tab stops for individual paragraphs just as you do multiple paragraphs. To set a left tab stop for the first heading paragraph only:

Step 1	***Click***	in the heading paragraph beginning "TO:" to position the insertion point (this selects the paragraph)
Step 2	***Verify***	the Tab Alignment button is set for a left tab stop
Step 3	***Click***	the 1-inch position on the horizontal ruler
Step 4	***Observe***	that the first line of the first paragraph *only* moves right and aligns at the new custom tab stop position
Step 5	***Set***	a 1-inch left-aligned custom tab stop for the remaining heading paragraphs
Step 6	***Deselect***	the text
Step 7	***Save***	the document

You now key the paragraph text in the body of the memo and then organize the expense analysis data in columns using tab formatting characters and tab stops on the horizontal ruler.

5.c Setting Center Tab Stops

Center-aligned tab stops center text over the tab stop, which is appropriate for creating column headings. Figure 5-1 includes text in five columns separated by tab formatting marks. The last four columns include column headers. You key the first body paragraph and the column headings. To key the first body paragraph:

Step 1	*Key*	the first body paragraph from Figure 5-1 on the second line following the SUBJECT: heading line
Step 2	*Press*	the ENTER key twice

Next you set custom center-aligned tab stops for the expense analysis column headings and key the headings.

Step 3	*Click*	the Tab Alignment button until the center-aligned tab icon appears
Step 4	*Click*	the 2.5-, 3.5-, 4.5-, and 5.5-inch positions on the horizontal ruler to insert the center-aligned tab icons
Step 5	*Press*	the TAB key
Step 6	*Key*	January
Step 7	*Press*	the TAB key
Step 8	*Key*	February
Step 9	*Press*	the TAB key
Step 10	*Key*	March
Step 11	*Press*	the TAB key
Step 12	*Key*	April
Step 13	*Press*	the ENTER key

When you press the ENTER key to create a new paragraph, Word remembers the previous paragraph tab stop settings. Because you use different tab stop settings for the text you key in the columns, you should remove the center-aligned tab icons from the ruler for this paragraph. To remove the center-aligned tab icons:

Step 1	*Drag*	each tab stop for the current paragraph off the ruler
Step 2	*Save*	the document and leave it open

C

5.d Setting Decimal Tab Stops

You want the expense data to align on the decimal point in each column when you key the data in the columns. This makes reading columns of numbers easier. A **decimal tab** stop aligns numbers at the decimal point. If a number does not contain a decimal point, it is aligned at the rightmost position. Decimal tabs do not affect text. To set decimal tab stops and enter the expense data text in columns:

QUICK TIP

You can view numbers instead of ruler marks on the horizontal ruler by pressing and holding the ALT key as you click the horizontal ruler to position a tab icon.

MOUSE TIP

You can press and hold both the left and right mouse buttons while clicking the horizontal ruler to view numbers instead of ruler marks.

Step 1	*Click*	the Tab Alignment button until the decimal-aligned tab icon  appears
Step 2	*Press & hold*	the ALT key while you click the horizontal ruler at the 2.61-, 3.61-, 4.61-, and 5.61-inch positions to insert the decimal-aligned tab stops
Step 3	*Key*	Computer Equipment
Step 4	*Press*	the TAB key
Step 5	*Key*	$12,503.45
Step 6	*Press*	the TAB key
Step 7	*Key*	$14,325.10
Step 8	*Press*	the TAB key
Step 9	*Key*	$18,332.50
Step 10	*Press*	the TAB key
Step 11	*Key*	$5,320.98
Step 12	*Press*	the ENTER key

When you press the ENTER key, the next paragraph retains the tab stop settings from the previous paragraph. These tab stops are appropriate for the remaining rows of data. To create the remaining lines:

Step 1	*Key*	Office Supplies
Step 2	*Press*	the TAB key
Step 3	*Observe*	that the insertion point moves to the tab stop position and aligns on the decimal point of the number above it
Step 4	*Continue*	to add the remaining two lines of tabbed text and the rest of the memo, as shown in Figure 5-1
Step 5	*Save*	the document and close it

Bill asks you to update the Accounting Department telephone extension list and add the revision date at the right margin below the phone numbers. You can use a right-aligned tab stop to add the date.

5.e Setting Right Tab Stops

C

A **right-aligned tab** stop is appropriate for text that should be aligned at the right of the tab stop, such as a date at the right margin of a document. To position the date at the right margin, set a right-aligned tab stop, press the TAB key, and then key or insert the date. To set a right tab stop and right-align the date on the first line:

Step 1	*Open*	the *Telephone List* document located on the Data Disk
Step 2	*Move*	the insertion point to the bottom of the document and add two new blank lines
Step 3	*Click*	the Tab Alignment button to the left of the horizontal ruler until the right-aligned tab icon  appears
Step 4	*Click*	the 5½-inch position on the horizontal ruler to insert the right-aligned tab icon
Step 5	*Drag*	the right-aligned tab icon to the 6-inch position (the right margin)

Your screen should look similar to Figure 5-5.

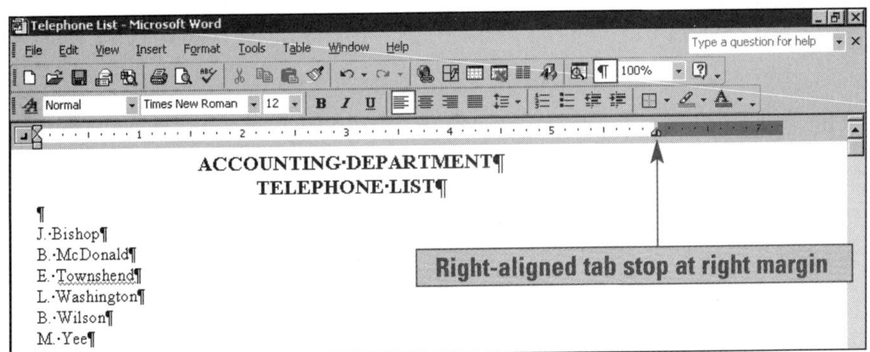

FIGURE 5-5
Right-Aligned Tab Stop

Step 6	*Press*	the TAB key
Step 7	*Key*	today's date
Step 8	*Observe*	that as you key the date the text flows left from the tab stop position
Step 9	*Save*	the document as *Telephone List Revised* and leave it open

Bill asks you to position each employee's name at the left margin and telephone number at the right margin in the telephone list document. He also wants you to insert a dotted or dashed line between the employee's name at the left margin and their extension at the right margin to help guide the reader's eye across the page. You can use right-aligned tab stops with tab leaders to do this.

5.f Setting Tab Stops with Leaders

Documents that have a large amount of white space between columns of text, such as a table of contents or a phone list, can be difficult for a reader's eye to follow across the page from column to column. **Tab leaders** are dashed or dotted lines you can add to a tab stop to provide a visual guide for readers as they follow the text from column to column. You add a leader character to a tab stop in the Tabs dialog box. Before you open the Tabs dialog box to set tab stops and add leaders, you must remember to select the appropriate paragraphs to be formatted. To set a right-aligned tab stop at the 6-inch position and add the second leader style:

Step 1	***Select***	the lines of text beginning with "J. Bishop" and ending with "M. Yee"
Step 2	***Click***	Format
Step 3	***Click***	Tabs

The Tabs dialog box on your screen should look similar to Figure 5-6.

FIGURE 5-6
Tabs Dialog Box

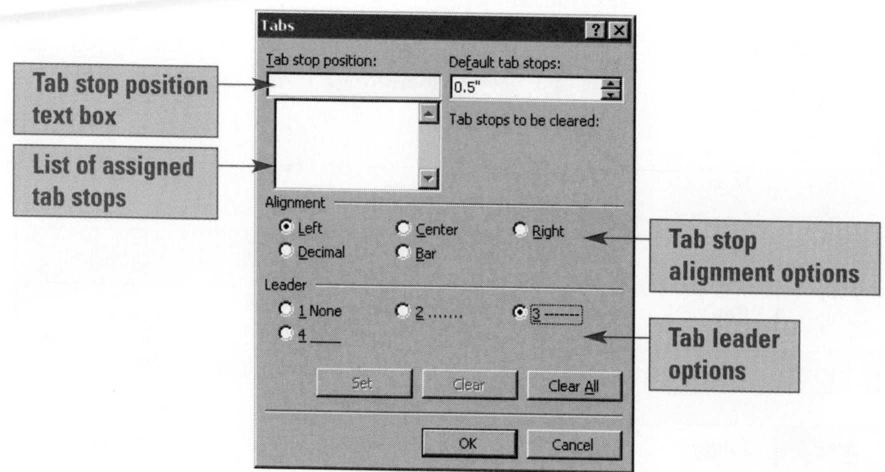

You can use the dialog box Help button to review the options in the dialog box. You set tab stops in the dialog box by keying the tab stop position and selecting an alignment option. Then, you can select a leader style.

Step 4	*Key*	6 in the Tab stop position: text box
Step 5	*Click*	the Right option button
Step 6	*Click*	the 2 .... leader option button
Step 7	*Click*	OK

With the tab stops and leader set, you can enter the tab formatting marks and telephone extensions for each item. To key the telephone extensions list:

Step 1	*Move*	the insertion point to the end of the J. Bishop text
Step 2	*Press*	the TAB key
Step 3	*Observe*	the leader characters that appear from the J. Bishop text to the tab stop
Step 4	*Key*	X388
Step 5	*Press*	the DOWN ARROW key to move the insertion point to the end of the B. McDonald text
Step 6	*Continue*	to key the telephone extensions to the document, pressing the TAB key between the name and extension B. McDonald, X391 E. Townshend, X402 L. Washington, X455 B. Wilson, X397 M. Yee, X405
Step 7	*Hide*	the nonprinting formatting marks
Step 8	*Save*	the document and close it

No matter what type of document you create, tab stops enable you to precisely align text in columns.

MOUSE TIP

You can use the Click and Type feature in Print Layout view or in Web Layout view to set a left tab stop anywhere in the document. Move the I-beam to the desired location. When you see the left-alignment icon next to the I-beam, double-click the document to insert a left tab stop at that position. When using the Click and Type feature to set multiple tab stops on the same text line, you can set center- and right-aligned tab stops as well.

Summary

- You can reposition and organize text in columns by setting tab stops on the horizontal ruler and inserting tab formatting marks in the text.
- Tab formatting marks are nonprinting characters you key in your document by pressing the TAB key.
- Tab stops are text-alignment icons positioned on the horizontal ruler that indicate where text should align.
- Left-aligned tab stops position text at the tab stop and then flow the text to the right.
- Right-aligned tab stops position text at the tab stop and then flow the text to the left.
- Center-aligned tab stops are appropriate for column headings; they position text at the tab stop and then flow the text left and right as necessary to center it at the tab stop.
- Decimal-aligned tab stops are appropriate for columns of numbers containing decimal points; they align the numbers on their decimal points.
- To assist the reader's eye in following text from column to column, you can add leader characters to a tab stop.

Commands Review

Action	Menu Bar	Shortcut Menu	Toolbar	Task Pane	Keyboard
Set custom tab stops	Format, Tabs		Click the Tab Alignment button to select an alignment icon, then click the horizontal ruler at the appropriate position		ALT + O, T

Concepts Review

Circle the correct answer.

1. Which of the following is not a tab stop alignment?
[a] Left
[b] Right
[c] Justify
[d] Decimal

2. To align text along the right margin by setting a tab stop on the horizontal ruler, select the:
[a] Left alignment icon.
[b] Justify alignment icon.
[c] Right alignment icon.
[d] Center alignment icon.

3. You can insert a tab formatting mark by pressing the:
[a] ENTER key.
[b] TAB key.
[c] HOME key.
[d] END key.

4. To quickly set custom tab stops that affect one paragraph, first:
[a] select the entire document.
[b] select multiple paragraphs.
[c] move the insertion point to the paragraph.
[d] click the horizontal ruler then select the paragraph.

5. The default tab stops are positioned every:
[a] ½ inch.
[b] 1 inch.
[c] ¾ inch.
[d] ¼ inch.

6. To assist the reader's eye in following text from column to column, you can add:
[a] length to the line.
[b] less space between the characters.
[c] leader characters.
[d] lending characters.

7. To view the tab formatting marks in a document, click the:
[a] Show Tabs button.
[b] Show/Hide button.
[c] Format Marks button.
[d] Tab Alignment button.

8. You can manually enter the tab stop position, change the default tab stop settings, and add leaders to tab stops with the:
[a] Format, Paragraph commands.
[b] Insert, Tabs commands.
[c] Tools, Options commands.
[d] Format, Tabs commands.

Circle **T** if the statement is true or **F** if the statement is false.

T F 1. The default setting for tab stops is every ⅓ inch.
T F 2. You can set tab stops with the mouse and the horizontal ruler.
T F 3. The Tab Alignment button has four alignment settings.
T F 4. Use a center-aligned tab stop to position text at the right margin.
T F 5. Use a left-aligned tab stop to start a new paragraph.
T F 6. When you create text column headings, you can use the decimal-aligned tab stop to center the headings over the column.
T F 7. You cannot remove tab stops with the mouse pointer.
T F 8. Tab leader characters can be added by clicking the Tab Alignment button.

Skills Review

Exercise 1 

1. Create a new, blank document and key the text in columns below, inserting a tab formatting mark between the text in each column.

	2001	*2002*	*2003*
Division 1	*$200,000*	*$90,000*	*$180,000*
Division 2	*212,000*	*205,000*	*79,000*
Division 3	*140,000*	*400,000*	*120,000*
Division 4	*304,000*	*107,000*	*105,000*
Division 5	*201,000*	*148,000*	*195,000*

2. Use right-aligned tab stops to align the numbers.
3. Use center-aligned tab stops to align the column headings.
4. Save the document as *Division Data*, and then preview, print, and close it.

Exercise 2 

1. Open the *Media Memo* document located on the Data Disk.
2. Replace the text "Current date" with the actual date.
3. Set the appropriate margins for an interoffice memorandum.
4. Insert tab formatting marks in the heading paragraphs so you can align the variable heading text.
5. Set a left-aligned tab stop at 1 inch on the horizontal ruler for all the heading paragraphs to align the variable heading text.
6. Insert a new line below R. F. Jones and then insert a tab formatting mark and key "Media Buyer" as the title.
7. Insert a new line below B. Wilson and then insert a tab formatting mark and key "Accounting Manager" as the title.
8. Check the spelling of the document.
9. Save the document as *Media Memo Revised*, and then preview, print, and close it.

Exercise 3 C

1. Create a new, blank document and key the text in columns below, inserting a tab formatting mark between the text in each column.

Branch	*Cheese*	*Meat*	*Produce*
Chicago	*$55,900*	*$125,000*	*$77,000*
Vancouver	*33,000*	*7,890*	*15,000*
London	*22,500*	*12,500*	*18,000*
Melbourne	*34,333*	*40,100*	*48,550*

2. Use right-aligned tab stops to align the numbers.
3. Use center-aligned tab stops to align the column headings.
4. Save the document as *Branch Sales*, and then preview, print, and close it.

Exercise 4 C

1. Open the *Vendor Phone List* document located on the Data Disk.
2. Select the four lines of text and set a right-aligned tab stop with the leader of your choice at the 6-inch position on the horizontal ruler.
3. Insert a new line at the top of the document and remove the right-aligned tab stop from the horizontal ruler.
4. Insert a tab formatting mark, key "Vendor" as the column title, insert a tab formatting mark, and key "Phone List" as the column title.
5. Set two center-aligned tab stops on the horizontal ruler to center the column titles attractively over their respective columns.
6. Use the CTRL key to select both column headings and underline them.
7. Save the document as *Vendor Phone List Revised*, and then preview, print, and close it.

Exercise 5 C

1. Create a new, blank document and key the text in columns below, inserting a tab formatting mark between the text in each column.

Sales District	*Telephone*	*Supplies*	*Misc.*
A	*$1,450.25*	*$744.33*	*$225.45*
B	*1,645.33*	*525.88*	*214.55*
C	*985.22*	*275.90*	*243.89*
D	*1,112.98*	*210.66*	*423.67*
E	*1,967.34*	*678.23*	*313.56*

2. Use decimal-aligned tab stops to align the telephone, supplies, and miscellaneous expense numbers.
3. Use center-aligned tab stops to align the column headings and the sales district numbers.
4. Use the CTRL key to select the column headings and bold them.
5. Save the document as *Sales District Expenses*, and then preview, print, and close it.

Exercise 6 C

1. Create a new, blank document and key the following text in columns, inserting a tab formatting mark between the text in each column.

Item	*Budget*	*Actual*	*Variance*
Executive Secretaries	*$1,234,000*	*$1,145,000*	*$(89,000)*
Administrative Assistants	*289,500*	*364,800*	*75,300*
Equipment	*850,000*	*730,000*	*(120,000)*
Telecommunications	*365,000*	*340,500*	*(24,500)*
Miscellaneous	*65,000*	*50,000*	*(15,000)*

2. Use the appropriate tab stops to center the column headings and align the budgeted, actual, and difference numbers.
3. Use the CTRL key to select the column headings and italicize them.
4. Save the document as *Budget Variance*, and then preview, print, and close it.

Exercise 7 

1. Open the *Regional Expenses Memo* document located on the Data Disk.
2. Replace the text "Current date" with the actual date.
3. Select the heading paragraphs and then set a left-aligned tab stop at 1½ inches on the horizontal ruler.
4. Move the left-aligned tab stop to 1 inch.
5. Insert the following columnar text separated by tab stops below the first body paragraph of the memo. Use center-aligned tab stops for the column titles. Use decimal-aligned tab stops for the direct sales, employee, and all other numbers. Remember to add a single blank line before and after the columnar text. Apply bold formatting to all the column titles.

Region	***Direct Sales***	***Employee***	***All Other***
Central	*$42,000.50*	*$2,210.00*	*$12,825.98*
Eastern	*32,545.78*	*3,412.44*	*7,890.66*
Midwest	*53,897.75*	*3,508.34*	*8,454.88*
Mountain	*49,154.33*	*6,974.76*	*5,221.44*
Southern	*34,675.21*	*11,242.88*	*15,111.75*
Western	*40,876.21*	*8,417.77*	*10,445.29*

6. Save the document as *Regional Expenses Memo Revised*, and then preview, print, and close it.

Exercise 8 C

1. Create the following interoffice memorandum.

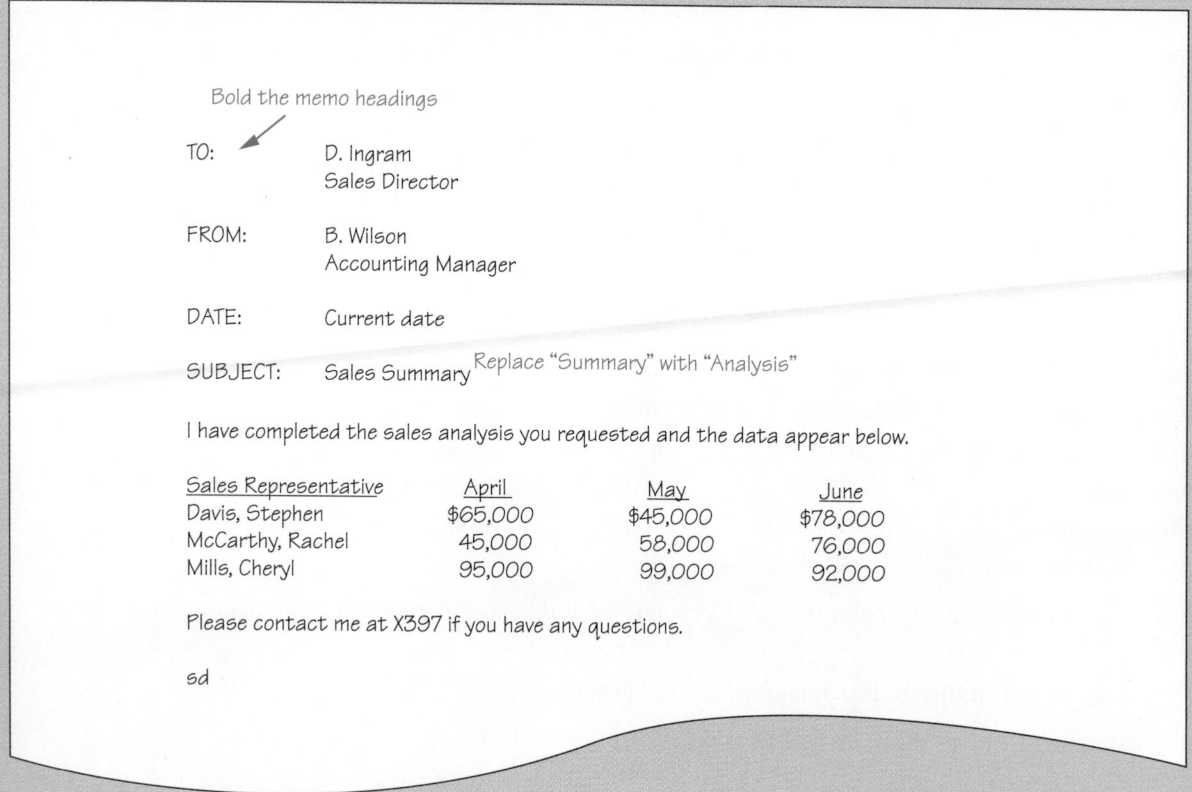

Bold the memo headings

TO: D. Ingram
Sales Director

FROM: B. Wilson
Accounting Manager

DATE: Current date

SUBJECT: Sales Summary Replace "Summary" with "Analysis"

I have completed the sales analysis you requested and the data appear below.

Sales Representative	April	May	June
Davis, Stephen	$65,000	$45,000	$78,000
McCarthy, Rachel	45,000	58,000	76,000
Mills, Cheryl	95,000	99,000	92,000

Please contact me at X397 if you have any questions.

sd

2. Key the current date in the memorandum using AutoComplete.
3. Set appropriate margins for an interoffice memorandum.
4. Set the appropriate tab stops for the memo headings and the text in columns.
5. Apply bold formatting to the TO:, FROM:, DATE:, and SUBJECT: headings.
6. Save the document as *Ingram Memo,* and then preview, print, and close it.

Case Projects

Project 1

Bill Wilson asks you to prepare an interoffice memorandum from him to all regional sales managers advising them of the semiannual sales meeting to be held in two weeks in the main conference room at corporate headquarters in Chicago. Everyone attending the meeting must contact you to arrange hotel accommodations, rental cars, and airline tickets. Use character and tab formatting features to make the memo interesting to read and professional in appearance. Save, preview, and print the document.

Project 2

You are preparing a sales analysis for Bill Wilson to take to the semiannual sales conference and you would like to change the default tab stop position from every ½ inch to every ¼ inch. Using the Ask A Question Box and the keyword "tabs" search for help topics on changing the default tab stop position in a document. Create an interoffice memorandum to Bill Wilson from yourself with the subject line "Default Tabs." Add at least two body paragraphs describing how to change the default tab settings. Save, preview, and print the document.

Project 3

Benji Hori, one of the accounting assistants, asks you if there is a way to vary the alignment of text in a single line. He needs to create a document with the document title, date, and page number all on the same line. He wants the document title left-aligned, the date center-aligned, and the page number right-aligned. If necessary, look up the "Troubleshoot paragraph formatting" topic in online Help using the Ask A Question Box and review how to align text differently on the same line. Create a sample document with the title "Quarterly Sales Report" left aligned, the current date center-aligned, and the text "Page Number" right-aligned. Save, preview, and print the document. With your instructor's permission, show a classmate how to align text differently on the same line.

Project 4

Before you begin keying a new accounting report for Bill Wilson, you want to practice setting and removing tab stops in a document. Open an existing document that contains tab stops and tab formatting marks. Remove all the tab stops for the entire document at one time. Explore using left-, center-, right-, and decimal-aligned tab stops to make the document easier to read. Save the document with a new name, and then preview and print it.

Project 5

Bill Wilson is planning an auto trip to Houston, Texas, and he asks you to use the Web to look up the mileage and print driving instructions and a city-to-city trip map from Chicago to Houston. Using the Internet, locate Web pages that help you plan auto trips by calculating the mileage and creating driving instructions and maps from city to city. Save and print the driving instructions and trip map. Create an interoffice memorandum to Bill outlining the mileage and driving instructions. Save, preview, and print the memorandum.

Project 6 

Katrina Levy, one of the accounting assistants, asks you for help. She has an old document with tab stops set differently for each paragraph. She wants to remove all the tab stops for the entire document at one time, but isn't certain how to do this. Open the Tabs dialog box and use the dialog box Help button to get more information about the Clear and Clear All buttons. Using the Ask A Question Box and the keywords "clear tabs," search online Help for information on clearing all the tab stops in a document. Create an interoffice memorandum to Katrina describing how to clear all the tab stops in the document at one time. Save, preview, and print the memo.

Project 7  

Kelly Armstead called to ask you how to find someone's e-mail address using the Web. Connect to the Internet, and search for Web pages that allow you to search for e-mail addresses. Print at least three pages. Create an interoffice memorandum to Kelly listing the Web pages you can use to search for e-mail addresses. Save, preview, and print the memo.

Project 8 

Bill Wilson is attending a meeting with the branch vice presidents to discuss the quarterly sales figures. He wants you to create a document he can hand out at the meeting. Using fictitious data for the Chicago, London, Melbourne, and Vancouver branches, create a document with two columns for branch names and total sales data for each branch. Use tab stops with leaders to organize the data attractively on the page. Save, preview, and print the document.

Formatting Paragraphs

Chapter Overview

Poorly arranged and formatted text can distract readers from the information in a document. When text is attractively spaced and positioned on the page, readers can concentrate on the document content. In this chapter, you use bullets and numbering, borders and shading, line spacing, alignment and indentation, and page breaks to format and position paragraph text. In addition, you use two other features to position paragraphs in a document: headers and footers, and outlining.

Case profile

After completing your assignment in the Accounting Department, you are asked to return to the Purchasing Department to help Kelly Armstead create and format the department's correspondence and reports. You begin by formatting the new audit report from the Melbourne branch office.

Learning Objectives

- Add bullets, numbering, borders, and shading
- Set line and paragraph spacing
- Align and indent paragraphs
- Insert page breaks
- Create and modify headers and footers
- Apply paragraph styles
- Create outlines

notes

For this chapter, the Define styles based on your formatting feature is turned off in the AutoFormat As You Type tab in the AutoCorrect dialog box.

Before beginning the activities in this chapter you should review the Formatting Tips for Business Documents appendix, if you have not already done so.

MENU TIP

You can automatically add numbers or bullets to selected text with options in the Bullets and Numbering dialog box, which you open by clicking the Bullets and Numbering command on the Format menu or a shortcut menu.

6.a Adding Bullets, Numbering, Borders, and Shading

There are several ways to format text paragraphs to make them stand out in a document. You can precede lists of text paragraphs with special symbols called bullets, or with numbers. You also can add a border to a paragraph and add shading to a paragraph. All of these formats add interest and emphasis to paragraphs.

Adding Bullets and Numbering

The *Melbourne Audit Report* document contains two groups of short paragraphs to which Kelly wants you to add bullets and numbers. To begin, you open the document and set the appropriate margins for an unbound report. To open the document, set the margins, and add bullets to the first groups of paragraphs:

MOUSE TIP

You can double-click a bullet symbol or number in a list to open the Bullets and Numbering dialog box.

Step 1	***Open***	the *Melbourne Audit Report* document located on the Data Disk
Step 2	***Set***	2-inch top and 1-inch left and right margins consistent with an unbound report document
Step 3	***Click***	the Show/Hide button on the Formatting toolbar
Step 4	***Select***	the three paragraphs beginning with "Insufficient quality control" and ending with "Poor communication"
Step 5	***Click***	the Bullets button on the Formatting toolbar
Step 6	***Deselect***	the text
Step 7	***Observe***	that the paragraphs are moved to the right, are preceded by bullet symbols, and include a tab formatting mark that moves the paragraph text ¼ inch from the bullet

Numbered lists are used to organize items sequentially. You want to create a numbered list from the second group of paragraphs. To create a numbered list:

Step 1	***Select***	the three paragraphs beginning with "Appropriate goals…" and ending with "Employees are not…"
Step 2	***Click***	the Numbering button on the Formatting toolbar
Step 3	***Deselect***	the paragraphs
Step 4	***Observe***	that the paragraphs are moved to the right, are preceded by numbers, and include a tab formatting mark that moves the paragraph text ¼ inch from the number

Your screen should look similar to Figure 6-1.

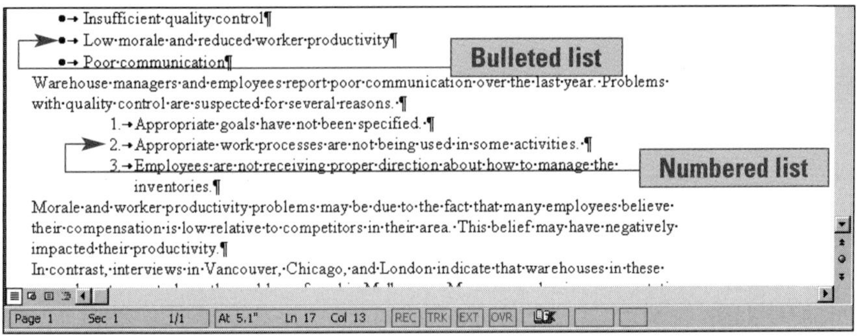

FIGURE 6-1
Bulleted and Numbered Paragraphs

Step 5	***Save***	the document as *Melbourne Audit Report Revised* and leave it open

Another way to add emphasis is with borders and shading.

Adding Borders and Shading

Kelly reviews the *Melbourne Audit Report Revised* and decides that you should add a title to the report. She suggests you emphasize the title by adding a border and shading to it. To add the report title:

Step 1	***Move***	the insertion point to the top of the document
Step 2	***Press***	the ENTER key twice to add two blank lines at the top of the document
Step 3	***Move***	the insertion point to the first blank line
Step 4	***Key***	Melbourne Audit Report and format it with the 14-point font size

MENU TIP

To change the bullet or numbering style, you can click the Bullets and Numbering command on the Format menu, click the appropriate tab, and select a different bullet or numbering style.

MOUSE TIP

You can apply border formatting to selected paragraphs with the Border button on the Formatting toolbar.

MOUSE TIP

You can remove the bullets or numbers from a list by selecting the list and clicking the Bullets or Numbering button on the Formatting toolbar.

You can quickly change a numbered list to a bulleted list and vice versa by selecting the bulleted or numbered paragraphs and then clicking the Bullets or Numbering button on the Formatting toolbar.

To add a border around the report title text:

Step 1	***Select***	the "Melbourne Audit Report" title text but do not select the paragraph mark
Step 2	***Click***	Format
Step 3	***Click***	Borders and Shading
Step 4	***Click***	the Borders tab, if necessary

The Borders and Shading dialog box on your screen should look similar to Figure 6-2.

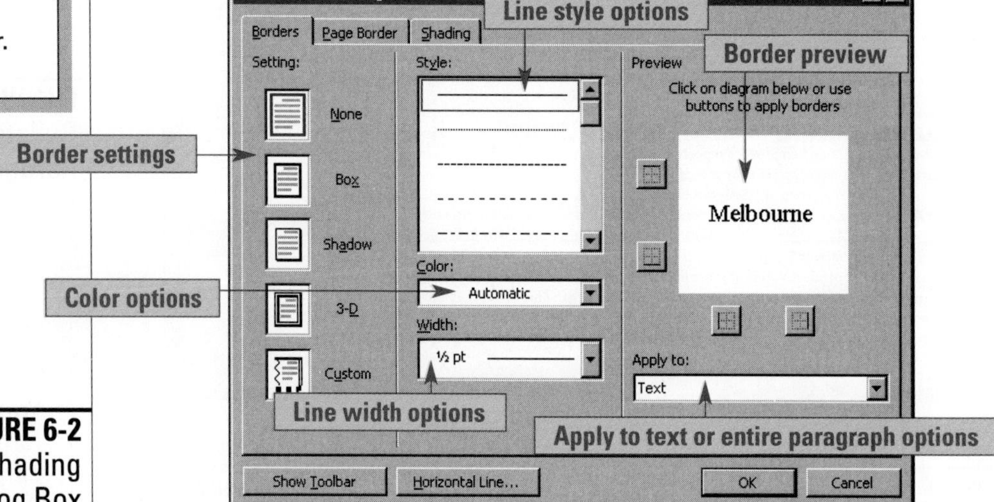

FIGURE 6-2
Borders and Shading Dialog Box

QUICK TIP

You can move an entire bulleted or numbered list to the left or right. Place the mouse pointer on a bullet symbol or a number and then click to select all the bullet symbols or numbers in the list (the text will not be selected). Place the mouse pointer on a selected bullet or number and drag the entire list to the left or right.

You can quickly apply or remove a border to either selected text or to an entire paragraph—from margin to margin—by clicking an option in the Setting: list and then clicking the Text or Paragraph option in the Apply to: list. You also can set the border style, color, and width before you apply the border formatting. Because you selected only the text (not including the paragraph mark) in the title paragraph, you apply a 1½ point box border to the selected text. To apply the border:

Step 1	***Click***	the Box setting
Step 2	***Click***	the Width: list arrow
Step 3	***Click***	1 ½ pt
Step 4	***Verify***	that Text appears in the Apply to: list
Step 5	***Observe***	the border in the Preview area

You can also apply shading in this dialog box. Because the document will be printed on a black-and-white printer, you can apply gray shading to the title for additional emphasis. To apply light gray shading to the report title:

Step 1	*Click*	the Shading tab
Step 2	*Click*	the Gray-12.5% square on the Fill color grid (the fourth square in the first row)
Step 3	*Verify*	that Text appears in the Apply to: list
Step 4	*Observe*	that the text in the Preview area has a border and shading
Step 5	*Click*	OK
Step 6	*Deselect*	the text
Step 7	*Save*	the document and leave it open

CAUTION TIP

If you select an entire paragraph including the paragraph mark or if you move the insertion point to a single paragraph, Word selects the entire paragraph for formatting. If you then open the Borders and Shading dialog box, the default option is to apply the borders and shading to the entire paragraph—from margin to margin.

To make the document easier to read, you can add more white space between the lines of text by adjusting the line and paragraph spacing.

6.b Setting Line and Paragraph Spacing

Line spacing indicates the vertical space between lines of text. The default setting for line spacing in Word is single spacing. The paragraph text in letters and memorandums is usually single-spaced. Double spacing is most often used for long reports so that they are easier to read. Also, the line spacing in documents in progress is often greater than single spacing, so reviewers can use the extra white space to write their comments and proofing notations. **Paragraph spacing** refers to the additional points of white space above and below a paragraph.

After reviewing your progress on the *Melbourne Audit Report Revised* document, Kelly suggests that spacing the report text 1.5 times single spacing and adding 6 points of additional white space after each paragraph would enable her supervisor and other reviewers to read it more easily. To space the report:

MENU TIP

You can change the line or paragraph spacing for selected paragraphs by clicking the Paragraph command on the Format menu or a shortcut menu and then setting line or paragraph spacing options on the Indents and Spacing tab of the Paragraph dialog box.

Step 1	*Select*	all the body text below the title document
Step 2	*Click*	the Line Spacing button list arrow on the Formatting toolbar

Your screen should look similar to Figure 6-3.

FIGURE 6-3
Line Spacing Options

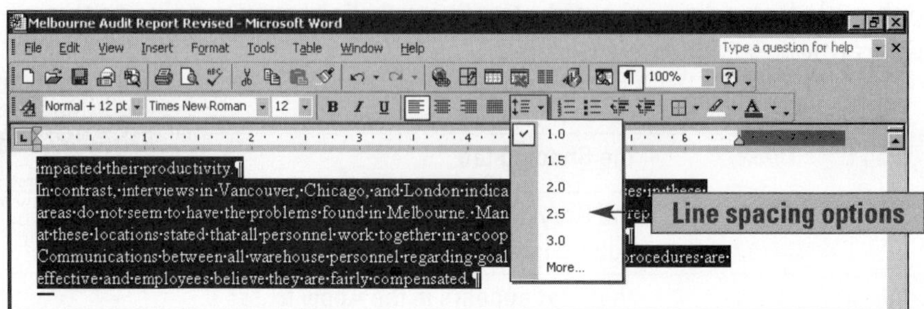

> **QUICK TIP**
>
> Line spacing is included in paragraph formatting, which means that whenever you change the line spacing, the new line spacing affects only the selected paragraphs. To change the spacing for a single paragraph, simply move the insertion point to that paragraph. To change the spacing for several paragraphs, you must first select the paragraphs. To set line spacing that affects all the paragraphs in a new document, set the line spacing before you begin keying the first paragraph.

Step 3	*Click*	1.5
Step 4	*Observe*	the new line spacing but do not deselect the text
Step 5	*Right-click*	the selected text
Step 6	*Click*	Paragraph
Step 7	*Click*	the Indents and Spacing tab, if necessary

The Paragraph dialog box on your screen should look similar to Figure 6-4. You can set horizontal alignment, line spacing, and paragraph spacing in this dialog box. Line spacing options available in the Paragraph dialog box include: At Least, which sets a minimum line spacing that adjusts for larger font sizes and graphics; Exactly, which sets a fixed line spacing that will not adjust; and Multiple, which sets the line spacing as a percentage of the single line space.

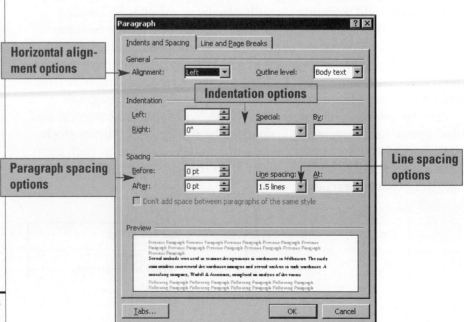

> **TASK PANE TIP**
>
> You can review and change both character and paragraph formatting in the Reveal Formatting task pane.

FIGURE 6-4
Paragraph Dialog Box

Step 8	*Key*	6 in the After: list box in the Spacing group
Step 9	*Click*	OK
Step 10	*Move*	the insertion point to the top of the document
Step 11	*Observe*	the additional white space between paragraphs
Step 12	*Save*	the document and leave it open

Next, you add to the text's readability by aligning and indenting paragraphs.

CAUTION TIP

You may need to zoom documents with narrow left and right margins to Page Width to see all the text at the right margin. For the remainder of this book it is assumed you have zoomed the document to Page Width, if necessary.

6.c Aligning and Indenting Paragraphs

Vertical alignment affects how the text is placed on the page in relation to the top and bottom margins. **Horizontal alignment** affects how the text is placed on the page in relation to the left and right margins. Sometimes it is useful to move text away from the left margin to set it off from the text that follows it. This is called **indenting** text. You can indent the first line, all the lines, or all lines *except* the first line of a paragraph.

Kelly and her supervisor have reviewed the *Melbourne Audit Report Revised* and they have a few final suggestions for making the report more attractive and easier to read. First, Kelly wants you to create a sample cover page document for the report. Next, she wants you to modify the report by centering the title paragraph between the left and right margins and then indenting the first line of each paragraph, indenting one of the paragraphs from both the left and right margins, and repositioning the bulleted and numbered lists at the left margin.

Aligning Paragraphs Vertically and Horizontally

Reports sometimes have a single cover page that provides the reader the name and date of the report and other important information. You can create a cover page as a separate document or you can create it as the first page of the report document. Because Kelly is undecided about using a cover page, she asks you to create a sample page as a separate document containing the report name and today's date centered vertically and horizontally on the page. You align text vertically on the page by changing the alignment options in the Layout tab of the Page Setup dialog box.

To create a cover page document with vertically aligned text:

Step 1	*Create*	a new, blank document

Step 2	***Set***	1-inch top, left, and right margins
Step 3	***Key***	Melbourne Audit Report
Step 4	***Press***	the ENTER key three times
Step 5	***Insert***	today's date
Step 6	***Format***	the text with the bold, 20-point font size
Step 7	***Click***	File
Step 8	***Click***	Page Setup
Step 9	***Click***	the Layout tab
Step 10	***Click***	the Vertical alignment: list arrow

The Page Setup dialog box on your screen should look similar to Figure 6-5.

FIGURE 6-5
Layout Tab in the Page Setup Dialog Box

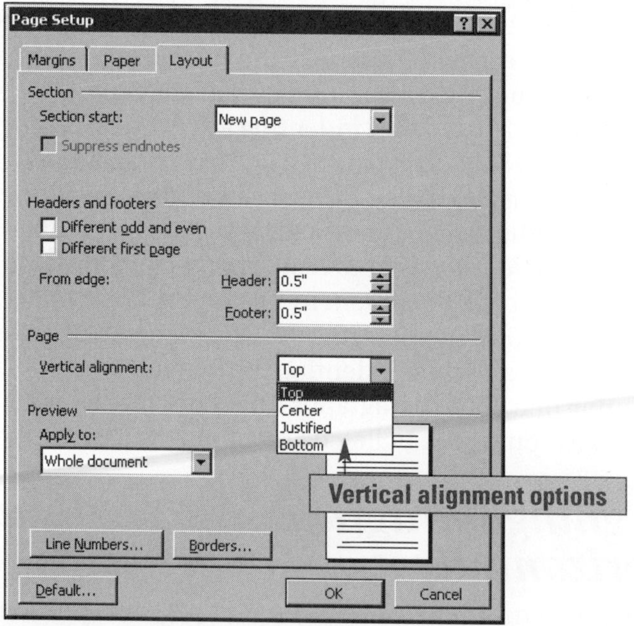

The **Top** vertical alignment option aligns text with the top margin. The **Center** vertical alignment option allows you to center the text between the top and bottom margins. This option is good for creating report title pages. The **Bottom** vertical alignment option aligns the text at the bottom margin, leaving the extra white space at the top of the page. The **Justified** vertical alignment option distributes full-page text evenly between the top and bottom margins by adding additional line spacing.

Step 11	***Click***	Center

Step 12	***Click***	OK
Step 13	***Switch to***	Print Layout view, if necessary
Step 14	***Zoom***	to Whole Page
Step 15	***Observe***	that the text is centered between the top and bottom margins

The four horizontal text alignment options are Left, Center, Right, and Justify. The default horizontal text alignment is left. **Left alignment** lines up the text along the left margin and leaves the right margin "ragged," or uneven. **Right alignment** lines up the text along the right margin and leaves the left margin "ragged." **Center alignment** centers the text between the left and right margins and leaves both margins "ragged." **Justified alignment** aligns the text along both the left and right margins; Word adjusts the spaces between words so that each line is even at both margins. The quickest way to change the alignment of selected paragraphs is to use the alignment buttons on the Formatting toolbar.

Center alignment is appropriate for single line paragraphs, such as cover page text, report titles, and paragraph headings. To center the cover page text horizontally:

Step 1	***Select***	all the lines of text
Step 2	***Click***	the Center button on the Formatting toolbar
Step 3	***Deselect***	the text
Step 4	***Observe***	that the cover page text is centered both vertically and horizontally between the margins
Step 5	***Zoom***	back to 100%
Step 6	***Switch to***	Normal view
Step 7	***Save***	the document as *Melbourne Audit Report Sample Cover Page* and close it

MENU TIP

You can change horizontal alignment by clicking the Alignment: list arrow on the Indents and Spacing tab in the Paragraph dialog box and selecting the appropriate alignment format.

You are ready to modify the alignment in the report.

Kelly asks you to center-align the title paragraph and use justified alignment for all the body text paragraphs in the document except the bulleted and numbered paragraphs.

To center the title paragraph:

Step 1	***Move***	the insertion point to the title paragraph
Step 2	***Click***	the Center button on the Formatting toolbar

The title paragraph is centered between the left and right margins. To justify all the paragraphs *except* the bulleted and numbered paragraphs:

Step 1	***Select***	all the body text paragraphs *except* the bulleted and numbered paragraphs, using the CTRL key
Step 2	***Click***	the Justify button on the Formatting toolbar
Step 3	***Deselect***	the paragraphs and scroll the document to verify that the paragraphs are justified
Step 4	***Save***	the document and leave it open

Now you want to indent the individual paragraphs.

Indenting Paragraphs

Indenting, or moving text away from the margin, helps draw attention to that text. Word indentation options position some or all lines of a paragraph to the right of the left margin (or to the left of the right margin). Indenting is part of paragraph formatting, which means only selected paragraphs are indented. The other paragraphs in the document remain unchanged.

There are four types of indents: first line, left, right, and hanging. A **First Line Indent** moves the first line of a paragraph to the right or the left. A **Left Indent** moves all the lines of a paragraph to the right, away from the left margin. A **Right Indent** moves all lines of a paragraph to the left, away from the right margin. A **Hanging Indent** leaves the first line of the paragraph at the left margin and moves the remaining lines to the right, away from the left margin. Hanging Indents are often used to create bulleted lists, numbered lists, and bibliographies.

The easiest way to indent selected paragraphs is to drag the First Line, Hanging Indent, or Left Indent marker to the desired location on the horizontal ruler.

You can use the First Line Indent marker on the horizontal ruler to indent just the first line of a paragraph, leaving the remaining lines in their original position. You often see first-line indents in long text documents, such as books and reports. You decide to indent the first line of each body text paragraph in the report. To indent the first line of the first paragraph of the report with the First Line Indent marker:

QUICK TIP

Right-aligned paragraphs are lined up along the right margin. Right alignment is appropriate for dates, page numbers, or to add a special effect to short one-line paragraphs. You can right-align paragraphs with the Align Right button on the Formatting toolbar or with the Right alignment option on the Indents and Spacing tab in the Paragraph dialog box.

Step 1	***Move***	the insertion point to the first body text paragraph
Step 2	***Move***	the mouse pointer to the First Line Indent marker on the horizontal ruler

Your screen should look similar to Figure 6-6.

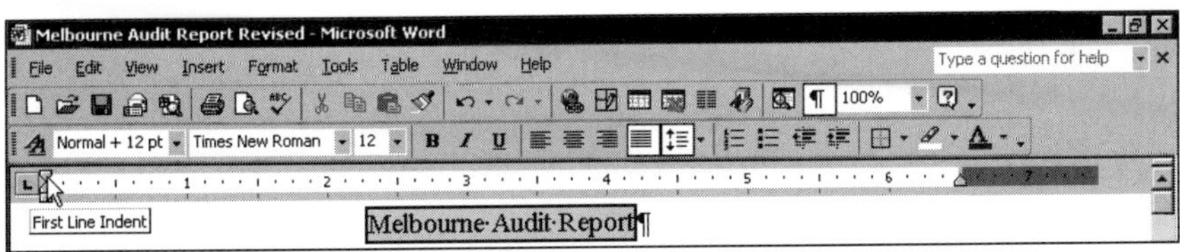

FIGURE 6-6
First Line Indent Marker

Step 3	***Drag***	the First Line Indent marker to the ¼-inch position on the horizontal ruler
Step 4	***Observe***	that the first line of the paragraph is indented to the ¼-inch position

MOUSE TIP

You can increase and decrease the left indent for selected paragraphs by clicking the Increase Indent and Decrease Indent buttons on the Formatting toolbar.

Another way to move the First Line Indent is with the TAB key. To indent the first line of the next paragraph using the TAB key:

Step 1	***Move***	the insertion point in front of the "T" in "The" in the second body paragraph
Step 2	***Press***	the TAB key
Step 3	***Observe***	that the first line is indented to the ¼-inch position

MENU TIP

You can indent paragraphs from the left or right margins by keying the indent positions on the Indents and Spacing tab in the Paragraph dialog box.

In addition, the First Line Indent marker on the ruler is positioned at ¼ inch and the AutoCorrect Options button appears. To review the AutoCorrect Options:

Step 1	***Move***	the mouse pointer to the AutoCorrect Options button to view the list arrow
Step 2	***Click***	the AutoCorrect Options button list arrow to view the menu

Your screen should look similar to Figure 6-7.

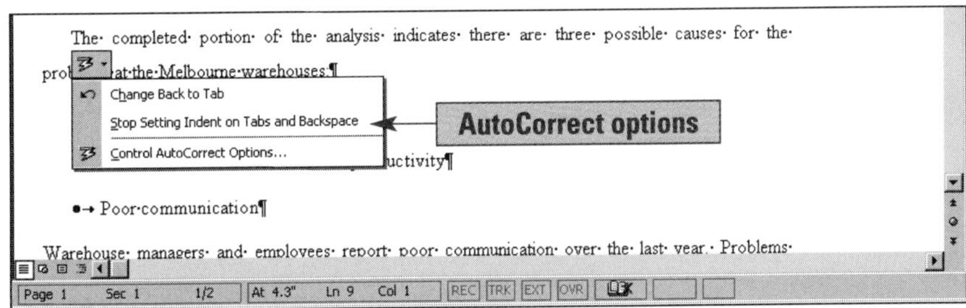

FIGURE 6-7
AutoCorrect Options Menu

You can change the indent back to a simple tab formatting mark, turn off the automatic indentation feature, or view additional AutoCorrect Options. You want to change the indent back to a tab.

CAUTION TIP

A tab stop and an indent are very different formatting features. When you press the TAB key, before you key text, Word inserts a nonprinting tab formatting mark and moves only that line to the next tab stop on the horizontal ruler. When you apply an indent option (before or after you key text), you can specify which lines to move and how many spaces to move them.

By default, the option is turned on to press the TAB and BACKSPACE keys to increase and decrease indents for text that's already keyed. (The setting is found in the AutoFormat As You Type tab in the AutoCorrect dialog box.) If you move the insertion point to a line of existing text and press the TAB key, Word indents the text by moving the First Line Indent marker on the horizontal ruler to the next tab stop on the horizontal ruler. When you press the TAB key *before* you key text, Word inserts a tab formatting mark.

Step 3	***Click***	Change Back to Tab
Step 4	***Observe***	that a tab formatting mark is inserted and the First Line Indent marker on the ruler returns to the left margin

The AutoCorrect Options button appears again. If desired, you can remove the tab formatting mark and replace it with a First Line Indent with a command on the AutoCorrect Options menu. To change the tab formatting mark back to an indent:

Step 1	***Display***	the AutoCorrect Options menu
Step 2	***Click***	Redo First Indent
Step 3	***Observe***	that the tab formatting mark is replaced with a First Line Indent
Step 4	***Continue***	to indent the first line of the each paragraph (except the bulleted and numbered paragraphs) by dragging the First Line Indent marker to the ¼-inch position on the ruler
Step 5	***Save***	the document and leave it open

You can modify an indent for selected paragraphs by dragging the indent markers to a new position on the horizontal ruler. You can remove an indent by dragging the indent markers back to the left margin. Kelly wants the numbered and bulleted paragraphs to be positioned at the left margin. When you applied the bullets and numbering formatting, Word indented the paragraphs with a Hanging Indent. To position the paragraphs at the left margin, you can drag the Left Indent marker, which moves all components of the indent marker, to the left until the First Line Indent marker is positioned at the left margin. This retains the Hanging Indent but repositions the first line of each paragraph at the left margin. To move the indents:

Step 1	***Select***	the bulleted paragraphs
Step 2	***Move***	the mouse pointer to the Hanging Indent marker on the horizontal ruler
Step 3	***Drag***	the left tab stop off the Hanging Indent marker
Step 4	***Drag***	the Left Indent marker to the left until the First Line Indent marker is at the left margin
Step 5	***Observe***	that the bulleted paragraphs are repositioned at the left margin
Step 6	***Select***	the numbered paragraphs
Step 7	***Follow***	Steps 2 through 4 to position the numbered paragraphs at the left margin

Step 8	*Observe*	that the numbered paragraphs are repositioned at the left margin
Step 9	*Deselect*	the text

Sometimes it is preferable to indent a paragraph from both the left and the right to draw the readers' attention to the paragraph or to set off quoted material. After reviewing your changes, Kelly asks you to indent the paragraph beginning "Morale..." 1 inch from the left and right margins. First you need to remove the First Line Indent from the paragraph. To remove the First Line Indent and then indent the paragraph from both the left and right margins:

Step 1	*Move*	the insertion point to the "Morale..." paragraph
Step 2	*Drag*	the First Line Indent marker back to the left margin to remove the First Line Indent
Step 3	*Observe*	that the paragraph is no longer indented
Step 4	*Drag*	the Left Indent marker to the right to the 1-inch position on the horizontal ruler
Step 5	*Observe*	that all the lines of the paragraph are indented 1 inch from the left margin
Step 6	*Move*	the mouse pointer to the Right Indent marker on the ruler

Your screen should look similar to Figure 6-8.

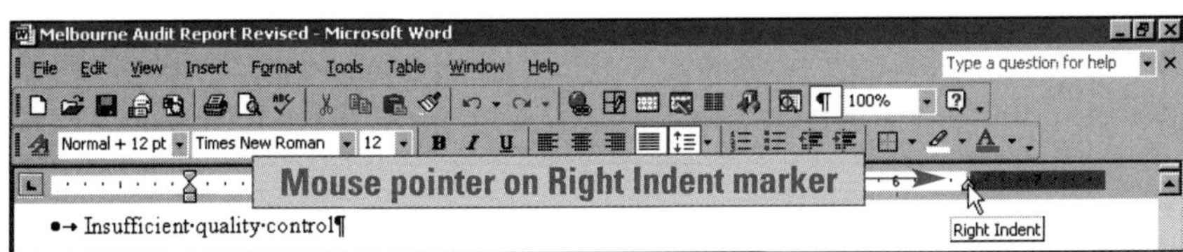

FIGURE 6-8
Right Indent Marker

Step 7	*Drag*	the Right Indent Marker to the left 1 inch from the right margin
Step 8	*Observe*	that the paragraph is indented from both the left and right margins
Step 9	*Save*	the document and leave it open

Another way to control the arrangement of paragraphs on each page is to control where the text ends on one page and begins on the next page.

CAUTION TIP

It's easy to drag the First Line, Hanging, or Left Indent markers on the ruler beyond the document's left margin. In Normal view, if you can still see the indent marker, drag it back to the appropriate position and then click the scroll box on the horizontal scroll bar to reposition the screen. If you can no longer see the indent markers, switch to Print Layout view, drag the indent markers to the right, and then return to Normal view.

C

6.d Inserting Page Breaks

QUICK TIP

The quickest way to insert a manual page break is to move the insertion point where you want to insert the page break and press the CTRL + ENTER keys.

CAUTION TIP

If you add or remove pages, edit text, or replace formatting, any manual page breaks you inserted may then be incorrect. You can move a manual page break by dragging it to a new position with the mouse pointer. You can delete a manual page break by selecting it and pressing the DELETE key or by moving the insertion point to the left margin below the dotted line and pressing the BACKSPACE key.

Word determines how much text will fit on a page based on the margins, font, font size, and paper size. A **page break** identifies where one page ends and another begins. There are two types of page breaks: a soft, or automatic, page break and a hard, or manual, page break. Word inserts an **automatic page break** when a page is full of text. In Normal view, an automatic page break appears as a dotted horizontal line from the left to the right margins. You can create a **manual page break** at any point on a page; a manual page break appears as a dotted horizontal line from the left to right margins with the words "Page Break" in the center. Manual page breaks are used to force paragraphs to the next page.

Adjusting the line and paragraph spacing in the *Melbourne Audit Report Revised* document causes an automatic page break to occur immediately above the next-to-last paragraph. This forces the last two paragraphs—containing just a few lines of text—to the second page. Kelly decides that she wants to more evenly distribute the text by moving the paragraph beginning "Morale…" to the second page. Changing the position of the page breaks in a document is called **repagination**. To repaginate the document, you cannot move or delete the automatic page break Word inserted. Instead, you must insert a manual page break above the automatic page break. Word then repaginates the entire document from the position of the manual page break.

To insert a manual page break before the "Morale…" paragraph:

Step 1	***Scroll***	to view the automatic page break, a single dotted line, below the "Morale…" paragraph
Step 2	***Move***	the insertion point to the left margin in front of the "M" in "Morale", if necessary
Step 3	***Click***	Insert
Step 4	***Click***	Break

The Break dialog box on your screen should look similar to Figure 6-9.

FIGURE 6-9
Break Dialog Box

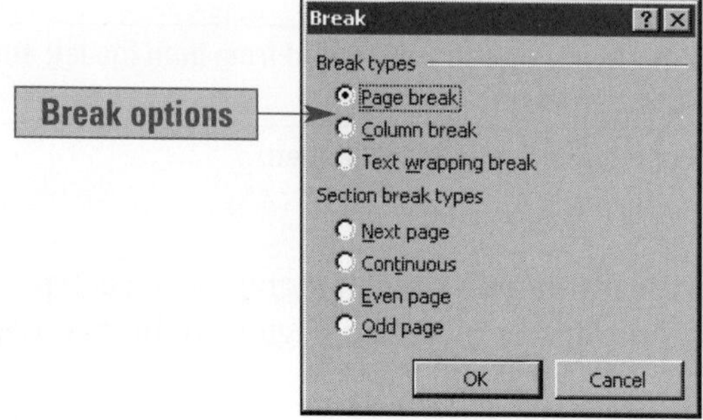

The default option, Page Break, is already selected.

Step 5	*Click*	OK
Step 6	*Observe*	the manual page break above the "Morale…" paragraph
Step 7	*Observe*	that Word repaginated the document and removed the automatic page break
Step 8	*Save*	the document and leave it open

To wrap up the *Melbourne Audit Report Revised* document, Kelly asks you to add page numbers in a footer and the department name and today's date in a header.

6.e Creating and Modifying Headers and Footers

Sometimes you need to have short, one-line paragraphs appear at the top or the bottom of document pages. For example, perhaps you want to include the date and preparer's name at the top of each page of a report and the document filename and page number at the bottom of each page. You use header text and footer text to position these short, one-line paragraphs at the top or bottom of a page above or below the top and bottom margins and body text area. **Header** text, often called **headers**, appears at the top of each page and **footer** text, also called **footers**, appears at the bottom of each page. You can specify that headers or footers print on every page or only on certain pages. For example, you can create headers and footers for every page except the first page or for even- or odd-numbered pages. You can view headers and footers in Print Layout view or Print Preview, but not in Normal view.

Inserting Page Numbers

Page numbers are always inserted at the top or bottom of a document in a header or footer. One way to insert and format page numbers is to first create the header or footer and then use buttons on the Header and Footer toolbar to insert and format the page numbers. A quick way to insert page numbers is to click the Page Numbers command on the Insert menu, select header or footer, specify the horizontal alignment, indicate whether to show the number on the first page, and select a number format.

QUICK TIP

To format part of a document with different margins, such as a title page, you can insert a section break. A **section break** stores the section formatting such as the margin settings and appears as a double dotted line with the words "Section Break" in the center of the line. Word inserts section breaks when you format a portion of a document with different margins, headers, footers, columns, or page orientation. You also can insert a manual section break with the Break command on the Insert menu and then apply the formatting.

Kelly asks you to insert a center-aligned page number in a footer on all pages of the document. To insert the page number:

Step 1	*Move*	the insertion point to the top of the document
Step 2	*Click*	Insert
Step 3	*Click*	Page Numbers

The Page Numbers dialog box on your screen should look similar to Figure 6-10.

FIGURE 6-10
Page Numbers Dialog Box

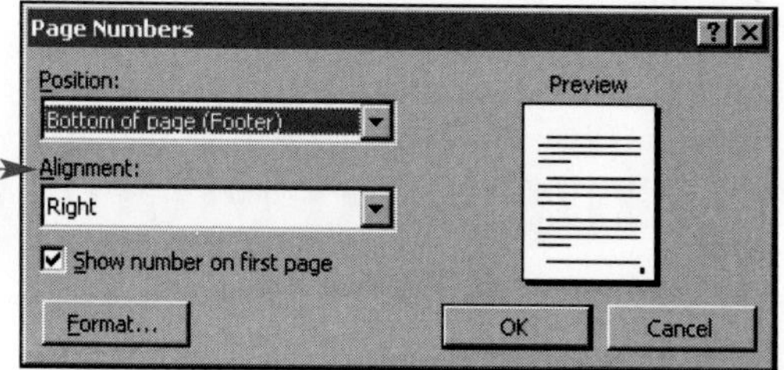

Page number position and alignment options

CAUTION TIP

Be careful when working in large documents that contain both manual and automatic page breaks. Adding text, changing margins, or inserting and deleting manual page breaks results in repagination. When Word repaginates a document, it cannot move or delete your manual page breaks, which may result in pagination errors. To be sure the pagination is correct, always use Print Preview to review the pagination of documents before printing them.

You select the position of the page numbers and their alignment in this dialog box. You also can turn on or off the page number on the first page and change the number format in this dialog box.

Step 4	*Verify*	that Bottom of page (Footer) appears in the Position: list
Step 5	*Click*	the Alignment: list arrow
Step 6	*Click*	Center
Step 7	*Click*	the Show number on first page check box to insert a check mark, if necessary
Step 8	*Click*	OK

Word switches to Print Layout view so you can see the footer.

Step 9	*Scroll*	to view the page numbers in the footer on both pages then return to the top of the document

Now you want to create the header.

Creating and Modifying a Header

Kelly asks you to insert the department name and today's date at the top of every page. You do this in a header. To create the header:

Step 1	*Click*	View
Step 2	*Click*	Header and Footer

Your screen should look similar to Figure 6-11.

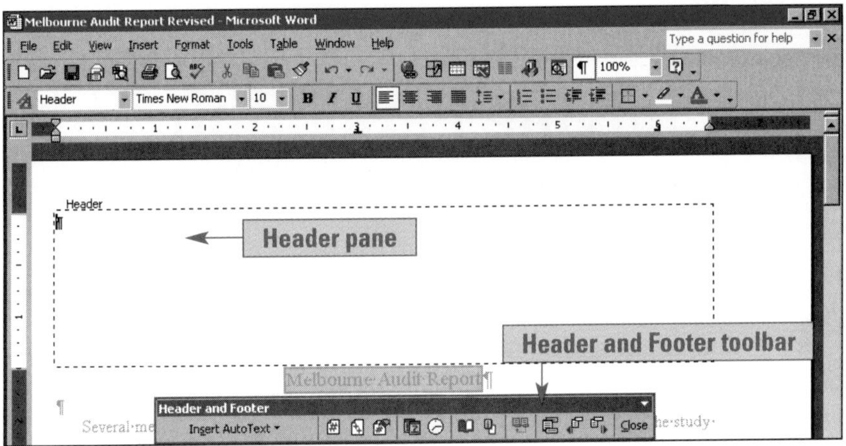

FIGURE 6-11
Header Pane in Print Layout View

The Header pane is visible and contains the insertion point. The Header and Footer toolbar automatically appears. You can use buttons on the Header and Footer toolbar to insert and format page numbers, insert the date and time, and switch between the Header and Footer panes among other tasks.

The horizontal ruler displays a center tab stop set at the 3-inch position and a right tab stop set at the 6-inch position. These are default tabs set for the Header and Footer panes. Because you want to insert today's date at the right margin, you do not need the center tab stop and you need to reposition the right tab stop at the right margin.

Step 3	*Drag*	the Center tab stop off the ruler to remove it
Step 4	*Drag*	the Right tab stop to the right margin to reposition it
Step 5	*Key*	Purchasing Department in the Header pane at the left margin
Step 6	*Press*	the TAB key
Step 7	*Click*	the Insert Date button on the Header and Footer toolbar to insert today's date

Step 8	*Observe*	that the department name and today's date are inserted in the header
Step 9	*Click*	the Close button  on the Header and Footer toolbar
Step 10	*Zoom*	the document to Whole Page and observe the completed header and footer
Step 11	*Switch to*	Normal view
Step 12	*Save*	the document and close it

You can quickly apply multiple paragraph formats at once with paragraph styles.

C

6.f Applying Paragraph Styles

Kelly is pleased with the formatting of the *Melbourne Audit Report Revised* document and wants you to reformat a similar document. She needs this document reformatted quickly and suggests you try using built-in paragraph formatting, called styles, to reformat it. A **paragraph style** contains multiple formatting attributes, such as line spacing, alignment, and indentations, that affect the way text looks on the page. When you use a style, you can quickly apply the multiple paragraph formatting attributes at one time.

Your first step is to open the *Chicago Draft* document and then set the appropriate margins for an unbound report document. You then use a paragraph style to automatically format the title, the body text, paragraph headings, and the bulleted and numbered lists. Like character styles, you can quickly apply paragraph styles using the Styles and Formatting task pane. To set the appropriate margins and view the Styles and Formatting task pane:

Step 1	*Open*	the *Chicago Draft* document located on the Data Disk
Step 2	*Set*	a 2-inch top margin and 1-inch left and right margins, consistent with an unbound report document
Step 3	*Click*	the Styles and Formatting button on the Formatting toolbar to view the Styles and Formatting task pane
Step 4	*Show*	All styles, if necessary

TASK PANE TIP

Word has several built-in list styles that contain bullets, numbering, and other formats you can apply to paragraphs from the Styles and Formatting task pane.

You can easily reapply formatting from formatted text to unformatted text using the Styles and Formatting task pane. When you apply formatting combinations to text manually using the Formatting toolbar or formatting dialog boxes, Word remembers those formatting combinations and displays them in the Available Formatting view of the Styles and Formatting task pane. You can then select unformatted text and click the formatting combination in the task pane you wish to apply.

To format the report title:

Step 1	*Move*	the insertion point to the top of the document, if necessary
Step 2	*Point to*	Title in the Pick formatting to apply list in the Styles and Formatting task pane (scroll to the bottom of the list to view this style)
Step 3	*Observe*	the ScreenTip that defines the formatting attributes contained in the style
Step 4	*Click*	the Title style in the Pick formatting to apply list in the Styles and Formatting task pane
Step 5	*Observe*	that the title text is centered, bolded, and changed to the 16-point font

To format the body text:

Step 1	*Select*	all the body text below the title
Step 2	*Click*	Body Text 2 in the Pick formatting to apply list in the Styles and Formatting task pane

To format the paragraph headings "Audit Methods," "Issues," "Issues Analyses," and "Summation":

Step 1	*Select*	the four paragraph headings, using the CTRL key
Step 2	*Click*	the Heading 3 style in the Pick formatting to apply list in the Styles and Formatting task pane

To format the bulleted and numbered lists:

Step 1	*Select*	the three paragraphs beginning "Outstanding management style" and ending "High morale and increased worker productivity"
Step 2	*Click*	the List Bullet style in the Pick formatting to apply list in the Styles and Formatting task pane
Step 3	*Select*	the paragraphs beginning "First, appropriate goals..." and ending "Finally, interviews..."
Step 4	*Click*	the List Number style in the Pick formatting to apply list in the Styles and Formatting task pane
Step 5	*Select*	the bulleted and numbered lists using the CTRL key
Step 6	*Double-space*	the lists using the Formatting toolbar
Step 7	*Close*	the Styles and Formatting task pane

MENU TIP

You can create custom list styles using options in the List Styles tab in the Bullets and Numbering dialog box. To view this tab, click the Bullets and Numbering command on the Format menu or a shortcut menu.

MOUSE TIP

You can apply paragraph styles (including list styles containing bullets, numbering, font, and other formats) with the Style button on the Formatting toolbar.

QUICK TIP

You can add spacing before and after a paragraph by applying a style such as the Body Text style that contains additional spacing formats.

Step 8	*Save*	the document as *Chicago Audit Report With Styles* and close it

Now that you have finished the *Chicago Audit Report With Styles* document, Kelly wants you to organize the text paragraphs in another document as an outline.

QUICK TIP

You can create an outline using headings styles in Outline view. For more information on using Outline view, see online Help.

6.g Creating Outlines

An outline, also called an outline numbered list, is a way to structure information logically. You can use an outline to organize the ideas and information into topics and subtopics for a large document, such as a report, proposal, or presentation. An **outline** consists of heading and body text paragraphs organized by level or importance. Body text is paragraph text below an outline heading. Major headings are called level one headings. Each major heading can have subheadings, called level two headings. Each level two heading can have its own subheadings at level three, and so forth. An outline is also a good way to construct multilevel lists. Using an outline numbered list is an easy way to indent paragraphs and add numbering. Kelly wants you to add paragraph numbering to a report and then create a formal topic outline for a business presentation.

Outlining Paragraphs

Numbered text paragraphs are often used in reports and proposals when it is useful to structure the report or proposal information logically. Kelly's supervisor is traveling to London on business next week and will be meeting with the London branch manager to discuss a research report on stores in the London branch. Kelly asks you to add paragraph numbering to the research report. To open the document and add paragraph numbering:

Step 1	*Open*	the *London Research* document located on the Data Disk
Step 2	*Select*	the entire document
Step 3	*Click*	Format
Step 4	*Click*	Bullets and Numbering
Step 5	*Click*	the Outline Numbered tab

You can select different numbering options for an outline in this tab. Your dialog box should look similar to Figure 6-12.

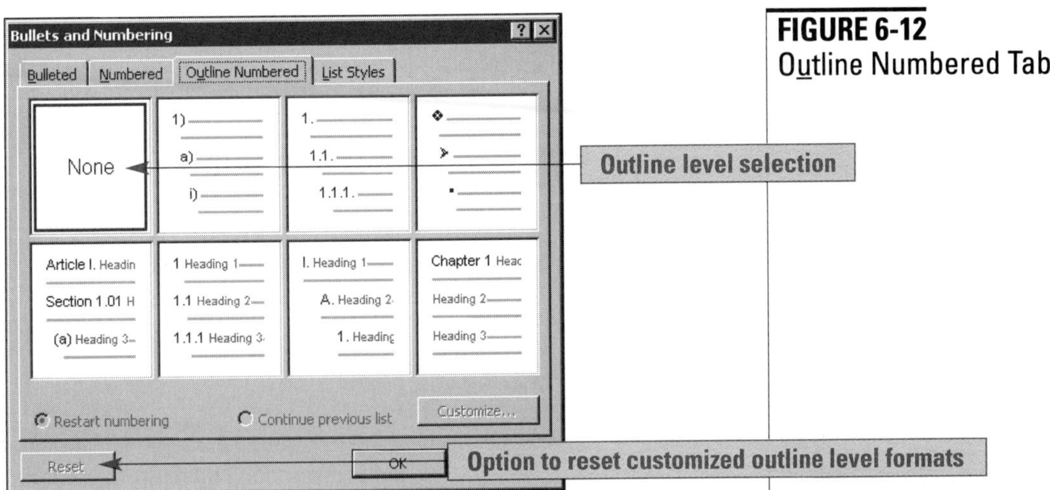

FIGURE 6-12
Outline Numbered Tab

Step 6	***Double-click***	the third option in the first row (1, 1.1, 1.1.1)
Step 7	***Deselect***	the text and review the new paragraph numbering

QUICK TIP

In some dialog boxes, you can double-click certain options to select them and close the dialog box in one step.

You can use the TAB key to demote outline numbered paragraphs to the next-lower outline level and the SHIFT + TAB keys to promote outline numbered paragraphs to the next-higher level. Paragraphs 3 and 4 are subparagraphs of paragraph 2, so you need to demote the paragraphs to the next-lower level. To demote paragraphs 3 and 4:

Step 1	***Select***	paragraphs 3 and 4
Step 2	***Press***	the TAB key
Step 3	***Deselect***	the paragraphs and observe the new subparagraph numbering (2.1 and 2.2)
Step 4	***Save***	the document as *London Research Revised* and close it

Creating a Formal Topic Outline

When you need to create a formal topic outline, you can use a modified Outline Numbered format. A short formal topic outline has a 1½-inch top margin and 2-inch left and right margins with an uppercase, centered title followed by three blank lines. Each major heading is numbered with Roman numerals followed by a period. The numerals are decimal aligned on the periods (for example, the I. and IV. heading numbers are aligned on the period). You double-space before and after each major heading. The subheadings are single-spaced and the number for each new subheading level (A., 1.) begins immediately below the text of the previous heading.

While in London, Kelly's supervisor will be making a presentation to a group of clients. She wants you to create a formal topic outline for the presentation. Kelly will expand the outline later by adding the appropriate body text and formatting. To create the margins and title of a formal outline:

Step 1	*Create*	a new, blank document
Step 2	*Set*	a 1½-inch top margin and 2-inch left and right margins
Step 3	*Center*	the title "PRESENTATION OUTLINE" on the first line
Step 4	*Press*	the ENTER key four times
Step 5	*View*	the formatting marks, if necessary
Step 6	*Click*	the Align Left button on the Formatting toolbar to move the insertion point to the left margin

CAUTION TIP

Options in the Outline Numbered tab in the Bullets and Numbering dialog box may contain custom formatting previously set. The Reset button is active whenever you click an option that has been customized. It is a good idea to reset that option to its default settings before you begin to create a new outline.

Next you select and customize an Outline Numbered format. To create and customize the formal outline:

Step 1	*Open*	the Outline Numbered tab in the Bullets and Numbering dialog box
Step 2	*Click*	the second outline option (1, a, i) in the first row
Step 3	*Click*	Reset to return the second outline option to its default formatting settings, if necessary
Step 4	*Click*	Customize

Your dialog box should look similar to Figure 6-13.

FIGURE 6-13
Customize Outline Numbered List Dialog Box

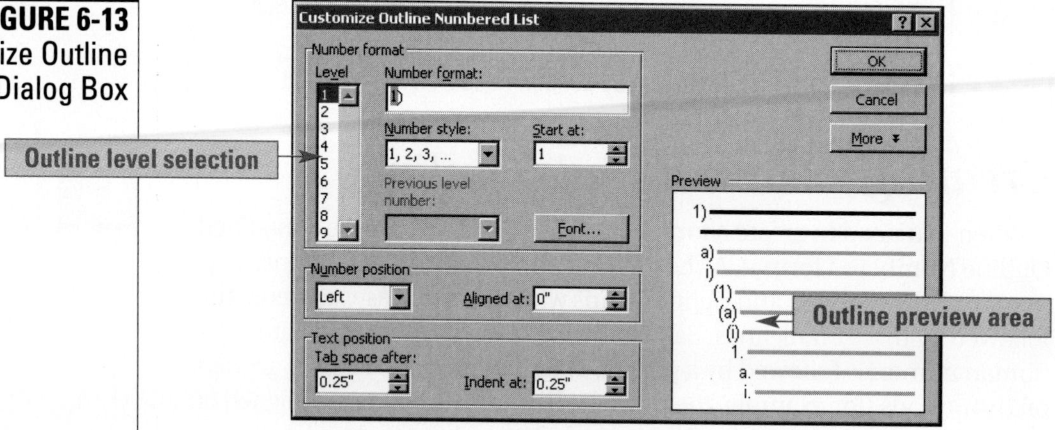

You can change the number format, number style, and number or text positioning for each level in a formal outline in this dialog box. To conform to the formatting standards for a formal topic outline, you must change the number style to Roman numerals for level one, uppercase alphabetic characters for level two, and Arabic numbers for level three. The character following the number to must be changed to a period. The level one number alignment must be changed to right-aligned so that the numbers align on the period at the end of each number. The indentation for levels two and three must be modified to line up the number with the text above it. You modify the outline format for level one:

Step 5	*Verify*	that 1 is selected in the Level list
Step 6	*Click*	the Number style: list arrow
Step 7	*Click*	I, II, III, ...
Step 8	*Click*	in the Number format: text box
Step 9	*Replace*	the closing parenthesis with a period
Step 10	*Change*	the Number position to Right
Step 11	*Change*	the Aligned at: text box to .25
Step 12	*Change*	the Tab space after: text box to .4 inch
Step 13	*Change*	the Indent at: text box to .5 inch
Step 14	*Observe*	the changes to the level one heading in the Preview

You repeat the same series of actions for the level two headings. To modify the level two indentations, numbering style and following character:

Step 1	*Click*	2 in the Level list
Step 2	*Change*	the Number style to A, B, C, ...
Step 3	*Replace*	the closing parenthesis with a period in the Number format: text box
Step 4	*Change*	the Aligned at: text box to .4 inch
Step 5	*Change*	the Tab space after: text box to .75 inch
Step 6	*Change*	the Indent at: text box to 1.2 inch

To modify the level three indentations, numbering style, and following character:

Step 1	*Click*	3 in the Level list
Step 2	*Change*	the Number style to 1, 2, 3, ...

Step 3	*Change*	the closing parenthesis to a period
Step 4	*Change*	the Aligned at: text box to .75 inches
Step 5	*Change*	the Indent at: text box to 1.45 inches
Step 6	*Click*	OK

The indented first number appears. When you press the ENTER key, the next heading line is automatically created with the next number at the same level. To double-space between the major heading and any subheadings, you can insert a New Line formatting mark that adds a blank line without outline numbers by pressing the SHIFT + ENTER keys. A **New Line formatting mark** creates a new line inside an existing paragraph formatting mark. You then press the ENTER key to create a new paragraph and begin the next numbered heading line. You promote or demote headings by clicking the Increase and Decrease Indent buttons on the Formatting toolbar or by pressing the TAB and SHIFT + TAB keys before you key the text.

To key the first heading:

Step 1	*Key*	MARKETING FORECAST
Step 2	*Press*	the SHIFT + ENTER keys to insert a New Line formatting mark (small return arrow) at the end of the MARKETING FORECAST heading and move the insertion point to a new line
Step 3	*Press*	the ENTER key to move the insertion point to the next line and continue the outline numbers

The next outline heading is automatically numbered at the same level, as the previous heading which is level one. However, you now want to key level two headings. You demote the insertion point to the next level.

Step 4	*Click*	the Increase Indent button on the Formatting toolbar to move the insertion point to the next level and insert the A. outline number
Step 5	*Key*	Projected Sales
Step 6	*Press*	the ENTER key
Step 7	*Key*	Sales Stars!
Step 8	*Press*	the ENTER key

Next, key the level three headings below "Sales Stars!"

Step 9	***Press***	the TAB key
Step 10	***Key***	Wilson, Betancourt, and Fontaine, pressing the ENTER key after each heading
Step 11	***Key***	Lu
Step 12	***Press***	the SHIFT + ENTER keys to insert a New Line formatting mark
Step 13	***Press***	the ENTER key

The next heading is level one. To promote the insertion point and key the second level one heading:

Step 1	***Click***	the Decrease Indent button twice on the Formatting toolbar
Step 2	***Key***	ADVERTISING CAMPAIGN
Step 3	***Press***	the SHIFT + ENTER keys to insert a New Line formatting mark
Step 4	***Press***	the ENTER key to create the next heading line
Step 5	***Press***	TAB key to demote the insertion point to level two
Step 6	***Key***	Media Budget
Step 7	***Press***	the ENTER key
Step 8	***Press***	the TAB key to demote the insertion point
Step 9	***Key***	TV, Radio, and Web banners, pressing the ENTER key after each heading
Step 10	***Press***	the SHIFT + TAB keys to promote the insertion point
Step 11	***Key***	Print Ads
Step 12	***Press***	the ENTER key
Step 13	***Press***	the TAB key to demote the insertion point
Step 14	***Key***	Newspapers and Magazines pressing the ENTER key after Newspapers
Step 15	***Switch to***	Print Layout view, if necessary
Step 16	***Zoom***	the document to see all of the text
Step 17	***Zoom***	the document back to 100%
Step 18	***Save***	the document as *Presentation Outline* and close it

Outlines provide a quick way to organize thoughts and topics.

Summary

- When applying paragraph formatting, you must select the paragraph or paragraphs to be formatted before you select the formatting option.
- Bullets, numbering, borders, and shading can add emphasis to paragraphs and draw a reader's attention to the paragraphs.
- You can select different line spacing options such as Single, Double, and 1.5 from the Line spacing: list in the Paragraph dialog box or from the Line Spacing button on the Formatting toolbar.
- You can add spacing before and after a paragraph by setting paragraph spacing options in the Paragraph dialog box.
- Paragraphs can be aligned vertically between the top and bottom margins and horizontally between the left and right margins.
- Paragraphs can be indented with options in the Paragraph dialog box, buttons on the Formatting toolbar, and by dragging the indent markers on the horizontal ruler. Indentation options include First Line, Hanging, Left, and Right Indents.
- Word inserts automatic page breaks whenever text fills a page. Although you cannot delete an automatic page break, you can insert manual page breaks to change the pagination of a document.
- Headers and footers position text such as names, dates, and page numbers, at the top and bottom of specific pages.
- You can apply paragraph styles to one or more paragraphs with options in the Styles and Formatting task pane.
- An outline is a way of organizing the ideas and information presented in a long document or presentation. You can create an outline by adding outline numbers to paragraphs, by setting custom outline numbering formats and keying the outline text, by using heading styles in Outline view, or by using outline paragraph numbering in the Paragraph dialog box.

Commands Review

Action	Menu Bar	Shortcut Menu	Toolbar	Task Pane	Keyboard
Apply or remove bullets and numbering to lists	Format, Bullets and Numbering	Right-click the selected text or at the insertion point, click Bullets and Numbering		Click the List link in the Bullets and Numbering group in the Reveal Formatting task pane	ALT + O, N Key a number, press the SPACEBAR or TAB key, and key the text Key an asterisk, press the SPACEBAR or TAB key, and key the text
Add borders and shading to text and entire paragraphs—from margin to margin	Format, Borders and Shading				ALT + O, B
Change line and paragraph spacing	Format, Paragraph	Right-click selected paragraph(s), click Paragraph		Click the Spacing link in the Paragraph group in the Reveal Formatting task pane	ALT + O, P CTRL + 1 (single) CTRL + 2 (double) CTRL + 5 (1.5)
Change vertical alignment	File, Page Setup			Click the Layout link in the Section group in the Reveal Formatting task pane	ALT + F, U
Change horizontal alignment	Format, Paragraph	Right-click selected paragraph(s), click Paragraph		Click the Alignment link in the Paragraph group in the Reveal Formatting task pane	ALT + O, P CTRL + L (Left) CTRL + E (Center) CTRL + R (Right) CTRL + J (Justify)
Indent paragraphs	Format, Paragraph	Right-click selected paragraph(s), click Paragraph	Drag the indent marker on the horizontal ruler	Click the Indentation link in the Paragraph group in the Reveal Formatting task pane	ALT + O, P CTRL + M (from Left) CTRL + T (Hanging)
Insert page breaks	Insert, Break				ALT + I, B CTRL + ENTER
Create headers and footers	View, Header and Footer		Various on the Header and Footer toolbar		ALT + V, H
Insert page numbers	Insert, Page Numbers				ALT + I, U
Apply paragraph styles	Format, Styles and Formatting		Normal	Click the style in the Pick a formatting to apply list in the Styles and Formatting task pane	ALT + O, S
Create an outline numbered list	Format, Bullets and Numbering				ALT + O, N
Remove formatting from selected text	Edit, Clear, Formats			Click Clear Formatting in the Pick a formatting to apply list in the Styles and Formatting task pane (Show Formatting in use)	ALT + E, A, F CTRL + Q (paragraph formatting) CTRL + SPACEBAR (character formatting)

Concepts Review

Circle the correct answer.

1. The default line spacing is:
- [a] Justified.
- [b] Single.
- [c] Double.
- [d] Center.

2. You can quickly apply a combination of formats to a paragraph by applying a paragraph:
- [a] template.
- [b] style.
- [c] task pane.
- [d] dialog box.

3. A page break:
- [a] moves all the lines of a paragraph to the right of the left margin.
- [b] centers text between the left and right margins.
- [c] identifies where one page ends and another begins.
- [d] adds emphasis to paragraphs.

4. Numbered lists are used to:
- [a] align paragraphs vertically on the page.
- [b] align paragraphs horizontally on the page.
- [c] organize paragraphs logically.
- [d] create headers and footers.

5. You cannot indent selected paragraphs by:
- [a] dragging an indent marker on the horizontal ruler.
- [b] clicking the Increase Indent button.
- [c] keying the indent position in the Paragraph dialog box.
- [d] keying the indent position in the Font dialog box.

6. A hanging indent moves:
- [a] all the lines of a paragraph to the right.
- [b] all the lines of a paragraph to the left.
- [c] only the top line.
- [d] all lines except the top line.

7. A header appears at the:
- [a] bottom of every page.
- [b] left margin of the first page.
- [c] top of every page.
- [d] the right margin of every page.

8. Page numbers are always inserted:
- [a] in headers or footers.
- [b] only on the first page.
- [c] at each new paragraph.
- [d] with the Break command on the Insert menu.

9. An outline is:
- [a] always double-spaced.
- [b] only created in Outline view.
- [c] used to organize paragraphs logically.
- [d] a way to quickly apply a combination of formats to paragraphs.

10. When document text aligns at the left margin and has a ragged right margin, the text is:
- [a] center-aligned.
- [b] left-aligned.
- [c] right-aligned.
- [d] justified.

Circle **T** if the statement is true or **F** if the statement is false.

T F 1. The default horizontal alignment is left alignment.

T F 2. You can set line spacing with the mouse and the horizontal and vertical ruler.

T F 3. Paragraph spacing allows you to add additional white space before and after a paragraph.

T F 4. Justified alignment means that text is aligned only along the left margin.

T F 5. The only way to indent a paragraph is to press the TAB key.

T F 6. A paragraph can be indented from the right margin.

T F 7. You can add borders and shading to text in paragraph or to the entire paragraph.

T F 8. You can set, modify, or delete automatic page breaks.

T F 9. Headers and footers are visible in Normal view.

T F 10. When applying paragraph formatting to an entire document that has already been keyed, only the first paragraph must be selected.

For the remainder of this text, when you open a letter or memo document from the Data Disk or key a new document from a figure, replace the text "Current date" with the actual date using the AutoComplete feature or the Date and Time command on the Insert menu.

Skills Review

SCANS

Exercise 1

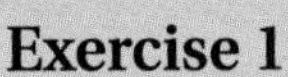

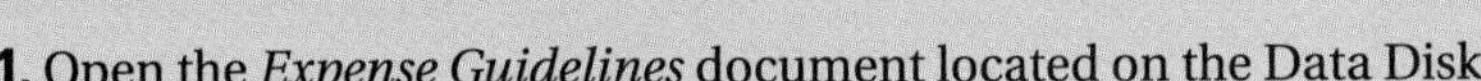

1. Open the *Expense Guidelines* document located on the Data Disk.
2. Set a 2-inch top margin and 1-inch left and right margins, as appropriate for an unbound report document.
3. Format the "Expense Guidelines" title to change the case to uppercase and apply bold, 14-point, centered alignment formats.
4. Add a 2¼ pt box border and Gray-10% shading to the Expense Guidelines title text. (*Hint:* Do not apply the formats to the entire paragraph.)
5. Justify the body paragraphs between the left and right margins.
6. Double-space the body paragraphs.
7. Indent the first line of each paragraph using the TAB key.
8. Save the document as *Expense Guidelines Revised*, and then preview and print it.
9. Remove the First Line Indents from all the body paragraphs *except* the first body paragraph by dragging the First Line Indent marker back to the left margin.
10. Create a numbered list using all the body paragraphs *except* the first body paragraph.
11. Save the document as *Expense Guidelines Numbered List*, and then preview and print it.
12. Change the numbered list to a bulleted list.

13. Create a footer containing your name at the left margin and the current date at the right margin.
14. Save the document as *Expense Guidelines With Bullets and Footer*, and then preview, print, and close it.

Exercise 2 

1. Open the *Interoffice Training Memo* located on the Data Disk.
2. Change the margins to the appropriate margins for an interoffice memorandum.
3. Set a tab stop to line up the heading paragraphs.
4. Change the case of the To, From, Date, and Subject headings to uppercase. (*Hint:* Don't forget to use the CTRL key to select all the items before you change the case.)
5. Change the line spacing for all the body paragraphs to 1.5 using the Formatting toolbar.
6. Indent the two paragraphs beginning "Samantha" and "Steve" ½ inch from both the left and the right margins.
7. Select the two indented paragraphs and add six points of spacing after the selected paragraphs by opening the Paragraph dialog box and changing the Spacing After: option to 6 pt.
8. Save the document as *Interoffice Training Memo Revised* and then preview and print it.
9. Remove the left and right indents from the two indented paragraphs and use outline numbering to number all the body paragraphs. The two paragraphs beginning "Samantha" and "Steve" are subparagraphs of the first body paragraph.
10. Save the document as *Interoffice Training Memo With Outline Numbering*, and then preview, print, and close it.

Exercise 3 

1. Open the *District C Sales Decline* document located on the Data Disk.
2. Set a 2-inch top margin and 1.5-inch left and right margins.
3. Double-space and justify the entire document.
4. Single-space all the stores paragraphs *except* store A5.
5. Create a bulleted list with the stores paragraphs.
6. Save the document as *District C Sales Decline With Bulleted List*, and then preview and print it.
7. Change the bulleted list to a numbered list.
8. Save the document as *District C Sales Decline With Numbered List*, and then preview, print, and close it.

Exercise 4 

1. Open the *Expense Guidelines* document located on the Data Disk.
2. Set the appropriate margins for an unbound report document.
3. Center-align the "Expense Guidelines" title, format it with the 14-point bold font, and delete the two blank lines that follow it.
4. Apply the Body Text paragraph style to the body paragraphs.
5. Indent the first line of each body paragraph ¼ inch using the First Line Indent marker on the horizontal ruler.
6. Save the document as *Expense Guidelines With Body Text*, and then preview and print it.
7. Remove the Body Text formatting from the body paragraphs. (*Hint:* Display the Formatting in use options in the Styles and Formatting task pane and clear the formatting.)

8. Justify all the paragraphs including the title paragraph vertically between the top and bottom margins.
9. Save the document as *Expense Guidelines With Vertical Justification*, and then preview, print, and close it.

Exercise 5

1. Open the *Vancouver Draft* document located on the Data Disk.
2. Set the appropriate margins for an unbound report document.
3. Apply the Body Text style to the entire document.
4. Center-align and format with Times New Roman 14 point bold the title "Vancouver Warehouse Report."
5. Justify the body paragraphs between the left and right margins.
6. Apply the Small caps effect and bold formatting to the paragraph heading "Audit Methods."
7. Copy the Small caps effect and bold formatting to the "Problems," "Problem Analyses," and "Summation" paragraph headings using the Format Painter.
8. Create a bulleted list with the three paragraphs beginning "Poor Communication" and then center-align the list.
9. Create a numbered list with the three paragraphs in the Problem Analyses section beginning "First," and ending with "Finally,".
10. Create a footer and insert the current date at the right margin using a button on the Header and Footer toolbar.
11. Save the document as *Vancouver Draft Revised*, and then preview, print, and close it.

Exercise 6 

1. Open the *Vancouver Draft Revised* document you created in Exercise 5.
2. Select the entire document.
3. Press CTRL + Q to remove the paragraph formatting.
4. Press CTRL + SPACEBAR to remove the character formatting.
5. Remove the Body Text style. (*Hint:* View the Formatting in use in the Styles and Formatting task pane and clear the formats.)
6. Triple-space the document.
7. Insert the page number in the center position in a footer on each page.
8. Create a manual page break above the "Summation" paragraph.
9. Save the document as *Vancouver Draft With Triple Spacing*, and then preview, print, and close it.

Exercise 7 

1. Open the *Sales Opportunities* document located on the Data Disk.
2. Change the text "Introduction," "Types of Stores," "Shopper Personalities," and "Conclusion" to all caps, bold, and Arial 14 point. (*Hint:* Use the CTRL key to select all the text before formatting it.)
3. Select the text beginning with "The Mall" and ending with "The Gourmet Store" and add bullets.
4. Select the text beginning with "The Sale Hunter" and ending with "The Catalog Shopper" and add bullets.
5. Create a header with your name at the right margin.

6. Insert a manual page break above the "Types of Stores," "Shopper Personalities," and "Conclusion" paragraphs.

7. Save the documents as *Sales Opportunities Revised*, and then preview, print, and close it.

Exercise 8 

1. Create a new, blank document and key the following text in a formal topic outline using customized outline numbering. Do not apply the italic formatting.

   Using the Proofing Tools

   Using the Spelling and Grammar Command

   Using the Thesaurus Command

   Using AutoCorrect

   Customizing AutoCorrect

   Setting AutoCorrect Exceptions

   Creating and Applying Frequently Used Text

   Inserting Standard AutoText

   Inserting Custom AutoText

   Editing, Saving, Printing, and Deleting AutoText

   Inserting Dates with AutoComplete

2. Save the document as *Proofing Topics*, and then preview, print, and close it.

Case Projects

Project 1 

Kelly asks you how to use different indent options using the Paragraph dialog box instead of the indent markers on the horizontal ruler. Using the Ask A Question Box, find and review information on indenting paragraphs. Create a new interoffice memorandum to Kelly with at least four paragraphs describing how to use the different indent options using the Paragraph dialog box, the indent markers on the horizontal ruler, and the Indent buttons on the Formatting toolbar. Save, preview, and print the document.

Project 2  

B. D. Vickers believes you can purchase and print postage over the Internet. Connect to the Internet, and search the Web for pages containing information about purchasing and printing postage on the Web. Create a favorite or bookmark for the home page at each site you visit. Create an interoffice memorandum to B. D. Vickers describing how to purchase and print postage from pages on the Web. Save, preview, and print the document.

Project 3 

One of the new employees in the Purchasing Department is having a problem creating evenly spaced lines in a document that contains large text characters on various lines. Using the Ask A Question Box, search for help topics on setting line spacing for this type of document. Create a new unbound report document with a title and a numbered list of instructions on how to change the line spacing to create evenly spaced lines with mixed-size characters. Save, preview, and print the document. With your instructor's permission, demonstrate these instructions to a classmate.

Project 4

Kelly asks you to prepare an interoffice memorandum to all Purchasing Department employees reminding them of the annual purchasing conference to be held in three weeks in Vancouver. All employees who plan to attend the conference must contact her no later than next Thursday to arrange for someone to handle their responsibilities while they are at the conference. Use character and paragraph formatting features to make the memo interesting to read and professional in appearance. Save, preview, and print the document.

Project 5  

You must complete Project 2 before beginning Project 5.

Kelly tells you that Word provides a special toolbar you can use to open your Web browser and load Web pages from inside Word. View the Web toolbar using the toolbar shortcut menu. Use the Favorites button to display a Web page with information about purchasing and printing postage on the Web. Create an interoffice memorandum to Kelly describing how to view and use the Web toolbar. Save, preview, and print the document.

Project 6

Kelly wants you to create a one-page cover sheet for an audit report on the Melbourne branch that she is completing. She wants the title of the report to contain B. D. Vickers name and title and the current date triple spaced, in a 16-point font, and centered vertically and horizontally on the page. Create the cover sheet for Kelly, and then save, preview, and print it.

Project 7 

Kelly asks you to present some troubleshooting tips on indenting text at the next meeting of the International Association of Executive Assistants. Using the Ask A Question Box, review how to indent text. Create a new document containing a list of at least five indenting troubleshooting tips. Save, preview, and print the document. With your instructor's approval, demonstrate these troubleshooting tips to several classmates.

Project 8 

You want to know more about how to use the keyboard to create bulleted and numbered lists automatically. Using the Ask A Question Box to research how to create bulleted and numbered lists automatically. Create a new document and practice creating bulleted and numbered lists automatically with the fictitious data of your choice. Save, preview, and print the document.

Word 2002

Previewing and Printing a Document

Chapter Overview

Previewing documents before printing them enables you to find errors you might otherwise not notice until you print. You can fix any problems you find right in Print Preview, whether they are text edits or formatting changes. In this chapter, you learn how to edit a document in Print Preview and set print options.

LEARNING OBJECTIVES

- Use Print Preview
- Print a document

Case profile

Worldwide Exotic Foods requires all employees to preview their documents and make necessary changes before printing to prevent reprinting and keep costs down. Kelly Armstead needs your help in previewing, editing, and printing a document she created previously. The printed document—an analysis report—then will be duplicated and distributed to the branch managers.

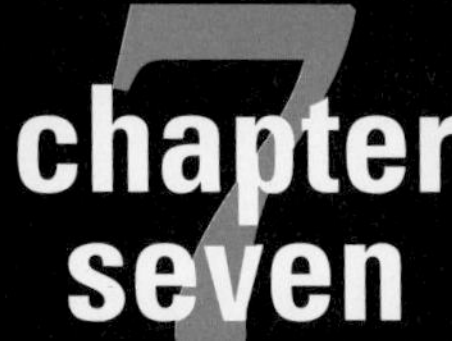

7.a Using Print Preview

Print Preview displays your document onscreen exactly as it will print on paper. When viewing a document in Print Preview, you can see one or more pages of your document. Headers, footers, margins, page numbers, text, and graphics can also be seen in Print Preview.

The document Kelly asks you to finalize and print is an *Analysis Report.* To open and preview a document:

Step 1	*Open*	the *Analysis Report* document located on the Data Disk
Step 2	*Verify*	that the insertion point is at the top of the document
Step 3	*Click*	the Print Preview button on the Standard toolbar
Step 4	*Click*	the One Page button on the Print Preview toolbar to view only the first page of the document, if necessary

MENU TIP

You can click the Print Preview command on the File menu to see how your document looks before it is printed.

The first page of the *Analysis Report* document appears in Print Preview. Your screen should look similar to Figure 7-1.

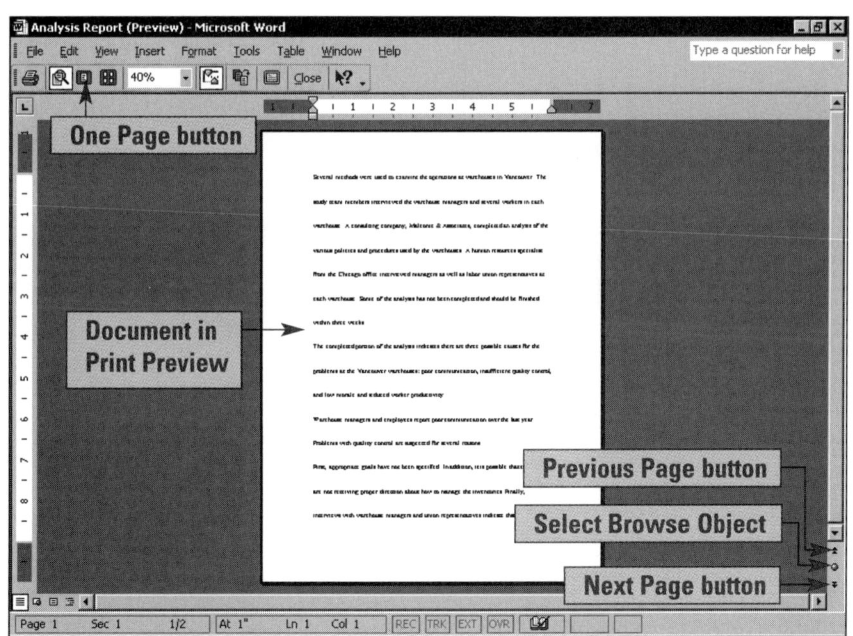

FIGURE 7-1
Print Preview

When only one page of a multiple-page document is viewed, you can use the vertical scroll bar or the Previous Page and Next Page buttons located below the vertical scroll bar to scroll between the pages.

MOUSE TIP

The Next and Previous buttons are controlled by the options in the Select Browse Object button. The default option is Page. When the Page option is selected in the Select Browse Object grid, the Next and Previous buttons have black arrows and are used to browse by page in all editing views, including Print Preview. When a different option is selected in the Select Browse Object grid, the Next and Previous buttons have blue arrows and become the Next and Previous browse buttons for the selected option. To reset the buttons to Next and Previous Page, click Page on the Select Browse Object grid.

Step 5	***Click***	the Next Page button below the vertical scroll bar to view the second page of the document
Step 6	***Click***	the Previous Page button below the vertical scroll bar to return to the first page

The One Page button on the Print Preview toolbar displays a single page at a time. You can use the Multiple Pages button on the Print Preview toolbar to view two or more small, thumbnail-sized pages. When you view several thumbnail-sized pages at one time, you can compare how the text appears on subsequent pages and where the page breaks occur. To view both pages of the *Analysis Report* document side by side:

Step 1	***Click***	the Multiple Pages button on the Print Preview toolbar to open the Multiple Pages grid
Step 2	***Point to***	the second square in the top row of the grid
Step 3	***Observe***	the 1 × 2 Pages notation at the bottom of the grid
Step 4	***Click***	the second square in the top row
Step 5	***Observe***	both pages of the document displayed side by side
Step 6	***Observe***	the dark blue border around the first page

The dark border indicates the active page of the document. Your screen should look similar to Figure 7-2.

FIGURE 7-2
Thumbnail Pages

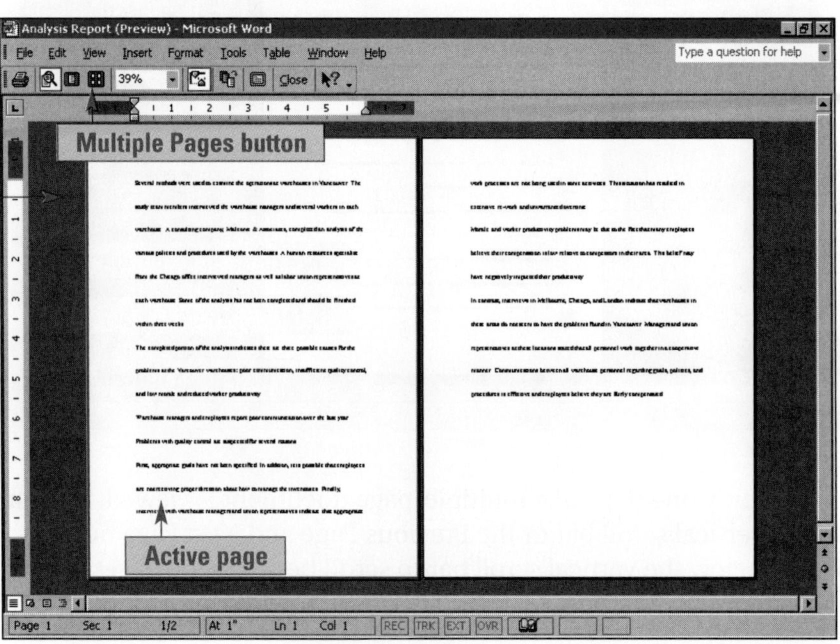

QUICK TIP

You can select and view individual pages of a multiple-page document by pressing the PAGE UP or PAGE DOWN keys.

You can zoom individual pages when viewing more than one page by first making a page the active page. To activate a page, you simply click it with the mouse pointer.

Step 7	*Click*	page 2
Step 8	*Observe*	the dark blue border around the page
Step 9	*Click*	page 1

MOUSE TIP

You can show additional toolbars in Print Preview with the toolbar shortcut menu or you can customize the Print Preview toolbar by clicking the Toolbar Options list arrow and then pointing to Add or Remove Buttons.

You also can edit your document in Print Preview. You can key text, apply formatting, set tab stops and paragraph indents, and change margins in Print Preview. For easier viewing, you can magnify, or zoom, a portion of the document with the zoom pointer or the Zoom button on the Print Preview toolbar.

The **Magnifier** button on the Print Preview toolbar is a toggle switch that turns on or off the zoom pointer. By default, the Magnifier button and the zoom pointer are turned on when you Print Preview a document. When the Magnifier button is turned on and the mouse pointer is positioned on a selected page, it changes into the zoom pointer. If multiple pages are displayed, you should first select a page by clicking it and then position the mouse pointer on it.

To view single pages and zoom the first page:

MENU TIP

You can close the Print Preview of the current document with the taskbar shortcut menu. This does not close the document. It returns you to previous Normal or Print Layout view.

Step 1	*Click*	the One Page button on the Print Preview toolbar
Step 2	*Move*	the mouse pointer to the beginning of the first paragraph on the page
Step 3	*Observe*	that the mouse pointer changes into a zoom pointer (a magnifying glass with a plus sign in the middle)

Your screen should look similar to Figure 7-3.

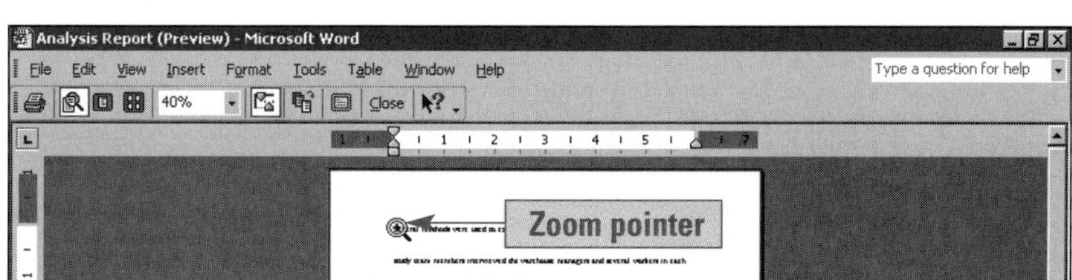

FIGURE 7-3
Zoom Pointer

Step 4	*Click*	the paragraph with the zoom pointer
Step 5	*Observe*	that the document is zoomed to 100% and you are viewing the portion of the first paragraph you clicked

Step 6	***Observe***	that the mouse pointer is still the zoom pointer (a magnifying glass with a minus sign in the middle)
Step 7	***Click***	the document with the zoom pointer

The document is zoomed to one page. You need to change the margins for the *Analysis Report* document. Because the document is in Print Preview, you can make the change here. The same formatting features that are available in Normal and Print Layout views are available in Print Preview. To set the margins for an unbound report:

Step 1	***Open***	the Margins tab in the Page Setup dialog box
Step 2	***Set***	the appropriate margins for an unbound report
Step 3	***Observe***	the new margins

To key or format selected text in Print Preview, you must first have an insertion point and an I-beam. When you turn off the Magnifier button, the insertion point appears and the mouse pointer becomes an I-beam when you position it over the document. To see the insertion point and the I-beam and zoom the document to 75%:

Step 1	***Click***	the Magnifier button on the Print Preview toolbar to turn off the zoom pointer
Step 2	***Move***	the mouse pointer to the top of the page
Step 3	***Observe***	that the mouse pointer is an I-beam and the small, flashing insertion point appears at the top of the document
Step 4	***Click***	the Zoom button list arrow 42% on the Print Preview toolbar
Step 5	***Click***	75%

Your screen should look similar to Figure 7-4. You can see the text well enough to edit it.

FIGURE 7-4
Document Zoomed to 75%

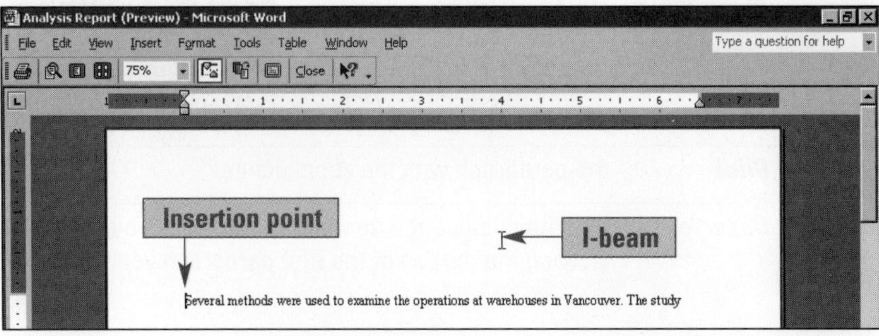

You want to indent the first line of all the paragraphs. You can show the horizontal and vertical rulers in Print Preview and then indent individual paragraphs or you can select the entire document, open the Paragraph dialog box, and indent all the paragraphs at the same time. To indent the first line of each paragraph ½ inch from the left margin:

Step 1	*Select*	the entire document
Step 2	*Open*	the Indents and Spacing tab in the Paragraph dialog box
Step 3	*Click*	the Special: list arrow
Step 4	*Click*	First line
Step 5	*Key*	.5 in the By: text box, if necessary
Step 6	*Click*	OK
Step 7	*Deselect*	the text

You want to zoom the document back to two pages so you can see your changes.

Step 8	*Click*	the Zoom button list arrow 42% on the Print Preview toolbar
Step 9	*Click*	Two Pages
Step 10	*Observe*	the indented paragraphs
Step 11	*Zoom*	the first page to 75%

The *Analysis Report* document should have a title. You can key and format that title when the Magnifier button is turned off and you see the insertion point and the I-beam. To key and format a title:

Step 1	*Insert*	a blank line at the top of the first page
Step 2	*Move*	the insertion point to the new blank line
Step 3	*Key*	Analysis Report
Step 4	*Select*	the title text using the I-beam
Step 5	*Format*	the title text with bold, 14-point font using a shortcut menu and the Font dialog box
Step 6	*Center*	the title text using a shortcut menu and the Paragraph dialog box
Step 7	*Deselect*	the title text

Step 8	*Zoom*	the first page to One Page
Step 9	*Insert*	page numbers centered at the bottom of each page

Your screen should look similar to Figure 7-5.

FIGURE 7-5
New Title, Indented Paragraphs, Page Numbers

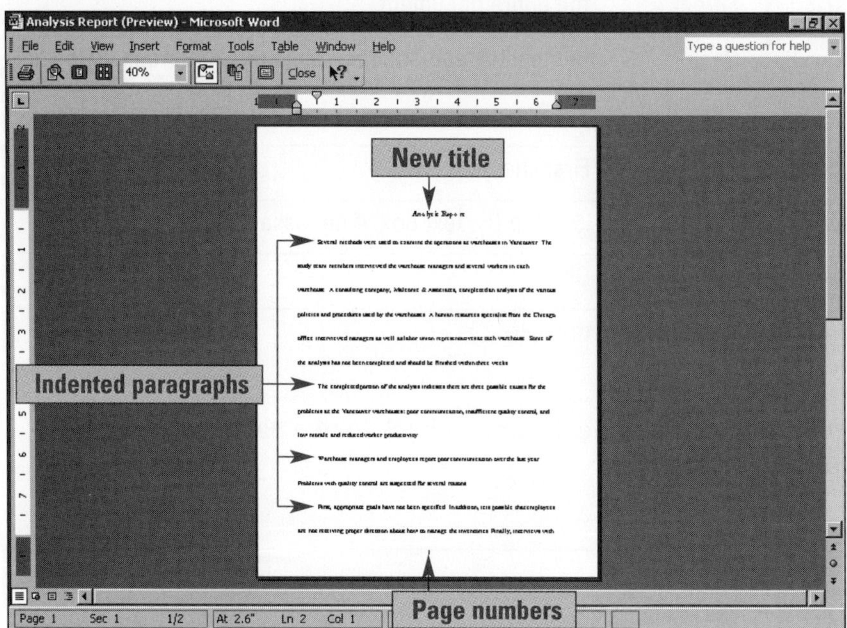

You can close Print Preview and save the document.

Step 10	*Click*	the Close button Close on the Print Preview toolbar
Step 11	*Save*	the document as *Revised Analysis Report* and leave it open

The document looks good with the correct margins, paragraph indentation, and title. You're ready to print it.

7.b Printing a Document

After you correct the margins and paragraph indentations, you are ready to print the document. Before you print it, however, you may need to change the paper size, paper orientation, or paper source. You can change these options in the Page Setup dialog box. Word provides a list of common paper sizes from which to choose, including Letter (8½ × 11 in), Legal (8½ × 14 in), and Executive (7½ × 10½ in).

You can also choose a paper **orientation** (the direction text is printed on the paper): Portrait or Landscape. **Portrait orientation** means that the short edge of the paper is the top of the page. **Landscape orientation** means that the long edge of the paper is the top of the page. To review the current settings in the Page Setup dialog box:

Step 1	*Open*	the Page Setup dialog box
Step 2	*Click*	the Paper tab

The dialog box on your screen should look similar to Figure 7-6.

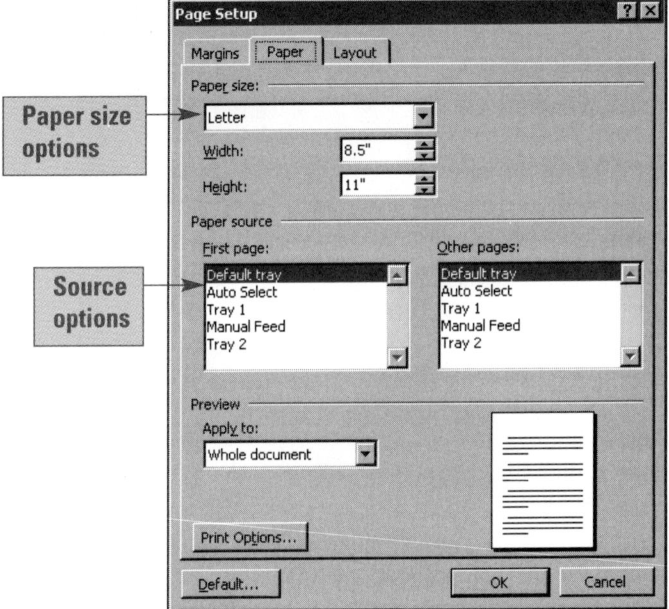

FIGURE 7-6
Paper Tab in the Page Setup Dialog Box

The Paper size: list box provides a list of preset paper sizes. You can also select a Custom size from the list, and then specify the paper dimensions in the Width: and Height: text boxes. By default, the paper size is Letter (8½ × 11 in). By default, the paper size settings apply to the whole document. You can change this option with the Apply to: list. As you change the options, the Preview area shows a sample of the document. You close the dialog box without making changes.

Step 3	*Click*	Cancel

Printing is usually your final activity in document creation. You can print a document by clicking the Print button on the Print Preview toolbar or the Standard toolbar. However, when you click the Print button, you do not get an opportunity to change the print options in the Print dialog box.

The Print command on the File menu opens the Print dialog box that contains options and print settings you can modify before printing a document. To set the print options for the *Revised Analysis Report*:

Step 1	***Click***	File
Step 2	***Click***	Print

The Print dialog box on your screen should look similar to Figure 7-7.

FIGURE 7-7
Print Dialog Box

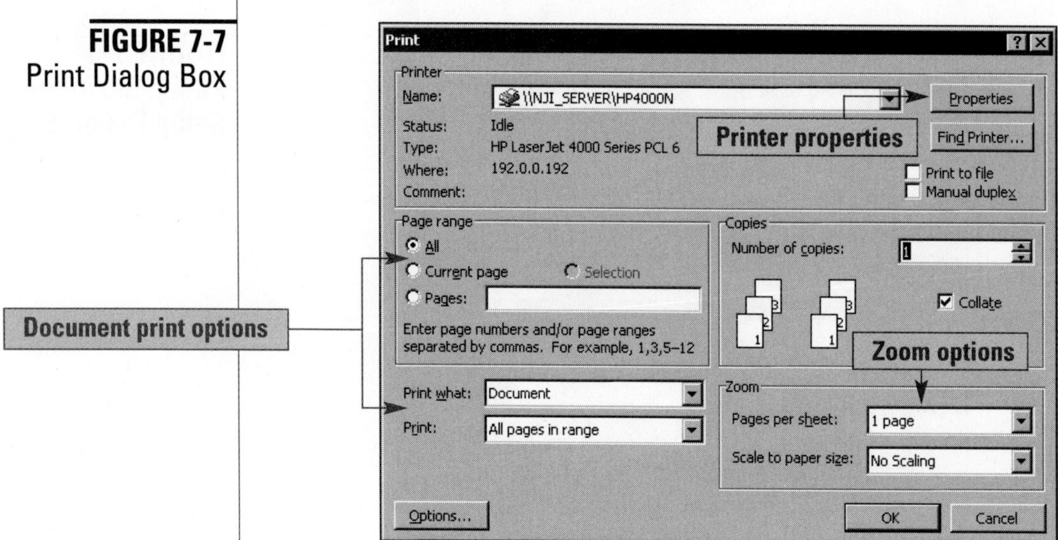

Document print options

QUICK TIP

You can print multiple consecutive pages, for example pages 3 through 6, by keying 3-6 in the Pages: text box in the Print dialog box. To print multiple, nonconsecutive pages—for example pages 3, 7, and 9—key the page numbers separated by a comma in the Pages text box.

By default, Word prints one copy of your entire document. The Print what: list box provides a list of items you can print other than your document. For example, to print a list of AutoText entries stored in the Normal template, select AutoText entries from this list.

You can specify the number of copies to print in the Number of copies: text box. The Page range group contains options for printing All pages, the Current page that contains the insertion point, the Selection of highlighted text, or the Pages you specify by page number. The Print: list box allows you to print only odd or even pages in a selected page range. By default, Word **collates** or prints copies of a multiple-page document in binding order as it prints. You can turn off the collating option by removing the check mark from the Collate check box.

Printing your document to a file is helpful if you want to print on a higher-quality printer at a different location or on a computer that does not have the Word program. You can print your document to a file on a disk rather than send it to a printer by inserting a check mark in the Print to file check box.

Sometimes you need to print on both sides of a sheet of paper. You can use the Manual duplex option to do that. For more information about printing on both sides of a sheet of paper or on folded paper, see online Help.

Text can be scaled to fit multiple pages on one sheet of paper or scaled to fit to various paper sizes in the Zoom group. Use this feature to scale larger documents to fit smaller paper or print several miniature document pages on one sheet of paper.

Selecting a Printer

The active printer is identified in the Name: list box. You can select from a list of available printers by clicking the list arrow and clicking the printer you want to use. You can view the properties such as default paper size, default page orientation, or graphics resolution for the selected printer with the Properties button.

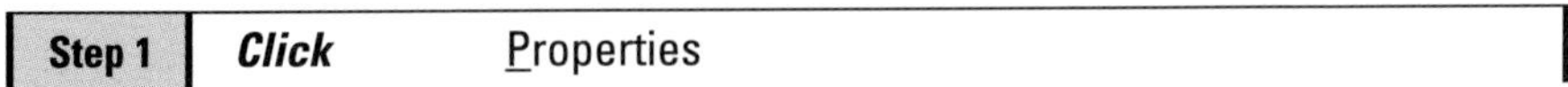

Step 1	*Click*	Properties

The Properties dialog box opens. Except for the printer name, which may be different, your dialog box should look similar to Figure 7-8.

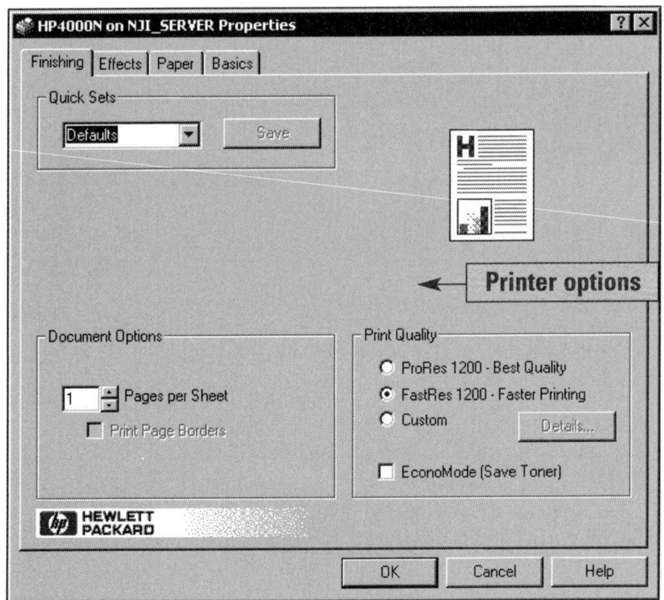

FIGURE 7-8
Printer Properties Dialog Box

After reviewing the printer properties, you can cancel the Properties dialog box.

Step 2	*Click*	Cancel

chapter seven

Kelly asks you to check the print options available for your printer.

Setting Print Options

You can specify a number of different print options by clicking the Options button in the Print dialog box or by clicking the Print tab in the Options dialog box. To review print options:

Step 1	*Click*	Options

The Print tab from the Options dialog box on your screen should look similar to Figure 7-9.

FIGURE 7-9
Print Tab from the Options Dialog Box

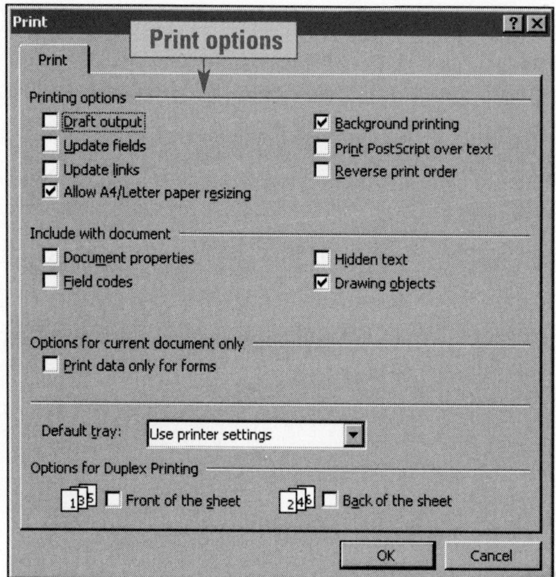

Step 2	*Review*	the options in the Print tab using the dialog box Help button
Step 3	*Close*	the Print (Options) and Print dialog boxes
Step 4	*Print*	the document
Step 5	*Save*	the document and close it

The printed *Revised Analysis Report* is ready to be duplicated and distributed to the Worldwide Exotic Foods branch managers.

Summary

- To save time and money, preview your document before printing to avoid printing a document that contains errors.
- You can view one page or multiple pages of your document in Print Preview.
- Print Preview displays headers, footers, margins, page numbers, text, and graphics.
- You can edit a document by keying text, applying formatting, setting tab stops, indenting paragraphs, and changing margins in Print Preview.
- You can turn off the Magnifier button in Print Preview and then key and edit text in the document.
- Documents can be zoomed in Print Preview by turning on the Magnifier button and clicking the document with the mouse pointer or by using the Zoom button on the Print Preview toolbar.
- You can set print and page setup options in the Print and Page Setup dialog boxes before you print your document.
- The Print button on the Print Preview or Standard toolbars prints the document without allowing you to review the settings in the Print dialog box. The Print command on the File menu opens the Print dialog box and allows you to confirm or change print options before printing a document.

Commands Review

Action	Menu Bar	Shortcut Menu	Toolbar	Task Pane	Keyboard
Preview a document	File, Print Preview				ALT + F, V CTRL + F2
View multiple pages in Print Preview					
View one page in Print Preview					
Magnify a document in Print Preview					
Print a document	File, Print				ALT + F, P CTRL + SHIFT + F12 CTRL + P

Concepts Review

Circle the correct answer.

1. By default, Print Preview displays your document:
- [a] in two pages.
- [b] in multiple pages.
- [c] exactly as it will print on paper.
- [d] in Landscape orientation.

2. The Magnifier button:
- [a] scrolls to a new page.
- [b] shows the horizontal and vertical rulers.
- [c] shows two pages side by side.
- [d] allows you to zoom your document with the mouse pointer.

3. You set the default print orientation in the:
- [a] printer Properties dialog box.
- [b] Page Setup dialog box.
- [c] Page Layout dialog box.
- [d] Options dialog box.

4. The default paper size and orientation is:
- [a] 11 × 18 inch, Portrait.
- [b] 8½ × 12 inch, Landscape.
- [c] 8½ × 11 inch, Portrait.
- [d] A4, Portrait.

5. To key or format selected text in Print Preview, you must use the:
- [a] zoom pointer.
- [b] horizontal ruler.
- [c] I-beam.
- [d] Magnifier button.

6. When Word collates a printed document, it:
- [a] saves the document to a file.
- [b] prints AutoText entries.
- [c] prints copies of multiple-page documents in binding order.
- [d] scales larger documents to fit on smaller paper.

7. The actions of the Next and Previous buttons in Print Preview are controlled by the:
- [a] vertical scroll bar.
- [b] Magnifier button.
- [c] Zoom button.
- [d] Select Browse Object button.

8. To key text in your document from Print Preview, you first:
- [a] minimize the window.
- [b] view multiple pages.
- [c] zoom the document.
- [d] turn off the Magnifier button.

9. You can view and change print options by clicking the:
- [a] Printer command on the File menu.
- [b] Options command on the Tools menu.
- [c] Print Options command on the Print Preview menu.
- [d] Set Print Options button in the Print dialog box.

10. The Print dialog box contains all of the following options except:
- [a] Print to file.
- [b] Collate copies.
- [c] Set the paper orientation.
- [d] Print selected text.

Circle **T** if the statement is true or **F** if the statement is false.

T F 1. To print only the page that contains the insertion point, you should select the All option in the Print dialog box.

T F 2. To print the entire document that you are currently editing, you should select the Current Page option in the Print dialog box.

T F 3. If you type "1-4" in the Pages text box in the Print dialog box, Word prints only pages 1 and 4 of the document.

T F 4. The Letter (8½ × 11 in) paper size is the default paper size.

T F 5. It is not possible to print only odd or even pages.

T F 6. You can change margins, tab stops, or paragraph indents in Print Preview.

T F 7. The Print button on the Print Preview toolbar opens the Print dialog box.

T F 8. By default, Word prints copies of a multiple-page document in binding order as it prints.

T F 9. You can view additional toolbars in Print Preview.

T F 10. It is possible to scale text to fit multiple pages on one sheet of paper or to fit various paper sizes.

Skills Review

SCANS

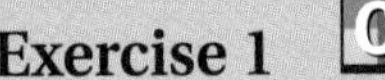

Exercise 1 

1. Open the *Vancouver Warehouse Report* document located on the Data Disk.

2. Print Preview the document.

3. Print only page 2 and close the document.

Exercise 2 C

1. Open the *Analysis Report* document located on the Data Disk.

2. Print the entire document using the Print button on the Standard toolbar in Normal view and close the document.

Exercise 3 C

1. Open the *Interoffice Meeting Memo* document located on the Data Disk.

2. Print Preview the document.

3. Apply bold formatting to the meeting day and time in the first body paragraph in Print Preview.

4. Save the document as *Interoffice Meeting Memo Edited.*

5. Print the document from Print Preview and close the document.

Exercise 4 C

1. Open the *New Expense Guidelines* document located on the Data Disk.
2. Print Preview the document.
3. Format the title with the Arial, 16-point font in Print Preview and leave the insertion point in the title paragraph.
4. Save the document as *New Expense Guidelines Revised.*
5. Print only the current page from Print Preview and close the document.

Exercise 5 C

1. Open the *Research Results* document located on the Data Disk.
2. Print Preview the document.
3. Change the top margin to 2 inches and the left and right margins to 1 inch in Print Preview.
4. Create numbered paragraphs with the last two single spaced paragraphs in Print Preview using a shortcut menu and the Bullets and Numbering dialog box.
5. Horizontally justify all the paragraphs in the document using a shortcut menu and the Paragraph dialog box.
6. Save the document as *Research Results Revised.*
7. Print the document from Print Preview and close the document.

Exercise 6 C

1. Open the *Understanding The Internet* document located on the Data Disk.
2. Print pages 1 and 3 in Normal view and close the document.

Exercise 7 C

1. Open the *Understanding The Internet* document located on the Data Disk.
2. Print Preview the document.
3. View the document in multiple pages with 4 pages on 2 rows.
4. Remove the bold, italic formatting and apply bold, small caps effect to the side (paragraph) headings in Print Preview. (*Hint:* After selecting and formatting the first bold, italic paragraph heading, use the CTRL + Y shortcut keys to copy the formatting to the other bold, italic paragraph headings.)
5. Save the document as *The Internet And The Web.*
6. Switch to Normal view and print pages 2, 4, and 6.
7. Use the Zoom options in the Print dialog box to print the entire document with two pages per sheet of paper and close the document.

Exercise 8 C

1. Create the following document.

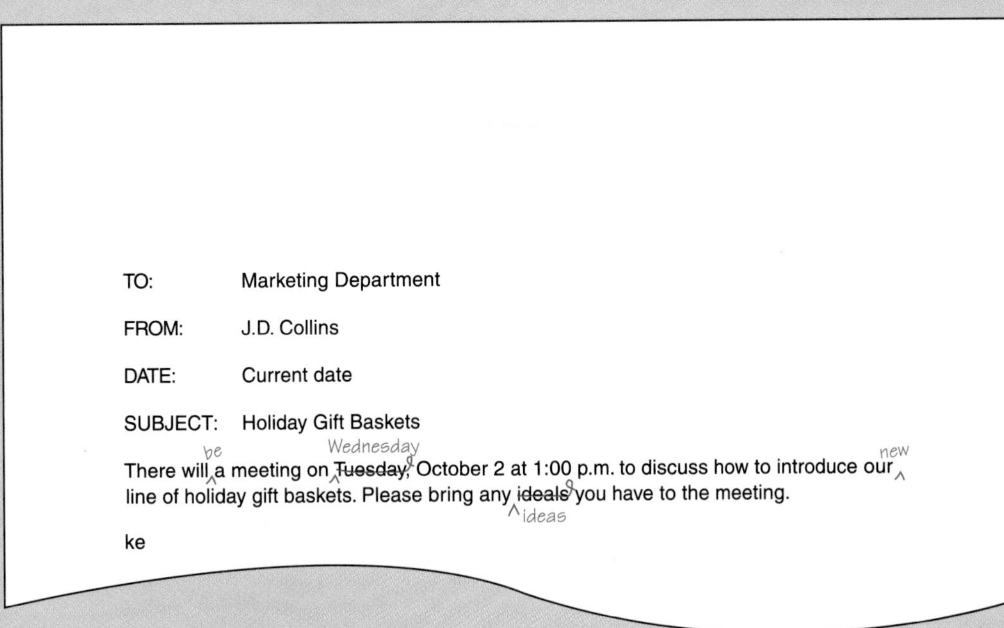

TO: Marketing Department

FROM: J.D. Collins

DATE: Current date

SUBJECT: Holiday Gift Baskets

There will be a meeting on Wednesday, October 2 at 1:00 p.m. to discuss how to introduce our new line of holiday gift baskets. Please bring any ideas you have to the meeting.

ke

2. Use the default margins and set the appropriate tab stops for the memo headings.
3. Print Preview the document.
4. Change the margins to the appropriate margins for an interoffice memorandum in Print Preview.
5. Change the font for the entire document to Arial, 12 point in Print Preview.
6. Apply bold formatting to the memo heading text "TO," "FROM," "DATE," and "SUBJECT" (do not include the colons) in Print Preview.
7. Save the document as *Holiday Gift Baskets.*
8. Print the document from Print Preview and close the document.

Case Projects

SCANS

Project 1  

Kelly wants you to review setting different print options and then create a memo to all summer interns describing the print options and how to set them. Using the Ask A Question Box, review setting print options. Create a new interoffice memorandum to all summer interns containing at least three paragraphs that describes how to use at least three print options. Save, preview, and print the document.

Project 2 

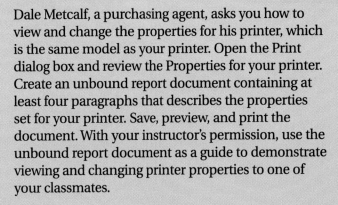

Dale Metcalf, a purchasing agent, asks you how to view and change the properties for his printer, which is the same model as your printer. Open the Print dialog box and review the Properties for your printer. Create an unbound report document containing at least four paragraphs that describes the properties set for your printer. Save, preview, and print the document. With your instructor's permission, use the unbound report document as a guide to demonstrate viewing and changing printer properties to one of your classmates.

Project 3  

You recently read an article in the company newsletter that describes Internet newsgroups (online discussion groups) and would like to know more about how to participate in them. Connect to the Internet and search for Web pages that contain information on newsgroups. Save at least two Web pages as favorites or bookmarks. Print at least two Web pages. Create an unbound report containing at least five paragraphs that describes newsgroups and how to subscribe to them. Use vertical and horizontal alignment, line spacing, and indentation options to give the report a professional appearance. Save, preview, and print the report.

Project 4  

B. D. Vickers needs to purchase several new laser printers for the Worldwide Exotic Foods and wants you to review the models that are currently available and make a recommendation. Connect to the Internet and search the Web for vendors who sell laser printers. Review information on two printers from at least three vendors. Create an interoffice memorandum to B. D. Vickers recommending one of the printers. Include each vendor's name and the printer price in the memo. Save, preview, and print the memo.

Project 5 

You are having lunch with Bob Garcia, the new administrative assistant, and he describes several problems he has when printing documents. He frequently gets a blank page at the end of his documents, sometimes the text runs off the edge of the page, he gets a "too many fonts" error when he prints a document, and occasionally the printed text looks different from the text on his screen. You offer to look into the problems and get back to him. Using the Ask A Question Box, search for troubleshooting tips for printing documents and find suggested solutions to Bob's problems. Write Bob a memo that describes each problem and suggests a solution to that problem. Save, preview, and print the memo.

Project 6 

Kelly wants a document she can use to train new employees how to set print options. She also wants to train the new employees to use the Zoom options in the Print dialog box. Open the Options dialog box and click the Print tab. Use the dialog box Help button to review each of the print options. Open the Print dialog box and review the Zoom options. Create an unbound report document titled "Print Options" and describe each of the options on the Print tab and the Print Zoom feature. Save, preview, and print the document. Attach a sample of a two-page document printed on one sheet of paper using the Zoom options.

Project 7 

You just purchased a new printer, but do not know how to set up it and define it as your default printer. Using the Ask A Question Box, research how to set up a new printer and define it as the default printer. Write Kelly Armstead a memo that discusses the process. Save, preview, and print the memo.

Project 8  

The Melbourne branch office manager is ill and B. D. Vickers wants to send flowers using a shop that accepts orders on the Web but isn't certain how to do this. Connect to the Internet, and search for Web pages with information about ordering and paying for flowers for international delivery to Melbourne, Australia. Print at least three Web pages. Create a memo to B. D. Vickers that describes how to order and pay for flowers on the Web. Save, preview, and print the memo. Attach the Web pages you printed to the memo.

Word 2002

Printing Envelopes and Labels

Chapter Overview

Every business depends on its correspondence. Letters and packages need to be sent daily. Each needs an envelope or mailing label before it can be mailed. In this chapter, you create, format, and print envelopes and labels.

LEARNING OBJECTIVES

- Print envelopes
- Print labels

Case profile

Kelly Armstead asks you to help print envelopes and labels for items that need to be mailed today. Worldwide Exotic Foods uses the U.S. Postal Service (USPS) guidelines for envelopes and mailing labels that do not have a corresponding letter. Otherwise, they follow the punctuation and case of the corresponding letter address. You create an envelope that does not have a corresponding letter, an envelope for an existing letter, an envelope and label from a list of addresses, and a sheet of return address labels for B. D. Vickers.

Because different printers have varying setup requirements for envelopes and labels, your instructor may provide additional printing instructions for the activities in this chapter.

8.a Printing Envelopes

Printing addresses on envelopes is a word processing task that almost everyone must perform at one time or another. Envelopes do not use the standard 8.5-inch × 11-inch paper on which you normally print letters and reports. A standard Size 10 business envelope is 4⅛ inches × 9½ inches, and a standard short Size 6¾ envelope is 3⅝ inches × 6½ inches. To create envelopes, you can open an existing letter and let Word identify the letter address as the envelope delivery address, or you can key the envelope delivery address in a blank document.

You can create an individual envelope by first creating a blank document. To create an envelope from a blank document:

QUICK TIP

Before you begin the activities in this chapter, you should review Appendix B, Formatting Tips for Business Documents, if you have not already done so.

Step 1	*Create*	a new, blank document, if necessary
Step 2	*Click*	Tools
Step 3	*Point to*	Letters and Mailings
Step 4	*Click*	Envelopes and Labels
Step 5	*Click*	the Envelopes tab, if necessary

The Envelopes and Labels dialog box on your screen should look similar to Figure 8-1.

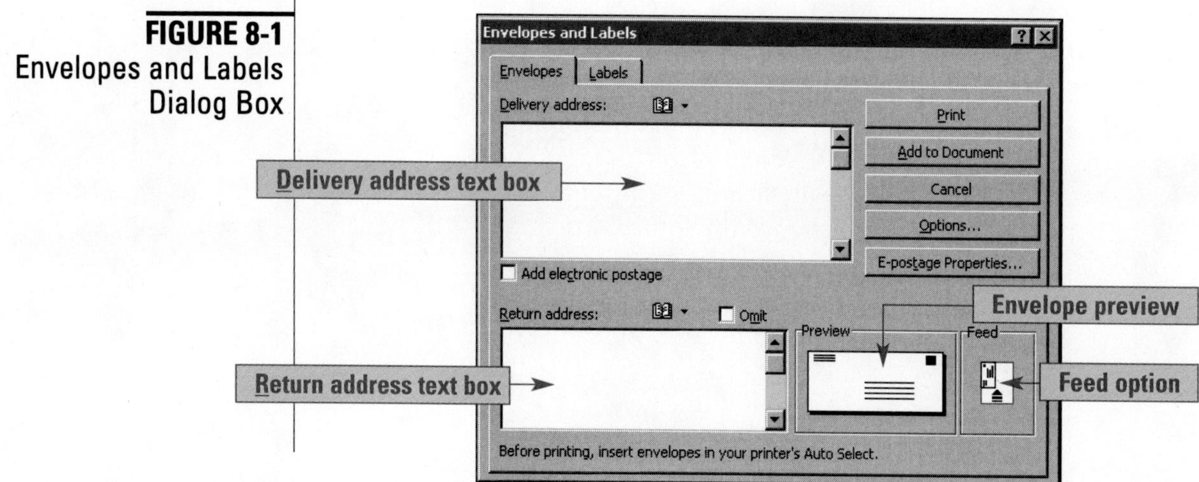

FIGURE 8-1
Envelopes and Labels Dialog Box

You key the delivery address in the Delivery address: text box. You can edit or key the return address in the Return address: text box, which contains information from the User Information tab in the Options dialog box. If you are using envelopes with a preprinted return address, you can omit printing the return address by inserting a check mark in the Omit check box. The Feed image illustrates how to insert envelopes in the current printer. You click the Options button to change envelope size, print the Delivery point barcode, add character formatting to the address text, select manual or tray feed for blank envelopes, or change the feed position. You send the envelope directly to the printer with the Print button. The Add to Document button attaches the envelope to the current document for saving and printing.

Word automatically formats the text you key in the Delivery address: text box with the Envelope Address style and the return address with the Envelope Return style. The Envelope Address style contains the sans serif Arial font with a 12-point font size. You key the delivery address using the USPS guidelines (see Appendix B). To key the envelope text:

QUICK TIP

You can change the font of the delivery or return address in the Envelopes and Labels dialog box by selecting the text and then opening the Font dialog box with a shortcut menu.

Step 1	***Verify***	that the insertion point is in the Delivery address: text box
Step 2	***Key***	MS ELAINE CHANG 719 EAST 35TH STREET ST PAUL MN 55117-1179

Because Worldwide Exotic Foods uses preprinted envelopes for all correspondence, you omit the return address. Then you select the envelope size.

Step 3	***Click***	the Omit check box to insert a check mark, if necessary
Step 4	***Click***	Options
Step 5	***Click***	the Envelope Options tab, if necessary

The Envelope Options dialog box on your screen should look similar to Figure 8-2. You can select the envelope size in the Envelope size: list box. Options for using the Facing Identification Mark (FIM-A) and Delivery point barcode to speed mail delivery are in the If mailed in the USA group. For a more detailed explanation of these two codes, see online Help. You can also change the font and position of the envelope addresses. You change the envelope size.

FIGURE 8-2
Envelope Options Dialog Box

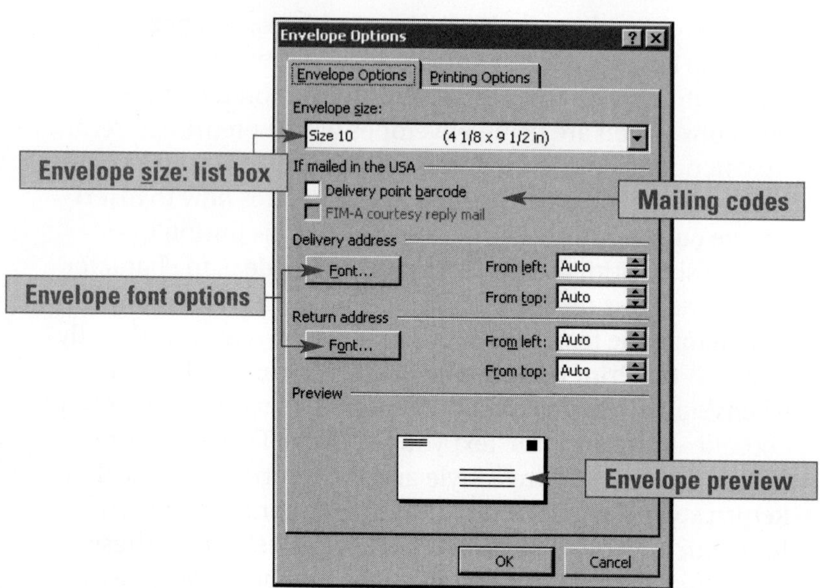

QUICK TIP

You can use the Add electronic postage check box in the Envelopes and Labels dialog box to add electronic postage to envelopes. However, before you can do this, you must have an electronic postage system installed on your computer. You can find links to electronic postage services such as Stamps.com on the Microsoft Office Update Web page. Once you have an electronic postage system installed on your computer, you can change the systems properties with the E-postage Properties button in the Envelopes and Labels dialog box. For more information on adding electronic postage to envelopes, see online Help.

Step 6	*Click*	the Envelope size: list arrow
Step 7	*Click*	Size 6¾ (3⅝ × 6½ in), if necessary
Step 8	*Observe*	that the sample envelope now displays the 6¾ size

You also set printing options in this dialog box. The current options are set for your printer. You can specify envelope rotation, face up or down, and manual or tray feed on this tab. You accept the current printing options and envelope size. To review print options:

Step 1	*Click*	the Printing Options tab
Step 2	*Observe*	the different Feed method options
Step 3	*Click*	OK

To print the envelope, you may have to manually feed a blank envelope or blank sheet of paper in your printer. If your instructor tells you to print the envelope, follow your printer's envelope setup instructions and print the envelope by clicking the Print button in the Envelopes and Labels dialog box. Otherwise you cancel the Chang envelope by closing the Envelopes and Labels dialog box.

Step 4	*Click*	Close

Another way to create an envelope is to open a document that contains a list of frequently used delivery addresses, move the insertion point to one of the addresses, and open the Envelopes and Labels dialog box. Word enters the delivery address for you. To open an address list document and create an envelope:

Step 1	***Open***	the *Envelope And Label List* document located on the Data Disk
Step 2	***Move***	the insertion point to the address for Elaine Fitzsimmons (scroll to view this address)
Step 3	***Click***	Tools
Step 4	***Point to***	Letters and Mailings
Step 5	***Click***	Envelopes and Labels

The Envelopes tab in the Envelopes and Labels dialog box opens with Elaine Fitzsimmons' address in the Delivery address: list box. Unless instructed to print the Fitzsimmons envelope by your instructor, you close the dialog box by canceling it.

Step 6	***Click***	Cancel
Step 7	***Close***	the document without saving any changes

When you open an existing letter and then open the Envelopes and Labels dialog box, Word selects the letter address exactly as it appears in the document and places it in the Delivery address: text box. B. D. Vickers' letter to Ms. Neva Johnson needs an envelope. To create and format an envelope for an existing letter:

Step 1	***Open***	the *Johnson Letter* document located on the Data Disk
Step 2	***Open***	the Envelopes tab in the Envelopes and Labels dialog box
Step 3	***Observe***	that the letter address is automatically placed in the Delivery address: text box
Step 4	***Click***	the Omit check box to remove the check mark, if necessary
Step 5	***Select***	all the text in the Return address: text box or move the insertion point to the text box if it is blank
Step 6	***Key***	B. D. Vickers Administrative Vice President Worldwide Exotic Foods, Inc. Gage Building, Suite 2100 Riverside Plaza Chicago, IL 60606-2000
Step 7	***Click***	Options and click the Envelope Options tab, if necessary

Step 8	*Click*	the Envelope size: list arrow
Step 9	*Click*	Size 6¾ (3⅝ × 6½ in), if necessary
Step 10	*Observe*	the envelope preview
Step 11	*Click*	OK

To add an envelope to the letter document so that you can edit or print both at the same time:

Step 1	*Click*	Add to Document

A confirmation dialog box opens, asking whether you want to save the new return address as the default return address for all future envelopes. If you click the Yes button, Word adds the return address information to the User Information tab in the Tools, Options dialog box. You do *not* want to change the default return address.

Step 2	*Click*	No

The envelope is added as Page 0 at the top of the document with a (Next Page) section break separating the envelope from the document. **Section breaks** divide your document into differently formatted parts. To view the envelope and letter in Print Layout view:

Step 1	*Verify*	that the insertion point is in the envelope text
Step 2	*Switch to*	Print Layout view

Your screen should look similar to Figure 8-3.

FIGURE 8-3
Envelope in Print Layout View

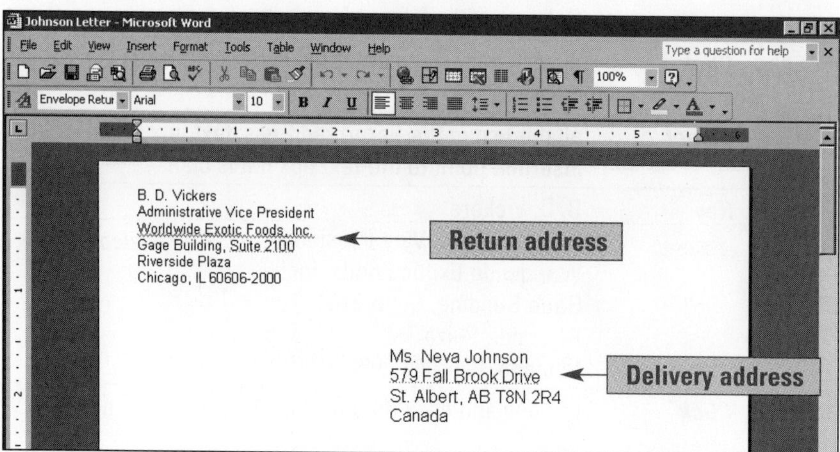

Step 3	***Scroll***	to view both the envelope and the letter, and then scroll to view just the envelope

If necessary, you can reposition the delivery address in Print Layout view by moving the frame that Word inserts around the address. A **frame** is a box added to text, graphics, or charts that you drag to reposition these items on a page. To view the frame:

Step 1	***Move***	the insertion point before the "M" in "Ms." in the delivery address

The frame around the delivery address appears. Your screen should look similar to Figure 8-4. You reposition the delivery address on the envelope by dragging and then deselecting the frame.

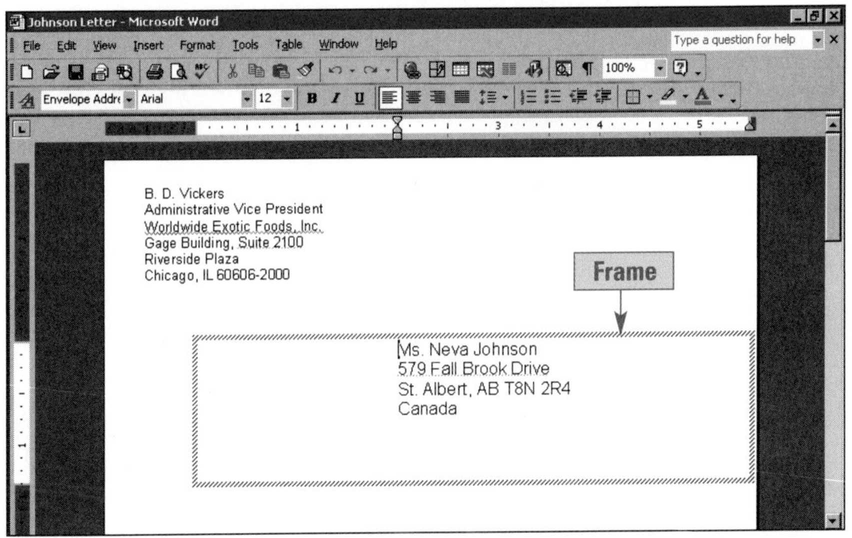

FIGURE 8-4
Frame Around the Delivery Address

Step 2	***Position***	the mouse pointer on the frame border (the mouse pointer becomes a move pointer)
Step 3	***Drag***	the frame ½ inch to the right
Step 4	***Click***	outside the frame
Step 5	***Observe***	the new position of the delivery address
Step 6	***Switch to***	Normal view
Step 7	***Save***	the document as *Johnson Letter With Envelope* and close it

Kelly also wants you to create a mailing label for an oversized envelope and to create a sheet of return address labels for B. D. Vickers.

8.b Printing Labels

You can create many different types of labels in many different sizes, such as mailing labels, name tags, file folder labels, and computer diskette labels, with the Envelopes and Labels command on the Tools menu. Word has built-in label formats for most types of labels. If you are not using a standard label, you can specify a similar label format, or you can create a custom label format.

QUICK TIP

There are labels for dot matrix printers and laser printers. Dot matrix printers use labels that pass through the printer by tractor feed. Laser and ink jet printers use labels on sheets that enter the printer through the sheet feeder. If you are using a laser printer, be sure to buy labels designed specifically for laser printers. Using labels made for a copier in a laser printer may damage your printer.

Printing Individual Labels

When you need just one label, you create it and then specify which label on a sheet of labels to use on the Labels tab in the Envelopes and Labels dialog box. Kelly asks you to create an individual label in the first row and first column on a sheet of Avery 5160 - Address labels. To create an individual label:

Step 1	***Open***	the *Envelope And Label List* document located on the Data Disk
Step 2	***Move***	the insertion point to the address for Debbie Gonzales
Step 3	***Open***	the Envelopes and Labels dialog box
Step 4	***Click***	the Labels tab
Step 5	***Observe***	that the address is inserted in the Address: text box

The default option is to print a full page of the same label. If you want to print a single label from a sheet of labels, you must specify the exact row and column position of the label. You can print a label that includes the return address in the User Information tab of the Options dialog box by inserting a check mark in the Use return address check box. As with envelopes, clicking the Options button enables you to select a label format or printer. Now you specify the label size and position.

Step 6	***Click***	the Single label option button
Step 7	***Verify***	that both the Row: and Column: text boxes contain 1, to print the label in the first row and first column of the sheet
Step 8	***Click***	Options

The Label Options dialog box on your screen should look similar to Figure 8-5. The Printer information group contains options for selecting a Dot matrix or Laser and ink jet printer, as well as Tray options. You use the Label products: list box to select an Avery or other label product list. The Product number: list box contains the list of label products by product number. The Label information group contains a description of the format for the label selected in the Product number: list box. Use the Details button to display margins, height, and width for the selected label. You also can change the pitch (the space between the labels) and the number of labels in each row or column with the Details button. Custom labels can be created and saved with the New Label button. When you create and save a custom label, it is added to the Product number: list.

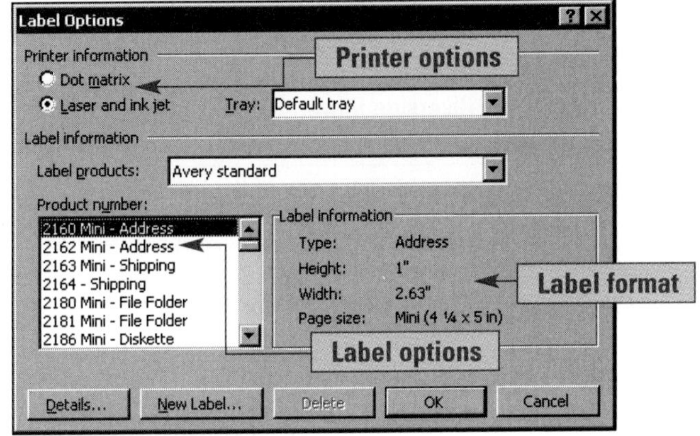

FIGURE 8-5
Label Options Dialog Box

Step 9	***Verify***	that Avery standard is in the Label products: list box
Step 10	***Click***	5160 - Address in the Product number: list box (scroll to view this option)
Step 11	***Observe***	that the label type, height, and width appear in the Label information group
Step 12	***Click***	OK

You are ready to print the label, if instructed to do so. Otherwise, cancel the Gonzales label by canceling the dialog box.

Step 13	***Click***	Cancel
Step 14	***Close***	the document without saving any changes

Next you create a sheet of return address labels for B. D. Vickers.

QUICK TIP

To quickly locate all the Avery standard labels in each numerical series, simply key the first number of the series. For example, to find the 5160 - Address label, key "5" when viewing the Product number: list in the Label options dialog box. Word scrolls the list to the series of labels that begins "5".You then can manually scroll all the labels in the 5XXX series to find the 5160 - Address label.

CAUTION TIP

The Word spelling checker does not work in the Envelopes and Labels dialog box so you should proof the address information you key very carefully.

QUICK TIP

You can use the AutoText feature to quickly insert an address in the Envelopes and Labels dialog box. Simply create the address and store it as AutoText. Then, open the Envelopes and Labels dialog box, key the AutoText name, and press the F3 key.

Printing a Sheet of Return Address Labels

The label product you use for B. D. Vickers' return address labels is the Avery 5260 - Address label. To create the labels you create a new, blank document, open the Labels tab in the Envelopes and Labels dialog box and key the address, select label options, and add the labels to the document. To create a sheet of address labels:

Step 1	*Create*	a new, blank document, if necessary
Step 2	*Open*	the Labels tab in the Envelopes and Labels dialog box
Step 3	*Verify*	that the insertion point is in the Address: text box
Step 4	*Key*	B. D. Vickers Administrative Vice President Worldwide Exotic Foods, Inc. Gage Building, Suite 2100 Riverside Plaza Chicago, IL 60606-2000
Step 5	*Verify*	that the Full page of the same label option is selected
Step 6	*Click*	Options
Step 7	*Click*	5262 - Address in the Product number: list box (scroll to view this option)
Step 8	*Click*	OK
Step 9	*Click*	New Document to create a document with labels

The new document containing a sheet of return address labels appears. Your screen should look similar to Figure 8-6.

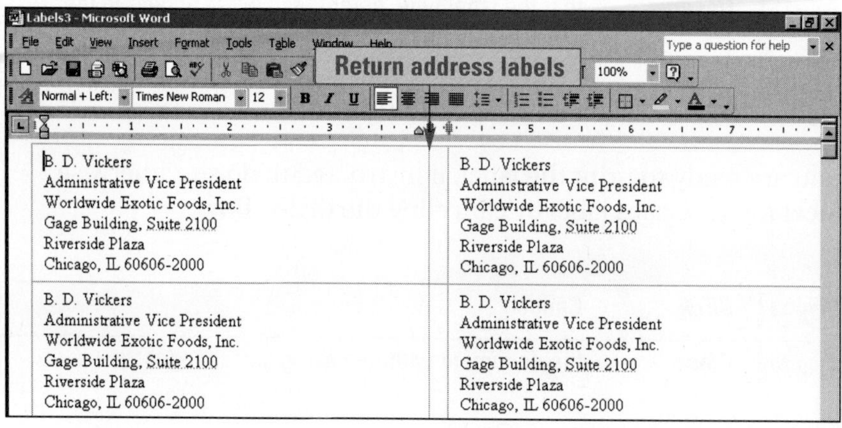

FIGURE 8-6
Sheet of Labels for B. D. Vickers

Word organizes label text in a series of columns and rows called a **table**. Each intersection of a column and row is called a **cell**. Each cell of the table represents a label that contains B. D. Vickers' return address. If you save the new label document, you can use it later to create more labels.

Step 10	***Save***	the document as *Return Address Labels* and close it

Because you saved the new label document, you can use it later to create more labels whenever B. D. Vickers runs out.

Summary

- You can send an envelope or a sheet of labels directly to a printer or you can add them to the current document. An individual label must be sent directly to the printer.
- You can create an envelope or label by keying the delivery address in the Envelopes or Labels dialog box or by selecting the delivery address in a document.
- When you create an individual envelope for a letter that is open, Word creates the delivery address from the letter address.
- Word inserts a frame or box around the delivery address on an envelope document that enables you to reposition the delivery address.
- Word adds the default return address from data found in the User Information tab of the Options dialog box, which you can change or omit.
- You can create a full sheet of the same label, or create individual labels at a specific position on the label sheet.
- You can select from a list of commonly used Avery labels, or you can create your own custom labels.

Commands Review

Action	Menu Bar	Shortcut Menu	Toolbar	Task Pane	Keyboard
Create an individual envelope, label, or sheet of the same label	Tools, Letters and Mailings, Envelopes and Labels				ALT +T, E, E

Concepts Review

Circle the correct answer.

1. To print a single label you must:
- [a] open a document that contains the label address.
- [b] specify the column and row on the label sheet.
- [c] change the return address in the User Information dialog box.
- [d] use a name tag label format.

2. A Size 10 business envelope is:
- [a] 3⅝ × 6½ inches.
- [b] 4⅛ × 9½ inches.
- [c] 3⅝ × 9½ inches.
- [d] 4⅛ × 6½ inches.

3. Labels are created and displayed in:
- [a] table format.
- [b] column format.
- [c] Landscape orientation.
- [d] only Print Preview.

4. You can modify the font, style, and size of addresses in the Envelopes and Labels dialog box with the:
- [a] Font command on the menu bar.
- [b] CTRL + Z keys.
- [c] Font command on the shortcut menu.
- [d] Change Formatting button in the Envelopes and Labels dialog box.

5. To reposition the delivery address for an envelope:
- [a] view the envelope in Print Preview.
- [b] drag the default frame to a new location.
- [c] delete the return address.
- [d] change the return address on the User Information tab in the Options dialog box.

6. The default formatting style that Word uses when you key the envelope delivery address is:
- [a] Normal.
- [b] Envelope Address.
- [c] Heading 1.
- [d] Envelope Return.

7. When you create a custom label, it is added to the:
- [a] Label products list.
- [b] Product number list.
- [c] Label options list.
- [d] Tray list.

Circle **T** if the statement is true or **F** if the statement is false.

T F 1. You can create file labels in the Envelopes and Labels dialog box.

T F 2. The return address can be omitted when creating envelopes.

T F 3. You can send an envelope directly to a printer or save it with the letter for printing later.

T F 4. If you save an envelope with the letter, Word places the envelope at the bottom of the letter.

T F 5. The USPS approved envelope format is mixed case with punctuation.

T F 6. You cannot create custom labels.

T F 7. Envelopes and labels must be printed on a laser printer.

T F 8. The Details button in the Labels tab allows you to change the margins, pitch, and number of labels on a sheet.

T F 9. The default envelope font is Times New Roman, 10 point.

T F 10. You can specify envelope rotation, face up or face down, and manual or tray feed in the Labels Options dialog box.

Skills Review

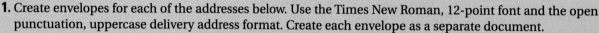

Exercise 1

1. Create envelopes for each of the addresses below. Use the Times New Roman, 12-point font and the open punctuation, uppercase delivery address format. Create each envelope as a separate document.

Mr. Thomas Williams	*Ms. Barbara Robins*
Williams Products Company	*Sunrise Orange Growers*
293 East Road	*698 Orange Grove Drive*
Houston, TX 77024-2087	*Miami, FL 33153-7634*

2. Use the Size 10 (4⅛ × 9½ in) envelope size.
3. Omit the return address.
4. Save the Williams envelope as *Williams Envelope*. Save the Robins envelope as *Robins Envelope*.
5. Preview and print the envelopes and close the documents.

Exercise 2

1. Create envelopes for each of the addresses below. Use the Arial 12-point font and open punctuation, uppercase delivery address format. Create each envelope as a separate document.

Mr. Alex Pyle	*Ms. Alice Yee*
Office Supplies, Inc.	*Raceway Park*
20343 Blue Sage Drive	*632 Raceway Drive*
Shreveport, LA 71119-3412	*Sebring, FL 33870-2156*

2. Use the Size 6¾ (3⅝ × 6½ in) envelope size.
3. Omit the return address.
4. Save the Pyle envelope as *Pyle Envelope*. Save the Yee envelope as *Yee Envelope*.
5. Preview and print the envelopes and close the documents.

Exercise 3

1. Create a sheet of labels for the following address. Use the Avery 5160 label product for laser printers.
   Ms. Ramona Mendez
   Southwest Services, Inc.
   3426 Main Street
   Dallas, TX 72345-1235
2. Format the address in the USPS style.
3. Add the labels to a new document.
4. Save the document as *Mendez Labels*, and then preview, print and close it.

Exercise 4 

1. Open the *Envelope And Label List* document located on the Data Disk.
2. Create a sheet of Avery 5260 product laser labels for John Delany as a new document.
3. Save the document as *Delany Labels*, and then preview, print, and close it.

Exercise 5 

1. Open the *Wilson Advertising Letter* document located on the Data Disk.
2. Create a Size 10 envelope.
3. Key your name and address as the return address.
4. Add the envelope to the document.
5. Do not save the new return address as the default return address.
6. Reposition the delivery address ½ inch to the right.
7. Save the document as *Wilson Advertising Letter With Envelope*, and then preview, print, and close it.

Exercise 6 

1. Open the *Wilson Advertising Letter* document located on the Data Disk.
2. Create a sheet of return labels using the Avery 5160 product for laser printers.
3. Format the labels with Times New Roman 10-point font and the uppercase and open punctuation style. (*Hint:* Remove the punctuation, select the address, right-click the address, and click Font.)
4. Add the labels to a new document.
5. Save the label document as *Wilson Labels*, preview and print the label document, and close both documents.

Exercise 7 

1. Create a sheet of nametag labels using the Avery 5362 product for laser printers. Add the labels to a new document.
2. Key the following names into the labels (*Hint:* Press the TAB key to move to the next label):
   Janice Greene
   Frances Carmichael
   Carlos Armondo
   Sarah Winters
   Felix Martinez
3. Select the entire document and change the font to Arial 20 point.
4. Apply the bold and center align formats.
5. Save the document as *Name Tags*, and then preview, print, and close it.

Exercise 8 

1. Create the following letter. Set the appropriate margins for a block-style letter.

Current date

Mr. Raul Rodriguez
Rodriguez Food Suppliers
355 Allen Drive
Houston, TX 77042-3354

Dear Mr. Rodriguez:

Congratulations on starting your own business. Given the growth of the specialty food industry, I know you will be successful.

Please send me a catalog explaining and illustrating your product lines. I hope we can do business together.

Yours truly,

Davita Washington
Purchasing Agent

ka

2. Create a Size 6¾ (3⅝ × 6½ in) envelope and format the delivery address in the approved USPS format.

3. Omit the return address.

4. Add the envelope to the document.

5. Save the document as *Solicitation Letter With Envelope.*

6. Create a sheet of return address labels using the Avery 2160 product for laser printers.

7. Add the labels to a new document.

8. Save the document as *Rodriguez Labels,* preview and print the sheet of labels, and close the documents.

Case Projects

Project 1

One of the Purchasing Department employees frequently creates return address labels and wants to be able to do this more quickly. You suggest using the AutoText feature. Create an AutoText entry for B. D. Vickers' return address. Using this AutoText entry, create a sheet of return address labels. Save, preview, and print the labels.

Project 2

You have been asked to add the POSTNET code and FIM-A code to an envelope. Using the Ask A Question Box, search online Help for information about these two codes. Create an unbound report document that describes these two codes and explains how to insert them on an envelope. Save, preview, and print the document. Attach a sample envelope with the codes inserted.

Project 3

Kelly Armstead wants to know how to print just the envelope attached to a document. Using the Ask A Question Box, research how to print only the envelope when it is attached to a document. Create an interoffice memorandum to Kelly explaining how to do this. Save, preview, and print the memorandum. Then, open an existing document with an attached envelope and print only the envelope, following the instructions in your memo to Kelly.

Project 4

At next week's "brown bag" lunch and training session for the Purchasing Department clerical staff, the discussion topic is "Printing Envelopes and Labels." You are presenting information on inserting an address from an electronic address book. Use the Ask A Question Box to locate information on your topic. Create an unbound report document that describes techniques for doing this. With your instructor's permission, explain the process to a group of classmates.

Project 5

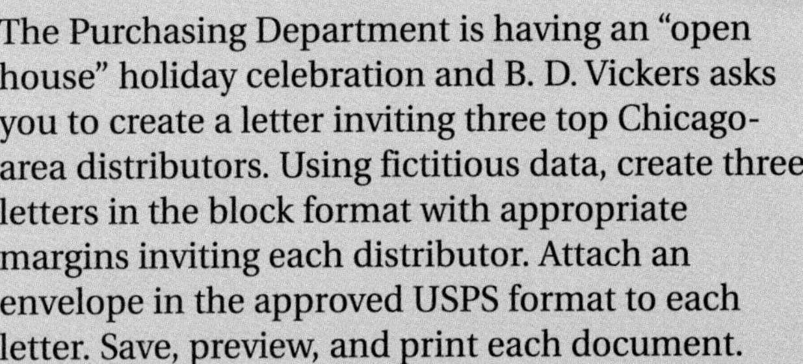

The Purchasing Department is having an "open house" holiday celebration and B. D. Vickers asks you to create a letter inviting three top Chicago-area distributors. Using fictitious data, create three letters in the block format with appropriate margins inviting each distributor. Attach an envelope in the approved USPS format to each letter. Save, preview, and print each document.

Project 6

Several important clients and their families are visiting the Chicago office next week and you have been asked to prepare a list of Chicago-area sites and facilities the families can enjoy during their visit. Connect to the Internet, and search for Chicago-area sites of interest to visitors. Print at least five Web pages. Create an interoffice memorandum to B. D. Vickers that describes the sites of interest. Save, preview, and print the memorandum.

Project 7

You have been asked to find out how to automatically add the company graphic logo to the return address each time you create an envelope. Use the Ask A Question Box to research how to do this. Create an interoffice memorandum to Kelly Armstead that describes how to add a graphic logo to the return address automatically. Save, preview, and print the memorandum.

Project 8

Worldwide Exotic Foods is going to sponsor an evening at a sports event for Chicago-area youth groups and you need to prepare a list of possible events. Connect to the Internet, and search for sports events in the Chicago area. Print at least three Web pages. Create an interoffice memorandum to Kelly Armstead that lists the sports events and Web site URLs. Save, preview, and print the memorandum.

Working with Columns, Pictures, Diagrams, and Charts

LEARNING OBJECTIVES

- Create and use newspaper columns
- Insert pictures
- Create diagrams
- Create and modify a data chart

Chapter Overview

Columns are used in many documents—from annual reports to brochures to newsletters. Often pictures, diagrams, and charts are added to documents to help explain a topic and to create an interesting and attractive format. In this chapter, you learn how to format text into columns, insert a picture, draw a diagram, and create a chart.

Case profile

Jody Haversham, in the Human Resources Department, asks you to help out for a few days. The Human Resources Department distributes the company newsletter each month. Jody assigns you the task of formatting the company newsletter for September. Jody wants the newsletter to be one page of text that includes a title and newspaper-style body text. Jody also asks you to insert appropriate pictures, a diagram, and a chart to add interest and draw attention to some aspects of the newsletter.

9.a Creating and Using Newspaper Columns

So far, you've worked with documents that are a single column, which extends from the left to the right margin. You can also create multicolumn documents, such as advertising brochures or newsletters, using **newspaper-style columns**, which divide a document into two or more vertical columns placed side-by-side on a page. When you format a document with columns, text fills the length of the first column before flowing into the next column. You can create two, three, four, or more newspaper-style columns of equal or unequal width for an entire document or for selected text in a document.

The Columns button on the Standard toolbar displays a grid from which you specify the number of equally spaced columns you want. By default, the Columns button applies column formatting to the whole document. To apply column formatting to a portion of the document, first select the text to be formatted and then select the number of columns from the Columns button grid. Word automatically inserts a continuous section break before and, if necessary, after the selected text in columns.

You begin by opening the newsletter draft document Jody prepared earlier and then you format the document text in columns. To format the text in columns, you first select the text. To open the September newsletter and format the text in columns:

Step 1	***Open***	the *September Newsletter* document located on the Data Disk
Step 2	***Select***	the text beginning "Happy Birthday!" to the end of the document
Step 3	***Click***	the Columns button on the Standard toolbar
Step 4	***Move***	the mouse pointer to the second column indicator on the grid
Step 5	***Observe***	the text "2 Columns" at the bottom of the grid
Step 6	***Click***	the second column indicator on the grid

Word creates the newspaper-style columns and automatically switches to Print Layout view, if necessary. You can view multiple columns in Print Layout view or Print Preview but not in Normal view. When the text in the first column reaches the bottom of the page, the remaining text shifts automatically to the next column. This can create uneven columns lengths. For example, the second column in the *September Newsletter* document is not as long as the first column.

MENU TIP

You can click the Columns command on the Format menu to specify the number of newspaper-style columns, set columns of equal or unequal width, add a vertical line between columns, or choose between five preset column formats.

QUICK TIP

You can insert an en dash to separate dates by pressing the CTRL + HYPHEN (-) keys. You can insert a nonbreaking space by pressing the CTRL + SHIFT + SPACEBAR keys.

To view the columns:

Step 1	*Deselect*	the text
Step 2	*Zoom*	the document to Whole Page to view the two newspaper-style columns

Your screen should look similar to Figure 9-1.

FIGURE 9-1
Text in Columns

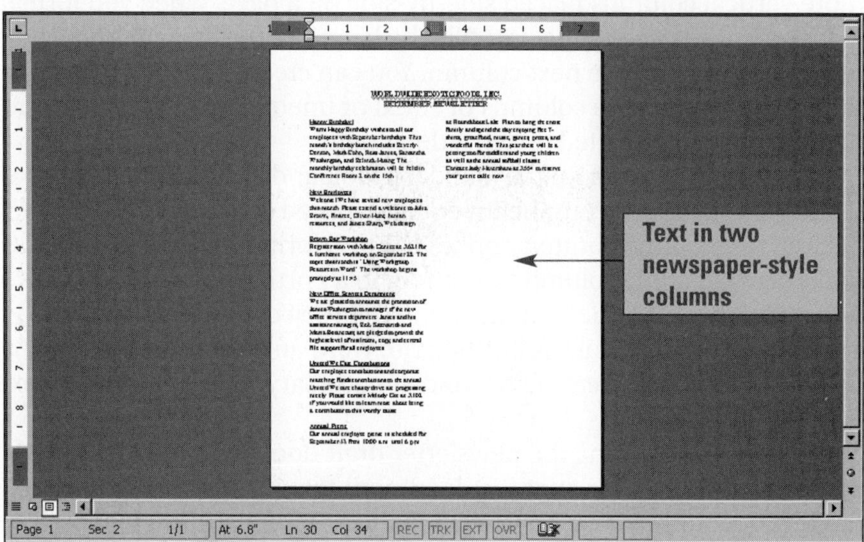

Step 3	*Zoom*	the document to 75% so you can read the text

Although the two-column format looks great, you decide to see how the document looks with other column formats.

Revising the Column Layout

The Columns dialog box provides a variety of formatting options that save you time creating newspaper-style columns. The five preset newspaper-style column formats are: One column, Two columns, Three columns, Left column, and Right column. The One, Two, and Three column formats create even column widths. The Left and Right column formats create uneven column widths. You can also add a horizontal line as a divider between the columns. To revise the column structure:

Step 1	*Move*	the insertion point into the two-column text, if necessary
Step 2	*Click*	Format
Step 3	*Click*	Columns

The Columns dialog box on your screen should look similar to Figure 9-2.

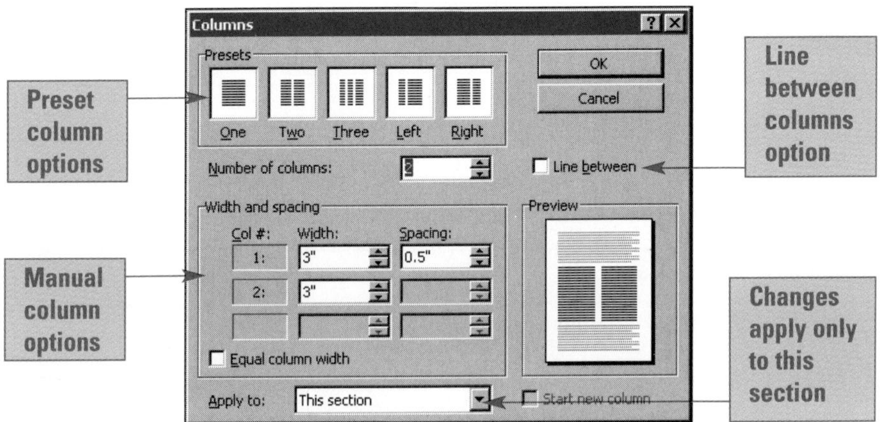

FIGURE 9-2
Columns Dialog Box

MOUSE TIP

You can change column widths by dragging the column indicator on the horizontal ruler with the mouse.

You try two newspaper-style columns with uneven widths.

Step 4	***Click***	Left in the Presets group
Step 5	***Click***	OK
Step 6	***Zoom***	the document to Whole Page and review the columns

The text is in a narrow left and a wide right column. You prefer two evenly spaced columns but want to add a vertical line between them. To change the column structure and add the line:

Step 1	***Open***	the Columns dialog box
Step 2	***Click***	Two in the Presets group
Step 3	***Click***	the Line between check box to insert a check mark
Step 4	***Click***	OK

QUICK TIP

Move the insertion point to the desired position and press the CTRL + SHIFT + ENTER keys to insert a column break.

Word cannot remove a manual column break when it applies a different column format to text. To reformat columns, you should remove any manual column breaks by moving the insertion point to the right of the column break and pressing the BACKSPACE key.

To make the newsletter more attractive, you can balance the column length.

Modifying Column Text Alignment

You can modify the text alignment within the columns by balancing the column length. To balance column length, you can insert manual column breaks that force text into the next column. Manual column breaks are inserted with an option in the Break dialog box. Manual column breaks can be deleted and reinserted, if necessary, as you

MENU TIP

You can also balance column length by inserting a continuous section break at the end of each column. To insert a continuous section break, click the Break command on the Insert menu.

continue to edit the document. To insert a manual column break in the *September Newsletter* document:

Step 1	***Move***	the insertion point to the left margin of the paragraph "United We Care Contributions"
Step 2	***Click***	Insert
Step 3	***Click***	Break
Step 4	***Click***	the Column break option button
Step 5	***Click***	OK
Step 6	***Zoom***	the document to 100%
Step 7	***Save***	the document as *September Newsletter Revised* and leave it open

To make the *September Newsletter Revised* document more interesting to readers, Jody asks you to add an appropriate picture to the Happy Birthday! and Annual Picnic paragraphs.

9.b Inserting Pictures

Word comes with a set of pictures you can access from the Clip Organizer. You can import pictures into the Clip Organizer from other sources, or you can insert pictures in your document from disk files without first importing them into the Clip Organizer.

MOUSE TIP

You can insert pictures from the Clip Organizer by clicking the Insert Clip Art button on the Drawing toolbar. You can insert pictures from your hard drive, network drive, or a diskette by clicking the Insert Picture button on the Drawing toolbar.

Your Clip Organizer might contain different pictures than the ones used in this chapter. If necessary, you can substitute pictures from those available in your Clip Organizer in the activities in this chapter.

Jody tells you that there are some great pictures in the Clip Organizer. You begin by opening the Clip Organizer using a button on the Drawing toolbar and then searching for the appropriate images. To display the Drawing toolbar and open the Clip Organizer:

Step 1	***Click***	the Drawing button on the Standard toolbar to view the Drawing toolbar
Step 2	***Observe***	the Drawing toolbar, which, by default, is docked at the bottom of the window above the status bar
Step 3	***Click***	the Insert Clip Art button on the Drawing toolbar

The Add Clips to Organizer dialog box may open. If you have additional picture, motion, or sound files located on your hard drive, you can catalog those files into the folders you specify and have the files appear in the Clip Organizer.

Step 4	*Click*	Later to close the Add Clips to Organizer dialog box, if necessary
Step 5	*Observe*	the Insert Clip Art task pane

Your screen should look similar to Figure 9-3.

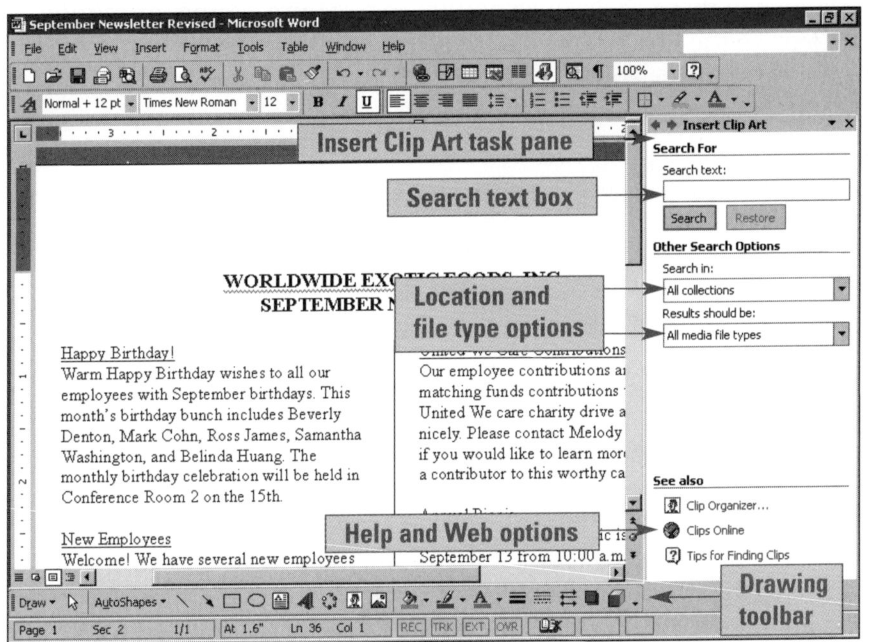

FIGURE 9-3
Drawing Toolbar and Insert Clip Art Task Pane

Clip Organizer picture, sound, and motion clips are stored in different folders, called catalogs or collections. Each picture, sound, or motion clip is associated with a series of keywords that help identify the clip. One way to locate suitable pictures in the Clip Organizer is to search for them by keyword. You can enter a keyword in the Search text: text box, select the collection in which to search from the Search in: list, and then select the type of file for which to search in the Results should be: list. To search for an appropriate birthday picture using the keyword "birthday":

Step 1	*Key*	birthday in the Search text: text box in the Insert Clip Art task pane
Step 2	*Verify*	that All collections appears in the Search in: list box in the Insert Clip Art task pane

MENU TIP

You can insert pictures located on your hard drive, network drive, or a diskette by clicking Insert, pointing to Picture, and clicking From File.

QUICK TIP

The Drawing toolbar also contains buttons you can use to draw lines and arrows, rectangles and squares, ovals and circles, and other shapes such as WordArt text, special charts, and AutoShapes.

TASK PANE TIP

You can insert pictures from the Clip Organizer using the Insert Clip Art task pane by clicking Insert, pointing to Picture, and then clicking Clip Art.

TASK PANE TIP

In addition to importing pictures from other sources, you can go directly to a special Web page containing additional pictures and import them directly into the Clip Organizer with the Clips Online link in the Insert Clip Art task pane. You can get online Help for the Clip Organizer by clicking the Tips for Finding Clips

Step 3	***Verify***	that All media file types appears in the Results should be: list box in the Insert Clip Art task pane
Step 4	***Click***	the Search button in the Insert Clip Art task pane
Step 5	***Observe***	that the Results: grid containing clips appears in the Insert Clip Art task pane (it may take a few seconds for the clips to appear)
Step 6	***Scroll***	the Results: grid in the Insert Clip Art task pane to see the available clips
Step 7	***Point to***	the first picture in the Results: grid in the Insert Clip Art task pane

When you move the mouse pointer to a picture, sound, or motion clip icon in the Results: grid, a list arrow and a ScreenTip containing the associated keywords, file type, and file size appear. Your screen should look similar to Figure 9-4.

FIGURE 9-4
Search Results in Clip Art Task Pane

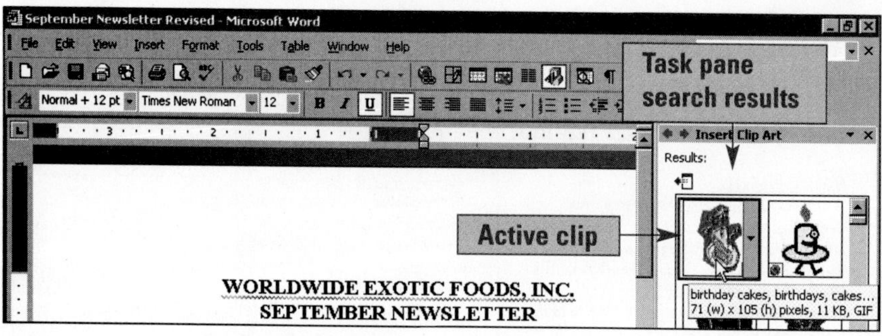

MOUSE TIP

When a picture object is selected, the Picture toolbar may appear automatically. If it does not appear, you can display it with a command on the toolbar shortcut menu. The Picture toolbar has buttons you use to edit the picture.

You can insert a selected picture or other clip in your document, copy it to the Office Clipboard, delete it from the Clip Organizer, move it to another collection, add or edit the keywords associated with the file, and view a picture's properties by clicking the list arrow.

A quick way to insert a picture is to drag it from the Insert Clip Art task pane into your document. To drag the birthday picture of your choice into the *September Newsletter* document:

Step 1	***Drag***	the birthday picture of your choice from the Insert Clip Art task pane to the left margin of the "Warm Happy…" paragraph in the first column
Step 2	***Close***	the Insert Clip Art task pane
Step 3	***Observe***	that the picture is inserted into the document as a selected object and that the Picture toolbar may appear

Your screen should look similar to Figure 9-5.

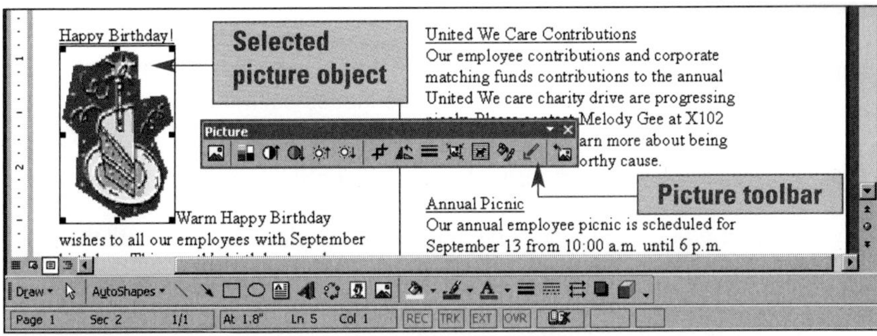

FIGURE 9-5
Selected Picture Object and Picture Toolbar

A Word document has a text "layer" in which the text and pictures appear and additional "layers" that allow you to position pictures and other objects in front of or behind the text. The default is for pictures to be inserted in the same "layer" as the text, or **in line** with the text, which means that the picture is on the same line as text that appears before or after it. When a picture is in line with text, you can position it with the alignment buttons on the Formatting toolbar, just as you would text. You can size a picture object proportionally by dragging a corner sizing handle. If you want to size a picture object proportionally while maintaining its center position, press and hold the CTRL key as you drag a corner sizing handle.

Now that the birthday picture is inserted in the text, you need to reposition and resize it. A picture object is automatically selected when it is inserted. You deselect a picture object by clicking in the document outside the picture object; you select a picture for editing, sizing, or repositioning by clicking the picture object. A selected picture object that is in line with the text has a border and eight sizing handles around the border. You can size a picture object with the mouse by dragging a sizing handle. To deselect and then select and size the birthday picture object:

Step 1	***Click***	in the document outside the picture object to deselect it
Step 2	***Click***	the picture object to select it
Step 3	***Drag***	the picture object's lower-right corner sizing handle diagonally up approximately ½ inch

You want to position the picture at the right margin of the paragraph and then let the text wrap down the left side of the picture. To edit the text wrapping and reposition the picture object:

Step 1	***Verify***	that the picture object is still selected

TASK PANE TIP

You can insert a clip at the insertion point by clicking the clip in the Insert Clip Art task pane.

MENU TIP

You can format a selected picture (including the text wrapping) with the Picture command on the Format menu or the Format Picture command

QUICK TIP

You can delete a picture, by selecting the picture and pressing the DELETE key.

chapter nine

Step 2	*Click*	the Text Wrapping button on the Picture toolbar
Step 3	*Click*	Square
Step 4	*Observe*	that the picture object now has clear round sizing handles, and that the mouse pointer becomes a move pointer when placed on the selected picture object
Step 5	*Drag*	the picture object to the right margin of the paragraph
Step 6	*Continue*	to reposition and resize the picture object until the picture object is attractively positioned at the right margin and the text wraps attractively down the left side of the picture
Step 7	*Deselect*	the picture object

Your screen should look similar to Figure 9-6.

FIGURE 9-6
Resized and Repositioned Picture

MOUSE TIP

When you want text to wrap around or through a picture, you use the Text Wrapping button on the Picture toolbar to select the Square, Tight, Behind Text, or In Front of Wrapping style. When you select one of these options, you can reposition the picture by dragging it to a new location with the mouse pointer.

Step 8	*Display*	the Insert Clip Art task pane and search for an appropriate picture for a "picnic"
Step 9	*Drag*	the picture to the "Our annual employee picnic…" paragraph
Step 10	*Wrap*	the text around the picture using the Square option
Step 11	*Resize*	and reposition the picture attractively in the paragraph
Step 12	*Save*	the document and leave it open
Step 13	*Close*	the Insert Clip Art task pane

Jody wants you to add a diagram to a paragraph.

9.c Creating Diagrams

Diagrams and organization charts are often used instead of, or in addition to, text to explain complex relationships and ideas. For example, cycle diagrams show a process with a continuous cycle, radial diagrams illustrate relationships to and from a central core element, pyramid diagrams show foundation-based relationships, Venn diagrams illustrate areas that overlap between elements, and a target diagram shows steps toward a goal. An organization chart illustrates hierarchical relationships between people in an organization. You use the Insert Diagram or Organization Chart button on the Drawing toolbar to turn on the drawing canvas and insert special diagrams. To insert a Venn diagram:

MENU TIP

You can insert a diagram chart object with the Diagram command on the Insert menu.

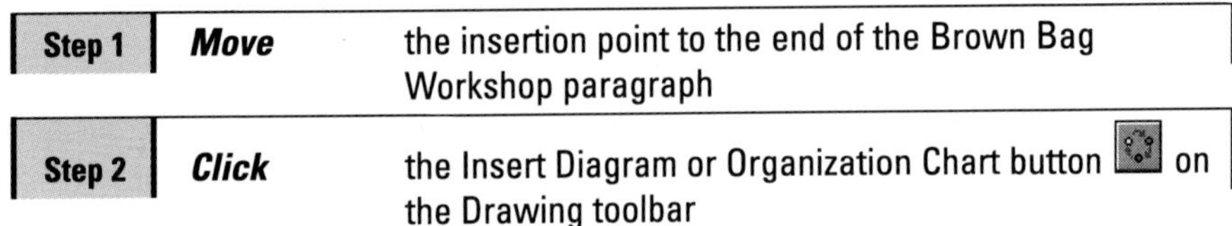

Step 1	*Move*	the insertion point to the end of the Brown Bag Workshop paragraph
Step 2	*Click*	the Insert Diagram or Organization Chart button on the Drawing toolbar

Your Diagram Gallery dialog box should look similar to Figure 9-7.

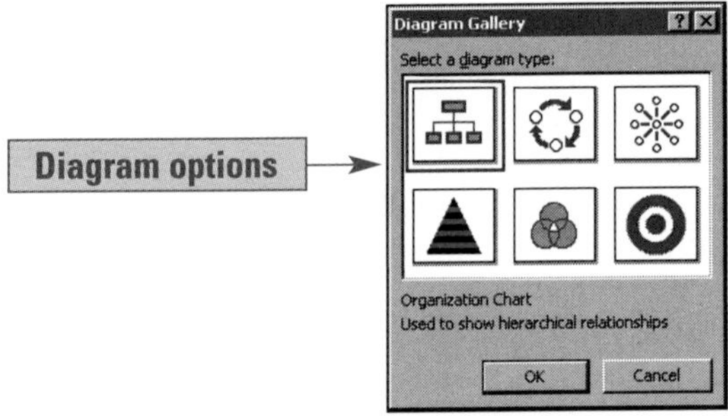

FIGURE 9-7
Diagram Gallery Dialog Box

Step 3	*Double-click*	the Venn Diagram icon (the second icon in the second row)

MOUSE TIP

You can change the diagram element shape, position, size, formatting, and text wrapping with buttons on the Diagram toolbar.

The Diagram toolbar appears and the drawing canvas contains the components of a Venn diagram. Your screen should look similar to Figure 9-8.

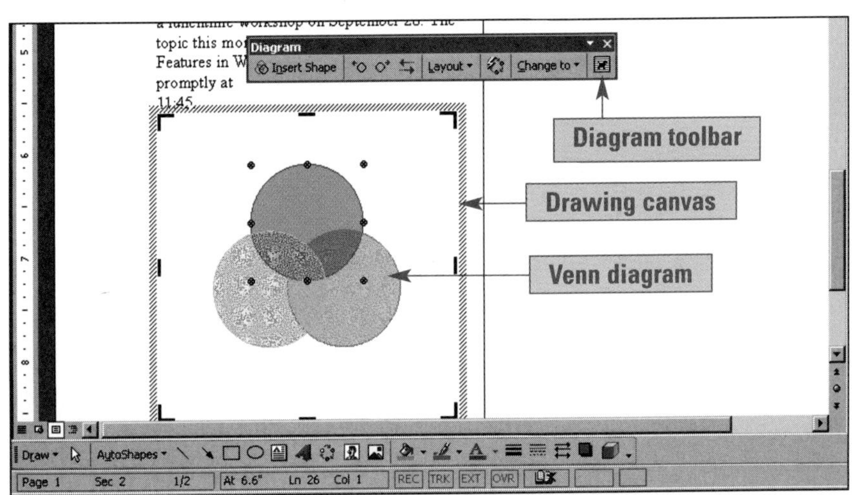

FIGURE 9-8
Drawing Canvas and Venn Diagram

chapter nine

You resize the diagram so you can better position it. To size the diagram from its center to approximately ⅙ its original size:

Step 1	***Click***	the Layout button on the Diagram toolbar
Step 2	***Click***	Scale Diagram
Step 3	***Observe***	the drawing canvas round sizing handles
Step 4	***Press & hold***	the CTRL key
Step 5	***Drag***	the lower-right sizing handle diagonally up and to the left to size the diagram to approximately ⅙ its original size

QUICK TIP

Word contains a drawing canvas that is used to create drawing objects such as diagrams and organization charts. The drawing canvas allows you to more easily position a diagram, organization chart, or other drawing objects in a Word document.

You can choose from a variety of diagram styles. To change the diagram format to remove the fill color and modify the line color:

Step 1	***Click***	the AutoFormat button on the Diagram toolbar

The Diagram Style Gallery dialog box on your screen should look similar to Figure 9-9. You select a style for your diagram from a variety of outline and fill styles in this dialog box.

FIGURE 9-9
Diagram Style Gallery Dialog Box

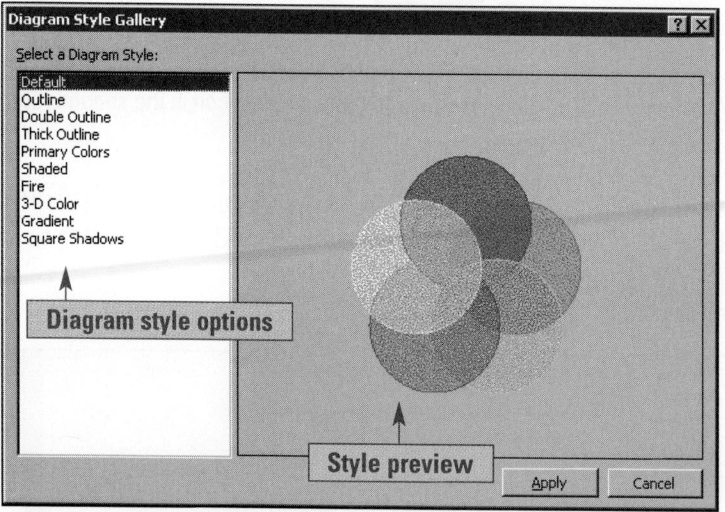

MOUSE TIP

You can preview a diagram by clicking it. You can double-click a diagram to edit it.

Step 2	***Double-click***	3-D color in the Select a Diagram Style: list

You now move the diagram into the "layer" behind the text and reposition it.

Step 3	***Click***	the Text Wrapping button on the Diagram toolbar
Step 4	***Click***	Behind Text
Step 5	***Drag***	the diagram to the center of the paragraph (place the mouse pointer on the diagram's border to see the move pointer)
Step 6	***Deselect***	the diagram
Step 7	***Observe***	that the diagram is visible behind the paragraph text

MOUSE TIP

You can click an individual diagram component to select it and then format it using buttons on the Drawing toolbar—such as the Fill Color, Line Color, Font Color, and Shadow Style buttons.

To finish the newsletter document you insert a chart comparing the actual employee and corporate contributions to the United We Care charity to the contribution goals.

9.d Creating and Modifying a Data Chart

CAUTION TIP

You can select a diagram placed behind the text by using the Special option in the Find dialog box to find a graphic image and the Highlight all items found in: option set to Text Boxes in Main Document.

Microsoft Graph is a supplementary application that comes with Office. With this application you can present numerical information as a **chart**, which is a pictorial representation of data or the relationship between sets of data. Common chart styles include bar charts, pie charts, and line charts.

Creating a Chart

You can create a Word chart by selecting data keyed in a table and then importing it into a chart datasheet or by keying the data directly into the chart datasheet. Jody gives you the data in Table 9-1, which you key into a chart datasheet.

TABLE 9-1
Chart Data

Label	Data
Employee Contributions	100,000
Corporate Contributions	50,000
Contribution Goal	250,000

To insert the data chart below the "Our employee contributions…" paragraph in the second column:

Step 1	***Move***	the insertion point to the end of the paragraph
Step 2	***Press***	the ENTER key

Step 3	*Click*	Insert
Step 4	*Click*	Object
Step 5	*Click*	the Create New tab in the Object dialog box, if necessary

Your Object dialog box should look similar to Figure 9-10.

FIGURE 9-10
Create New Tab in the Object Dialog Box

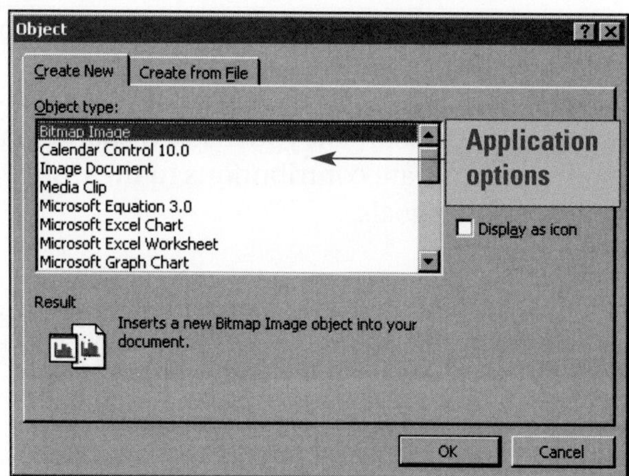

QUICK TIP

A datasheet contains many of the same features as an Excel worksheet; you enter, select, and edit data in the same way you would if you were working with an Excel worksheet.

Step 6	*Double-click*	Microsoft Graph Chart in the Object type: list (scroll to view this option, if necessary)

Word displays a chart based on the sample data contained in the datasheet. Your screen should look similar to Figure 9-11.

FIGURE 9-11
Sample Chart and Datasheet

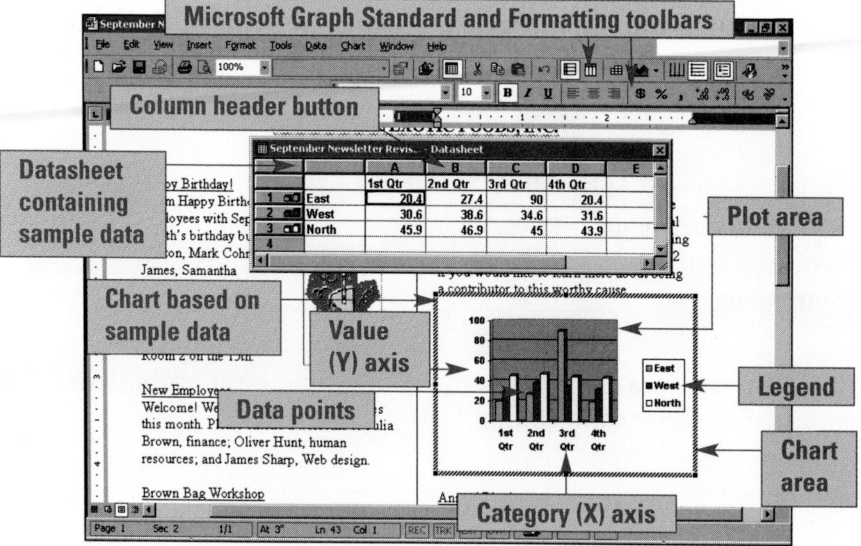

A datasheet is similar to a Word table and contains columns (A, B, C, etc.) and rows (1, 2, 3, etc.). The intersection of a column and row is called a cell. For example, cell A1 is at the intersection of column A and row 1. The unnumbered row immediately below the column header buttons is used to enter text labels for the columns. The remaining rows contain data and row labels for that data. The unlettered column immediately to the right of the row header buttons is used to enter text labels for the rows. You activate a cell to enter text or numbers by clicking the cell with the mouse pointer, which becomes a large white plus sign pointer when positioned in the datasheet. The active cell has a dark black border around it.

You can replace the sample data by keying new data in each cell or by deleting the sample data before you key the new data. To enter data in a cell, you activate the cell, key the data, and then press the ENTER key. To key the chart labels:

Step 1	*Click*	the first cell in column A (currently contains "1st Qtr")
Step 2	*Key*	Contributions
Step 3	*Press*	the ENTER key
Step 4	*Click*	the first cell in row 1 (currently contains East)
Step 5	*Key*	Employee
Step 6	*Press*	the ENTER key to enter the text and move the active cell indicator down to row 2
Step 7	*Key*	Corporate
Step 8	*Press*	the ENTER key to enter the text and move the active cell indicator down to row 3
Step 9	*Key*	Goal
Step 10	*Press*	the ENTER key

You follow the three-step process to enter the contribution values. To enter the values in column A:

Step 1	*Enter*	100,000 in the second cell in row 1 (currently contains 20.4)
Step 2	*Enter*	50,000 in the second cell in row 2 (currently contains 30.6)
Step 3	*Enter*	250,000 in the second cell in row 3 (currently contains 45.9)

MOUSE TIP

You can widen a column by placing the mouse pointer on the right boundary between column header buttons and dragging the boundary to the right or left.

QUICK TIP

You can move the datasheet out of the way, if necessary, by dragging its title bar.

QUICK TIP

Both Word charts and Excel charts are created using the Microsoft Graph features. This means that all the chart creation and editing features available in Excel are also available in Word when you open the Microsoft Graph application.

CAUTION TIP

Be careful when you use the double-click method to edit a chart object. Because the chart objects are positioned so closely, it's easy to accidentally double-click an adjacent object instead of the intended object. An alternative to double-clicking an object is to use the Chart Objects and Format Objects buttons on the Microsoft Graph Standard toolbar to select an object and open its formatting dialog box or to right-click an object and click the Format (selected object) command.

MOUSE TIP

You can select individual chart objects by clicking the Chart Objects button list arrow on the Microsoft Graph Standard toolbar and selecting a chart item from the list. Then you can open the formatting dialog box for that object by clicking the Format Object button on the Microsoft Graph Standard toolbar.

You can delete the remaining sample data or simply hide the columns. To hide columns B–D and view the chart in the newsletter document:

Step 1	***Double-click***	the Column B, C, and D header buttons
Step 2	***Observe***	the changes to the chart
Step 3	***Click***	in the document outside the chart area and datasheet
Step 4	***Observe***	the chart

Jody reviews the newsletter and suggests you modify the chart. To change the chart type to a simple column chart, remove the plot area color, and change the column colors.

Modifying a Data Chart

Microsoft Graph inserts a chart into a Word document as an embedded object. An **embedded object** must be edited with the tools of the application in which it was created, sometimes called the **source application**. To edit the embedded chart, you can double-click it to open Microsoft Graph and then edit each chart item, called a chart object—such as the legend, the data points (columns), the plot area, or the Category (X) or Value (Y) labels. To modify individual chart objects, you can double-click the object or right-click the object to open its formatting dialog box.

To modify the embedded chart:

Step 1	***Double-click***	the chart object to open Microsoft Graph
Step 2	***Click***	the Chart Type button list arrow on the Microsoft Graph Standard toolbar
Step 3	***Click***	Column Chart (first item in the third row)
Step 4	***Right-click***	the gray plot area
Step 5	***Click***	Format Plot Area to open the Format Plot Area dialog box

The Format Plot Area dialog box on your screen should look similar to Figure 9-12.

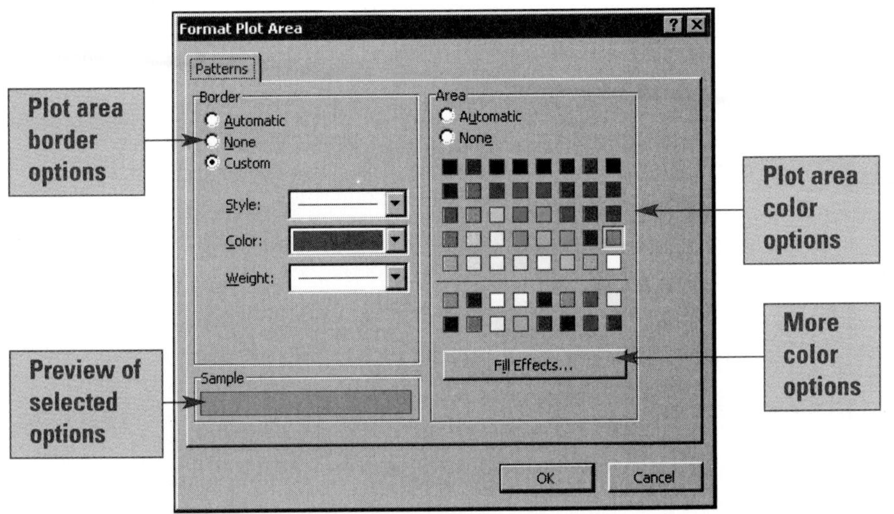

FIGURE 9-12
Format Plot Area Dialog Box

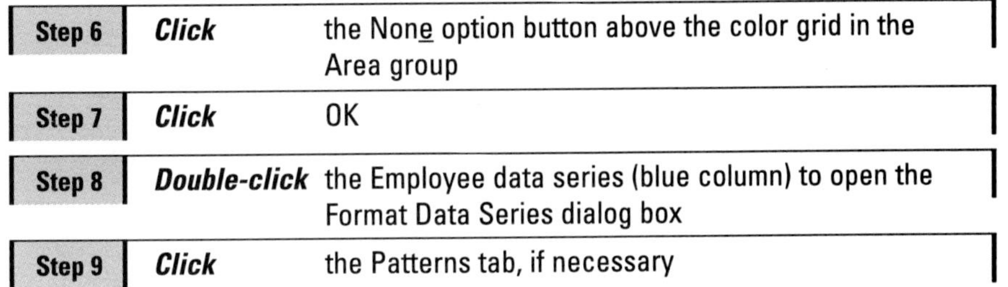

Step 6	***Click***	the None option button above the color grid in the Area group
Step 7	***Click***	OK
Step 8	***Double-click***	the Employee data series (blue column) to open the Format Data Series dialog box
Step 9	***Click***	the Patterns tab, if necessary

The Format Data Series dialog box on your screen should look similar to Figure 9-13.

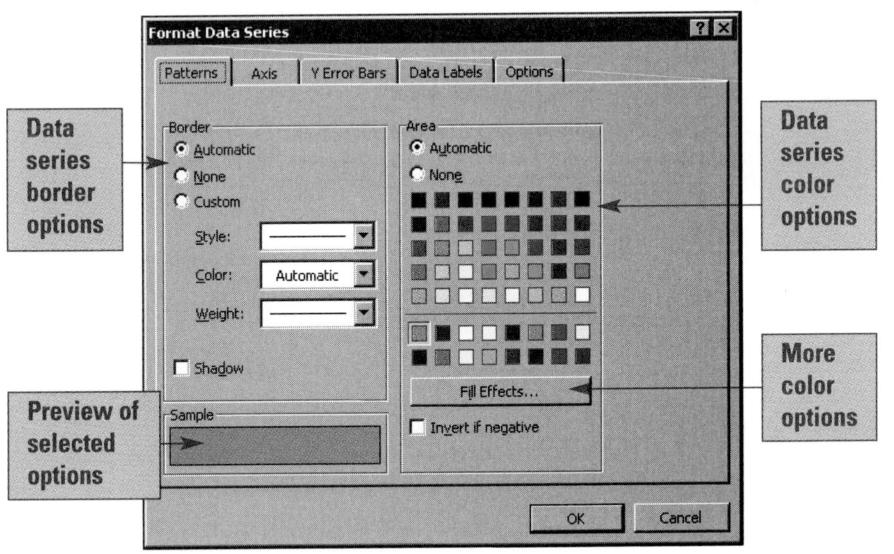

FIGURE 9-13
Format Data Series Dialog Box

Step 10	*Click*	the Red square (first color in the third row) in the Area color grid
Step 11	*Click*	OK
Step 12	*Change*	the Corporate data series (maroon column) to Blue (sixth color in the second row)
Step 13	*Change*	the Goal data series (yellow column) to Green (fourth color in the second row)
Step 14	*Deselect*	the chart

To view the completed newsletter document:

Step 1	*Print Preview*	the document

The previewed document on your screen should look similar to Figure 9-14.

FIGURE 9-14
Completed Document

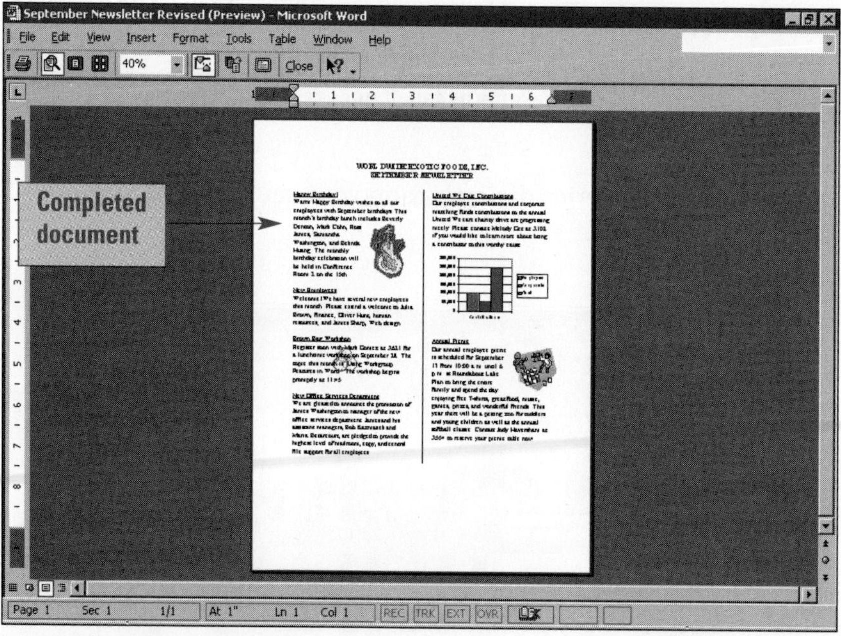

Step 2	*Close*	Print Preview
Step 3	*Close*	the Drawing toolbar
Step 4	*Save*	the document and close it

The September newsletter is completely formatted. Jody will have the newsletter copied and then distribute it appropriately.

Summary

- Newspaper-style columns are appropriate for documents such as brochures or newsletters.
- When you use newspaper-style columns, the text fills the length of the first column before flowing to the next column.
- Newspaper-style columns can be created for an entire document or a section of a document.
- You can select text and create columns from the selected text, or you can insert a section break and then create columns for the text in a specific section.
- Text columns can be viewed in Print Layout view or Print Preview, but cannot be viewed in Normal view.
- You can create columns of unequal width by using one of the two preset unequal-width column options or by specifying the exact column width in the Columns dialog box.
- A vertical divider line can be added between columns.
- You can insert pictures from the Clip Organizer using the Insert Picture button on the Drawing toolbar.
- You can insert and edit diagrams with the Insert Diagram or Organization Chart button on the Drawing toolbar.
- You can create a data chart object in Word using the Microsoft Graph application.
- You enter data into a chart by keying the data into the datasheet.
- A chart is inserted into a Word document as an embedded object that must be edited with options in Microsoft Graph, the source application.
- You can select individual chart items, called chart objects, and then format them.

Commands Review

Action	Menu Bar	Shortcut Menu	Toolbar	Task Pane	Keyboard
Create newspaper columns	Format, Columns				ALT + O, C
Insert a column break	Insert, Break				ALT + I, B CTRL + SHIFT + ENTER
Insert a picture	Insert, Picture, Clip Art Insert, Picture, From File			Drag a picture from the Results: section of the Insert Clip Art task pane into the document	ALT + I, P, C ALT + I, P, F

Action	Menu Bar	Shortcut Menu	Toolbar	Task Pane	Keyboard
Text wrapping for selected picture	Format, Picture	Right-click picture, click Format Picture			ALT + O, I
View the Drawing toolbar	View, Toolbars, Drawing	Right-click any toolbar, click Drawing			ALT + V, T
Insert a diagram	Insert, Diagram				ALT + I, G

Concepts Review

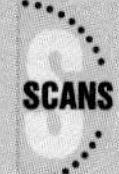

Circle the correct answer.

1. The Columns dialog box contains all of the preset options for creating columns except:
[a] Right.
[b] Center.
[c] Left.
[d] Two.

2. Which task pane is used to insert pictures, sound, and motion clips?
[a] Insert Media Clips
[b] Insert Picture Art
[c] Insert Clip Art
[d] Insert Clip Media

3. Word presents collections or catalogs of picture, sound, and motion clips in the:
[a] Clip Organizer.
[b] Media Organizer.
[c] Art Organizer.
[d] Picture Organizer.

4. When you use the Columns button to create newspaper-style columns, the columns are formatted into:
[a] unequal column widths.
[b] equal column widths.
[c] vertical column widths.
[d] justified column widths.

5. To balance columns of uneven length, you should insert a(n):
[a] page break.
[b] even page section break.
[c] column break.
[d] line break.

6. Which of the following is not a text wrapping option for picture objects?
[a] Near
[b] Square
[c] Tight
[d] Behind Text

7. The diagram that illustrates the relationship to and from a central element is:
[a] Venn.
[b] Pryamid.
[c] Radial.
[d] Cycle.

8. A datasheet is a(n):
[a] embedded object.
[b] source application.
[c] worksheet of columns and rows.
[d] picture object.

9. You can use sizing handles to:
[a] format picture objects.
[b] position text in newspaper-style columns.
[c] change the size and shape of picture objects.
[d] embed picture objects.

10. The drawing canvas is used to:
[a] position picture objects in line with the text.
[b] control the position of drawing objects such as diagrams.
[c] insert data charts.
[d] wrap text around picture objects.

Circle **T** if the statement is true or **F** if the statement is false.

T F 1. With default newspaper-style columns, text fills one column before flowing to the next column.

T F 2. Columns appear on the screen only in Print Layout view.

T F 3. You can redistribute text in columns by inserting a manual page break.

T F 4. A chart is a pictorial representation of numerical data or the relationship between sets of numerical data.

T F 5. The Microsoft Graph application is used to create charts in a Word document.

T F 6. You can view vertical lines between columns in Normal view.

T F 7. You can create a manual column break with the CTRL + SHIFT shortcut keys.

T F 8. Diagrams and charts are used to help readers understand complex relationships and ideas.

T F 9. A datasheet consists of rows, columns, and cells, and is similar to a Word table.

T F 10. You can size a picture object proportionally while maintaining its center position by pressing the CTRL key while dragging a corner sizing handle.

Skills Review

Exercise 1

1. Open the *Legislative Update* document located on the Data Disk.

2. Select all the text below the second title line "LEGISLATIVE UPDATE."

3. Format the selected text with two columns of even width.

4. Insert column breaks so that the columns are approximately the same length.

5. Add a vertical line between the columns.

6. Switch to Normal view and select the two lines of title text.

7. Expand the character spacing in the title text by 0.5 points. (*Hint:* Use the Character Spacing tab in the Font dialog box.)

8. Save the document as *Legislative Update With Columns*, and then preview, print, and close it.

Exercise 2

1. Create a new, blank document.

2. Center and bold the title "Targeted Sales by Department" in 14-point Times New Roman font and press the ENTER key twice.

3. Display the Drawing toolbar.

4. Insert a Target diagram.

5. Click the outside ring of the target to select it and then change the color to red. (*Hint:* Click the Fill Color button list arrow on the Drawing toolbar and click red on the color grid.)

6. Change the color of the middle ring to black and the center ring to white.

7. Click the "Click to add text" text box for the outside ring and key "A=1M." Key "B=2M" as the middle ring text and "C=3M" as the center ring text. Size the diagram appropriately.
8. Save the document as *Target Diagram*, and then preview, print, and close it.

Exercise 3 C

1. Open the *Announcements* document located on the Data Disk.
2. Find all instances of underlined text and replace it with no underline and Small caps effect. (*Hint:* use the Format button in the Find and Replace dialog box to find and replace formatting.)
3. Format the entire document in two columns of uneven width using the Right preset option.
4. Replace the "For Sale:" text with an appropriately sized and positioned picture.
5. Save the document as *Announcements Revised*, and then preview, print, and close it.

Exercise 4 C

1. Create a new, blank document.
2. Center the title "Radial Diagram" in Arial, 14-point, bold font and press the ENTER key twice.
3. Display the Drawing toolbar.
4. Insert a Radial diagram.
5. Add two additional elements. (*Hint:* Click the Insert Shape button on the Diagram toolbar once for each additional element you wish to add.)
6. Change the format to Primary Colors. (*Hint:* Use the AutoFormat button on the Diagram toolbar.)
7. Add the centered text of your choice formatted with the white color to each of the diagram elements. Click an element, click the Font Color button list arrow on the Drawing toolbar and click white in the color grid, then key the text. Reposition the diagram attractively below the heading text.
8. Save the document as *Radial Diagram*, and then preview, print, and close it.

Exercise 5 C

1. Open the *Chicago Warehouses Audit* report located on the Data Disk.
2. Select the body text (not the title) and format it in two columns of even width.
3. Insert a manual column break at the paragraph beginning "A consulting company…." to balance the columns.
4. Insert a vertical line between the columns.
5. Save the document as *Chicago Warehouses Audit With Columns*, and then preview, print, and close it.

Exercise 6 C

1. Open the *Travel Services* document located on the Data Disk.
2. Create newspaper-style columns for the body text beginning with "Pink Beach" paragraph heading.
3. Insert, size, and position (including wrapping the text attractively) an appropriate picture for each of the paragraphs.
4. Insert a manual column break as needed to balance the columns attractively.
5. Save the document as *Travel Services Revised*, and then preview, print, and close it.

Exercise 7 

1. Open the *Office Technology Society* document located on the Data Disk.
2. Create three columns of equal width for the body text (do not include the title) and insert appropriate manual column breaks. Add a vertical line between the columns.
3. Insert, format, and size the diagram of your choice and position it behind the text in column 2.
4. Save the document as *Office Technology Society Revised*, and then preview, print, and close it.

Exercise 8 

1. Open the *Training Commitment* document located on the Data Disk.
2. Move the insertion point to the second blank line following the second body paragraph.
3. Insert a data chart using the following data. Key the text "Employees" as the heading in the first cell below column A. Hide columns B–D.

Label	***Data***
Sales and Marketing	*35*
Accounting	*50*
Information Technology	*125*
All Other	*130*

4. Format the data chart as a Column Chart, change the Plot Area to white, change the data points to the colors of your choice.
5. Add data label values to the chart. Click the Chart Options command on the Chart menu and select the Value option on the Data Labels tab.
6. Position the chart legend below the Category (x) axis. Click the Chart Options command on the Chart menu and select the Bottom option on the Legend tab.
7. Center the chart object. After clicking in the document to close the Microsoft Graph application, click the chart to select it, and then click the Center button on the Formatting toolbar.
8. Save the document as *Training Commitment With Chart*, and then preview, print, and close it.

Case Projects

Project 1

You are the secretary for the local chapter of the Office Technology Society and you prepare a quarterly newsletter for all chapter members. Create a newsletter titled "OFFICE TECHNOLOGY BULLETIN" with two newspaper-style columns of body text containing fictitious data for the following paragraph headings: *Membership Drive*; *New Members*; *Annual Conference*; *User Tips for Word 2002*; and *Hot Internet Sites*. Add a line between the columns. Add an appropriate picture, sized and positioned attractively at the bottom of column 2. Save, preview, and print the document.

Project 2

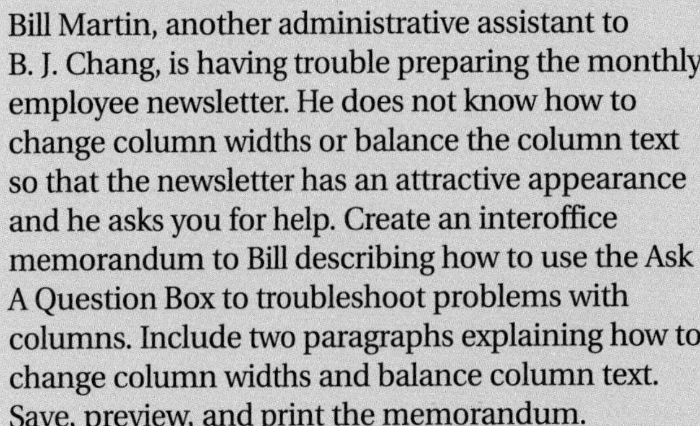

Bill Martin, another administrative assistant to B. J. Chang, is having trouble preparing the monthly employee newsletter. He does not know how to change column widths or balance the column text so that the newsletter has an attractive appearance and he asks you for help. Create an interoffice memorandum to Bill describing how to use the Ask A Question Box to troubleshoot problems with columns. Include two paragraphs explaining how to change column widths and balance column text. Save, preview, and print the memorandum.

Project 3  

Your new assignment in the Human Resources Department is to fill in for the corporate librarian while she is at a conference. Joe Beck in the Finance Department requests a list of investment-oriented online magazines and newsletters. Using the Internet and Internet search tools, search for investment-oriented online newsletters and magazines. Print at least two Web pages for each type. Create an interoffice memo to Joe describing the results of your search. Use two evenly spaced columns separated by a line for the Web page descriptions. Add an appropriate picture or diagram to the memo. Attach the Web pages you printed.

Project 4

Bill Martin drops by your desk to tell you about the different diagrams he discovered in Word. You want to experiment with creating these diagrams and then tell Kelly Armstead and Jody Haversham about them. Create a new, blank document. Display the Drawing toolbar, and explore creating at least three different diagrams and formatting them with buttons on the Diagram toolbar and the Drawing toolbar. Save, preview, and print the document.

Project 5

Chris Lofton, the manager of the Word Processing Department, calls and asks you to present a brief "brown bag" seminar on tips and tricks for inserting, sizing, positioning (including text wrapping) pictures in Word documents. Create an outline of the topics you will present at the seminar. Save, preview, and print the outline. Then, with your instructor's permission, use the outline to show several classmates how to insert, size, and position pictures in a Word document.

Project 6

The Human Resources Department is helping a neighborhood civic association to hold its annual fund-raising bake sale by providing clerical support for the association. You are asked to create a flyer that can be copied and posted at Create an 8½ × 11-inch flyer using fictitious data announcing the bake sale. Include appropriately sized and positioned pictures in the flyer. Save, preview, and print the flyer.

Project 7  

Bill Martin calls and asks you for help. B. J. Chang wants a list of Web-based training classes covering office technology topics and Bill is not familiar with the WWW. You agree to search for the Web sites and write a memo to Chang. Using the Internet and Internet search tools, search for Web sites providing online classes in office technology topics. Print at least three Web pages. Write an interoffice memorandum to B. J. Chang describing the results of your search. Use columns and pictures to make the memo more interesting. Save, preview, and print the memorandum. Attach the Web pages to the memorandum.

Project 8 

Your recent "brown bag" seminars for the word processing staff have been so well received that Chris Lofton, the manager of the Word Processing Department, asks you to prepare another seminar on inserting data charts into a Word document. Create a new, blank document and create a Word table containing fictitious data. Select the data and insert a Microsoft Graph data chart below the table. Experiment with modifying the chart using different chart types and experiment with the options in the Chart Options dialog box. Also experiment with ways to format the different chart objects and then close the document without saving it. Create an outline of the topics you will present at the seminar. Save, preview, and print the outline. With your instructor's permission, use the outline to show several classmates how to create and format charts in a Word document.

Creating Basic Tables

Chapter Overview

Certain columnar data included in a document, such as budgets and price lists, needs to be organized in a logical manner so that it is easier to read and understand. You could use tabs to organize this data, but usually it is simpler to place it in a table. In this chapter, you learn how to create and edit tables.

Learning Objectives

- Create and format tables
- Modify tables
- Position tables
- Apply AutoFormats to tables

Case profile

The Marketing and Sales Departments at Worldwide Exotic Foods, Inc. are getting ready for the busy holiday shopping season and need assistance preparing correspondence and reports. You are assigned to handle the work overflow for both departments. You begin by creating a letter containing a table of data for the media budget.

10.a Creating and Formatting Tables

R. D. Jacobson, the media director for the Marketing Department, gives you a page of handwritten notes and asks you to use the notes to create a letter to the advertising agency that develops the media buying plans for Worldwide Exotic Foods. The letter contains the media budget for this year's holiday season. Jacobson's executive assistant, Maria Betancourt, suggests you use a table to organize the budget data in the letter. You begin by creating a new, blank document and keying part of text. To create the letter:

Step 1	***Create***	a new, blank document
Step 2	***Set***	the appropriate margins for a block format letter
Step 3	***Key***	the current date, letter address, salutation, and first two body paragraphs shown in Figure 10-1

FIGURE 10-1
Completed Dynamic Advertising Letter

Current date

Ms. Sue Wong
Account Executive
Dynamic Advertising Agency
3268 West International Blvd.
Dallas, TX 75211-1052

Dear Ms. Wong:

Please extend our thanks and congratulations to everyone at the Dynamic Advertising Agency who works on the Worldwide Exotic Foods, Inc. account. Because of the outstanding media program developed by your team last year, we experienced exceptional holiday sales.

We anticipate holiday sales for this year to exceed last year. Therefore, we are increasing this year's media budget by 20%. The budget is detailed below:

Worldwide Exotic Foods, Inc. Media Budget			
Branch Office	**Holiday Baskets**	**Beverage Baskets**	**Gift Certificates**
Chicago	$133,175	$55,321	$11,500
London	74,768	46,987	10,589
Melbourne	97,509	30,890	1,561
Vancouver	458,321	138,079	15,345

We can discuss these budget figures in detail at our media program meeting next week.

Sincerely,

R. D. Jacobson
Media Director

xx

Step 4	*Press*	the ENTER key twice

The next part of the letter contains the table of information. A **table** is a grid organized into columns and rows. A **column** is a set of information that runs down the page. A **row** runs across the page. A **cell** occurs at the intersection of a column and row. First, you create the table grid and key the data in the table cells. Then, you can add or remove the table border and format the text using the same formatting features you use for the body text.

The Insert Table button on the Standard toolbar displays a grid from which you select the number of rows and columns for the table, simply by dragging the mouse pointer down and across the grid. To create a table with five rows and four columns:

Step 1	*Click*	the Insert Table button on the Standard toolbar
Step 2	*Move*	the mouse pointer to the upper-left square in the grid
Step 3	*Observe*	the text "1 × 1 Table" at the bottom of the grid, indicating that one row and one column are selected
Step 4	*Drag*	the mouse pointer down five rows and across four columns (until you see 5 × 4 Table at the bottom of the grid)
Step 5	*Release*	the mouse button to create the table
Step 6	*Scroll*	to view the table, if necessary
Step 7	*Save*	the document as *Dynamic Advertising Letter* and leave it open

The insertion point automatically appears in the first cell of the table. Whenever the insertion point is in the table, column markers also appear on the horizontal ruler. Word inserts table nonprinting formatting marks, called **end-of-cell** and **end-of-row marks**, in the table. You use these formatting marks to select cells, rows, and columns.

Step 8	*Click*	the Show/Hide button on the Standard toolbar to view the table formatting marks

Your screen should look similar to Figure 10-2.

MENU TIP

You can create a table by pointing to the Insert command on the Table menu and clicking Table.

MOUSE TIP

You can create a table with the Insert Table button on the Tables and Borders toolbar or the Insert Table button on the Standard toolbar.

FIGURE 10-2
Table Grid, Column Markers, and Formatting Marks

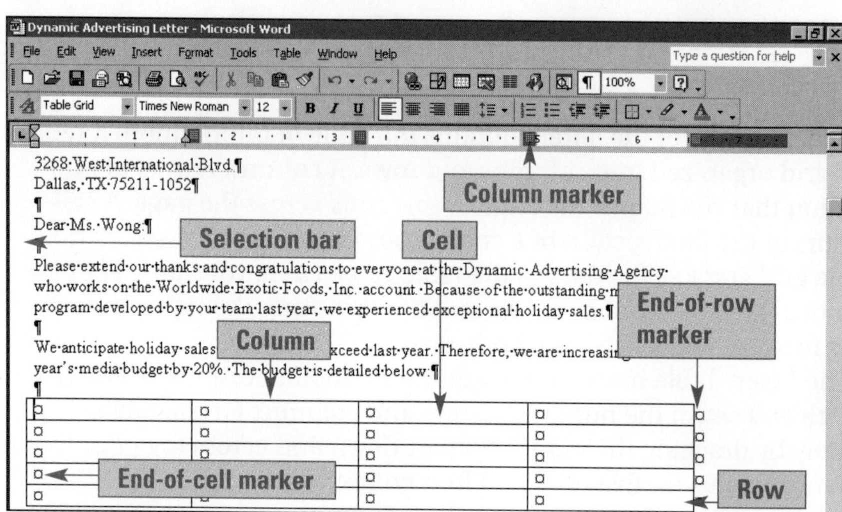

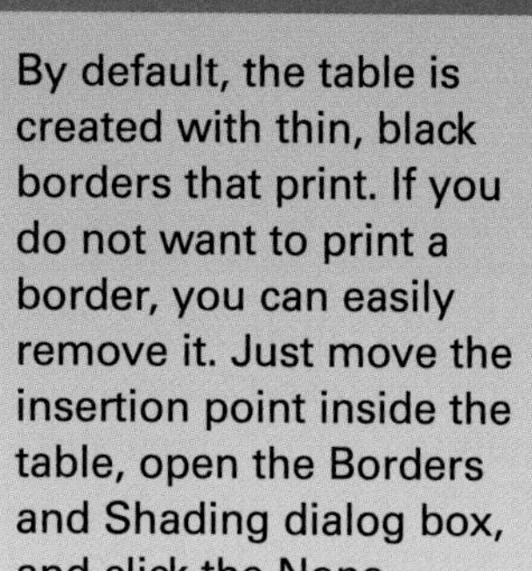

CAUTION TIP

By default, the table is created with thin, black borders that print. If you do not want to print a border, you can easily remove it. Just move the insertion point inside the table, open the Borders and Shading dialog box, and click the None preset option on the Borders tab.

To key text in a table you must move the insertion point from cell to cell.

Moving the Insertion Point in a Table

You can use the I-beam and the keyboard to move the insertion point from cell to cell in a table. You do not press the ENTER key. Pressing the ENTER key creates a new paragraph inside the table cell. To move the insertion point with the I-beam, just click in the appropriate cell.

To use the keyboard, press the appropriate ARROW key, press the TAB key to move one cell to the right, or press the SHIFT + TAB keys to move one cell to the left. Table 10-1 lists methods for moving the insertion point in a table using the keyboard.

TABLE 10-1
Table Movement Keys

Location	Keys	Location	Keys
One cell down	DOWN ARROW	**First cell in a row**	ALT + HOME
One cell right	TAB (RIGHT ARROW, if the cell is empty)	**Last cell in a row**	ALT + END
One cell left	SHIFT + TAB (LEFT ARROW, if the cell is empty)	**First cell in a column**	ALT + PAGE UP
One cell up	UP ARROW	**Last cell in a column**	ALT + PAGE DOWN

To move the insertion point in the table:

Step 1	*Click*	the middle of the first cell in the second row
Step 2	***Press***	the UP ARROW key

Step 3	*Continue*	to practice moving the insertion point in the table, using Table 10-1 as your guide
Step 4	*Move*	the insertion point to the first cell (upper-left corner) in the table

You are ready to key the text in the table.

Keying Text in Tables

You key the column headings in the first row of the table, called the **heading row**, and then key the media budget data in the following rows. As you key the numbers, do not attempt to align them in the cells; you do that later. If you accidentally press the ENTER key while keying data in a cell, press the BACKSPACE key to remove the paragraph mark and blank line from the cell.

To key the column headings:

Step 1	*Verify*	that the insertion point is in the first cell in the first row
Step 2	*Key*	Branch Office
Step 3	*Press*	the TAB key
Step 4	*Key*	Holiday Baskets
Step 5	*Press*	the TAB key
Step 6	*Key*	Beverage Baskets
Step 7	*Press*	the TAB key
Step 8	*Key*	Gift Certificates
Step 9	*Press*	the TAB key

The insertion point moves to the first cell in the second row. Now you can key the rest of the data for the table.

Step 10	*Key*	Chicago
Step 11	*Press*	the TAB key
Step 12	*Continue*	to key the remaining data in the Branch Office, Holiday Baskets, Beverage Baskets, and Gift Certificates columns for the Chicago, London, Melbourne, and Vancouver branches, as shown in Figure 10-1 (do not align the budget amounts at this time)
Step 13	*Save*	the document and leave it open

MENU TIP

You can point to the Select command on the Table menu and then click Table, Column, Row, or Cell to select all or part of the table containing the insertion point.

QUICK TIP

You can use the SHIFT + Click and CTRL + Click methods to select contiguous and noncontiguous rows, columns, and cells in the same way you do body text.

In addition to moving the insertion point from cell to cell, you also select cells, rows, and columns to format or delete the contents or to insert or delete the cells, rows, and columns.

Selecting Cells, Rows, and Columns

Before you can format the table contents, you must select the cells that contain the text. If you move the mouse pointer to the lower-left corner of a cell, to the selection bar to the left of a row, or to the top of a column, the mouse pointer becomes a selection pointer. You can also select parts of a table with the keyboard. Table 10-2 lists mouse pointer and keyboard selection techniques.

TABLE 10-2
Table Selection Methods

Selection	Mouse	Keyboard
Cell	Move the mouse pointer inside the left boundary of a cell and click	Move the insertion point to the cell and press the SHIFT + END keys
Several cells	Drag across the cells with the selection pointer or the I-beam	Move the insertion point to the first cell, press and hold the SHIFT key, and then press the UP, DOWN, LEFT, or RIGHT ARROW key
Column	Move the mouse pointer to the top of the column until it becomes a vertical selection pointer, then click (or hold down the ALT key and click) a cell in the column with the I-beam pointer	Move the insertion point to the first cell in the column, hold down the SHIFT key, and press the ALT + PAGE DOWN keys
Row	Click the selection bar at the left of the row, or double-click any cell in a row with the selection pointer	Move the insertion point to the first cell in the row, hold down the SHIFT key, and press the ALT + END keys
Table	Drag to select all rows or all columns (including the end-of-row marks) with the selection pointer	Move the insertion point to any cell, press the NUMLOCK key on the numeric keypad to turn off the Number Lock feature, and press the ALT + 5 keys (the 5 key on the numeric keypad).

QUICK TIP

You can delete both the contents of a table and the table grid. To delete the contents of a cell, row, or column, simply select the cell, row, or column and press the DELETE key. To delete the entire table grid or a cell, row, or column, you must use a menu command. First move the insertion point to the table column, row, or cell, point to the Delete command on the Table menu, and click Table, Columns, Rows, or Cells.

To select a row, column, and cell in the table:

Step 1	***Move***	the mouse pointer to the left of the first row in the selection bar
Step 2	***Click***	the selection bar
Step 3	***Move***	the mouse pointer to the top of the second column (the mouse pointer becomes a small black selection pointer)

Step 4	*Click*	the column with the selection pointer
Step 5	*Move*	the mouse pointer just inside the left cell boundary in last cell in the last row (the mouse pointer becomes a small black selection pointer)
Step 6	*Click*	the cell with the selection pointer
Step 7	*Continue*	to select cells, rows, columns, and the entire table, using Table 10-2 as your guide
Step 8	*Move*	the insertion point to the first cell in the first row

You are ready to format the table text.

Changing Cell Formats

You format text in a table just as you do in the body of a document. To help distinguish the column labels from the rest of the data, you can shade, bold, and center them. You also can use the alignment buttons on the Formatting toolbar to align the numbers in their cells.

To bold and center the column headings and right-align the numbers:

Step 1	*Select*	the first row containing the column headings
Step 2	*Click*	the Bold button on the Formatting toolbar
Step 3	*Click*	the Center button on the Formatting toolbar
Step 4	*Click*	any cell to deselect the row
Step 5	*Select*	the cells that contain the budget numbers
Step 6	*Click*	the Align Right button to align the numbers to the right
Step 7	*Deselect*	the cells
Step 8	*Save*	the document and leave it open

Later you shade the cells. To complete the table contents you need to add the heading row.

CAUTION TIP

When you select all or part of a table and then press the DELETE key, only the contents in the selected part of the table are deleted. To use the DELETE key to delete an entire table, you must also select a portion of the text or a blank line above or below the table before you press the DELETE key.

QUICK TIP

You can set tab stops on the horizontal ruler to align text and numbers in cells in the same way you use tab stops to align text and numbers in the body of a document. Select the cells, set the tab alignment you want, and then click the horizontal ruler where you want to insert the tab stop.

To insert a tab formatting mark in a cell, press the CTRL + TAB keys.

10.b Modifying Tables

Once you create a table, you often need to modify it by inserting rows or columns for additional data, or deleting unused rows and columns. For the table in the letter, you need to insert a row at the top of the table for the table heading, a row at the bottom of the table for the column totals, and a column at the right of the table for the row totals.

MENU TIP

To insert a row or column, you can click the Insert command on the Table menu to insert the rows or columns above or below a selected row and left or right of a selected column. You also can use a shortcut menu to insert rows or columns.

MOUSE TIP

You can use the Insert Table button on the Standard toolbar to insert rows and columns. When you select a table row, the Insert Table button on the Standard toolbar becomes the Insert Rows button. When you select a cell or column, the Insert Table button becomes the Insert Cell or Insert Column button.

Inserting Rows and Columns

To insert rows or columns, first select the number of rows or columns you wish to insert. For example, to insert two rows, select two rows in the table. The new row you insert retains the formatting from the original row. If you don't specify where you want to insert rows or columns, Word automatically inserts rows above the selected row and inserts columns to the left of the selected column.

You want to add a row at the top of the table in which you can key a heading for the table. To add a new row at the top of the table using the Table menu:

Step 1	***Move***	the insertion point to any cell in the first row
Step 2	***Click***	Table
Step 3	***Point to***	Insert
Step 4	***Click***	Rows Above

A new row is inserted at the top of the table.

A table heading in the first row helps identify the data in the table. Currently the first row has four cells, one for each column. You only need one cell for a table heading.

Merging Cells

You can combine, or **merge**, cells vertically or horizontally by first selecting the cells to be merged and then clicking the Merge Cells command on the Table menu or a shortcut menu. You also can divide, or **split**, cells vertically or horizontally. Before you key and format the table heading, you want to merge the five cells in the first row into one cell. To merge the cells in the first row:

Step 1	***Select***	the first row, if necessary
Step 2	***Right-click***	the selected row
Step 3	***Click***	Merge Cells

The first row of the table now contains one large cell. To create the two-line table heading:

Step 1	***Key***	Worldwide Exotic Foods, Inc.
Step 2	***Press***	the ENTER key to create a new line in the cell
Step 3	***Key***	Media Budget

Step 4	*Observe*	that the two-line table heading is centered and bold, and the row height increases to accommodate the second line of the heading

Using AutoFit to Change Column Width

Once the table contents are complete, you want to resize the widths to fit the data. A quick way to resize the table is to use the AutoFit options on the Table menu. You can have Word size or fit each column to match the column's contents. This method creates a column width that accommodates the widest cell contents in that column. Word also can resize the entire table to fit within the document margins or format rows for uniform height and columns for uniform width.

To have Word automatically fit the entire table with evenly distributed columns (columns with the same width):

Step 1	*Verify*	that the insertion point is in the table
Step 2	*Click*	Table
Step 3	*Point to*	AutoFit
Step 4	*Click*	AutoFit to Contents

You decide to see how the table looks without a border and with shaded column label cells.

Adding Borders and Shading to Tables

Borders and shading can make a table more attractive and easier to read. When you create a table using the Insert Table button on the Standard toolbar or Insert Table command on the Table menu, Word adds a border around each cell in the table. You can modify or remove this border and add shading from the Borders and Shading dialog box. To open the Borders and Shading dialog box:

Step 1	*Right-click*	the table
Step 2	*Click*	Borders and Shading
Step 3	*Click*	the Borders tab, if necessary

The border options for tables appear in the Borders tab. You can select one of the five preset border options or customize the table border. If you remove the table's printing border, the table appears with light gray gridlines. These nonprinting **gridlines** provide a visual

QUICK TIP

To insert a column at the end of the table, first select the end-of-row marks just like you select a column. When you add a new column, the overall size of the table doesn't change but the column widths adjust to accommodate the new column.

You can easily add as many rows to a table as you need by pressing the TAB key to create each new row as you key the data. You also can quickly insert multiple rows at the end of a table by moving the insertion point to the blank line immediately below the table, clicking the Insert Rows button on the Standard toolbar, and specifying the number of rows to add.

MENU TIP

You can split a cell vertically and horizontally by first selecting the cell and then clicking the Split Cells command on the Table menu.

> **QUICK TIP**
>
> You can resize individual rows and columns by setting row height or column width properties in the appropriate tabs in the Table Properties dialog box. To open the dialog box, click the Table Properties command on the Table menu.

guide as you work in a table. The nonprinting gridlines can be turned on or off with the Show Gridlines or Hide Gridlines commands on the Table menu. You remove the border and view the nonprinting gridlines.

Step 4	*Click*	the None preset border option in the Setting: group
Step 5	*Click*	OK

The light gray nonprinting gridlines should appear. However, if the gridlines were previously turned off they do not appear. To turn on the gridlines, if necessary, and Print Preview the document:

Step 1	*Click*	Table
Step 2	*Click*	Show Gridlines, if necessary
Step 3	*Print Preview*	the document
Step 4	*Observe*	that the light gray gridlines do not print
Step 5	*Close*	Print Preview

> **MOUSE TIP**
>
> You can merge cells with the Merge Cells button on the Tables and Borders toolbar or you can split a cell vertically and horizontally by first selecting the cell and then clicking the Split Cells button on the Tables and Borders toolbar.
>
> You can drag the column boundaries inside a table or the column markers on the horizontal ruler to change the width of a column.

The information in the table was easier to read with the default border. To reapply the default border and add shading to the column label row:

Step 1	*Open*	the Borders tab in the Borders and Shading dialog box
Step 2	*Click*	the Grid option
Step 3	*Click*	OK
Step 4	*Select*	the second row, which contains the column heading text
Step 5	*Open*	the Shading tab in the Borders and Shading dialog box
Step 6	*Click*	the Gray-10% square on the color grid (the third square in the first row)
Step 7	*Click*	OK
Step 8	*Deselect*	the row

10.c Positioning Tables

You can horizontally align a table in relation to the edge of the page, the margins, or column boundaries. Tables can also be vertically aligned in relation to the top and bottom of the page, the top and bottom margins, or the top and bottom of a paragraph. The Table tab in the Table Properties dialog box provides options for positioning a table on the page. To position the table using the Table Properties dialog box:

Step 1	*Right-click*	the table
Step 2	*Click*	Table Properties
Step 3	*Click*	the Table tab, if necessary

Your Table Properties dialog box should look similar to Figure 10-3.

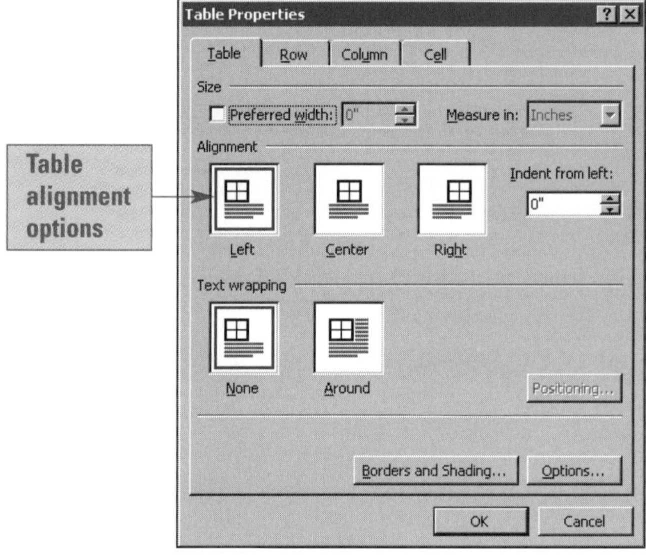

FIGURE 10-3
Table Properties Dialog Box

MOUSE TIP

You can quickly align a table at the left or right margin or center the table by selecting the entire table *including the end-of-row marks* and clicking an alignment button on the Formatting toolbar.

Step 4	*Click*	the Center alignment option
Step 5	*Click*	OK

The table is centered between the left and right margins. The table is complete and you need to finish the letter. To key the remaining body text and closing:

Step 1	*Move*	the insertion point to the blank line below the table
Step 2	*Press*	the ENTER key
Step 3	*Key*	the last body paragraph, closing, and your initials, using Figure 10-1 as your guide
Step 4	*Save*	the document

MENU TIP

When you have a long table that flows over to another page, you can repeat the heading row of the table on each page by moving the insertion point to the heading row and clicking the Heading Rows Repeat command on the Table menu.

Maria asks you to reformat the table.

10.d Applying AutoFormats to Tables

One way to quickly format a table is to apply a Table AutoFormat, also called a table style, which is a table format that includes preset borders and shading. Many of the automatic formats can be modified by turning on or off special formatting for the heading row, the first and last column, and the last row. To apply a Table AutoFormat:

Step 1	*Click*	anywhere inside the table to position the insertion point
Step 2	*Click*	Table
Step 3	*Click*	Table AutoFormat

Your Table AutoFormat dialog box should look similar to Figure 10-4.

FIGURE 10-4
Table AutoFormat Dialog Box

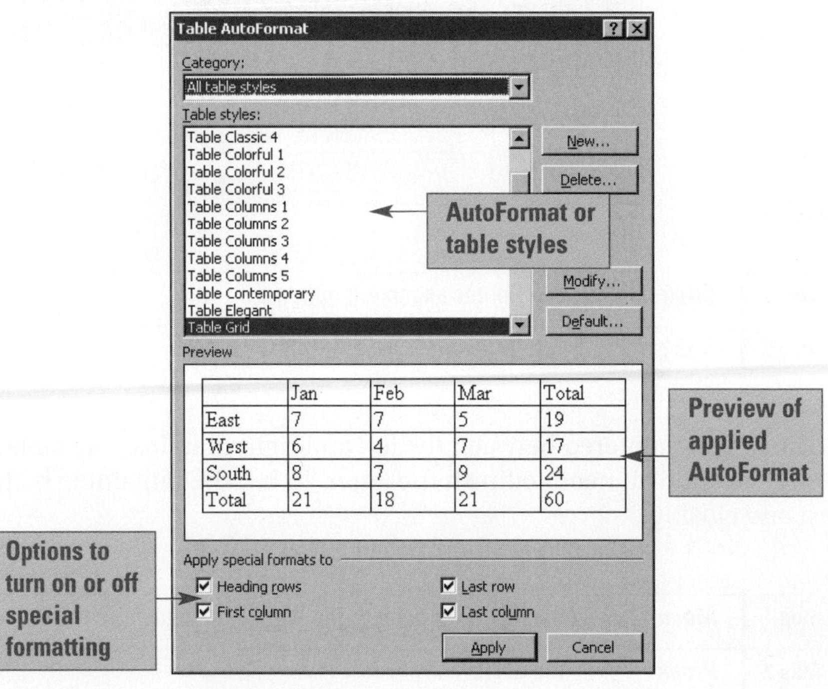

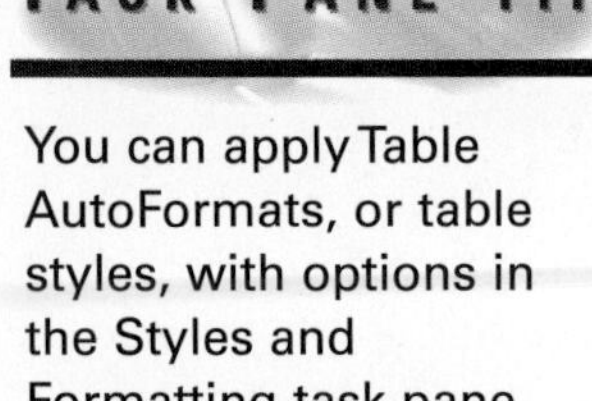

TASK PANE TIP

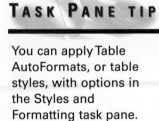

You can apply Table AutoFormats, or table styles, with options in the Styles and Formatting task pane.

You can select from a variety of automatic formats or styles in the Table styles: list and then preview what the document table would look like with the selected AutoFormat (table style) applied. To apply special formatting to the heading rows, first column, last row, or last column, you click the appropriate check box.

Step 4	***Click***	Table 3D effects 3 in the Table styles: list
Step 5	***Observe***	the table preview
Step 6	***Preview***	several other table styles

You want to use the Table Classic 3 style with heading row and first column formatting. To apply the Table Classic 3 style:

Step 1	***Click***	Table Classic 3 in the Table styles: list
Step 2	***Click***	the Heading rows and First column check boxes to insert check marks and remove any check marks from the Last row and Last column check boxes, if necessary
Step 3	***Observe***	the table preview
Step 4	***Click***	Apply

The table will look better centered between the left and right margins. To quickly center the table horizontally:

Step 1	***Select***	the entire table (including the end-of-row marks)
Step 2	***Click***	the Center button on the Formatting toolbar
Step 3	***Deselect***	the table
Step 4	***Save***	the document as *Dynamic With Table AutoFormat* and close it

The AutoFormats provide a variety of looks that you can use to quickly format a table.

QUICK TIP

If you use a particular AutoFormat for most of your tables, you can open the Table AutoFormat dialog box, select the desired table style and then click the Default button to make that AutoFormat the default format for all tables in the current document or all tables in documents based on the Normal template.

Summary

- Data in a Word document can be placed in a table so that it is easier to read and understand.
- A table is a grid organized into rows and columns.
- A column is a set of information that runs down a page, and a row is a set of information that runs across a page.
- A cell is the intersection of a column and a row.
- You can format text in table cells just as you format paragraph text.
- You can merge multiple cells into one cell.
- You can use the mouse or keyboard to move the insertion point between cells in a table.
- You can select cells, rows, and columns in a table; you can then format them, insert and delete rows or columns, or shift cells.
- You can change the widths of one or more columns in a table with the mouse or use the AutoFit commands on the Table menu.
- You can view nonprinting gridlines when working in a table.
- You can add printable borders and gridlines to a table.
- Word has many automatic table formats you can apply to an existing table.

Commands Review

Action	Menu Bar	Shortcut Menu	Toolbar	Task Pane	Keyboard
Create a table	Table, Insert, Table or Draw Table				ALT + A, I, T or W
Delete a table or columns, rows, or cells	Table, Delete, Table, or Columns or Rows or Cells	Right-click selected table component, click Delete			ALT + A, D, T or C or R or E
Insert rows, columns, or cells in a table	Table, Insert, Columns to the Left or Columns to the Right or Rows Above or Rows Below or Cells	Right-click selected table component, click Insert			ALT + A, I, L or R or A or B or E
Merge cells	Table, Merge Cells	Right-click selected cells, click Merge Cells			ALT + A, M
Split cells	Table, Split Cells	Right-click cell, click Split Cells			ALT + A, P
Change column width for selected column(s)	Table, Table Properties Table, AutoFit, AutoFit to Contents or AutoFit to Window or Fixed Column Width or Distribute Rows Evenly or Distribute Columns Evenly		Drag the column boundary or the column marker on the horizontal ruler		ALT + A, R ALT + A, A, F or W or X or N or Y

Action	Menu Bar	Shortcut Menu	Toolbar	Task Pane	Keyboard
Add borders and shading to a table	Format, Borders and Shading	Right-click table, Borders and Shading			ALT + O, B
Show or hide Table Gridlines	Table, Show Gridlines				ALT + A, G
Align text horizontally and vertically		Right-click cell, click Cell Alignment			
Position a table on the page	Table, Table Properties	Right-click a table, click Table Properties			ALT + A, R
Repeat a heading row on all pages of the table	Table, Heading Rows Repeat				ALT + A, H
Apply a Table AutoFormat	Table, Table AutoFormat				ALT + A, F

Concepts Review

Circle the correct answer.

1. A table:
- [a] is a grid organized in columns and rows.
- [b] must be created with a button on the Standard toolbar.
- [c] cannot be formatted with character formats like bold and paragraph formats like borders and shading.
- [d] is created without a printable border.

2. You cannot change the width of a column in a table by:
- [a] pressing the TAB key.
- [b] dragging a row boundary between two rows.
- [c] clicking the Column Width command on the Table menu.
- [d] dragging a column boundary on the horizontal ruler.

3. When you create a new table, the insertion point automatically appears:
- [a] in the last cell.
- [b] below the table.
- [c] in the first cell.
- [d] in the second row.

4. A cell is:
- [a] a set of information that runs down a page.
- [b] a set of information that runs across the page.
- [c] the intersection of a column and row.
- [d] a grid of columns and rows.

5. You cannot move the insertion point in a table with the:
- [a] I-beam.
- [b] TAB key.
- [c] UP ARROW and DOWN ARROW keys.
- [d] SPACEBAR.

6. To select a cell using the keyboard, press the:
- [a] SHIFT + ALT keys.
- [b] ALT + END keys.
- [c] SHIFT + END keys.
- [d] ALT + 5 keys.

7. To delete a table grid, you must:
- [a] press the F8 key.
- [b] use a menu command.
- [c] use a shortcut menu.
- [d] press the DELETE key.

8. Combining cells is also called:
[a] splitting them.
[b] deleting them.
[c] merging them.
[d] formatting them.

9. The best way to align the numbers 973, 734, 1,034 in a table column is to:
[a] left-align the numbers.
[b] justify the numbers.
[c] right-align the numbers.
[d] center the numbers.

10. To automatically resize column widths so that all the columns in the table have enough space for the largest cell in the column, use the:
[a] AutoFit to Height command.
[b] AutoFit to Width command.
[c] AutoFit to Size command.
[d] AutoFit to Contents command.

Circle **T** if the statement is true or **F** if the statement is false.

T F 1. A table column contains text in a vertical arrangement down the page.

T F 2. To delete a table's contents, first select the table and then press the DELETE key.

T F 3. Rows can be inserted above or below the selected rows.

T F 4. Cells can be merged horizontally but not vertically.

T F 5. To move the insertion point to the next cell, press the ENTER key.

T F 6. You set tab stops for table cells in the same manner as body text.

T F 7. The default table border cannot be removed or modified.

T F 8. Nonprinting gridlines can provide a visual guide when you are working in a table.

T F 9. The ALT + TAB keys move the insertion point one cell to the left.

T F 10. Before you format the contents of a table, you must first select the cells, rows, or columns to be formatted.

Skills Review

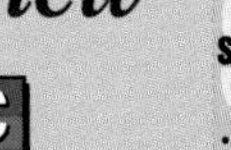

Exercise 1 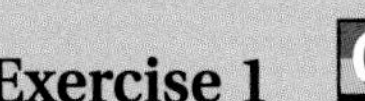

1. Create a new, blank document.
2. Change the top margin to 1½ inches and the left and right margins to 1 inch.
3. Create a 5 × 4 Table and key the following text in the table.

Branch	*2001*	*2002*	*2003*
Chicago	*300,000*	*100,000*	*210,000*
London	*323,000*	*306,000*	*89,000*
Melbourne	*250,000*	*500,000*	*130,000*
Vancouver	*405,000*	*108,000*	*206,000*

4. AutoFit the table to its contents.
5. Center and bold the column headings.
6. Right-align the numbers in their cells.
7. Insert a new first row, merge the cells, and key the following heading text in the new row.
Worldwide Exotic Foods, Inc.
Annual Beverage Sales
($000)

8. Bold and center the heading text.
9. Add 10% gray shading to the column headings.
10. Add a grid border to the table.
11. Save the document as *Annual Sales Data*, and then preview and print it.
12. Apply the Table AutoFormat of your choice and center the table horizontally.
13. Save the document as *Annual Sales With AutoFormat*, and then preview, print, and close it.

Exercise 2 C

1. Open the *Regional Deli Sales* document located on the Data Disk.
2. Insert a row between North and East regions using the Insert Rows button on the Standard toolbar.
3. Key the following text in the row: Central, 28,975.33, 54,333.45, and 78,125.54.
4. Insert a column at the end of the table. (*Hint:* View and select the end-of-row marks and insert a column to the left.)
5. Key "Beverages" in the first cell of the column.
6. Key the following text in the column: $30,456.78, 11, 300.56, 23,678.99, 97,234.55, and 59,112.45. (*Hint:* Use the DOWN ARROW to move to the next cell in the column.)
7. Right-align the numbers in the cells.
8. Adjust the column widths by dragging the column boundaries with the mouse pointer so that each column is just wide enough for the largest cell contents. (*Hint:* Place the mouse pointer on the right column boundary until it changes shape to a sizing pointer and then drag the boundary to the left.)
9. Center and bold the heading row.
10. Insert a new row at the top of the table, merge the cells, and then key, bold, and center the following text in the row: Regional Deli Sales.
11. Center the table between the left and right margins using the Table Properties dialog box.
12. Save the document as *Regional Deli Sales Revised*, and then preview, print, and close it.

Exercise 3 

1. Create a new, blank document.
2. Create 5×4 Table and key the following text in the cells. Use the TAB key to insert a new row at the bottom of the table each time you need one.

Pastries	*June*	*July*	*August*
Éclairs	*1,500*	*3,000*	*2,600*
Danish	*7,800*	*5,600*	*9,300*
Croissants	*13,000*	*15,000*	*10,500*
Butter Biscuits	*30,000*	*45,000*	*26,450*
Lemon Tarts	*5,600*	*3,500*	*3,450*
Truffle Torte	*850*	*1,200*	*635*
Raspberry Charlotte Torte	*1,300*	*1,475*	*2,300*
Sweet Pretzels	*75,000*	*65,000*	*80,000*
German Chocolate Brownies	*125,000*	*150,000*	*210,000*

3. Size the columns attractively using the mouse. (*Hint:* Drag a right column border to the left or right to size a column.)

4. Bold and center the column headings.

5. Insert a new row at the top of the table, merge the cells, and key the following as boldfaced centered heading text.

   Vancouver Branch
   Pastries Sales

6. Remove the grid border from the table.

7. Add Gray-12.5 % shading to the top row.

8. Center the table between the left and right margins using the mouse pointer. (*Hint:* Select the entire table *including the end-of-row marks* and click the Center button.)

9. Save the document as *Vancouver Pastries Sales*, and then preview, print, and close it.

Exercise 4 C

1. Create a new, blank document.

2. Create a 1×4 Table and key the data below. Use the TAB key to add additional rows as you key the data.

District	*Selling*	*Employee*	*Overhead*
Central	*$49,100.60*	*$12,421.00*	*$13,921.99*
Eastern	*41,756.72*	*5,523.42*	*8,992.33*
Midwest	*64,871.86*	*4,819.89*	*9,655.76*
Mountain	*59,256.36*	*7,085.07*	*6,332.99*
Southern	*45,817.32*	*12,253.57*	*16,322.86*
Western	*51,857.52*	*9,528.88*	*11,661.30*

3. Select the first row, and then bold and center the text.

4. AutoFit the table to the contents.

5. Right-align the numbers.

6. Insert a row at the top of the document, merge the cells, and key the following title text in bold Arial 14-point font.

   Worldwide Exotic Foods, Inc.
   District Expense Report
   Fourth Quarter

7. Add a 1½-point grid border to the table.

8. Align the table at the right margin.

9. Save the document as *District Expense Report*, and then preview, print, and close it.

Exercise 5 C

1. Open the *Adjusted Costs Memo* document located on the Data Disk.

2. Create a 7×4 Table with no border below the memo body text.

3. Merge the cells in the first row.

4. Key the following heading text (boldface and centered) in two lines in the first row.

   EXECUTIVE SUPPORT DIVISION
   Adjusted Costs for Second Fiscal Quarter

5. Key the following data in the remaining rows.

Item	*Budgeted*	*Actual*	*Difference*
Executive Secretaries	*$2,455,000*	*$2,256,000*	*-$199,000*
Administrative Assistants	*390,600*	*475,900*	*85,300*
Equipment	*960,000*	*840,000*	*-120,000*
Telecommunications	*476,000*	*450,600*	*-25,400*
Miscellaneous	*76,000*	*60,000*	*-16,000*

6. Right align the numbers.
7. Underline and center the column heading text in the second row.
8. AutoFit the table to the contents.
9. Shade the Difference column with 10% gray.
10. Center the table between the left and right margins.
11. Save the document as *Adjusted Costs Memo Revised*, and then preview, print, and close it.

Exercise 6 

1. Create a new, blank document and insert the text "TRIVIA INFORMATION ABOUT SELECTED STATES" centered in 14-point Times New Roman font at the top of the document.
2. Create a 2×2 Table on two lines below the title and key the following information in 12-point Times New Roman font in the table. Use the TAB key to add additional rows to the end of the table as necessary.

Arkansas	*The Natural State*
Arizona	*Grand Canyon State*
Colorado	*Centennial State*
Connecticut	*Constitution State*
Nebraska	*Cornhusker State*
New Mexico	*America's Land of Enchantment*
Texas	*The Lone Star State*
Washington	*The Evergreen State*

3. Change the first column width to 1.5 inches and the second column width to 3.5 inches. (*Hint:* Select the column and change the width on the Column tab in the Table Properties dialog box.)
4. Center the table between the left and right margins.
5. Center the contents of each column.
6. Add 10% gray shading to each alternate row beginning with the first row. (*Hint:* You can use the CTRL key to select multiple, noncontiguous rows.)
7. Save the document as *State Trivia*, and then preview, print, and close it.

Exercise 7 

1. Open the *Burns Letter* document located on the Data Disk.
2. Insert a row at the top of the table, merge the cells, and key the following text.
   Vancouver Office Expense Report
   Second Quarter
3. Select the first two rows and the first column cells, bold and center the contents, and add 12.5% gray shading. (*Hint:* Use the CTRL key to select the table rows and cells before formatting them.)
4. Right-align the numbers and key "$" before each number in the first and last rows.

5. Center the table horizontally between the left and right margins.
6. Save the document as *Burns Letter With Formatted Table*, and then preview, print, and close it.

Exercise 8

1. Create a new, blank document.
2. Add the title "NEW TELEPHONE LIST" centered in 14-point Times New Roman font at the top of the page.
3. Create a 2×2 Table on the third line below the table and key the following text in 12-point Times New Roman font in the table.

NAME	*EXTENSION*
Maria Sanchez	*X3316*
Michael Chin	*X3201*
Susan Hernandez	*X3455*
Marshall Collins	*X4453*
Frances Robinson	*X3233*

4. Add a blank row at the bottom of the table and merge the cells.
5. Key the following information in a bulleted list in the new row.
   - *Fax Number (713) 555-3456*
   - *Dial 0 for the operator*
   - *Dial 9 for an outside line*
   - *Dial 8 for long distance calls*
6. Modify the bulleted list hanging indent so that the bullets are at the left margin of the row.
7. Center the table between the left and right margins.
8. AutoFit the table to the contents.
9. Italicize the table column headings.
10. Save the document as *New Telephone List*, and then preview, print, and close it.

Case Projects

Project 1

A Marketing Department coworker, Ella Cohen, wants to know how to insert information from a database or other data source into a Word document as a table. Use the Ask A Question Box to locate online Help topics about inserting information from other applications. Write an interoffice memorandum to Ella describing the process. Save, preview, and print the memo.

Project 2

R. D. Jacobson asks you to create an interoffice memo to five Vancouver sales representatives advising them of the profit (sales minus expenses) for the third quarter on the Extravaganza Basket product. Use a table to present the data for the five sales representatives by listing the sales, expenses, and profit for each. Use fictitious data. Format and position the table attractively on the page. Save, preview, and print the memo.

Project 3

Maria Betancourt does not understand the concept of Word fields, such as the formula field or date and time field, and asks for your help. Use the Ask A Question Box to search online Help for information on Word fields. Print and review the information. Open the Options dialog box and use the Help button to review the Field options in the View tab. Create an interoffice memorandum to Maria describing Word fields and how to use the options on the View tab to view the fields. Use a table to organize the information about the View tab options. Save, preview, and print the memo.

With your instructor's permission, use the memo as a guide to describe Word fields to a classmate. Then open a document that contains a date and time or formula field and demonstrate how to use the View tab field options.

Project 4  

R. D. Jacobson asks you to help locate a list of firms that provide Web-based advertising. Connect to the Internet, and search for companies that provide advertising services on the Web. Print at least five home pages. Create an interoffice memorandum to R. D. Jacobson listing your Web sources and a brief description of their services. Organize your Web source list in an attractively formatted and positioned table. Save, preview, and print the memo.

Project 5 C

Create letter and an accompanying envelope to the president of WholeSale Food Distributors from M. D. Anderson, Sales Director, advising the president of the first quarter sales data for five products. Use an attractively formatted and positioned table to itemize the product sales for January, February, and March. Use fictitious data. Save, preview, and print the letter.

Project 6 C

You have been asked to present a 15-minute brown bag luncheon presentation on mouse and keyboard selection techniques with Word tables. Create a new document and use a table to organize your ideas for the presentation. Save, preview, and print the document. Then, with your instructor's permission, use the document to demonstrate the table selection techniques to a classmate.

Project 7  

R. D. Jacobson assigns you to write a memorandum to all Sales and Marketing Department employees advising them how to save a Word document to the company FTP site on the Internet. Use the Ask A Question Box to research how to save a Word document to an FTP site. Create a memorandum that describes an FTP site and provides step-by-step instructions on how to save a document to an FTP site. Use a table to organize the steps. Save, preview, and print the document.

Project 8 C

During lunch, Maria Betancourt tells you that the Tables and Borders toolbar is a great tool. You want to explore using it. Create a new, blank document and display the Tables and Borders toolbar by clicking the Tables and Borders button on the Standard toolbar. Use the What's This? Help pointer to review the buttons on the toolbar. Explore using each of the buttons. Create a new document with a table that lists each button and what it does. Save, preview, and print the document.

Using Templates and Wizards

Chapter Overview

Templates help reduce the time you need to format documents you create repeatedly, such as schedules, fax cover sheets, or reports. Word has several built-in templates you can use to create new documents or you can create a custom template. Additionally, Word has several step-by-step processes called wizards you can use to create special documents. This chapter shows you how to use built-in templates and wizards, as well as how to create and modify custom templates.

Learning Objectives

- Create a document using a template
- Create a custom template
- Create a document using a wizard

Case profile

The public affairs officer, Viktor Winkler, handles investor and customer inquiries from around the world. Winkler's assistant is out of the office for two weeks and you are chosen to be her replacement. Winkler asks you to prepare several documents using both templates and wizards.

chapter eleven

11.a Creating a Document Using a Template

Every document you create in Word is based on a template. A **template** is a master document or model that contains any text, formats, styles, and AutoText that you want to include in a particular kind of document. Templates enable you to prepare documents more quickly because they supply many of the settings that you would otherwise need to create—such as margins, tabs, alignment, and formatted nonvariable text. Each time you click the New Blank Document button on the Standard toolbar you create a new document based on the Normal template. Another example of a template is a letter template that contains the margin settings for a block-format letter, the date field, and a standard closing that includes the writer's signature area.

There are two types of templates: global templates and document templates. The Normal template is an example of a **global template**, which means its settings are available for all documents. **Document templates** supply settings that affect only the current document and help you format letters, faxes, memos, reports, manuals, brochures, newsletters, and special documents, such as Web pages. Word provides many built-in document templates and you can easily create your own.

notes

It is assumed that the Word templates used in the activities and exercises in this chapter are already installed on your computer. See your instructor if the templates are not installed.

Viktor Winkler sends many faxes in response to customer and investor inquiries. He asks you to create a fax cover sheet. A quick way to do this is to base your new cover sheet document on one of the Word fax templates.

To create a fax cover sheet based on a template:

Step 1	*Click*	File
Step 2	*Click*	New to view the New Document task pane
Step 3	*Click*	the General Templates link in the New Document task pane
Step 4	*Click*	the Letters & Faxes tab

TASK PANE TIP

You can click the *Templates on Microsoft.com* link in the New Document task pane to download templates from the Microsoft Office Template Gallery. You can also click the Templates on my Web Sites link to access templates stored on a Web server.

QUICK TIP

To use settings from another template, you can load it as a global template and attach it to your document. For more information on using and attaching global templates, see online Help.

chapter eleven

The Templates dialog box on your screen should look similar to Figure 11-1.

FIGURE 11-1
Letters & Faxes Tab in the Templates Dialog Box

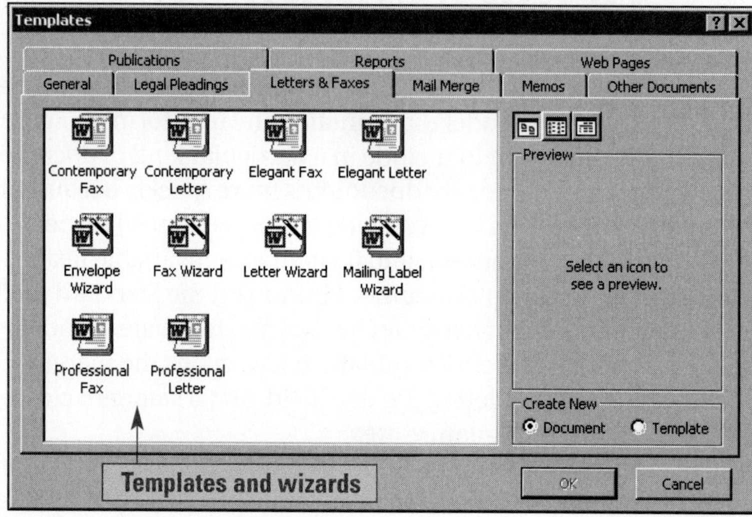

QUICK TIP

You can create a new document based on a template or a new custom template based on another template using the Templates dialog box. To create a new custom template based on an existing template, first click the template icon on which you wish to base the new custom template and then click the Template option button.

You can select several different letter or fax templates on the Letter & Faxes tab. You want to use the Contemporary Fax template.

Step 5	***Double-click***	the Contemporary Fax icon
Step 6	***Observe***	that a new document is created based on the Contemporary Fax template and Word switches to Print Layout view
Step 7	***Zoom***	the document to Page Width, if necessary

Your screen should look similar to Figure 11-2.

FIGURE 11-2
Document Based on the Contemporary Fax Template

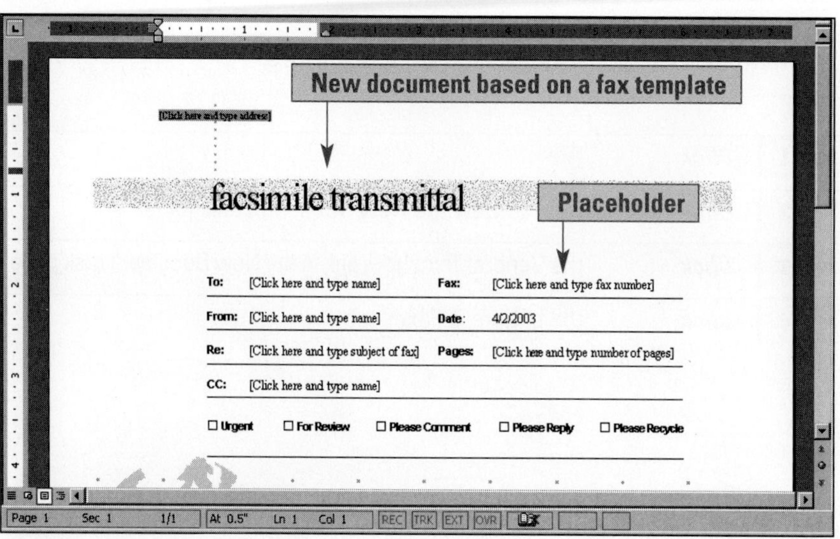

The document is preformatted with graphics, text boxes, heading text, lines, and placeholders. **Placeholders** are areas in which you key the variable information. All you need to do to complete the fax is to key the appropriate variable information in the [Click here and type…] placeholders. After you click a variable text placeholder to select it, you key the appropriate text. You can press the F11 key to move to the next placeholder. To key the company name and address and other variable text:

Step 1	***Observe***	that the current date already appears in the Date: placeholder because the date area contains a Date field
Step 2	***Click***	the address placeholder text box in the upper-left corner of the document
Step 3	***Key***	Worldwide Exotic Foods, Inc. Gage Building, Suite 1200 Riverside Plaza Chicago, IL 60606-2000
Step 4	***Press***	the F11 key to select the next placeholder
Step 5	***Key***	John Washington, Software Inc.
Step 6	***Press***	the F11 key
Step 7	***Key***	311-555-0098 in the Fax: placeholder
Step 8	***Press***	the F11 key
Step 9	***Key***	Viktor Winkler in the From: placeholder
Step 10	***Press***	the F11 key twice
Step 11	***Key***	Speaking Engagement in the Re: placeholder
Step 12	***Press***	the F11 key
Step 13	***Key***	2 in the Pages: placeholder
Step 14	***Press***	the F11 key
Step 15	***Press***	the Delete key to delete the CC: placeholder
Step 16	***Press***	the F11 key
Step 17	***Key***	X in the Urgent placeholder check box
Step 18	***Select***	the Notes: text below the check box placeholders (do not select the word and colon "Notes:")
Step 19	***Key***	I am happy to accept your invitation to speak at the Software Inc. executive committee luncheon tomorrow. Attached is a draft of my speech.
Step 20	***Save***	the document as *Washington Fax* and close it

QUICK TIP

You can press the SHIFT + F11 keys to move back to a previous placeholder.

During the day, Viktor Winkler asks you to create several fax cover sheets for him. It takes several minutes to create each cover sheet using the fax template. To save time, you decide to create a custom fax cover sheet template that already contains the company name, address, and Viktor Winkler's name.

QUICK TIP

By default, custom templates are stored in the Templates folder located in the Application Data\Microsoft directory. An icon for each template stored in the Templates folder appears on the General tab in the Templates dialog box, making it easy to create documents from a custom template. You can create additional tabs in the Templates dialog box by creating folders inside the Templates folder. The folder name is the tab name. Any Word document (.doc file extension) saved in the Templates folder can be used as a template.

You can change the default location for templates from the Templates folder by changing the User Templates location in the File Locations tab in the Options dialog box. For more information about storing templates, see online Help.

11.b Creating a Custom Template

You can create your own templates by making changes to the current document and saving it as a template. You can also use one of the Word templates as a basis for your custom template.

You use the Contemporary Fax template as the basis for the Winkler fax template. To create a custom template:

Step 1	*Open*	the Letters & Faxes tab in the Templates dialog box
Step 2	*Click*	the Template option button to create a new template based on another template
Step 3	*Double-click*	the Contemporary Fax icon

A template document named Template1 – Fax Coversheet opens. You can replace the placeholders with text that never changes. To add text to the template:

Step 1	*Click*	the address placeholder text box in the upper-right corner of the document
Step 2	*Key*	Worldwide Exotic Foods, Inc. Gage Building, Suite 1200 Riverside Plaza Chicago, IL 60606-2000
Step 3	*Press*	the F11 key three times
Step 4	*Key*	Viktor Winkler
Step 5	*Delete*	the Notes: text (do not delete the word and colon "Notes:")

Next you customize the heading text at the top of the document.

Step 6	*Select*	the text "facsimile transmittal" near the top of the document
Step 7	*Key*	Fax Cover Sheet

Like a document, you need to save the changes you made to the template. To save the template:

Step 1	*Open*	the Save As dialog box
Step 2	*Observe*	that Save in: location defaults to the Templates folder
Step 3	*Observe*	that the file type is Document Template
Step 4	*Save*	the template as *Winkler Fax Template* and close it

The next time Viktor asks for a fax cover sheet, you can create one quickly based on the *Winkler Fax Template* template. To test the custom template:

Step 1	*Open*	the General tab in the Templates dialog box
Step 2	*Observe*	the new *Winkler Fax Template* template icon
Step 3	*Click*	the Document option button, if necessary
Step 4	*Double-click*	the *Winkler Fax Template* template icon
Step 5	*Create*	a one-page fax to Beryl Davis, 311-555-7890, for review with a note confirming receipt of the new brochure listing government offices in the Chicago area
Step 6	*Save*	the fax as *Davis Fax* and close it

When you no longer use a template, you can delete it by opening the Templates dialog box, right-clicking the template icon, and clicking Delete. Your fax assignments for Viktor are complete so you want to delete the template. To delete the *Winkler Fax Template* template:

Step 1	*Open*	the General tab in the Templates dialog box
Step 2	*Right-click*	the *Winkler Fax Template* icon
Step 3	*Click*	Delete
Step 4	*Click*	Yes to confirm the deletion, if necessary
Step 5	*Cancel*	the Templates dialog box

You can also modify the Normal template to change the default settings. Common defaults that users change are the font style, font size, and margin settings. Viktor Winkler uses the same margins and fonts for all public affairs correspondence. You can create a custom template

TASK PANE TIP

A link to the most recently used templates is added to the New from template section of the New Document task pane.

QUICK TIP

Another quick way to create a template is to use an existing document. Simply open the document, make any necessary changes or deletions, then save the document as a template by changing the file type to Document Template in the Save as type: list box in the Save As dialog box.

The nonvariable portion of a template is called **boilerplate text** or **fixed text**.

for Viktor Winkler's correspondence or you can modify the margins and font settings in the Normal template so that every document you create contains the preferred margin and font settings.

Changing the Normal Template

The Normal template contains default formats and settings that are appropriate for most common documents. If, like Viktor Winkler, you use a different font and margins in most documents you create, it would be easier to modify the Normal template rather than to manually change the font and margins for each new document. One way to change the Normal template settings is to open the Normal template, change the settings, and then save the template with the changes. The most common changes to the Normal template are to the font and font size and margin settings. These changes can be made to the Normal template from the Font and Page Setup dialog boxes.

To change the default font in the Normal template from Times New Roman 12 point to Arial 12 point, the top margin to 2 inches, and the left and right margins to 1 inch:

Step 1	*Create*	a new, blank document, if necessary
Step 2	*Open*	the Font tab in the Font dialog box
Step 3	*Change*	the font to Arial
Step 4	*Click*	Default
Step 5	*Click*	Yes to confirm the font change to the Normal template
Step 6	*Open*	the Margins tab in the Page Setup dialog box
Step 7	*Change*	the top margin to 2 inches and the left and right margins to 1 inch
Step 8	*Click*	Default
Step 9	*Click*	Yes to confirm the font change to the Normal template

After you modify a template, you should test it to make sure the new settings appear correctly. You verify the changes to the Normal template.

Step 10	*Switch to*	Print Layout view, if necessary
Step 11	*Create*	a new, blank document
Step 12	*Observe*	the new margin settings and the new font

Step 13	*Repeat*	Steps 2 through 9 to return the font and margin settings to Times New Roman font, 1-inch top margin and 1.25-inch left and right margins
Step 14	*Close*	all open documents without saving changes

Another quick way to create special documents is to use a wizard.

11.c Creating a Document Using a Wizard

A **wizard** is a series of dialog boxes that take you through a step-by-step process to create a document. You can choose from several different Word wizards that help you create letters, legal documents, calendars, resumes, and other documents. Viktor Winkler asks you to create an attractive calendar for the month of December (current year) that he can put on the employees bulletin board. He suggests you use the Calendar Wizard to quickly do this. You select a document wizard in the Templates dialog box.

To create a calendar for the month of December:

Step 1	*Open*	the Templates dialog box
Step 2	*Click*	the Other Documents tab
Step 3	*Click*	the Document option button, if necessary
Step 4	*Double-click*	the Calendar Wizard icon

The first wizard dialog box opens. As you work through the wizard steps, you can use the Next> button to go forward to the next step, the Back> button to go back to a previous step, the Cancel button to stop the wizard process, and the Finish button to complete the wizard process. You go to the next step.

Step 5	*Click*	the Next> button

The second wizard dialog box on your screen should look similar to Figure 11-3.

FIGURE 11-3
Second Calendar Wizard Dialog Box

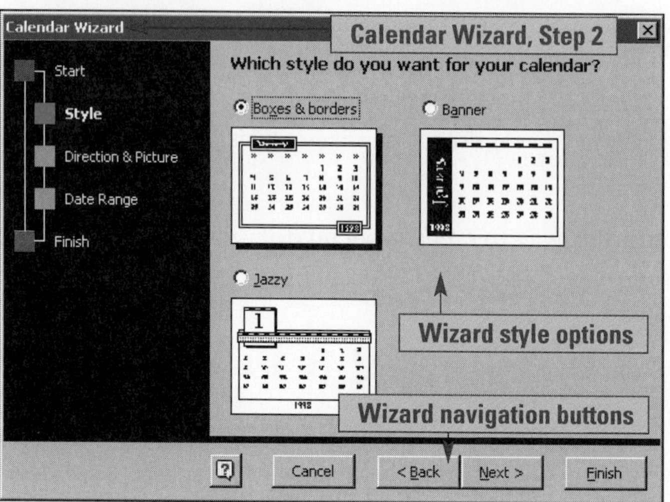

In this and subsequent dialog boxes, you select the options necessary to create a December calendar in landscape orientation.

Step 6	***Click***	the Banner option button, if necessary
Step 7	***Click***	the Next> button
Step 8	***Click***	the Landscape option button, if necessary
Step 9	***Click***	the No option button, if necessary
Step 10	***Click***	the Next> button
Step 11	***Click***	the Start: month list arrow
Step 12	***Click***	December
Step 13	***Click***	the Start: year spin box arrow to select the current year
Step 14	***Change***	the End: month and year to December and the current year
Step 15	***Click***	the Next> button
Step 16	***Click***	the Finish button
Step 17	***Print Preview***	the calendar document
Step 18	***Save***	the calendar document as *December Calendar* and close it

Wizards and templates make it simple to create consistently formatted documents quickly, letting you focus on the content of your documents.

Summary

- A template is a model document. The default model is the Normal template.
- You can modify the Normal template by opening it and making changes to it. Also, you can change the font, font size, and margin settings in the Normal template in the Font and Page Setup dialog boxes.
- Word has many letter, fax, Web page, and other templates you can use to create your own documents.
- You can create a custom template by example from other Word documents or by using a Word template as the basis for the new custom template.
- A wizard is a step-by-step series of dialog boxes you can use to create special documents, such as a fax cover sheet.

Commands Review

Action	Menu Bar	Shortcut Menu	Toolbar	Task Pane	Keyboard
Base a document on a Word template	File, New			Click the General Templates link in the New Document task pane	ALT + F, N
Create a template from a Word document	File, Save As (change the file type to Document Template)				ALT + F, A
Go to the next field in a document based on a Word template					F11
Go to the previous field in a document based on a Word template					SHIFT + F11
Base a document on a Word wizard	File, New			Click the General Templates link in the New Document task pane	ALT + F, N

Concepts Review

Circle the correct answer.

1. You can access Word templates by clicking a link in the:
- [a] Save As dialog box.
- [b] New Document task pane.
- [c] New Document dialog box.
- [d] New Template task pane.

2. To move from placeholder to placeholder in a document based on a template, press the:
- [a] F12 key.
- [b] F10 key.
- [c] F11 key.
- [d] F13 key.

3. The template that contains the default margin and formatting settings for a basic Word document is the:
- [a] Fax template.
- [b] Document template.
- [c] Wizard template.
- [d] Normal template.

4. A template is a:
- [a] place to store documents.
- [b] tool to apply multiple formats at once.
- [c] model document.
- [d] step-by-step series of dialog boxes.

5. A wizard is a:
- [a] template.
- [b] way to apply multiple formats at one time.
- [c] task pane.
- [d] step-by-step process to create a document.

6. Two basic types of templates are:
- [a] global and fax.
- [b] fax and letter.
- [c] document and fax.
- [d] global and document.

7. A template does not include:
- [a] styles.
- [b] formatting.
- [c] text.
- [d] task panes.

8. You can download additional templates from the Microsoft Office:
- [a] Web Warehouse.
- [b] Style Gallery.
- [c] Template Gallery.
- [d] Internet Gallery.

Circle **T** if the statement is true or **F** if the statement is false.

T F 1. A global template's settings are available for all documents.

T F 2. Placeholders are areas in a document based on a template that cannot be used for text.

T F 3. You can change the margins and font in the Normal template just once.

T F 4. Each time you click the New Blank Document button on the Standard toolbar, you are creating a document based on the Contemporary Document template.

T F 5. Any Word document (.doc file extension) that is saved in the Microsoft Office\Templates folder can be used as a template.

T F 6. You can use buttons in each wizard dialog box to move forward to the next wizard step or back to the previous wizard step.

T F 7. When you no longer need a custom template, you can delete it from the Templates dialog box.

T F 8. You can create a custom template by saving a Word document with the Document Template file type or by basing the custom template on an existing template.

Skills Review

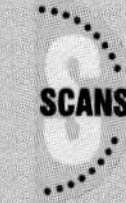

Exercise 1

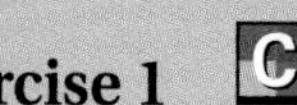

1. Use the Resume Wizard located on the Other Documents tab in the Templates dialog box to create your own professional style resume. Select the wizard options you desire as you go through the wizard dialog boxes.
2. Save the document as *My Personal Resume*, and then preview, print, and close it.

Exercise 2 

1. Use the Mailing Label Wizard on the Letters & Faxes tab in the Templates dialog box to create a page of the same Avery 5260-Address mailing labels for the following address.
   Mr. James Daniels
   President
   Nevada Lumber
   1177 Wickshire Street
   Reno, NV 89501-4899
2. Save the document as *Daniels Mailing Labels*, and then preview, print, and close it.

Exercise 3 

1. Use the Elegant Fax template on the Letters & Faxes tab in the Templates dialog box to create a fax cover sheet with the following information.

Company Name	*Worldwide Exotic Foods, Inc.*
To	*Becky Hardcastle*
From	*Yourself*
Company	*Hardcastle Specialties*
Date	*Current Date*
Fax #	*311-555-2345*
# of pages	*1*
Phone #	*311-555-2346*
Sender reference	*None*
Re:	*Order # 56A5678*
Your reference	*None*
Please reply	*X*
Notes/Comments	*The captioned order was shipped to your Denver warehouse on March 15. Please confirm receipt of the order.*
Return Address	*Gage Building, Suite 1200* *Riverside Plaza* *Chicago, IL 60606-1200*

2. Save the document as *Hardcastle Fax*, and then preview, print, and close it.

Exercise 4 

1. Use the Calendar Wizard on the Other Documents tab in the Templates dialog box to create a March calendar for the current year in the Jazzy format and in Portrait orientation.
2. Save the document as *March Calendar*, and then preview, print, and close it.

Exercise 5 

1. Use the Contemporary Memo template on the Memos tab in the Templates dialog box as the basis for a custom template.
2. Key "Ben Adams" in the CC: placeholder and your name in the From: placeholder.
3. Save the document with the Document Template file type in the location specified by your instructor with the filename *Custom Memo Template.*
4. Preview, print, and close the template.

Exercise 6 

1. Use the *Custom Memo Template* you created in Exercise 5 (if you have not created the template, do so now) to create a new memo. Use the following information in the memo.

To:	*Alex Cruz*
Re:	*Vacation*
Text	*Your vacation scheduled for May 5-10 is approved. Please see Marla about getting another staff member to cover your client calls while you are out.*

2. Save the memorandum as *Cruz Memo*, and then preview, print, and close it.

Exercise 7 

1. Create a new fax cover sheet based on the Professional Fax template and insert the following information.

Return Address	*Gage Building, Suite 1200* *Riverside Plaza* *Chicago, IL 60606-1200*
Company Name	*Worldwide Exotic Foods, Inc.* (resize the cell to avoid word wrap)
To	*B. J. Chang*
From	*Bill Martin*
Fax #	*312-555-1345*
# of pages	*1*
Phone #	*312-555-1346*
Date	*Current Date*
Re:	*Sales Meeting*
CC:	*None*
Urgent	*X*
Comments	*I cannot attend the next sales meeting and I am sending Barbara Belville in my place. She will make the quarterly sales results presentation for me.*

2. Save the document as *Chang Fax*, and then preview, print, and close it.

Exercise 8 

1. Open the *Marketing Memo* document located on the Data Disk.
2. Remove all the variable information such as the addressee, reference, and text information and replace the current date with the date field. (*Hint:* Insert the date as a field.)
3. Save the document with the Document Template file type as *Marketing Memo Template* in the location specified by your instructor, and then preview, print, and close the template.
4. Create a new memo document using the *Marketing Memo Template* and the fictitious data of your choice.
5. Save the new document as *Marketing Memo Document*, and then preview, print, and close it.

Case Projects 

Project 1 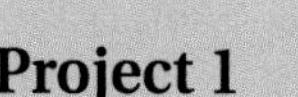

Viktor Winkler's assistant, Bob Thackery, returns from vacation and is impressed with the documents you have created. He wants to know how to use the built-in templates and how to create custom templates. Use the Ask A Question Box to research using built-in templates and creating custom templates. Write Bob an interoffice memorandum based on a memo template explaining how he can create documents with built-in and custom templates. Save, preview, and print the memo.

Project 2 

The Human Resources Department frequently receives unsolicited resumes from people around the world who want to work for Worldwide Exotic Foods. Company policy is to thank the sender for the resume and advise them that their resume will be kept on file for six months. If a position becomes available, the sender will be contacted to arrange for an interview. To save time in responding to unsolicited resumes, B. J. Chang asks you to create a block format custom letter template with B. J. Chang's signature line. The only variable data keyed in documents based on this new custom template is the letter address and the name portion of the salutation. The date, the "Dear" portion of the salutation, the body text, the closing, the signature line, and the typist's initials are fixed text in the template. Create, save, preview, and print the template. Then, create two letters, including attached envelopes to fictitious persons using the new custom letter template. Save, preview, and print the letters and envelopes.

Project 3  

Viktor Winkler needs a list of government Web sites containing information of interest to Worldwide Exotic Foods, Inc. management and employees. Connect to the Internet, and search the Web for government Web pages of interest. Print at least five Web pages. Use a report template of your choice to create a report on the Web sites you found. Save, preview, and print the report.

Project 4

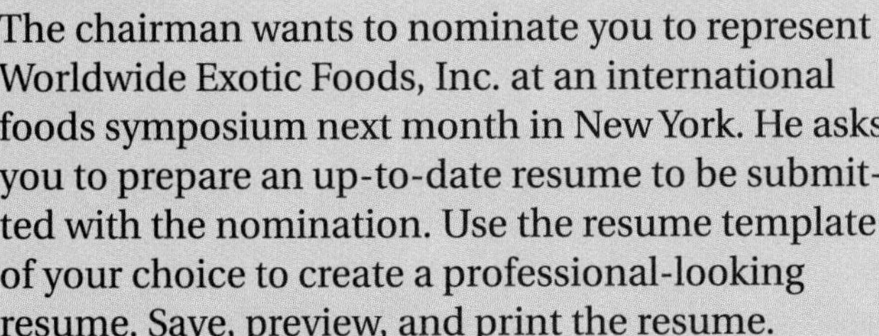

The chairman wants to nominate you to represent Worldwide Exotic Foods, Inc. at an international foods symposium next month in New York. He asks you to prepare an up-to-date resume to be submitted with the nomination. Use the resume template of your choice to create a professional-looking resume. Save, preview, and print the resume.

Project 5  

Viktor Winkler wants to include current U.S. government international travel warnings in a bulletin he wants faxed to each branch office and posted in the employee lounge area to warn traveling employees. He asks you use the Internet to locate the government page where international warnings are posted and then print the page. Create a document using an appropriate template and list the travel warnings you printed out. Save, preview, and print the document.

Project 6 

To save time in creating interoffice memos, Lydia Cruz asks you to create a human resources interoffice memorandum template. She wants you to use the Professional Memo template as the basis for the custom template but she does not want the page number at the bottom of the page. Create the custom memo template, making any other changes to styles, layout, and formatting you think appropriate. Save, preview, and print the document.

Project 7  

Viktor Winkler is so impressed with your work with templates and the amount of time you have saved by using them. He asks you to go to the Microsoft Office Template Gallery Web site and check the kinds of Word templates available there. Use a Word template to create a document describing what you find at the Web site. With your instructor's permission, download two new templates and create a new document based on each template. Save, preview, and print the documents.

Project 8  

Jody Haversham calls to ask for your help. She needs a list of expert information exchange Web sites to post in the employee cafeteria. Use the Internet to locate expert information exchange Web sites such as Ask.com. Then use an appropriate template to create a document listing at least four expert information Web sites. Save, preview, and print the document.

Comparing and Merging Documents

Chapter Overview

It is common to edit documents and keep track of the changes made and to compare and combine different documents. In this chapter, you edit a document, track your editing changes, and then insert an internal document notation called a comment. Next you compare your edited document with a similar document and merge both documents into a new, third document. Finally, you preview the resulting document as a Web page and then save it as a Web page.

Learning Objectives

- Track changes to a document
- View and edit comments
- Compare and merge documents
- Convert documents into Web pages

Case profile

After your successful two weeks assisting Viktor Winkler, the Human Resources Department asks you to spend a few days updating a document to be saved as a Web page. Your first assignment is to edit an existing document in a way that your supervisor can review the original document and the changes you have made.

chapter twelve

12.a Tracking Changes to a Document

To make it easier to review changes to documents, you can use the Track Changes feature. The Track Changes feature enables a reviewer to suggest changes to a document by actually keying the changes into the document. Then the document with changes can be reviewed online or in printed hard copy. When the document is reviewed online the changes can be accepted or rejected either individually or all at once. When reviewing the tracked changes to a document online, the reviewer can choose to view all the changes at once, or limit the kind of changes that are displayed. For example, you might want to see only the additions and deletions first without viewing any formatting changes. Some of the tracked changes are displayed inline with the original text and others are displayed in the document margin in a balloon-style notation.

Setting the Track Changes Options

You can determine the formatting style for tracked changes by setting options in the Track Changes tab of the Options dialog box or in the Track Changes dialog box. Your supervisor asks you to make some revisions in the *About the Internet* document and track your changes. Before you edit the document, you need to review the Track Changes options. To review the Track Changes options:

Step 1	***Create***	a new, blank document, if necessary
Step 2	***Right-click***	the TRK mode indicator on the status bar
Step 3	***Click***	Options

You set the formatting for the type of mark and the color for inserted text and reformatted text in this dialog box. You also can turn on or off the use of the balloon-style notations and specify their size and position. If you are printing the balloons, you can specify the paper orientation. Finally, you can indicate which lines are changed by positioning a mark at the margin of the changed line. The Track Changes dialog box on your screen "remembers" the last setting changes.

You want any text you insert to be changed to red and any reformatted text to have a double underline. You also want the balloons in the right margin and the changed lines mark to be positioned at the left margin of the line. To set the Track Changes options:

Step 1	***Click***	Color only in the Insertions: list, if necessary

MENU TIP

You can review the Track Changes options by clicking the Options command on the Tools menu and clicking the Track Changes tab.

MOUSE TIP

You can set options for tracking changes and turn on or off the Track Changes feature with the TRK mode indicator on the status bar. You can also click the Options command on the Show button list on the Reviewing toolbar to set the Track Changes options.

Step 2	*Click*	Red in the Color: list, if necessary
Step 3	*Click*	Double underline in the Formatting: list, if necessary
Step 4	*Insert*	check marks in the Use balloons in Print and Web Layout and Show lines connecting to text check boxes, if necessary
Step 5	*Key*	2.5" in the Preferred width: text box, if necessary
Step 6	*Click*	Inches in the Measure in: list, if necessary
Step 7	*Click*	Preserve in the Paper orientation: list, if necessary
Step 8	*Click*	the Left border in the Mark: list, if necessary

The Track Changes dialog box on your screen should look similar to Figure 12-1.

FIGURE 12-1
Track Changes Dialog Box

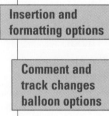

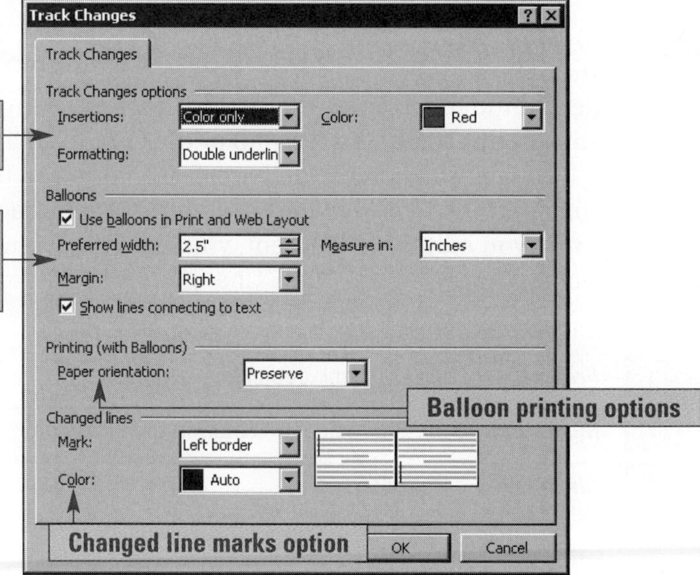

MOUSE TIP

You can also display the Reviewing toolbar with the toolbar shortcut menu.

Step 9	*Click*	OK

Tracking Changes

You can use the Track Changes command on the Tools menu to display the Reviewing toolbar and turn on the Track Changes feature. You can also use the TRK mode indicator on the status bar to turn on or off the Track Changes feature and to turn on the Reviewing toolbar. You use buttons on the Reviewing toolbar to manage the Track Changes process.

You can preview a document with tracked changes in several ways: Final mode shows how the document would look with all the editing changes; Final Showing Markup mode shows deleted text in balloons

MENU TIP

You can turn on or off the view of tracked changes with the Markup command on the View menu.

and inline inserted text and all formatting changes applied; Original mode shows the original unedited document; and Original Showing Markup mode shows the original document with inline deleted text and inserted text and formatting changes in balloons. You use the Display for Review button on the Reviewing toolbar to select your reviewing option.

To turn on the Track Changes feature and begin modifying the document:

Step 1	***Open***	the *About the Internet* document located on the Data Disk
Step 2	***Double-click***	the TRK mode indicator on the status bar
Step 3	***Observe***	the bolded TRK mode indicator on the status bar and the Reviewing toolbar
Step 4	***Dock***	the Reviewing Toolbar below the Formatting toolbar, if necessary

When you are editing or reviewing a document with tracked changes, you should use the Final Showing Markup view. To change the reviewing display:

Step 1	***Click***	the Display for Review button list arrow [Final Showing Markup] on the Reviewing toolbar
Step 2	***Click***	Final Showing Markup, if necessary

To edit the document:

Step 1	***Switch to***	Print Layout view, if necessary
Step 2	***View***	the nonprinting formatting marks, if necessary
Step 3	***Zoom***	the document to 75%
Step 4	***Delete***	the "Introduction to the Internet" paragraph heading
Step 5	***Bold***	the text "World Wide Web" in the first body paragraph
Step 6	***Replace***	the word "computer" in the last line of the first body paragraph with "multimedia"
Step 7	***Select***	all of the paragraph headings using the CTRL key
Step 8	***Change***	the formatting to Small caps effect
Step 9	***Move***	the insertion point to the top of the document
Step 10	***Observe***	the tracked changes, including the single vertical lines at the left margin that indicates changes

MOUSE TIP

You can turn on or off the display of insertions and deletions or formatting changes with the Show button on the Reviewing toolbar. You can turn on or off the track changes feature with the Track Changes button on the Reviewing toolbar. Finally, you can show or hide a separate changes reviewing pane with the Reviewing Pane button on the Reviewing toolbar.

QUICK TIP

You can select a tracked change in Normal view with the mouse pointer just as you would select any text. In Print Layout view or Web Layout view, you can select a tracked change by clicking or right-clicking the tracked change balloon. When you select a tracked change in Print Layout or Web Layout view, the dotted line from the source of the change to the balloon becomes a solid line and reformatted text, if applicable, appears selected.

Your screen should look similar to Figure 12-2.

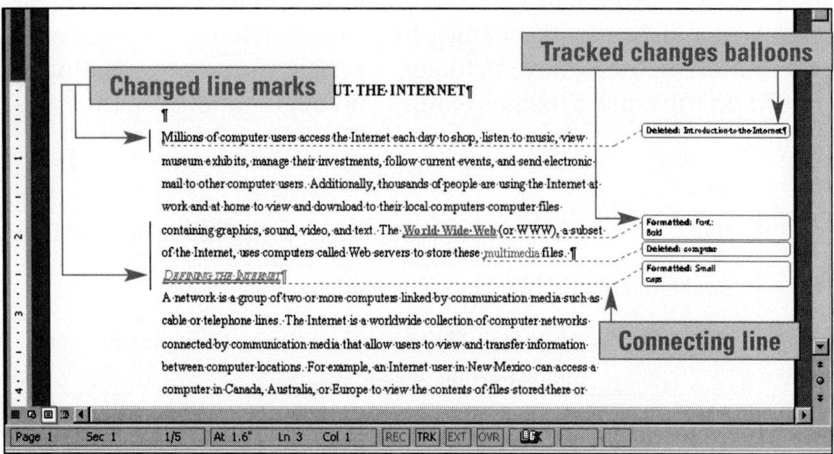

FIGURE 12-2
Tracked Changes Marked in a Document

Step 11	***Save***	the document as *Internet With Tracked Changes* and leave it open

> **CAUTION TIP**
>
> To view the Track Changes balloon-style notations you must be in Print Layout or Web Layout view or in Print Preview.

Accepting or Rejecting Tracked Changes

You can accept or reject individual changes or all changes with the Accept Change and Reject Change/Delete Comment buttons on the Reviewing toolbar. You also can use a shortcut menu to accept or reject individual changes. Your supervisor reviews all your changes and approves them. To accept all the changes:

Step 1	***Click***	the Accept Change button list arrow on the Reviewing toolbar
Step 2	***Click***	Accept All Changes in Document
Step 3	***Double-click***	TRK mode indicator on the status bar to turn off the Track Changes feature
Step 4	***Turn off***	the view of formatting marks, if necessary
Step 5	***Save***	the document as *Internet With Accepted Changes* and leave it open

Your supervisor asks you to insert an internal document notation that can be viewed by others when they read the document online.

12.b Viewing and Editing Comments

A **comment** is an internal notation in a document. Comment text is displayed in a balloon, if the balloon feature is turned on. Otherwise, the comment text is keyed in the Reviewing Pane. Your supervisor wants you to add a comment to the document title reminding employees to call the Human Resources Department for a list of new training classes. To add the comment to the document:

Step 1	*Zoom*	the document to 100%, if necessary
Step 2	*Move*	the insertion point to the end of the title text "ABOUT THE INTERNET"
Step 3	*Click*	the New Comment button  on the Reviewing toolbar
Step 4	*Scroll*	the document horizontally to view the Comment balloon containing the insertion point
Step 5	*Key*	Call the Human Resources Department for a list of new training classes.

Your screen should look similar to Figure 12-3.

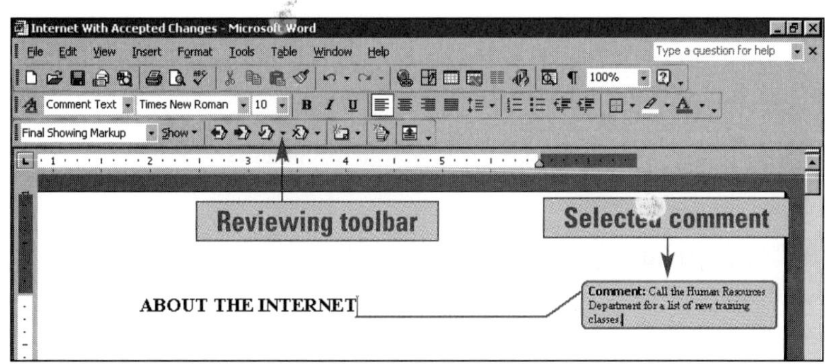

FIGURE 12-3
Comment Balloon and Text

The insertion point remains in the Comment balloon. If you move the insertion point to another position in the document, you can move it back into the Comment balloon simply by clicking inside the balloon. You can select, edit, and format text or add and delete text in a Comment balloon just as you would in the body of a document.

After reading the comment you decide to edit the comment text to add the Human Resources Department telephone extension. To edit the comment text:

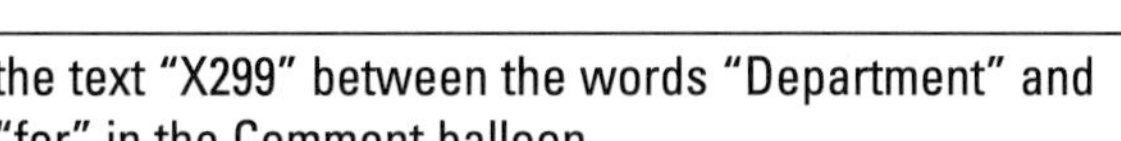

Step 1	*Insert*	the text "X299" between the words "Department" and "for" in the Comment balloon

C

MOUSE TIP

You can edit or delete a selected comment by clicking the New Comments button list arrow on the Reviewing toolbar. You also can delete an individual comment or all document comments by clicking the Reject Change/Delete Comment button on the Reviewing toolbar.

To view and edit a comment in Normal view, turn on the Reviewing Pane with the Reviewing Pane button on the Reviewing toolbar.

MENU TIP

You can insert a comment by using the Comment command on the Insert menu. You can delete an individual comment by right-clicking the comment balloon and clicking Delete Comment.

Step 2	*Save*	the document as *Internet With Edited Comment* and close it

Your supervisor wants you to merge your document with a similar document she created earlier.

C

12.c Comparing and Merging Documents

QUICK TIP

If your computer is equipped with a sound card and a microphone, you can create sound or voice comments. Voice comments are added to a document as sound objects inline with the text.

MOUSE TIP

To compare two documents and display only what changed between them, click the Legal blackline check box in the Compare and Merge Documents dialog box. Word accepts any previously tracked changes before showing the changes and then displays the changes in a new document. Do not use the Legal blackline option when comparing changes from multiple reviewers.

When merging two documents, Word compares the documents and then uses the Track Changes feature to illustrate the changes. Word identifies the document to be compared and merged as the **current document** (the document that is open) and the **target document** (the document you choose for comparison). During the comparison and merging process, you can choose one of three locations in which to merge the documents and display the document differences: into the current document; into the target document; or into a new, third document. You make the choice when you open the Compare and Merge Documents dialog box using the Compare and Merge Documents command on the Tools menu.

To compare and merge the documents:

Step 1	*Open*	the *Supervisors Document* document located on the Data Disk
Step 2	*Click*	Tools
Step 3	*Click*	Compare and Merge Documents

The Compare and Merge Documents dialog box, which is similar to the Open dialog box, opens. You select the target document and your merge option in this dialog box.

Step 4	*Switch to*	the disk drive and folder where your files are stored
Step 5	*Click*	the *Internet With Edited Comment* filename (do not double-click)
Step 6	*Click*	the Merge button list arrow to view the merge options
Step 7	*Click*	Merge into new document
Step 8	*Observe*	that a new, third document containing tracked changes opens
Step 9	*Scroll*	the document to review all the suggested changes

You review the tracked changes with your supervisor who suggests you reject the change from "multimedia" to "computer" and the title change, but accept all the remaining changes. To reject the "multimedia" deletion, the "computer" insertion, and the title change:

Step 1	***Right-click***	~~multimedia~~
Step 2	***Click***	Reject Deletion
Step 3	***Reject***	the "computer" insertion using the shortcut menu
Step 4	***Reject***	both title changes using the shortcut menu
Step 5	***Click***	the Accept Change button list arrow  on the Reviewing toolbar
Step 6	***Click***	Accept All Changes in Document
Step 7	***Hide***	the Reviewing toolbar
Step 8	***Save***	the document as *Compared and Merged Internet* and leave it open
Step 9	***Close***	the *Supervisors Document* document without saving changes

Your supervisor wants you to save the document as a Web page so that other employees can view it via the company intranet.

notes

It is assumed you have read Chapter 3 in the Office unit before starting this section. It is also assumed that you are using the Internet Explorer Web browser. If you are using a different browser, your instructor may modify the following activities.

12.d Converting Documents into Web Pages

You can quickly convert an existing Word document to a Web page to be later uploaded to a Web server and then viewed by others on a local intranet or on the Internet using a Web browser. You do this by simply saving the document as a Web page. Before you save a Word document as a Web page, it is a good idea to first preview it in your Web browser to see how it will look.

QUICK TIP

After you open the Compare and Merge Documents dialog box, click the Merge button list arrow and then click the Merge command to merge changes from the current document into the target document, which then becomes active. You click the Merge into current document command in the Merge button list to merge the changes from the target document into the current document.

C

To preview the *Compared and Merged Internet* document in a Web browser:

Step 1	***Click***	File
Step 2	***Click***	Web Page Preview
Step 3	***Observe***	that the Internet Explorer Web browser opens and contains the document
Step 4	***Maximize***	the Internet Explorer window, if necessary
Step 5	***Scroll***	to review the document
Step 6	***Move***	the mouse pointer to the Comment notation following the document title
Step 7	***Observe***	the ScreenTip containing the Comment text
Step 8	***Close***	the Internet Explorer window

The document is formatted for viewing as a Web page, so you can save it. To save the document as a Web page:

Step 1	***Click***	File
Step 2	***Click***	Save As Web Page

The Save As dialog box opens and the file type is changed to Web Page. Before you save the document you can create a descriptive page title that appears in the title bar of the Web browser when the page is viewed. To change the page title:

Step 1	***Click***	the Change Title button
Step 2	***Key***	About the Internet in the Page title: text box in the Set Page Title dialog box
Step 3	***Click***	OK
Step 4	***Save***	the Web page as *About the Internet Web Page* and close it

It's easy to compare and merge different documents, accept or reject the differences, and then preview and save the resulting document as a Web page.

CAUTION TIP

When you save a Word document as a Web page, Word may create an additional folder in the location where the Web page is stored. This folder contains any special instructions and graphic images needed by the Web browser to properly display the Web page. Do not delete this folder unless you are also deleting the associated Web page. Also, if you move the Web page to a different location, remember to move its associated folder to the new location.

QUICK TIP

Because Web page viewers prefer to quickly scan text for information, large sections of densely worded text may need to be reformatted by using paragraph headings, line spacing, bulleted lists, and so forth to make the text easier to read and scan online.

Summary

- The Track Changes feature makes it easier to review document changes either online or in hard copy.
- Tracked changes are identified by different formatting or by balloon-style notations in the margin.
- You can change the formatting style of tracked changes in the Track Changes tab of the Options dialog box or in the Track Changes dialog box.
- You can turn on the Track Changes feature with a menu command, a button on the Reviewing toolbar, or the TRK mode indicator on the status bar.
- When reviewing a document that contains tracked changes, you can accept or reject changes with buttons on the Reviewing toolbar or with a shortcut menu.
- A comment is an internal document note that appears in a balloon-style notation.
- You can compare and merge two documents by merging the changes into the currently open document, the target document (the document being compared to), or a new, third document.
- When you compare and merge two documents, the differences are shown as tracked changes.
- You can preview a Word document as a Web page to see how it will look when viewed in a Web browser before saving it as a Web page.
- You can easily convert an existing Word document into a Web page by saving it as a Web page.

Commands Review

Action	Menu Bar	Shortcut Menu	Toolbar	Task Pane	Keyboard
Set the Track Changes options	Tools, Options	Right-click the TRK mode indicator on the status bar, click Options	Click the Options command on Show list		ALT + T, O
Turn on the Track Changes feature	Tools, Track Changes	Right-click the TRK mode indicator on the status bar, click Track Changes	Double-click the TRK mode indicator on the status bar		ALT + T, T CTRL + SHIFT+ E
Select a tracked change			In Normal view: drag to select the changed text In Print Layout or Web Layout view: click or right-click the tracked change balloon		
Accept tracked change		Right-click change, click Accept (Insertion or Deletion or Formatting Change)			
Reject tracked change		Right-click change, click Reject (Insertion or Deletion or Formatting Change)			
Create a comment	Insert, Comment				ALT + I, M
View the Reviewing Pane (View and edit comments in Normal view)					
Edit a comment in Print Layout or Web Layout view			Click Edit Comment on the list		Key, delete, and edit comment text inside the balloon-style notation or in the Reviewing Pane
Delete a comment		Right-click the comment balloon and click Delete Comment	Click Delete Comment on the list		
Compare and Merge documents	Tools, Compare and Merge Documents				ALT + T, D
Preview an existing Word document as a Web page	File, Web Page Preview				ALT + F, B
Save an existing Word document as a Web page	File, Save as Web Page				ALT + F, G

Concepts Review

Circle the correct answer.

1. You can turn on or off the Track Changes feature by double-clicking the:
[a] Turn On/Off Track Changes button.
[b] TRK mode indicator.
[c] OVR mode indicator.
[d] Insert Track Changes button.

2. You can manage tracked changes and comments with buttons on the:
[a] Track Changes toolbar.
[b] Comments and Changes toolbar.
[c] Reviewing toolbar.
[d] Compare and Merge Documents toolbar.

3. You cannot see the track change balloon in:
[a] Print Layout view.
[b] Web Layout view.
[c] Print Preview.
[d] Normal view.

4. A comment is a(n):
[a] tracked change.
[b] internal document notation.
[c] formatting option.
[d] target document.

5. To edit comments in Normal view, you must:
[a] display the Reviewing Pane.
[b] click the comment balloon.
[c] turn on the Edit Comment feature in the Options dialog box.
[d] first compare the document to another document.

6. When comparing and merging two documents, Word illustrates the changes with the:
[a] Comment feature.
[b] Compare feature.
[c] Track Changes feature.
[d] Merge feature.

7. When comparing and merging two documents, the document you choose for comparison is called the:
[a] comparison document.
[d] original document.
[c] current document.
[d] target document.

8. Before you save an existing Word document as a Web page, it is a good idea to first:
[a] format the document.
[b] compare the document to another document.
[c] track changes to the document.
[d] preview the document as a Web page in your Web browser.

Circle **T** if the statement is true or **F** if the statement is false.

T F 1. You can view and change the options for formatting and displaying tracked changes in the Options or Track Changes dialog box.

T F 2. You can change the view of tracked changes with the Display for Review or Show buttons on the Track Changes toolbar.

T F 3. You can use a shortcut menu to delete a comment in Print Layout view.

T F 4. The Track Changes dialog box "remembers" its previous settings.

T F 5. To view tracked changes in Normal view, you can display the Reviewing Pane.

T F 6. When comparing and merging two documents, the document that is open is called the original document.

T F 7. You can merge two documents into a new, third document.

T F 8. When you save a Word document as a Web page, Word creates a new folder containing special Web browser instructions associated with the Web page.

Skills Review

Exercise 1 C

1. Open the *Preparing For A Speech* document located on the Data Disk.
2. Preview the document as a Web page.
3. Scroll to review the document, and then close the Web browser.
4. Center the document title and apply Arial, bold formatting.
5. Using the CTRL key, select the paragraph headings "Overcoming Fear" and "Make Your Talk Interesting," and apply Arial, bold formatting.
6. Using the CTRL key, select all the paragraphs following the "Overcoming Fear" paragraph heading and all the paragraphs following the "Make Your Talk Interesting" paragraph heading.
7. Create bulleted lists from the selected paragraphs.
8. Select all the text below the document title and change the line spacing to 1.5 lines.
9. Preview the document as a Web page, review the new look and the improved readability, and close the Web browser.
10. Save the document as a Web page with the title "Speaking Tips" and the filename *Preparing For A Speech*, and then preview, print, and close it.

Exercise 2 C

1. Open the *Security Policy* document located on the Data Disk and view the document in Print Layout view.
2. Open the Track Changes dialog box using the TRK mode indicator on the status bar.
3. Change the insertion formatting option to Italic, Bright Green; change the balloon position to the Left margin; change the Paper orientation for printing with balloons to Force Landscape (to print in Landscape orientation without changing the document orientation); and view the changed line mark at the Right border.
4. Turn on the Track Changes feature and display the Reviewing toolbar using the TRK mode indicator on the status bar.
5. Change the Warning! line to bold, uppercase.
6. Delete the word "clearance" in the first line of the body paragraph; change the security level from "8" to "10"; and change "this level" in the second line to "this area."
7. Turn off the Track Changes feature.
8. Save the document as *Security Policy With Tracked Changes*, and then preview, print, and close it. (*Hint:* Click Yes if warned that the margins in section 1 are outside the printable area of the page.)

Exercise 3 C

1. Open the *Security Policy With Tracked Changes* document you created in Exercise 2. If you have not completed Exercise 2, do so now.
2. Switch to Print Layout view, if necessary, and hide the Reviewing toolbar.

3. Right-click the document title tracked change balloon and accept the change.
4. Use the shortcut menu method to accept the "clearance" deletion, the "level" deletion, and the "area" insertion.
5. Use the shortcut menu method to reject the "8" deletion and the "10" insertion.
6. Save the document as *Security Policy With Accepted Changes*, and then preview, print, and close it.

Exercise 4 C

1. Open the *Vancouver Warehouse Report* document located on the Data Disk and switch to Print Layout view, if necessary.
2. Change the Track Changes options to view all insertions with Color only in Red; formatting changes with a single Underline; balloons at the Right margin; changed line marks at the Left border; and change the Printing (with Balloons) paper orientation option in the Track Changes dialog box to Force Landscape, if necessary.
3. Compare the current document to the *London Warehouse Report* target document located on the Data Disk and merge the changes into the current document.
4. Select Final using the Display for Review button on the Reviewing toolbar and review how the document would look if all changes were accepted then switch back to the Final Showing Markup display.
5. Reject all the formatting changes *except the numbered list change* with the shortcut menu.
6. Accept all the remaining changes with the Accept Change button on the Reviewing toolbar.
7. Save the document as *Vancouver Warehouse Report With Accepted Changes*, and then preview, print, and close it.

Exercise 5 C

1. Open the *Winter Schedule* document located on the Data Disk.
2. Preview the document as a Web page.
3. Italicize the two lines beginning "Dates:" and set left-aligned tab stops for the two lines at 1.5, 3, and 4.5 inches on the horizontal ruler using the mouse pointer. (*Hint:* When changing the formatting for multiple areas of the document in the same way, don't forget to use the CTRL key to select the multiple areas.)
4. Select the document title and the three paragraph headings and apply Arial, bold formatting.
5. Change the document title font size to 14 point.
6. Preview the document as a Web page and observe the different formatting.
7. Save the document as a Web page with the title "Winter Schedule" and the filename *Winter Schedule Web Page*; print, and close it.

Exercise 6 C

1. Open the *Automation Society* document located on the Data Disk.
2. Switch to Normal view and display the Reviewing toolbar, if necessary.
3. Change the Printing (with Balloons) paper orientation option in the Track Changes dialog box to Force Landscape, if necessary.
4. Insert a comment containing the following after the document title using the New Comment button on the Reviewing toolbar. (*Hint:* In Normal view, the Reviewing Pane opens when you insert the comment. Key the comment text in the Reviewing Pane at the position of the insertion point, then click the Reviewing Pane button on the Reviewing toolbar to close the Reviewing Pane.)

   Jody, please review this document and give me a call at X367 if you have any questions or comments.

5. Observe the red comment icon at the end of title text.
6. Save the document as *Automation Society With Comment*, and then preview and print it.
7. Switch to Print Layout view and observe the comment balloon.
8. Edit the comment to replace "Jody" with "Helen" and "X367" with "X450."
9. Save the document as *Automation Society With Edited Comment*, and then preview, print, and close it.

Exercise 7 

1. Open the *Policy #152* document located on the Data Disk.
2. Compare the current document to the *Security Policy With Accepted Changes* document you created in Exercise 3 and merge the changes to a new, third document. If you have not completed Exercise 3, do so now.
3. Reject the title formatting change and accept all the remaining changes.
4. Save the document as *Compared And Merged Security Policy*, and then preview, print, and close it.
5. Close the *Policy #152* document.

Exercise 8 

1. Open the *Compared And Merged Security Policy* document you created in Exercise 7. If you have not completed Exercise 7, do so now.
2. Preview the document as a Web page and then close the Web browser.
3. Make formatting changes you feel are appropriate to make the document more attractive or easier to read in the Web browser.
4. Save the document as a Web page with the title "Security Policy" and the filename *Security Policy Web Page*; and then print and close it.

Case Projects

Project 1 

One of the Purchasing Department employees has a new assignment that requires him to compare and then merge two documents. He asks for your help. Using the Ask A Question Box, search online Help for information on comparing and merging documents. Then create a document containing at least two paragraphs that describe the compare and merge process. Save, preview, and print the document.

Project 2 

Your supervisor has asked you to make a short presentation on how to use the Track Changes feature at the next staff meeting. Use the Ask A Question Box to review online Help topics related to tracking changes. Then create an outline of the topics you plan to cover. Save, preview, and print the outline. With your instructor's permission, use your outline to demonstrate the Track Changes feature to two classmates.

Project 3 

Kelly Armstead calls you for help. She has displayed the Reviewing toolbar and wants to know how to use each of the buttons. She is also curious about how to use the TRK mode indicator on the status bar. Using the What's This? Help tool and the Ask A Question Box, review the Reviewing toolbar and the TRK mode indicator online Help topics. Then write Kelly an interoffice memo containing a brief explanation of the toolbar buttons and mode indicator. Save, preview, and print the memo.

Project 4

At next week's "brown bag" lunch and training session for the Purchasing Department clerical staff, the discussion topic is "Saving a Word Document as a Web Page" and you have been asked to make the presentation. Use the Ask A Question Box to locate information on your topic. Create an outline containing information for your presentation. Save, preview, and print the outline. With your instructor's permission, use the outline to describe the process of previewing and saving a Word document as a Web page to a group of classmates.

Project 5

Marcia Davenport, in the Finance Department, needs to make changes to an existing document and then send the document to her supervisor for review online. Her supervisor wants to see both the original document and Marcia's changes and then be able to accept or reject the changes as he is reviewing the document online. Neither Marcia nor her supervisor knows where to start with this project, so she calls you. Create an interoffice memorandum to Marcia describing how to change the Track Changes options, how to turn on the Track Changes features, and how to accept or reject changes using both the toolbar and shortcut menu method while the document is being reviewed online. Save, preview, and print the memo.

Project 6

Your supervisor asks you to find out what different compare and merge software programs might be available. Using the Internet and the keywords "compare and merge" search for other software vendors that offer file compare and merge software. Print at least three Web pages. Create an interoffice memorandum to your supervisor describing three different compare and merge software applications including vendor name and URL, package features, and package prices. Save, preview, and print the memo and attach the three printed Web pages.

Project 7

Chris Lofton calls and requests your help. Several of his new Word Processing Department employees are having problems using the comment, tracked changes, and compare and merge documents features. The most common problems include:

1. Word not tracking all the changes made to a document.
2. Problems rejecting changes made to a bullet list.
3. Comment text not appearing in a ScreenTip.
4. Merging changes into the wrong document.

Using online Help, troubleshoot problems working with comments, tracked changes, and comparing and merging documents. Then create an interoffice memorandum to Chris, which details each problem and its possible solution. Save, preview, and print the document.

Project 8

While attending the monthly meeting of the Administrative Assistants Group, you overhear two other attendees discussing Office "document libraries." You want to know more about document libraries, so you decide to check online Help. Using the Ask A Question Box, review the online Help topics related to document libraries. Then create a report-style document containing at least three paragraphs describing document libraries and how you might use them when working with Word documents. Save, preview, and print the document.

Word 2002

Integrating Word with Other Office Applications

LEARNING OBJECTIVES

- Use Excel data in a Word document
- Share data with PowerPoint
- Use Access tables or queries in a Word document
- Create and modify charts using data from other applications

Chapter Overview

A very important feature of the Word application is the ability to integrate data with other Office applications. This means you can create documents with the application most suited to that information, such as analyzing and calculating numerical data in Excel, and then use that same information in other application documents. In this chapter, you learn to use Excel, PowerPoint, and Access data in Word documents.

Case profile

Marisa DaFranco, the executive assistant to the chairperson, asks for your help in preparing documents for the third quarter sales meeting. Working with Marisa, you combine information from Excel worksheets, PowerPoint slide show presentations, and Access database information with Word documents.

13.a Using Excel Data in a Word Document

The Excel application is designed to analyze and perform calculations on numerical data rather than prepare text documents. You enter data in Excel **workbooks** that contain **worksheets** consisting of columns and rows similar to Word tables. Then you use Excel special features, which are more flexible and comprehensive than Word table features, to analyze and format the numerical data. When you have a large set of numerical data that includes calculations, you should use an Excel worksheet instead of a Word table to take advantage of Excel's special features.

It is possible to enter, format, and calculate numerical data in an Excel worksheet and then integrate that data into a Word document in several ways. You can:

1. Insert an Excel file into a Word document.
2. Copy and paste Excel worksheet data or a chart into a Word document.
3. Embed Excel data or a chart in a Word document.
4. Link Excel data or a chart in a Word document.
5. Import Excel data into a Microsoft Graph Chart datasheet and place the chart object in a Word document.

When you **insert** an Excel file into a Word document, the data is placed in a Word table that must be edited with Word table features.

When you use the Copy and Paste commands, the data are pasted into a Word table. Neither option maintains a link to the original Excel data—that is, the Word document includes a copy of the data, but it does not maintain any connection to the Excel workbook. Any changes you make to the data in the Word document do *not* appear in the original Excel workbook. Use the insert or copy and paste option when you want to include Excel data in a Word document in a table format, and when you want to edit the data with Word editing features. Do not use these options if you want to edit the data with Excel editing features or if you want to edit the data in the original Excel workbook.

When you **embed** Excel data, you place a copy of the data in a Word document as an object that you can edit only with Excel menu commands and toolbar buttons. However, the embedded data maintains no link or connection with the original Excel workbook. Any changes you make to the data in the Word document do *not* appear in the original Excel workbook. Use the embed method when you want to include Excel data in a Word document and want to edit the data with the Excel features (instead of Word features) without affecting the original Excel data.

QUICK TIP

When sharing data between Excel and Word, Excel is usually the **source**, or originating application and Word is usually the **destination**, or target application. However, you can embed and link Word text into an Excel worksheet. For example, you can paste Word text such as a date into the Excel formula bar; or, you can "paste link" a lengthy piece of text from a Word document into a worksheet cell or paste Word text into a text box on a worksheet.

When you **link** Excel worksheet data to a Word document, the data are displayed in the Word document but stored and edited in the Excel workbook. You must make any changes to the data in the original Excel workbook. When you open the Word document, the data is automatically updated to reflect the changes in the original Excel workbook. Use the link method when the Excel workbook data changes frequently.

The activities in this chapter assume you are familiar with the Excel, PowerPoint, and Access applications. Your instructor may provide additional information about these applications before you begin these activities.

Copying and Pasting Excel Data into a Word Document

To include Excel data in a Word document and then edit the data with Word editing features, you can copy the data from an Excel worksheet and then paste it into a Word document. You use this method to paste data from an Excel worksheet located in the *Worldwide Exotic Foods Sales Report* workbook into the *Worldwide Memo* document. To open the Excel and Word files:

Step 1	***Open***	the *Worldwide Memo* document located on the Data Disk
Step 2	***Move***	the insertion point to the end of the document
Step 3	***Open***	the Excel application and the *Worldwide Exotic Foods Sales Report* Excel workbook located on the Data Disk and maximize the Excel window, if necessary
Step 4	***Click***	the Sales Data sheet tab, if necessary

You want to use the data in the group of cells (called a **range**) that start in cell A1 and end in cell F10. To copy the worksheet data to the Office Clipboard:

Step 1	***Move***	the insertion point to cell A1 (the cell pointer becomes a large white plus pointer)
Step 2	***Drag***	down and to the right to cell F10 to select the range of cells A1:F10
Step 3	***Right-click***	the selected range of cells
Step 4	***Click***	Copy

QUICK TIP

A hyperlink is text or an image associated with the location or path to another page. You can create hyperlinks to link Word documents to each other or to link documents created in other Office applications, such as Excel or PowerPoint. You can also create hyperlinks between two Word documents. This is an excellent alternative to embedding or linking data maintained in other Office applications.

You create hyperlinks with the Hyperlink command on the Insert menu or the Insert Hyperlink button on the Standard toolbar. You can also create a hyperlink to a Web page or Office document by keying the URL or network path and pressing the SPACEBAR. The option to automatically create hyperlinks as you type is in the AutoFormat as You Type tab in the AutoCorrect dialog box.

The Excel data is stored on the Office Clipboard and the Clipboard task pane may appear. To switch to the Word application and paste the data into the *Worldwide Memo* document in Word's default table format:

Step 1	***Click***	the *Worldwide Memo* document button on the taskbar
Step 2	***Display***	the Clipboard task pane, if necessary
Step 3	***Click***	the Worldwide Exotic Foods, Inc. copied item in the Click an item to paste: list in the Clipboard task pane
Step 4	***Observe***	the Excel data pasted into the Word document

To reformat the table with Word's commands and features:

Step 1	***Turn on***	the gridlines, if necessary
Step 2	***Double-click***	the right boundary of the Branch, Meat, Cheese, Produce, Beverage, and Total columns in the table to AutoFit each column's width
Step 3	***Right-align***	the dollar values in the cells
Step 4	***Right-align***	the Meat, Cheese, Produce, Beverage, and Total column headings
Step 5	***Delete***	the blank row below the three table heading rows
Step 6	***Merge***	the three table heading rows
Step 7	***Center***	the table horizontally
Step 8	***Hide***	the gridlines
Step 9	***Click***	the Clear All button Clear All on the Clipboard task pane
Step 10	***Click***	the Close button on the Clipboard task pane title bar
Step 11	***Move***	the insertion point to the end of the document, if necessary
Step 12	***Scroll***	to view the table, if necessary

Your screen should look similar to Figure 13-1.

QUICK TIP

You can insert an Excel file into a Word document. Open a Word document and then click the File command on the Insert menu. Select the workbook file, the desired worksheet, and any range of cells if appropriate, then insert the data. The data are inserted into a Word table that often requires substantial formatting to provide a professional presentation of the data. For more information on inserting an Excel worksheet into a Word document, see online Help.

TASK PANE TIP

You can display the Clipboard task pane by clicking Office Clipboard on the Edit menu or by pressing the CTRL + C keys twice.

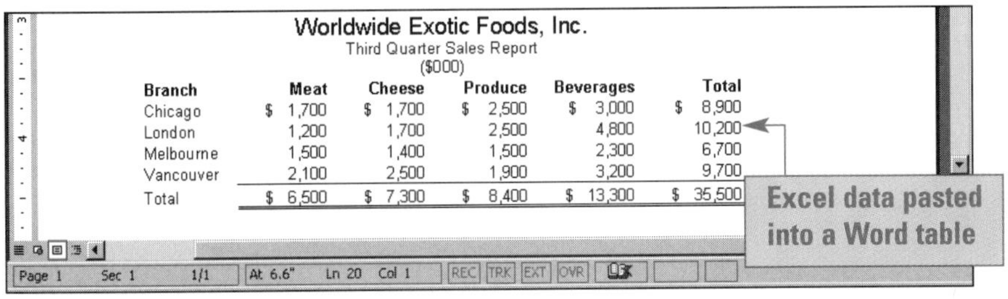
Worldwide Exotic Foods, Inc.
Third Quarter Sales Report
($000)
Branch Meat Cheese Produce Beverages Total
Chicago $ 1,700 $ 1,700 $ 2,500 $ 3,000 $ 8,900
London 1,200 1,700 2,500 4,800 10,200
Melbourne 1,500 1,400 1,500 2,300 6,700
Vancouver 2,100 2,500 1,900 3,200 9,700
Total $ 6,500 $ 7,300 $ 8,400 $ 13,300 $ 35,500
Excel data pasted into a Word table
Page 1 Sec 1 1/1 At 6.6" Ln 20 Col 1 REC TRK EXT OVR

FIGURE 13-1
Excel Data Pasted into a Word Table

chapter thirteen

MENU TIP

You can embed Excel worksheet data in a Word document with the Object command on the Insert menu. You can also use the Copy and Paste Special commands on the Edit menu.

Step 13	*Save*	the document as *Worldwide Memo With Pasted Data* and close it (leave the Excel application and workbook open)

Embedding Excel Worksheet Data in a Word Document

Sometimes you need to share data between Excel and Word but still want to edit the data with the Excel menus and toolbars. In this case, you insert the Excel worksheet data into the Word document as an embedded object. Embedding leaves the data in its original Excel format and you must edit it with Excel features.

You need to reopen the *Worldwide Memo* document and then copy and paste the Excel data into it as an embedded object using the Paste Special command. To create an embedded object:

CAUTION TIP

Remember that simply pasting Excel data into a Word document places the data in a Word table. To create an embedded Excel object, use the Paste Special command not the Paste command, Clipboard task pane, or Paste button.

Step 1	*Open*	the *Worldwide Memo* document located on the Data Disk
Step 2	*Move*	the insertion point to the end of the document
Step 3	*Switch to*	the Excel application and worksheet using the taskbar
Step 4	*Copy*	the selected range A1:F10
Step 5	*Switch to*	Word and the document using the taskbar
Step 6	*Click*	Edit
Step 7	*Click*	Paste Special

The Paste Special dialog box on your screen should look similar to Figure 13-2.

FIGURE 13-2
Paste Special Dialog Box

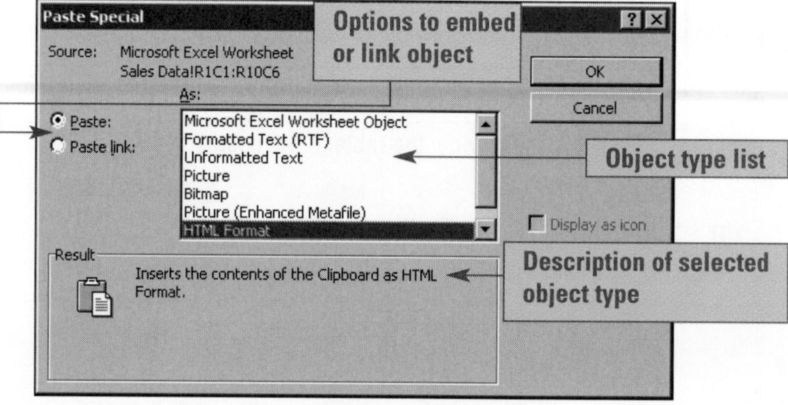

The eight data types allow you to embed or link the Excel worksheet data in the Clipboard as an Excel object, data in a table, pictures, or HTML format. You can click a data type in the As: list box and view its description in the Result box. The Display as icon option inserts an icon representing the worksheet data in the Word document. Double-clicking the icon in the destination document displays the worksheet data. To embed the worksheet data:

Step 1	***Click***	the Paste: option button, if necessary
Step 2	***Double-click***	Microsoft Excel Worksheet Object in the As: list box
Step 3	***Observe***	the embedded Excel object in the document
Step 4	***Click***	the embedded Excel object to select it
Step 5	***Observe***	the eight sizing handles on the object's border
Step 6	***Center***	the selected object horizontally using the Formatting toolbar
Step 7	***Deselect***	the object
Step 8	***Save***	the document as *Worldwide Memo With Embedded Data* and leave it open

You can edit an embedded worksheet object by double-clicking the object to view the Excel menu bar, toolbars, and worksheet grid. When you edit an embedded object, you are editing the data *only* in the Word document (although you use the Excel features). You are *not* editing the data in the original Excel source workbook.

You need to update the London meat expense in the worksheet object and then verify that no changes are made to the data in the Excel source file. To edit the embedded worksheet object:

Step 1	***Double-click***	the Excel embedded object to view the Excel features
Step 2	***Observe***	the Excel menu bar and toolbars and the data in an Excel worksheet grid
Step 3	***Observe***	that the title bar indicates you are still working in the Word application

To turn off the gridlines and edit the data in cell B7:

Step 1	***Click***	Tools
Step 2	***Click***	Options and click the View tab, if necessary

QUICK TIP

When you embed data or a chart from an Excel worksheet in a Word document, the entire workbook is embedded. When you activate the embedded Excel object for editing, you can view different worksheets by clicking the individual sheet tabs.

MENU TIP

You can edit a selected embedded Excel object by pointing to the Worksheet Object command on the Edit menu and clicking Edit. You can also right-click an embedded Excel object, point to Worksheet Object, and click Edit.

QUICK TIP

Sometimes you may have a few lines of numerical data to enter directly into a Word document and you would like to use the more comprehensive Excel features to format the data or perform calculations on it. Instead of first entering and formatting the data in an Excel workbook and then creating an embedded Excel object in the Word document, you can simply insert a blank Excel worksheet object directly into the Word document and key and format the data in the blank worksheet object. You use the Object command on the Insert menu or the Insert Microsoft Excel Worksheet button on the Standard toolbar to do this.

Step 3	*Click*	the Gridlines check box to remove the check mark
Step 4	*Click*	OK
Step 5	*Click*	cell B7 (column B and row 7) to make it the active cell
Step 6	*Key*	2500
Step 7	*Press*	the ENTER key
Step 8	*Observe*	the recalculated totals in cells F7, B10, and F10
Step 9	*Click*	anywhere in the document outside the embedded worksheet object to deselect it

The data in the worksheet object have changed. To verify that no changes have been made to the original Excel workbook:

Step 1	*Switch to*	the Excel application and workbook using the taskbar
Step 2	*Observe*	that the gridlines still appear and that the data in B7 and the totals in F7, B10, and F10 did not change
Step 3	*Switch to*	the Word application and document using the taskbar
Step 4	*Save*	the document and close it

Linking Excel Worksheet Data to a Word Document

When you link data between an Excel worksheet and a Word document, the Word destination file contains only a reference, or pointer, to the data—although the data are visible in the document. The data exist only in the Excel source file. When you edit linked data, you actually open the source application and file and do all your editing in the source file. When you change data in the source file, the data displayed in the destination file are updated.

You want to insert a linked Excel object in the *Worldwide Memo* document and then edit the original source worksheet to update the linked document. To begin:

Step 1	*Open*	the *Worldwide Memo* document located on the Data Disk
Step 2	*Move*	the insertion point to the end of the document
Step 3	*Switch to*	the Excel application and workbook using the taskbar
Step 4	*Save*	the workbook as *Sales Report 2*

Step 5	*Select*	the range A1:F10, if necessary
Step 6	*Copy*	the selected range
Step 7	*Switch to*	the Word application and document using the taskbar

To paste the Excel data as a linked object:

Step 1	*Open*	the Paste Special dialog box
Step 2	*Click*	the Paste link: option button
Step 3	*Double-click*	Microsoft Excel Worksheet Object in the As: list
Step 4	*Observe*	that a linked Excel worksheet object appears in the *Worldwide Memo* document
Step 5	*Center*	the object

By default, any changes you make to the source Excel worksheet are updated automatically in the Word document each time you open the document. However, you can require that the linked Excel object be updated manually. This allows you more control over whether or not to show the most current changes in the original Excel worksheet when you open the Word document. When you no longer want the Excel object to be linked to the original Excel workbook, you can break the link. If the original Excel workbook is moved to a new location, you can redirect the link. You make these changes in the Links dialog box.

You want to be able to control the updating process for the linked Excel object. To change the link status:

Step 1	*Right-click*	the linked Excel object
Step 2	*Point to*	Linked Worksheet Object
Step 3	*Click*	Links to open the Links dialog box

Except for the location of the Excel workbook file, the Links dialog box on your screen should look similar to Figure 13-3.

CAUTION TIP

It is a good idea to link data between files when you do not need a copy of the data in the destination file. Linking data between files saves disk space because the same information is not duplicated in both the source file and the destination file. However, the source file must be available at all times to provide the data for the destination file. If you move or rename the source file without updating the link in the destination file, an error may occur when the destination file looks for the linked data. For more information on breaking, modifying, and reestablishing links, see online Help.

FIGURE 13-3
Links Dialog Box

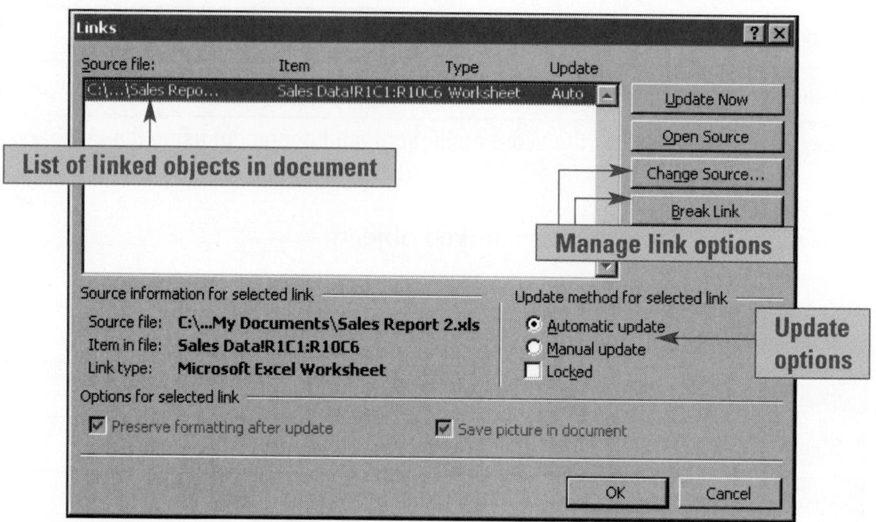

MENU TIP

You can manage the Excel links in a Word document by selecting the linked object, clicking the Edit command, pointing to Linked Worksheet Object, and then clicking the desired subcommand.

Step 4	***Click***	the Manual update option button
Step 5	***Click***	OK
Step 6	***Save***	the document as *Worldwide Memo With Linked Data* and close it

MOUSE TIP

You can open the Excel application and source workbook file by double-clicking a linked Excel object.

The Excel object in the *Worldwide Memo With Linked Data* is a reference to the *Sales Report 2* Excel source workbook file. The data does not exist in Word document and cannot be edited in the Word document.

Marisa asks you to change the Vancouver branch produce sales to $2,500 in the *Sales Report 2* Excel workbook and then update the *Worldwide Memo With Linked Data* document. To edit the Excel workbook:

Step 1	***Switch to***	the Excel application and workbook using the taskbar
Step 2	***Click***	cell D9 to make it the active cell
Step 3	***Key***	2500
Step 4	***Press***	the ENTER key to enter the data in the cell
Step 5	***Save***	the workbook and close the Excel application and the workbook
Step 6	***Open***	the *Worldwide Memo With Linked Data* document
Step 7	***Right-click***	the linked Excel object
Step 8	***Click***	Update Link
Step 9	***Observe***	that the value for Vancouver's produce is updated to $2,500

Step 10	***Deselect***	the linked Excel object
Step 11	***Save***	the document as *Worldwide Memo With Edited Linked Data* and close it

In addition to using Excel data in Word, you can share data between PowerPoint and Word.

13.b Sharing Data with PowerPoint

The PowerPoint application provides tools for creating slides and audience handout materials for presentations. You can integrate a PowerPoint presentation with Word in several ways. You can copy and paste PowerPoint information into Word documents, or you can embed or link PowerPoint slides into a Word document just as you can with Excel worksheet data or charts. You can send PowerPoint items, such as slides, notes pages, or an outline to Word to be edited or printed. In addition, you can create a PowerPoint presentation from a Word outline.

Creating a PowerPoint Presentation from a Word Outline

You can create a Word outline using outline level headings and then send that outline to PowerPoint to create slides. When you send a Word outline to PowerPoint, the Level 1 heading formatted text creates a new Text slide containing a bulleted list. The remaining lower-level headings create the individual bulleted text items on the slide.

You can create an outline in Outline view by selecting text and then applying an outline level heading to the text or by using toolbar buttons to demote or promote selected text to different outline levels. To open a Word document and view it in Outline view:

Step 1	***Open***	the *Worldwide Outline* document located on the Data Disk
Step 2	***Click***	the Outline View button to switch to Outline view
Step 3	***Observe***	that the Outlining toolbar opens
Step 4	***Dock***	the Outlining toolbar below the Formatting toolbar, if necessary

Your screen should look similar to Figure 13-4.

QUICK TIP

You can update the links in a selected linked Excel object by pressing the F9 key. You can choose to update links when the Word document is printed by turning on the Update links option on the Print tab in the Options dialog box.

MOUSE TIP

You can use the drag-and-drop method to link Excel worksheet data in a Word document by right-dragging the selected worksheet range to the Word document and clicking the Link Excel object here.

FIGURE 13-4
Document in Outline View

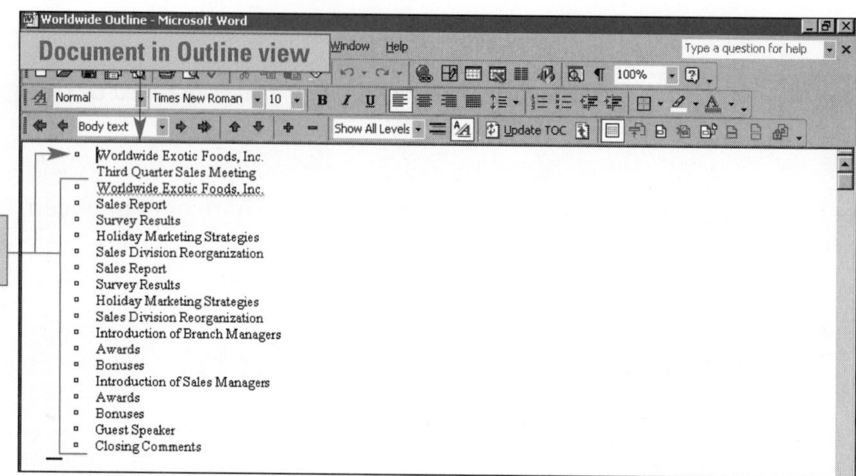

MENU TIP

You can also use the Outline level: formatting feature in the Paragraph dialog box to format text for a specific outline level. You must be in Normal or Print Layout view to do this.

There are 18 short paragraphs in the document. Paragraphs 1–2, 7–11, 14, and 17–18 will be used to create new slides. Paragraphs 3–6,12–13, and 15–16 will be used to create bulleted list text. To apply the outline level headings to the text:

Step 1	***Select***	paragraphs 1–2, 7–11, 14, and 17–18 using the CTRL key
Step 2	***Click***	the Outline Level button list arrow [Level 1] on the Outlining toolbar
Step 3	***Click***	Level 1
Step 4	***Select***	paragraphs 3–6, 12–13, and 15–16, using the CTRL key
Step 5	***Click***	the Outline Level button list arrow [Level 1]
Step 6	***Click***	Level 2
Step 7	***Deselect***	the text

MOUSE TIP

You can use buttons on the Outlining toolbar to promote selected text to a higher outline level or demote selected text to a lower outline level. You can also move selected text up or down to a new position in the outline and change the view of outline levels with buttons on the Outlining toolbar.

Now that the Word document is properly formatted with outline level headings, you are ready to create a PowerPoint presentation by sending the Word document to PowerPoint. To send the Word document to PowerPoint:

Step 1	***Click***	File
Step 2	***Point to***	Send to
Step 3	***Click***	Microsoft PowerPoint
Step 4	***Observe***	that the PowerPoint application opens in Normal view and contains Text slides based on the Word outline

Your screen should look similar to Figure 13-5.

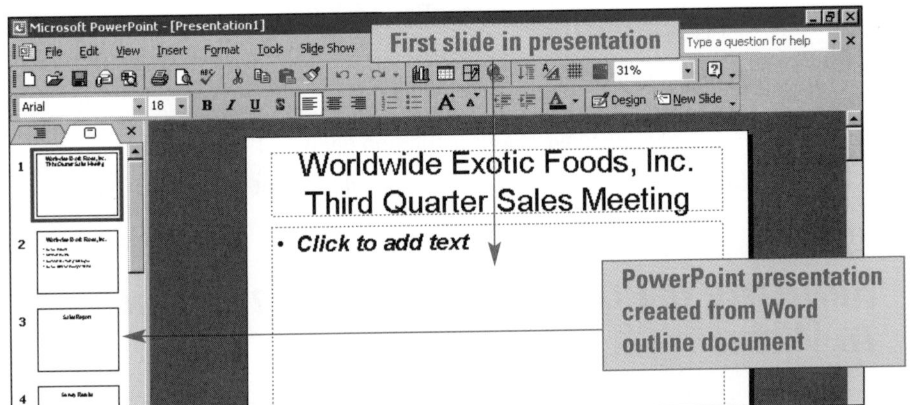

FIGURE 13-5
New PowerPoint Presentation from Word Outline

PowerPoint creates a new bulleted list text slide for each topic formatted with the Level 1 outline heading and a bulleted list detail item for text formatted with the Level 2 outline heading. You edit text on a PowerPoint slide just like you edit text in Word. You can change the general format of a slide, called the slide layout, if necessary. The general format or layout of the first slide should be a Title Slide. To convert the first text slide to a Title Slide, you open the Slide Layout task pane and then click the Title Slide layout format. You work with task panes in PowerPoint in the same way you work with them in Word.

To change the slide layout:

Step 1	***Click***	Format
Step 2	***Click***	Slide Layout
Step 3	***Click***	the Title Slide layout (first layout, first row) in the Text Layouts group in the Apply slide layout: section of the Slide Layout task pane
Step 4	***Observe***	the change to the layout of the text on the slide
Step 5	***Close***	the Slide Layout task pane
Step 6	***Click***	the Next Slide button below the vertical scroll bar
Step 7	***Observe***	that the second slide is in the Text slide layout and has title text (the Word Level 1 text) and four bullet items (the Word Level 2 text that immediately follows the Level 1 text)
Step 8	***Review***	the remaining slides using the Next Slide button
Step 9	***Scroll***	the vertical scroll bar to view the first slide

MENU TIP

You can also bring a Word outline into PowerPoint by clicking the Open command on the PowerPoint File menu (or the Open button on the Standard toolbar), and then changing the Files of type: list to All Outlines. Switch to the appropriate disk drive and folder and open the Word outline. For more information, see PowerPoint online Help.

QUICK TIP

You can link or embed individual slides or an entire presentation to a Word document with options in the Object dialog box. To embed or link a single slide from a PowerPoint presentation into a Word document, select the slide icon in PowerPoint Normal or Slide Sorter view, use the Copy and Paste Special commands, and then Paste or Paste Link the slide object.

To make the slides more attractive, you can use PowerPoint features to format the text, add a color-coordinated design theme to the slides, insert graphic images, and so forth. For now, you save the presentation.

Step 10	***Save***	the presentation as *Worldwide Sales Meeting* and leave the presentation open
Step 11	***Close***	the *Worldwide Outline* document without saving any changes

Sending a PowerPoint Presentation to Word

Another way to integrate a PowerPoint presentation with Word is to send part of a presentation to Word. Marisa wants a copy of the *Worldwide Sales Meeting* presentation in a format suitable for manually adding notations about how to format and enhance the presentation. She asks you to send the *Worldwide Sales Meeting* presentation to Word to create the document she needs. To send the *Worldwide Sales Meeting* presentation to Word:

Step 1	***Switch to***	the PowerPoint application and presentation using the taskbar
Step 2	***Click***	File
Step 3	***Point to***	Send To
Step 4	***Click***	Microsoft Word

The Send To Microsoft Word dialog box on your screen should look similar to Figure 13-6.

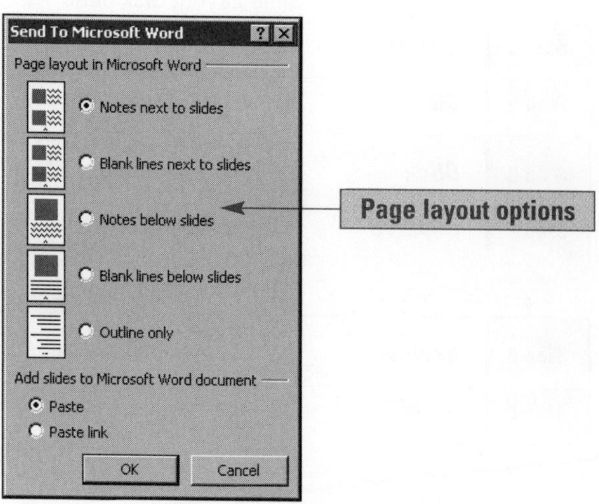

FIGURE 13-6
Send To Microsoft Word Dialog Box

This dialog box has options for the Word document format as well as for whether to embed or link the slides to the Word document. You select the Blank lines next to slides format and embed the slides.

Step 5	*Click*	the Blank lines next to slides option button
Step 6	*Click*	the Paste option button, if necessary
Step 7	*Click*	OK

In a few seconds, the application creates a Word document that contains a large table. Each row is used to display an individual slide. The first column contains the slide number, the second column contains the embedded slide object, and the third column contains the blank lines.

Step 8	*Switch to*	Print Layout view and zoom the document to Whole Page
Step 9	*Observe*	that the embedded slide objects are inserted into a table
Step 10	*Zoom*	to 100% view and switch to Normal view
Step 11	*Save*	the document as *Worldwide Sales Meeting Notes* and close it
Step 12	*Close*	the PowerPoint application and presentation

You also can integrate data stored in an Access table or query with a Word document.

13.c Using Access Tables or Queries in a Word Document

Data in an Access database is maintained in **Access tables**. An **Access query** is a subset of an Access table that meets specific criteria. For example, an Access table may include data for all sales representatives and an Access query created from that table may include only the sales representatives from a specific division. Data from an Access table or query can be inserted into a Word document. You also can use an Access database table or query as the data source in the mail merge process or import a Word document converted to a text file into the Access application.

Inserting an Access Query into a Word Document

Worldwide Exotic Foods, Inc. maintains information about its branch office vice presidents and sales managers in an Access database. You want to add a list of the vice presidents to an interoffice memorandum created by Marisa. To open the memorandum:

Step 1	***Open***	the *Confidential Memo* document located on the Data Disk
Step 2	***Move***	the insertion point to the end of the document

Next you need to get the data from the Access database. To insert an Access query:

Step 1	***Display***	the Database toolbar using the toolbar shortcut menu and dock it below the Formatting toolbar, if necessary
Step 2	***Click***	the Insert Database button on the Database toolbar

The Database dialog box on your screen should look similar to Figure 13-7.

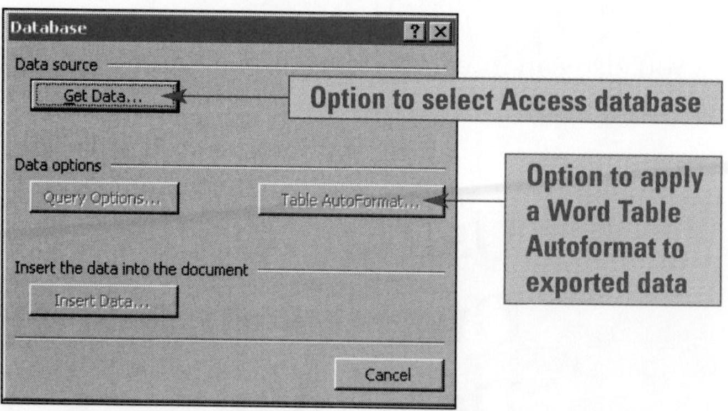

FIGURE 13-7
Database Dialog Box

You insert the Vice President query data in the *Worldwide Sales* database located on the Data Disk.

Step 3	***Click***	the Get Data button

The Select Data Source dialog box, which is very similar to the Open dialog box, opens.

Step 4	*Switch to*	the Data Disk
Step 5	*Click*	Access Databases in the Files of type: list
Step 6	*Double-click*	*Worldwide Sales*
Step 7	*Double-click*	Vice President Query in the Select Table dialog box

The Access table data will be inserted into the Word document as a Word table. You can either format the table after it is inserted, using table formatting features, or apply a Table AutoFormat now. To apply a Table AutoFormat and insert the data:

Step 1	*Click*	the Table AutoFormat button
Step 2	*Double-click*	Colorful 2 in the Formats: list box
Step 3	*Click*	the Insert Data button in the Database dialog box

The Insert Data dialog box opens from which you select which data records to insert.

Step 4	*Click*	the All option button, if necessary
Step 5	*Click*	OK in the Insert Data dialog box to insert all the records
Step 6	*Observe*	that the Access query data appear in your document as a formatted Word table
Step 7	*AutoFit*	the table to the window using the table shortcut menu
Step 8	*Save*	the document as *Confidential Memo With Vice President Data* and close it
Step 9	*Hide*	the Database toolbar

Exporting Access Data to Word

You can also send (or **export**) an Access table or query to Word for formatting or to use as a data source in a Word mail merge. When you export Access table or query data to a Word document, Access creates a Rich Text Format (.rtf) file (a text file containing the formatting) and stores the file in the default document folder specified in the File Locations tab in the Options dialog box or in the folder that is open when the data is exported.

The *Worldwide Sales* database includes information on sales managers that you want to send to a Word document. To specify the destination folder, open the database, and send the query data to Word:

Step 1	***Open***	the Access application and the *Worldwide Sales* database located on the Data Disk
Step 2	***Click***	Queries in the Objects bar, if necessary
Step 3	***Select***	the Sales Managers Query, if necessary
Step 4	***Click***	the OfficeLinks button list arrow  on the Access Database toolbar
Step 5	***Click***	Publish It with Microsoft Word

In a few seconds, the Sales Managers Query data is sent to Word as a Rich Text Format file named *Sales Managers Query*. (The file is stored in the last opened folder or the default documents folder.)

Step 6	***View***	the new *Sales Managers Query* document using the taskbar, if necessary
Step 7	***Center***	the table horizontally
Step 8	***Save***	the document as *Worldwide Sales Managers* as a Word document type and close it
Step 9	***Close***	the Access application and database
Step 10	***Delete***	the *Sales Managers Query* (.rtf) document from the default documents folder or the folder that was open when the data was exported

Access and Excel also can supply the data when you create charts in Word.

C 13.d Creating and Modifying Charts Using Data from Other Applications

You can use data from Excel or Access to create charts in Word. To do this, you can import Excel data into the Microsoft Graph datasheet or export Access to Word and use the resulting table to create a chart. Marisa wants you to create a document that shows a chart of the third quarter pastries sales. You import the data from an Excel worksheet into the Microsoft Graph datasheet and create a chart based on the imported data.

To create a new document and create a chart:

Step 1	*Create*	a new, blank document
Step 2	*Key*	Pastries Sales
Step 3	*Format*	the text as 14-point, bold, Times New Roman, center-aligned
Step 4	*Press*	the ENTER key twice
Step 5	*Click*	Insert
Step 6	*Click*	Object
Step 7	*Click*	the Create New tab
Step 8	*Double-click*	Microsoft Graph Chart in the Object type: list

MENU TIP

You can import Excel data into a Microsoft Graph datasheet with the Import File command on the Edit menu in Microsoft Graph.

You also can insert an embedded Excel chart object in a Word document using the Microsoft Excel Chart option on the Create New tab in the Object dialog box by clicking the Object command on the Insert menu.

The datasheet opens and contains sample data. You replace the sample data with the imported data. To import the data from the Excel worksheet:

Step 1	*Click*	the Import File button on the Standard toolbar

The Import File dialog box, which is quite similar to the Open dialog box, opens.

Step 2	*Switch to*	the Data Disk
Step 3	*Double-click*	the *Quarterly Pastries Sales* Excel workbook filename on the Data Disk

The Import Data Options dialog box on your screen should look similar to Figure 13-8.

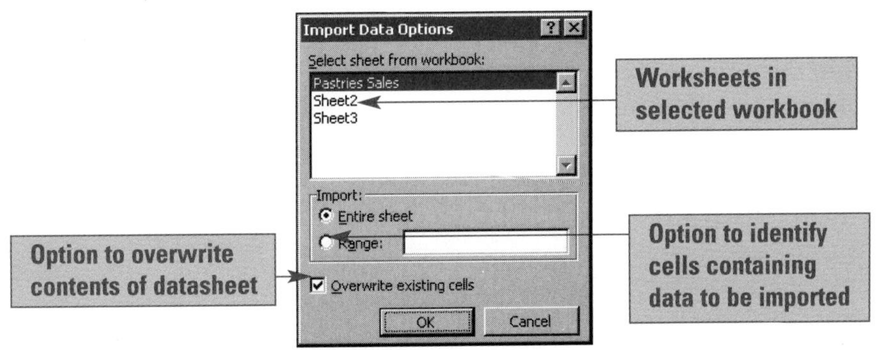

FIGURE 13-8
Import Data Options Dialog Box

chapter thirteen

You specify the worksheet and data range to import in this dialog box. The data you want to import begins in cell A5 (column A, row 5) and ends in cell D9 (column D, row 9) in the Pastries Sales worksheet in the workbook. The group of cells beginning in A5 and ending in D9 is called a range and is written as A5:D9.

QUICK TIP

You can copy an existing Excel chart in an Excel workbook and then embed or link the chart in a Word document by using the Paste Special command.

Step 4	*Click*	Pastries Sales in the Select sheet from workbook: list, if necessary
Step 5	*Click*	the Range option button
Step 6	*Key*	A5:D9 in the Range: text box
Step 7	*Click*	the Overwrite existing cells check box to insert a check mark, if necessary
Step 8	*Click*	OK
Step 9	*Observe*	that the pastries sales data replaces the sample data in the datasheet
Step 10	*Click*	the View Datasheet button to hide the datasheet
Step 11	*Deselect*	the chart object and return to the document

You can format the chart object by double-clicking it to activate the Microsoft Graph application and then selecting individual chart objects for formatting. For this document, however, all that's left to do is to finish sizing it so that all the Category (X) labels are visible. To resize the chart object:

Step 1	*Select*	the chart object, if necessary
Step 2	*Drag*	the middle-right sizing handle to the right until three months (July, August, September) appear in the Category (X) axis
Step 3	*Deselect*	the chart object
Step 4	*Save*	the document as *Pastries Sales With Chart* and close it

Integrating existing data from Excel, PowerPoint, and Access into Word documents increases document flexibility and saves time by eliminating duplicate data entry.

Summary

- You can insert an Excel worksheet into a Word document as a Word table and you can copy and paste Excel data into a Word document as a Word table.
- Embedding data in a Word document inserts a copy of the data in its original source format and the data must be edited with the source application features.
- Linking data in a Word document places a reference or pointer in the Word document, but the data continue to reside in the source application and must be edited in the source application.
- A PowerPoint presentation can be based on an imported Word outline created with outline level headings.
- You can send a PowerPoint presentation to Word to create notes or handout materials.
- Data from a database application, such as Access, can be inserted into a Word document as a Word table.
- You can open an Access database and publish a selected table or query to a Rich Text Format document.
- You can import Excel data into the Microsoft Graph datasheet to create a chart in Word.

Commands Review

Action	Menu Bar	Shortcut Menu	Toolbar	Task Pane	Keyboard
Insert Excel worksheet data as a Word table	Edit, Copy Edit, Paste Insert, File	Right-click selected worksheet range, click Copy Right-click at insertion point, click Paste		Use the Clipboard task pane features to paste copied Excel data into a Word document Use the Paste Options features to set the formatting for a pasted object	ALT + E, C ALT + E, P ALT + I, L CTRL + C CTRL + V
Create hyperlinks between Word and Office documents	Insert, Hyperlink				ALT + I, I CTRL + K
Embed Excel worksheet data into a Word document	Insert, Object Edit, Copy Edit, Paste Special, Paste				ALT + I, O ALT + E, C ALT + E, S, P
Link Excel worksheet data to a Word document	Edit, Paste Special, Paste Link	Right-drag and click Link Excel object here			ALT + E, S, L
Manage links to Excel linked object in a Word document	Edit, Linked Worksheet Object	Right-click object, point to Linked Worksheet Object			ALT + E, O
Manually update a selected linked Excel object	Edit, Update	Right-click object, click Update Link			ALT + E, D F9

Commands Review

Action	Menu Bar	Shortcut Menu	Toolbar	Task Pane	Keyboard
Create a blank embedded Excel object	Insert, Object				ALT + I, O
Apply outline level heading formatting to selected text	Format, Paragraph				ALT + O, P
Create a PowerPoint presentation from a Word outline	File, Send To, Microsoft PowerPoint				ALT + F, D, P
Import a Word outline to create a PowerPoint slide show	From PowerPoint: File, Open, All Outlines				ALT + F, O, O
Link a PowerPoint presentation to a Word document	Edit, Copy Edit, Paste Special				ALT + E, C ALT + E, S
Send a PowerPoint presentation to Word	From PowerPoint: File, Send To, Microsoft Word				ALT + F, D, W
Import an Access table or query into a Word document					
Send an Access table or query to Word	From Access: File, Save As/Export				ALT + F, A

Concepts Review

Circle the correct answer.

1. **You can link Excel worksheet data to a Word document with the:**
   [a] Copy and Paste buttons on the Standard toolbar.
   [b] Copy and Paste Special commands.
   [c] Link button on the Standard toolbar.
   [d] Link command on the Edit menu.

2. **When you insert an Excel file into a Word document, the data are:**
   [a] linked.
   [b] embedded.
   [c] hyperlinked.
   [d] placed in a Word table.

3. **To edit data in an embedded Excel worksheet object in a Word document, you use the:**
   [a] Excel menu bar and toolbars in Word.
   [b] Excel menu bar and toolbars in Excel.
   [c] Word menu bar and toolbars in Word.
   [d] Word menu bar and toolbars in Excel.

4. **When you link data maintained in another Office application to Word, the Word document:**
   [a] cannot be edited.
   [b] contains a copy of the actual data.
   [c] contains a hyperlink.
   [d] contains a reference to the original source document and application.

5. **You can use the drag-and-drop method to embed Excel worksheet data in a Word document by:**
   [a] dragging Excel data to the Word button on the taskbar while pressing the CTRL key.
   [b] displaying both applications side-by-side and dragging Excel data into the Word application window while pressing the ALT key.
   [c] dragging Excel data to the Word button on the taskbar while pressing the SHIFT key.
   [d] dragging Excel data to the Word button on the taskbar while pressing the SPACEBAR.

6. When you want to insert a blank embedded Excel object in a Word document, you can click the:

[a] Object command on the Insert menu.
[b] Create Worksheet button on the Formatting toolbar.
[c] Import Excel command on the File menu.
[d] Office Links button on the Word Standard toolbar.

7. When you create a PowerPoint presentation from a Word outline, the Word outline must be:

[a] linked to a PowerPoint presentation.
[b] formatted with outline level formats.
[c] copied to PowerPoint first.
[d] sent to PowerPoint with the Send Word command on the File menu.

8. If you use the Paste command to place Excel data in a Word document, you create a(n):

[a] Word table.
[b] embedded Excel object.
[c] linked Excel object.
[d] hyperlink.

Circle **T** if the statement is true or **F** if the statement is false.

T F 1. When you link an Excel worksheet object to a Word document, the data must be edited in the Word application with Excel features.

T F 2. If you want to modify the data only in the Word document using the source application's tools, you should embed the data.

T F 3. When you paste Excel data into a Word document, the data is placed in a Word table.

T F 4. To have data in the destination application automatically reflect changes made in the source application, you should embed the data.

T F 5. You can send a PowerPoint presentation to Word to create speaker notes and handout materials.

T F 6. When you embed data, any changes you make to the original data are reflected in the embedded object.

T F 7. An Access query is a subset of an Access table.

T F 8. You can import Access data into a Microsoft Graph datasheet.

Skills Review

SCANS

Exercise 1 

1. Open the *Vancouver Sales Memo* document located on the Data Disk.
2. Open the Excel application and the *Vancouver Branch Sales* workbook located on the Data Disk.
3. Copy the Sales Report data in the range A1:F10 and paste the data into a Word table below the body paragraph using the Clipboard task pane.
4. AutoFit the Meat, Cheese, Produce, Beverages, and Total columns.
5. Right-align the dollar values and the Meat, Cheese, Produce, Beverages, and Total column headings.
6. Delete the blank row below the three rows of table titles.
7. Center the table horizontally.
8. Save the document as *Vancouver Sales Memo With Pasted Data*, and then preview, print and close it.
9. Close the Excel application and workbook.

Exercise 2 

1. Open the *Vancouver Sales Memo* document located on the Data Disk.
2. Open the Excel application and the *Vancouver Branch Sales* workbook located on the Data Disk.
3. Save the workbook as *Modified Vancouver Branch Sales.*
4. Copy the Sales Report data in the range A1:F10 and paste the data as a linked object below the body paragraph using the Paste Special dialog box.
5. Center the object.
6. Change the object's update option to manual.
7. Save the document as *Vancouver Sales Memo Revised,* and then preview, print, and close it.
8. Edit Excel worksheet to right-align the column headings in cells B5:F5 using the Align Right button on the Formatting toolbar and change the sales figures for Meat to 1,000 for North, 800 for South, 1,300 for East, and 900 for West.
9. Save the workbook and close the Excel application.
10. Open the *Vancouver Sales Memo Revised* and update the linked object.
11. Preview, print, and close the Word document without saving changes.
12. Close Excel and the workbook.

Exercise 3 

1. Open the *Australia Outline* document located on the Data Disk.
2. Switch to Outline view.
3. Format paragraphs 2-4, 7, 9, and 14 with outline heading Level 1.
4. Format paragraphs 5-6, 8, 10-13, and 15-17 with outline heading Level 2.
5. Save the document as *Formatted Australia Outline,* and then preview and print it.
6. Send the Word outline document to PowerPoint to create a presentation.
7. Change the layout of the first slide to Title Slide.
8. Save the presentation as *Australia Highlights.*
9. Print the presentation slides and close PowerPoint and the presentation. (*Hint:* Click Print on the File menu to open the Print dialog box.)
10. Close the Word document without saving any changes.

Exercise 4 

1. Open the *Vancouver Sales Memo* document located on the Data Disk.
2. Open the Excel application and the *Vancouver Branch Sales* workbook located on the Data Disk.
3. Copy the Sales Report data in the range A1:F10 and embed the object below the body paragraph using the Paste Special dialog box.
4. Center the embedded object horizontally.
5. Save the document as *Vancouver Sales Memo With Embedded Data,* and then preview and print it.
6. Edit the embedded Excel object to remove the bold formatting from the District, Meat, Cheese, Produce, Beverages, and Total headings using the Formatting toolbar. (*Hint:* Remember to double-click the object to activate it for editing.)
7. Select the three table heading rows and italicize the heading text. (*Hint:* Drag down across the row 1, 2, and 3 buttons at the left of the activated worksheet object to select the rows and then use the Formatting toolbar to italicize the text in the rows.)
8. Click outside the object to deselect it.
9. Save the document as *Vancouver Sales Memo With Edited Data,* and then preview, print, and close it.

Exercise 5

1. Open the PowerPoint application and the *Australia Highlights* presentation you created in Exercise 3.
2. Send the presentation to Word and use the Blank lines next to slides and Paste options.
3. Save the Word document as *Australia Handout*, and then preview, print, and close it.
4. Close the PowerPoint application and presentation.

Exercise 6

1. Open the *District A Sales Decline* document located on the Data Disk.
2. Double-space the document. Center and single-space the Store A1–Store A4 paragraphs.
3. Save the document as *Modified Sales Decline.*
4. Open the Excel application and open the *District A Sales Report* workbook located on the Data Disk.
5. Copy the District A Sales Report data in the range A1:H11 and paste the data as an embedded worksheet object below the document text.
6. Edit the embedded object to change the sales figures for Store A5 to 68,000 for November, 59,100 for December, 57,850 for January, 59,150 for February, 58,000 for March, 67,100 for April, and 66,900 for May.
7. Save the document, and then preview, print, and close it.
8. Close the Excel application and workbook without saving any changes.

Exercise 7

1. Open Access and the *London Personnel* database located on the Data Disk.
2. Publish the Employees table to a Word document.
3. Edit the Word table to apply the Table AutoFormat of your choice editing features.
4. Save the document as *London Personnel* as a Word document type, and then preview, print and close it.

Exercise 8

1. Create a new, blank document.
2. Key "Third Quarter Bread Sales" as the title and apply 14-point, bold, center-aligned formatting.
3. Insert two blank lines after the title.
4. Create a Microsoft Graph Chart object and import the data from the *Third Quarter Bread Sales* workbook, Sales Unit worksheet, cell range A1: D4. Overwrite the sample data in the datasheet.
5. Edit the chart as desired and widen the chart object as necessary.
6. Save the document as *Third Quarter Bread Sales Chart*, and then preview, print, and close it.

Case Projects

Project 1

Marisa DaFranco calls to tell you that whenever she double-clicks a linked Excel object in one of her Word documents, see gets a "cannot edit" error message. Using the Ask A Question Box, research troubleshooting linked and embedded objects. Create a memo to Marisa telling her how to solve the problem. Save and print the memo.

Project 2

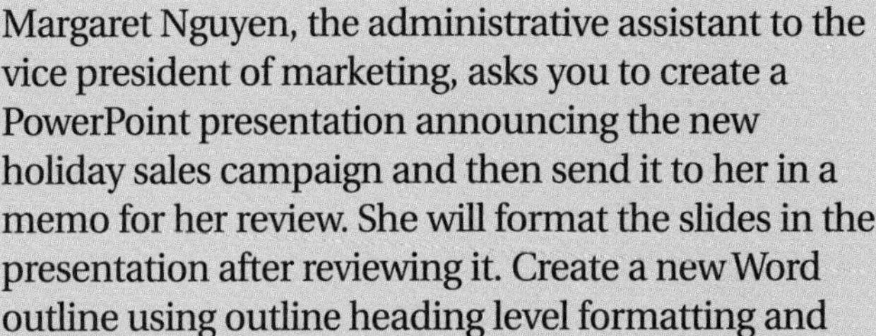

Margaret Nguyen, the administrative assistant to the vice president of marketing, asks you to create a PowerPoint presentation announcing the new holiday sales campaign and then send it to her in a memo for her review. She will format the slides in the presentation after reviewing it. Create a new Word outline using outline heading level formatting and containing fictitious sales campaign topics. Then create a PowerPoint slide presentation from the outline. Save and print the presentation slides. Create a memo to Margaret from inside Word and attach the presentation file. Save and print the memo.

Project 3

Chris Lofton, the word processing manager, asks you to give a short presentation to the word processing specialists on the difference between embedding and linking objects. Use online Help to review the explanation of linked objects and embedded objects. Then create a Word outline of the topics you plan to cover in the presentation using outline level formatting. Send the Word outline to PowerPoint to create a presentation. Format the presentation as desired and print it. Send the PowerPoint presentation to Word using an output format of your choice. Save and print the Word document. With your instructor's permission, open the PowerPoint presentation and, using the presentation and the Word handout document, explain the difference between linked and embedded objects to a group of classmates.

Project 4

Jody Haversham asks for your help in managing the linked Excel objects in her documents. She has linked objects to source application files that have been moved to a new location, linked objects that are updated automatically when she wants to update them manually, and linked objects that she no longer wants linked to the source file. Using the Ask A Question Box, search for and review topics related to linked objects. After reviewing the topics, write Jody a memo providing some suggestions to help her manage linked objects. Save and print the memo.

Project 5

Kelly Armstead has a Word document that contains a list of contact names and addresses. She wants to import the Word information into her Outlook Contacts folder. Use online Help to research how to do this, then write Kelly a memo describing what she needs to do. Save and print the memo.

Project 6

Marisa DaFranco wants to know if there is any shortcut method to create linked objects, shortcuts, or hyperlinks when sharing information between Word and other Office documents. You think she can use the right-drag technique to do this. Using the Word document and Excel workbook of your choice, practice creating linked objects, shortcuts, and hyperlinks using right-drag. Write Marisa a memo explaining how to create each of these items using the right-drag method. Save and print the memo.

Project 7

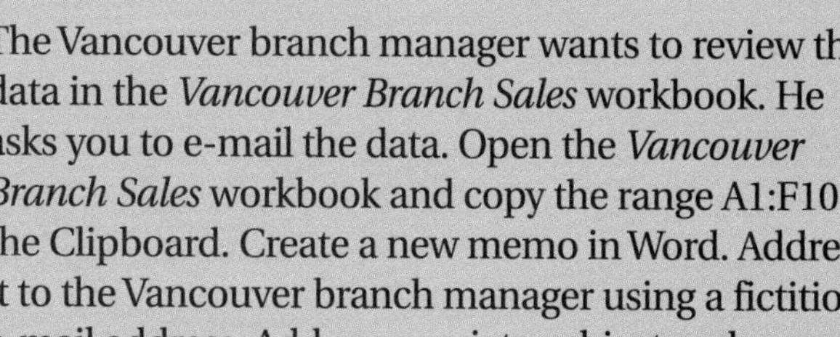

The Vancouver branch manager wants to review the data in the *Vancouver Branch Sales* workbook. He asks you to e-mail the data. Open the *Vancouver Branch Sales* workbook and copy the range A1:F10 to the Clipboard. Create a new memo in Word. Address it to the Vancouver branch manager using a fictitious e-mail address. Add appropriate subject and message text and paste the copied data into a Word table. Save and print the memo.

Project 8

You want to know what online Help is available from the Web. Connect to the Internet and click the Office on the Web command on the Help menu. Review the available help topics. Send a memo to several classmates describing what they can expect to find when they click the Office on the Web command. Save and print the memo.

Working with Windows 2000

Appendix

Appendix Overview

The Windows 2000 operating system creates a workspace on your computer screen, called the desktop. The desktop is a graphical environment that contains icons you click with the mouse pointer to access your computer system resources or to perform a task such as opening a software application. This appendix introduces you to the Windows 2000 desktop by describing the default desktop icons and showing how to access your computer resources, use menu commands and toolbar buttons to perform a task, and review and select dialog box options.

LEARNING OBJECTIVES

- Review the Windows 2000 desktop
- Access your computer system resources
- Use menu commands and toolbar buttons
- Use the Start menu
- Review dialog box options
- Use Windows 2000 shortcuts
- Understand the Recycle Bin
- Shut down Windows 2000

A appendix

A.a Reviewing the Windows 2000 Desktop

Whenever you start your computer, the Windows 2000 operating system automatically starts. You are prompted to log on with your user name and password, which identify your account. Then the Windows 2000 desktop appears on your screen. To view the Windows 2000 desktop:

Step 1	*Turn on*	your computer and monitor

The Log On to Windows dialog box opens, as shown in Figure A-1.

FIGURE A-1
Log On to Windows Dialog Box

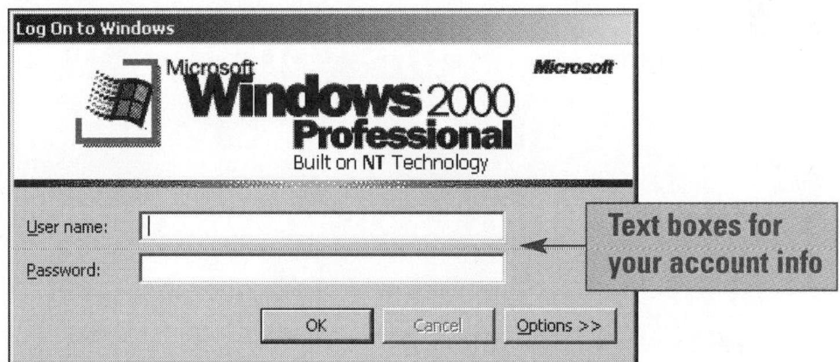

QUICK TIP

If you don't see the Log On to Windows dialog box, you can open the Windows Security window at any time by pressing the CTRL + ALT + DELETE keys. From this window, you can log off the current user and log back on as another user. You can also change passwords, shut down Windows 2000 and your computer, and use the Task Manager to shut down a program.

Step 2	*Key*	your user name in the User name: text box
Step 3	*Key*	your password in the Password: text box
Step 4	*Click*	OK
Step 5	*Click*	the Exit button in the Getting Started with Windows 2000 dialog box, if necessary
Step 6	*Observe*	the Windows 2000 desktop work area, as shown in Figure A-2

The Windows 2000 desktop contains three elements: icons, background, and taskbar. The icons represent Windows objects and shortcuts to opening software applications or performing tasks. Table A-1 describes some of the default icons. The taskbar, at the bottom of the window, contains the Start button and the Quick Launch toolbar, and tray. The icon types and arrangement, desktop background, or Quick Launch toolbar on your screen might be different.

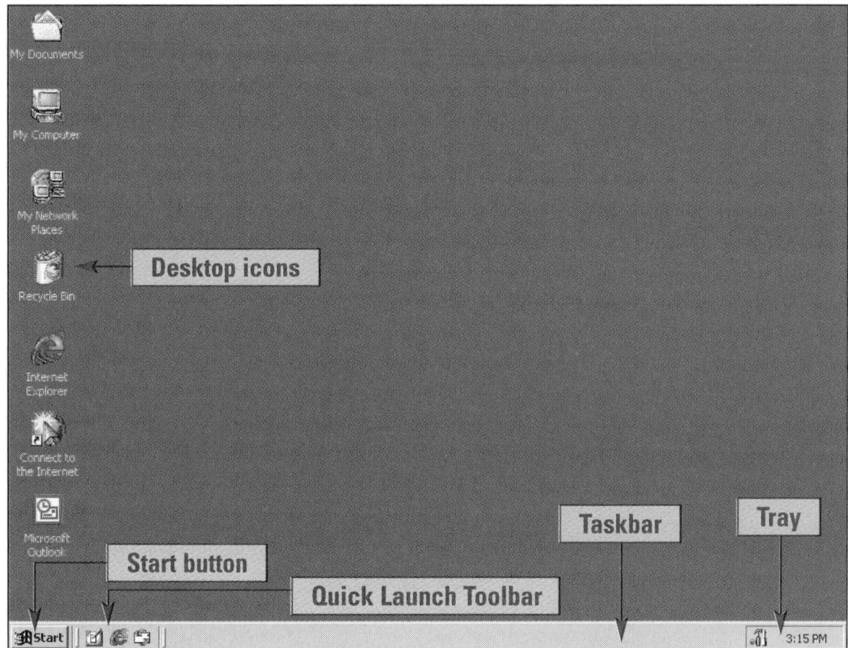

FIGURE A-2
Windows 2000 Desktop

TABLE A-1
Common Desktop Icons

Icon	Name	Description
	My Computer	Provides access to computer system resources
	My Documents	Stores Office documents (by default)
	Internet Explorer	Opens Internet Explorer Web browser
	Microsoft Outlook	Opens Outlook 2002 information manager software
	Recycle Bin	Temporarily stores folders and files deleted from the hard drive
	My Network Places	Provides access to computers and printers net worked in your workgroup

The Start button on the taskbar displays the Start menu, which you can use to perform tasks. By default, the taskbar also contains the **Quick Launch toolbar**, which has shortcuts to open the Internet Explorer Web browser and Outlook Express e-mail software, and to switch between the desktop and open application windows. You can customize the Quick Launch toolbar to include other shortcuts.

QUICK TIP

An **active desktop** can contain live Web content. You can create an active desktop by adding windows to the desktop that contain automatically updated Web pages. To add Web pages to your desktop, right-click the desktop, point to Active Desktop, click Customize my Desktop, and click the Web tab in the Display Properties dialog box. For more information on Active Desktop features, see online Help.

A.b Accessing Your Computer System Resources

The My Computer window provides access to your computer system resources. Double-click the My Computer desktop icon to open the window. To open the My Computer window:

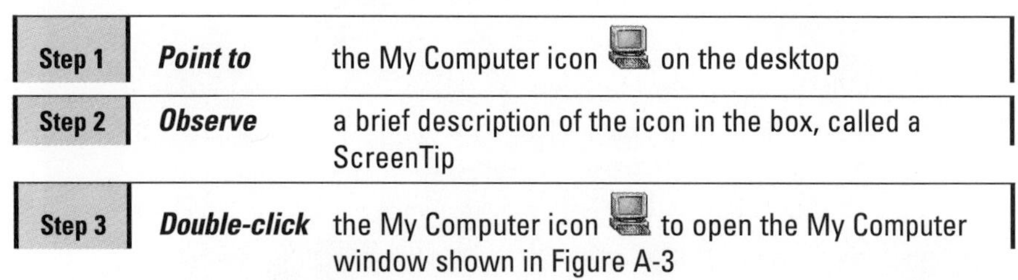

Step 1	*Point to*	the My Computer icon on the desktop
Step 2	*Observe*	a brief description of the icon in the box, called a ScreenTip
Step 3	*Double-click*	the My Computer icon to open the My Computer window shown in Figure A-3

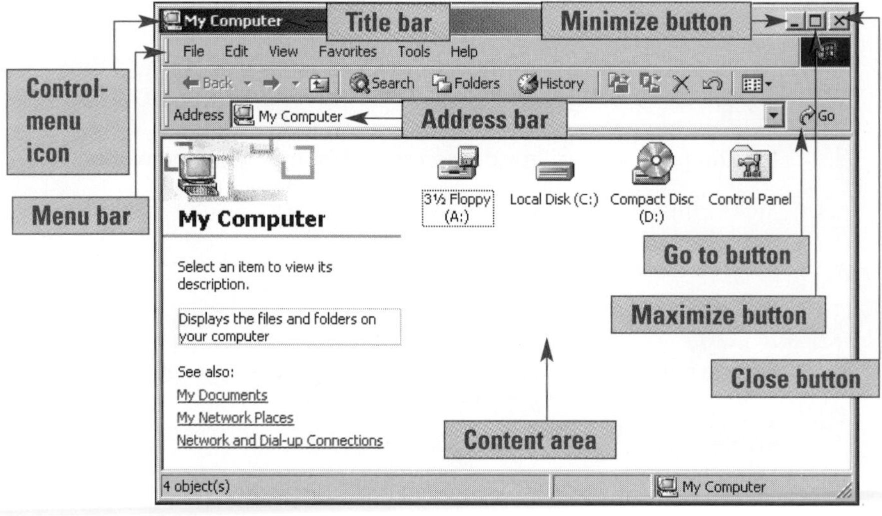

FIGURE A-3
My Computer window

A window is a rectangular area on your screen in which you view operating system options or a software application, such as Internet Explorer. Windows 2000 has some common window elements. The **title bar**, at the top of the window, includes the window's Control-menu icon, the window name, and the Minimize, Restore (or Maximize), and Close buttons. The **Control-menu icon**, in the upper-left corner of the window, accesses the Control menu that contains commands for restoring, moving sizing, minimizing, maximizing, and closing the window. The **Minimize** button, near the upper-right corner of the window, reduces the window to a taskbar button. The **Maximize** button, to the right of the Minimize button, enlarges the window to fill the entire screen viewing area above the taskbar. If the window is already maximized, the Restore button

appears in its place. The **Restore** button reduces the window size. The **Close** button, in the upper-right corner, closes the window. To maximize the My Computer window:

Step 1	***Click***	the Maximize button on the My Computer window title bar
Step 2	***Observe***	that the My Computer window completely covers the desktop

When you want to leave a window open, but do not want to see it on the desktop, you can minimize it. To minimize the My Computer window:

Step 1	***Click***	the Minimize button on the My Computer window title bar
Step 2	***Observe***	that the My Computer button remains on the taskbar

The minimized window is still open but not occupying space on the desktop. To view the My Computer window and then restore it to a smaller size:

Step 1	***Click***	the My Computer button on the taskbar to view the window
Step 2	***Click***	the Restore button on the My Computer title bar
Step 3	***Observe***	that the My Computer window is reduced to a smaller window on the desktop

You can move and size a window with the mouse pointer. To move the My Computer window:

Step 1	***Position***	the mouse pointer on the My Computer title bar
Step 2	***Drag***	the window down and to the right approximately ½ inch
Step 3	***Drag***	the window back to the center of the screen

Several Windows 2000 windows—My Computer, My Documents, and Windows Explorer—have the same menu bar and toolbar features. When you size a window too small to view all its icons, a vertical or horizontal scroll bar may appear. A scroll bar includes scroll arrows and a scroll box for viewing different parts of the window contents.

QUICK TIP

This book uses the following notations for mouse instructions. **Point** means to place the mouse pointer on the command or item. **Click** means to press the left mouse button and then release it. **Right-click** means to press the right mouse button and then release it. **Double-click** means to press the left mouse button twice very rapidly. **Drag** means to hold down the left mouse button as you move the mouse pointer on the mouse pad. **Right-drag** means to hold down the right mouse button as you move the mouse pointer on the mouse pad. **Scroll** means to use the application scroll bar features or the IntelliMouse scrolling wheel.

MOUSE TIP

You can display four taskbar toolbars: Address, Links, Desktop, and Quick Launch. The Quick Launch toolbar appears on the taskbar by default. You can also create additional toolbars from other folders or subfolders and you can add folder or file shortcuts to an existing taskbar toolbar. To view other taskbar toolbars, right-click the taskbar, point to Toolbars, and then click the desired toolbar name.

To size the My Computer window:

Step 1	*Position*	the mouse pointer on the lower-right corner of the window
Step 2	*Observe*	that the mouse pointer becomes a black, double-headed sizing pointer
Step 3	*Drag*	the lower-right corner boundary diagonally up until the horizontal scroll bar appears and release the mouse button
Step 4	*Click*	the right scroll arrow on the horizontal scroll bar to view hidden icons
Step 5	*Size*	the window to a larger size to remove the horizontal scroll bar

You can open the window associated with any My Computer icon by double-clicking it. The windows open in the same window, not separate windows. To open the Control Panel Explorer-style window:

Step 1	*Double-click*	the Control Panel icon
Step 2	*Observe*	that the Address bar displays the Control Panel icon and name, and the content area displays the Control Panel icons for accessing computer system resources

A.c Using Menu Commands and Toolbar Buttons

You can click a menu command or toolbar button to perform specific tasks in a window. The **menu bar** is a special toolbar located below the window title bar that contains the File, Edit, View, Favorites, Tools, and Help menus. The **Standard Buttons toolbar**, located below the menu bar, contains shortcut "buttons" you click with the mouse pointer to execute a variety of commands. You can use the Back and Forward buttons on the Standard Buttons toolbar to switch between My Computer and the Control Panel. To view My Computer:

Step 1	*Click*	the Back button on the Standard Buttons toolbar to view My Computer
Step 2	*Click*	the Forward button on the Standard Buttons toolbar to view the Control Panel
Step 3	*Click*	View on the menu bar
Step 4	*Point to*	Go To
Step 5	*Click*	the My Computer command to view My Computer

Step 6	*Click*	the Close button [X] on the My Computer window title bar

A.d Using the Start Menu

The **Start button** on the taskbar opens the Start menu. You use this menu to access several Windows 2000 features and to open software applications, such as Word or Excel. To open the Start menu:

Step 1	*Click*	the Start button [Start] on the taskbar to open the Start menu, as shown in Figure A-4

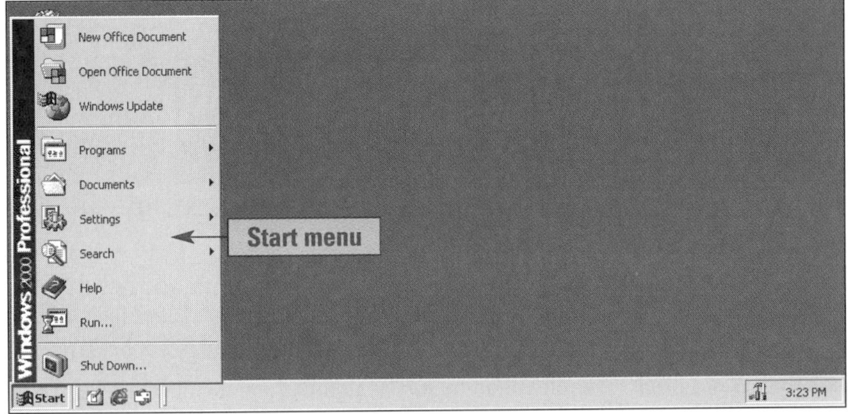

FIGURE A-4
Start Menu

Step 2	*Point to*	Programs to view the software applications installed on your computer
Step 3	*Click*	the desktop outside the Start menu and Programs menu to close them

A.e Reviewing Dialog Box Options

A **dialog box** is a window that contains options you can select, turn on, or turn off to perform a task. To view a dialog box:

Step 1	*Right-click*	the desktop
Step 2	*Point to*	Active Desktop

QUICK TIP

You can use Start menu commands to create or open Office XP documents, connect to the Microsoft Web site to download operating system updates, open software applications, open a favorite folder or file, or open one of the last fifteen documents you worked on. You can also change the Windows 2000 settings, search for files, folders, and resources on the Internet, get online Help, run software applications, log off a network, and shut down Windows 2000.

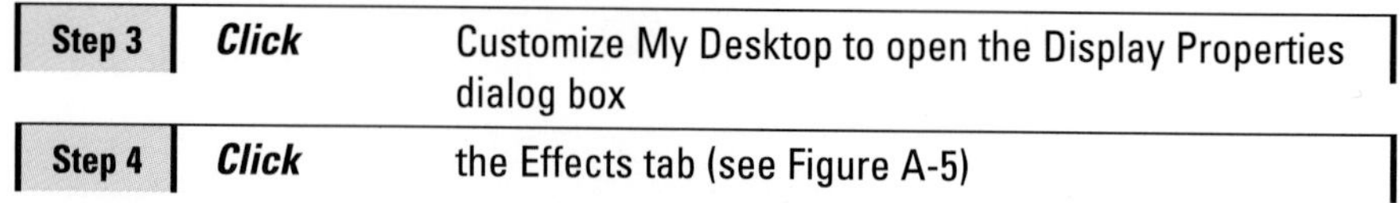

Step 3	*Click*	Customize My Desktop to open the Display Properties dialog box
Step 4	*Click*	the Effects tab (see Figure A-5)

> **QUICK TIP**
>
> Many dialog boxes contain sets of options on different pages organized on **tabs** you click. Options include drop-down lists you view by clicking an arrow, text boxes in which you key information, check boxes and option buttons you click to turn on or off an option, and buttons that access additional options.

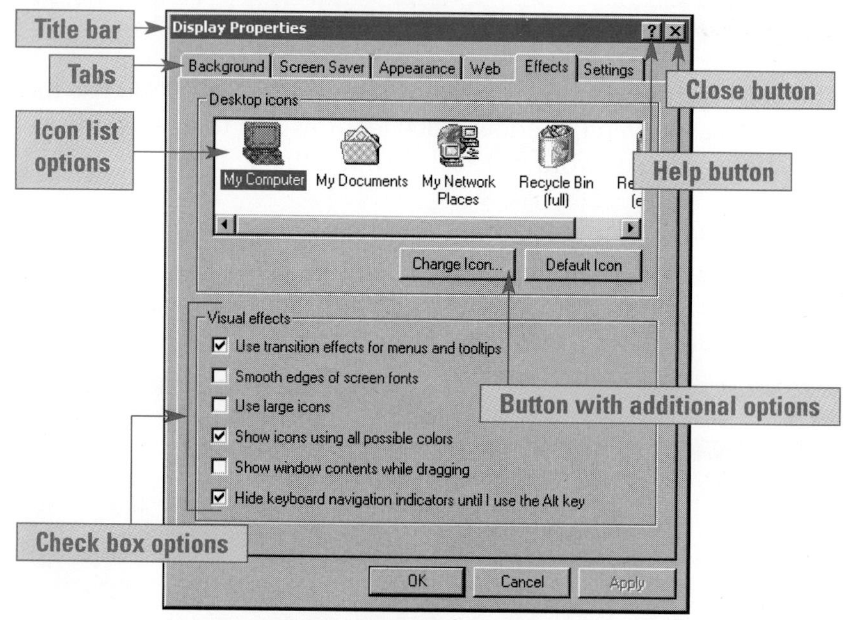

FIGURE A-5
Effects Tab in the Display Properties Dialog Box

Step 5	*Click*	each tab and observe the different options available *(do not change any options unless directed by your instructor)*
Step 6	*Right-click*	each option on each tab and then click What's This? to view its ScreenTip
Step 7	*Click*	Cancel to close the dialog box without changing any options

> **MOUSE TIP**
>
> One way to speed up tasks is to single-click (rather than double-click) a desktop icon just like you single-click a Web page hyperlink. You can create a Web-style, single-click environment by opening the Folder Options dialog box from the Tools menu in any Windows 2000 window or the Control Panel from the Settings command on the Start menu. The Single-click to open an item (point to select) and Underline icon titles consistent with my browser options add an underline to icon titles, similar to a hyperlink.

A.f Using Windows 2000 Shortcuts

You can use the drag-and-drop method to reposition or remove Start menu commands. You can also right-drag a Start menu command to the desktop to create a desktop shortcut. To reposition the Windows Update item on the Start menu:

Step 1	*Click*	the Start button Start on the taskbar
Step 2	*Point to*	the Windows Update item
Step 3	*Drag*	the Windows Update item to the top of the Start menu

To remove the Windows Update shortcut from the Start menu and create a desktop shortcut:

Step 1	*Drag*	the Windows Update item to the desktop
Step 2	*Observe*	that the desktop shortcut appears after a few seconds
Step 3	*Verify*	that the Windows Update item no longer appears on the Start menu

To add a Windows Update shortcut back to the Start menu and delete the desktop shortcut:

Step 1	*Drag*	the Windows Update shortcut to the Start button Start on the taskbar and then back to its original position when the Start menu appears
Step 2	*Close*	the Start menu
Step 3	*Drag*	the Windows Update shortcut on the desktop to the Recycle Bin

You can close multiple application windows at one time from the taskbar using the CTRL key and a shortcut menu. To open two applications and then use the taskbar to close them:

Step 1	*Open*	the Word and Excel applications (in this order) from the Programs menu on the Start menu
Step 2	*Observe*	the Word and Excel buttons on the taskbar (Excel is the selected, active button)
Step 3	*Press & hold*	the CTRL key
Step 4	*Click*	the Word application taskbar button (the Excel application taskbar button is already selected)
Step 5	*Release*	the CTRL key
Step 6	*Right-click*	the Word or Excel taskbar button
Step 7	*Click*	Close to close both applications

You can use the drag-and-drop method to add a shortcut to the Quick Launch toolbar for folders and documents you have created. To create a new subfolder in the My Documents folder:

Step 1	*Double-click*	the My Documents icon on the desktop to open the window
Step 2	*Right-click*	the contents area (but not a file or folder)

CAUTION TIP

Selecting items in a single-click environment requires some practice. To **select** (or highlight) one item, simply point to the item. *Be careful not to click the item; clicking the item opens it.*

You can use the SHIFT + Click and CTRL + Click commands in the single-click environment. Simply *point to* the first item. Then press and hold the SHIFT or CTRL key and *point to* the last item or the next item to be selected.

MENU TIP

In the Windows environment, clicking the right mouse button displays a **shortcut menu** of the most commonly used commands for the item you right-clicked. For example, you can use a shortcut menu to open applications from the Programs submenu. You can right-drag to move, copy, or create desktop shortcuts from Start menu commands.

Step 3	*Point to*	New
Step 4	*Click*	Folder
Step 5	*Key*	Example
Step 6	*Press*	the ENTER key to name the folder
Step 7	*Drag*	the Example folder to the end of the Quick Launch toolbar (a black vertical line indicates the drop position)
Step 8	*Observe*	the new icon on the toolbar
Step 9	*Close*	the My Documents window
Step 10	*Position*	the mouse pointer on the Example folder shortcut on the Quick Launch toolbar and observe the ScreenTip

You remove a shortcut from the Quick Launch toolbar by dragging it to the desktop and deleting it, or dragging it directly to the Recycle Bin. To remove the Example folder shortcut and then delete the folder:

Step 1	*Drag*	the Example folder icon to the Recycle Bin
Step 2	*Open*	the My Documents window
Step 3	*Delete*	the Example folder icon using the shortcut menu
Step 4	*Click*	Yes
Step 5	*Close*	the My Documents window

MENU TIP

You can open the Recycle Bin by right-clicking the Recycle Bin icon on the desktop and clicking Open. To restore an item to your hard drive after opening the Recycle Bin, click the item to select it and then click the Restore command on the File menu. You can also restore an item by opening the Recycle Bin, right-clicking an item, and clicking Restore.

To empty the Recycle Bin, right-click the Recycle Bin icon and then click Empty Recycle Bin.

A.g Understanding the Recycle Bin

The **Recycle Bin** is an object that temporarily stores folders, files, and shortcuts you delete from your hard drive. If you accidentally delete an item, you can restore it to its original location on your hard drive if it is still in the Recycle Bin. Because the Recycle Bin takes up disk space you should review and empty it regularly. When you empty the Recycle Bin, its contents are removed from your hard drive and can no longer be restored.

A.h Shutting Down Windows 2000

It is very important that you follow the proper procedures for shutting down the Windows 2000 operating system when you are finished, to allow the operating system to complete its internal "housekeeping" properly. To shut down Windows 2000 correctly:

Step 1	*Click*	the Start button on the taskbar
Step 2	*Click*	Shut Down to open the Shut Down Windows dialog box shown in Figure A-6

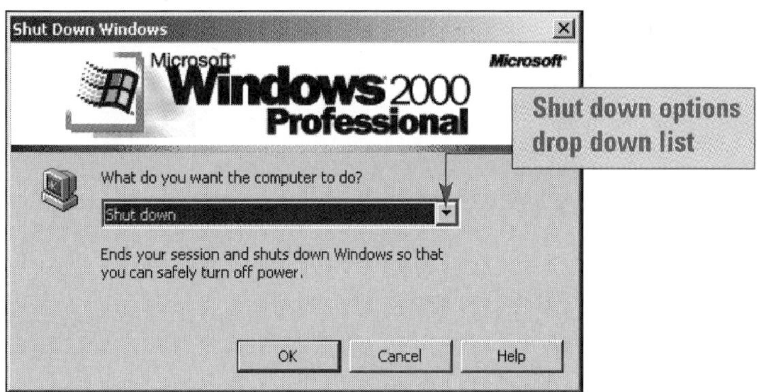

FIGURE A-6
Shut Down Windows Dialog Box

You can log off, shut down, and restart from this dialog box. You want to shut down completely.

Step 3	*Click*	the Shut down option from the drop-down list, if necessary
Step 4	*Click*	OK

Appendix

Formatting Tips for Business Documents

LEARNING OBJECTIVES

- Format letters
- Insert mailing notations
- Format envelopes
- Format interoffice memorandums
- Format formal outlines
- Use style guides
- Use proofreader's marks

Appendix Overview

Most organizations follow specific formatting guidelines when preparing letters, envelopes, memorandums, and other documents to ensure the documents present a professional appearance. In this appendix you learn how to format different size letters, interoffice memos, envelopes, and formal outlines. You also review a list of style guides and learn how to use proofreader's marks.

B.a Formatting Letters

Most companies use special letter paper with the company name and address (and sometimes a company logo or picture) preprinted on the paper. The preprinted portion is called a **letterhead** and the paper is called **letterhead paper**. When you create a letter, the margins vary depending on the style of your letterhead and the length of your letter. Most letterheads use between 1 inch and 2 inches of the page from the top of the sheet. There are two basic business correspondence formats: block format and modified block format. When you create a letter in **block format**, all the text is placed flush against the left margin. This includes the date, the letter address information, the salutation, the body, the complimentary closing, and the signature information. The body of the letter is single spaced with a blank line between paragraphs.[1] Figure B-1 shows a short letter in the block format with standard punctuation.

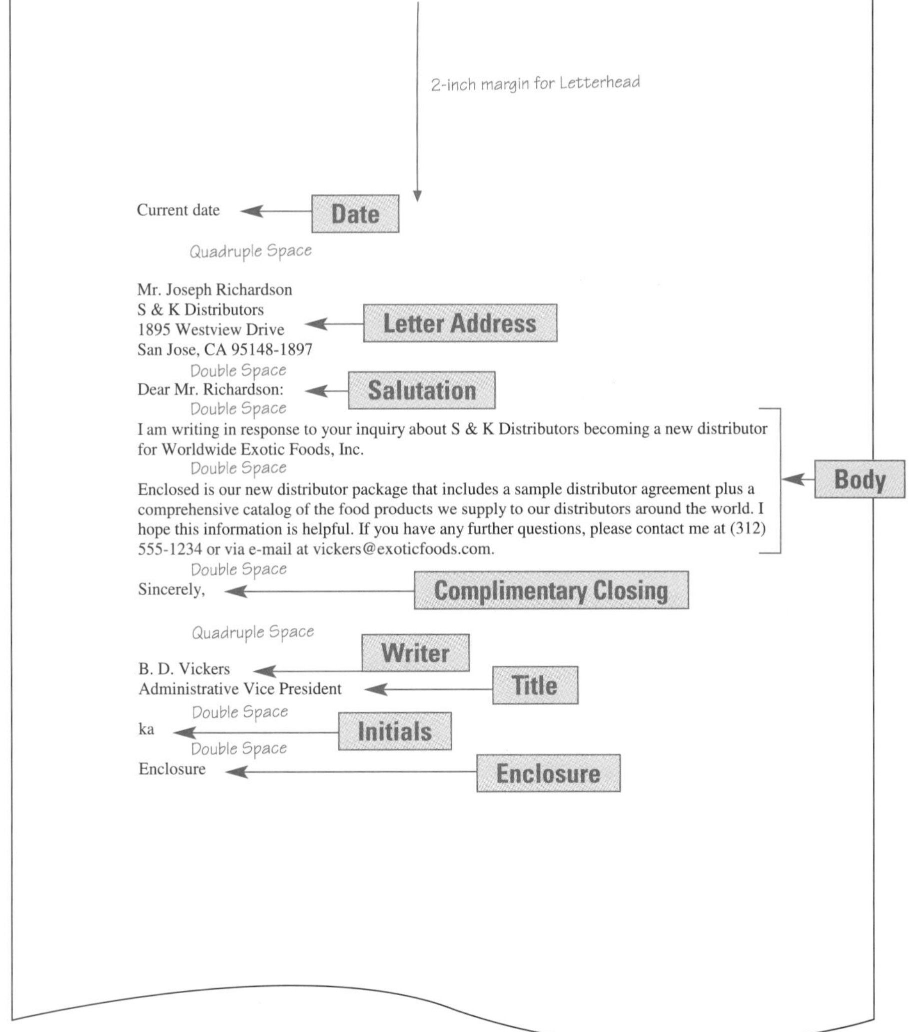
2-inch margin for Letterhead

Current date

Quadruple Space

Mr. Joseph Richardson
S & K Distributors
1895 Westview Drive
San Jose, CA 95148-1897

Double Space

Dear Mr. Richardson:

Double Space

I am writing in response to your inquiry about S & K Distributors becoming a new distributor for Worldwide Exotic Foods, Inc.

Double Space

Enclosed is our new distributor package that includes a sample distributor agreement plus a comprehensive catalog of the food products we supply to our distributors around the world. I hope this information is helpful. If you have any further questions, please contact me at (312) 555-1234 or via e-mail at vickers@exoticfoods.com.

Double Space

Sincerely,

Quadruple Space

B. D. Vickers
Administrative Vice President

Double Space

ka

Double Space

Enclosure

FIGURE B-1
Block Format Letter

QUICK TIP

The quality and professionalism of a company's business correspondence can affect how customers, clients, and others view a company. That correspondence represents the company to those outside it. To ensure a positive and appropriate image, many companies set special standards for margins, typeface, and font size for their business correspondence. These special standards are based on the common letter styles illustrated in this section.

appendix B

In the **modified block format**, the date begins near the center of the page or near the right margin. The closing starts near the center or right margin. Paragraphs can be either flush against the left margin or indented. Figure B-2 shows a short letter in the modified block format with standard punctuation.

FIGURE B-2
Modified Block Format Letter

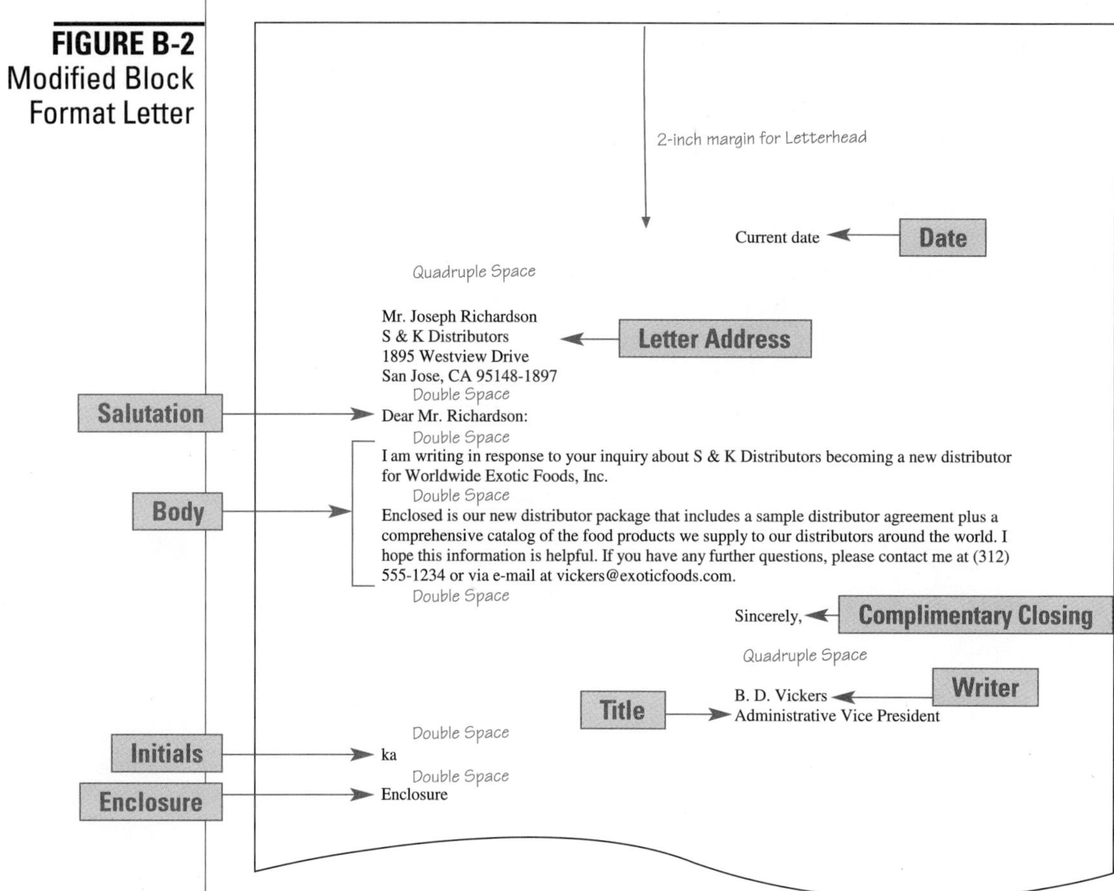

QUICK TIP

When you key a letter on plain paper in the modified block format, the return address usually appears near the right margin and above the date, with one blank line between the return address and the date.

Both the block and modified block styles use the same spacing for the non-body portions. Three blank lines separate the date from the addressee information, one blank line separates the addressee information from the salutation, one blank line separates the salutation from the body of the letter, and one blank line separates the body of the letter from the complimentary closing. There are three blank lines between the complimentary closing and the writer's name. If a typist's initials appear below the name, a blank line separates the writer's name from the initials. If an enclosure is noted, the word "Enclosure" appears below the typist's initials with a blank line separating them. Finally, when keying the return address or addressee information, one space separates the state and the postal code (ZIP+4).

B.b Inserting Mailing Notations

Mailing notations add information to a business letter. For example, the mailing notations CERTIFIED MAIL or SPECIAL DELIVERY indicate how a business letter was sent. The mailing notations CONFIDENTIAL or PERSONAL indicate how the person receiving the letter should handle the letter contents. Mailing notations should be keyed in uppercase characters at the left margin two lines below the date.[2] Figure B-3 shows a mailing notation added to a block format business letter.

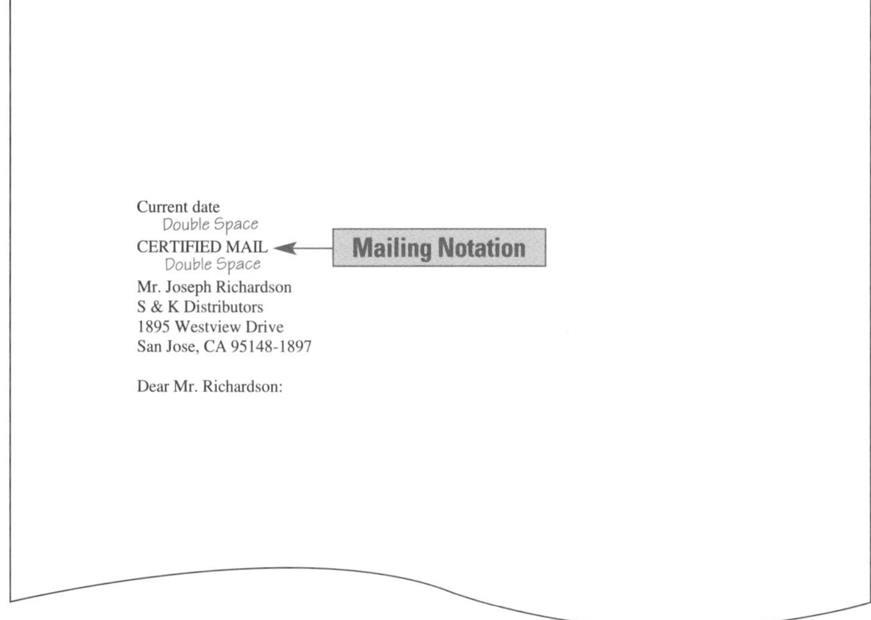

FIGURE B-3
Mailing Notation on Letter

B.c Formatting Envelopes

Two U.S. Postal Service publications, *The Right Way* (Publication 221), and *Postal Addressing Standards* (Publication 28) available from the U.S. Post Office, provide standards for addressing letter envelopes. The U.S. Postal Service uses optical character readers (OCRs) and barcode sorters (BCSs) to increase the speed, efficiency, and accuracy in processing mail. To get a letter delivered more quickly, envelopes should be addressed to take advantage of this automation process.

Table B-1 lists the minimum and maximum size for letters. The post office cannot process letters smaller than the minimum size. Letters larger than the maximum size cannot take advantage of automated processing and must be processed manually.

TABLE B-1
Minimum and Maximum Letter Dimensions

Dimension	Minimum	Maximum
Height	3½ inches	6⅛ inches
Length	5 inches	11½ inches
Thickness	.007 inch	¼ inch

The delivery address should be placed inside a rectangular area on the envelope that is approximately ⅝ inch from the top and bottom edge of the envelope and ½ inch from the left and right edge of the envelope. This is called the **OCR read area.** All the lines of the delivery address must fit within this area and no lines of the return address should extend into this area. To assure the delivery address is placed in the OCR read area, begin the address approximately ½ inch left of center and on approximately line 14.[3]

The lines of the delivery address should be in this order:

1. any optional nonaddress data, such as advertising or company logos, must be placed above the delivery address
2. any information or attention line
3. the name of the recipient
4. the street address
5. the city, state, and postal code (ZIP+4)

The delivery address should be complete, including apartment or suite numbers and delivery designations, such as RD (road), ST (street), or NW (northwest). Leave the area below and on both sides of the delivery address blank. Use uppercase characters and a sans serif font (such as Arial) for the delivery address. Omit all punctuation except the hyphen in the ZIP+4 code.

Figure B-4 shows a properly formatted business letter envelope.

QUICK TIP

Foreign addresses should include the country name in uppercase characters as the last line of the delivery address. The postal code, if any, should appear on the same line as the city.

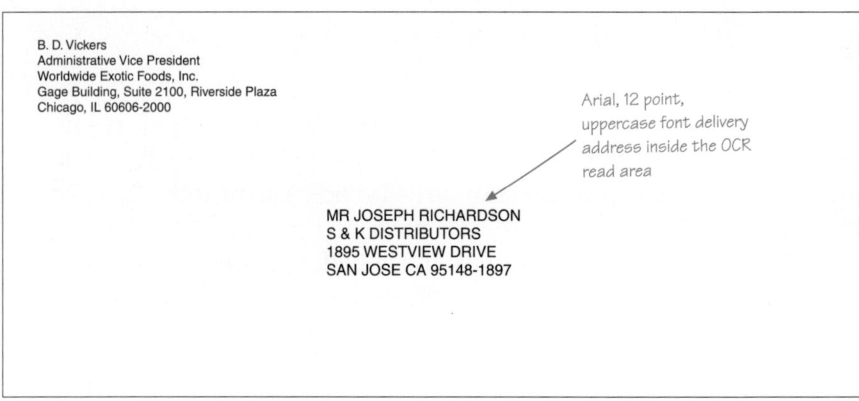

FIGURE B-4
Business Letter Envelope

B.d Formatting Interoffice Memorandums

Business correspondence that is sent within a company is usually prepared as an **interoffice memorandum**, also called a **memo**, rather than a letter. There are many different interoffice memo styles used in offices today, and word processing applications usually provide several memo templates based on different memo styles. Also, just as with business letters that are sent outside the company, many companies set special standards for margins, typeface, and font size for their interoffice memos.

A basic interoffice memo should include lines for "TO:", "FROM:", "DATE:", and "SUBJECT:" followed by the body text. Memos can be prepared on blank paper or on paper that includes a company name and even a logo. The word MEMORANDUM is often included. Figure B-5 shows a basic interoffice memorandum.

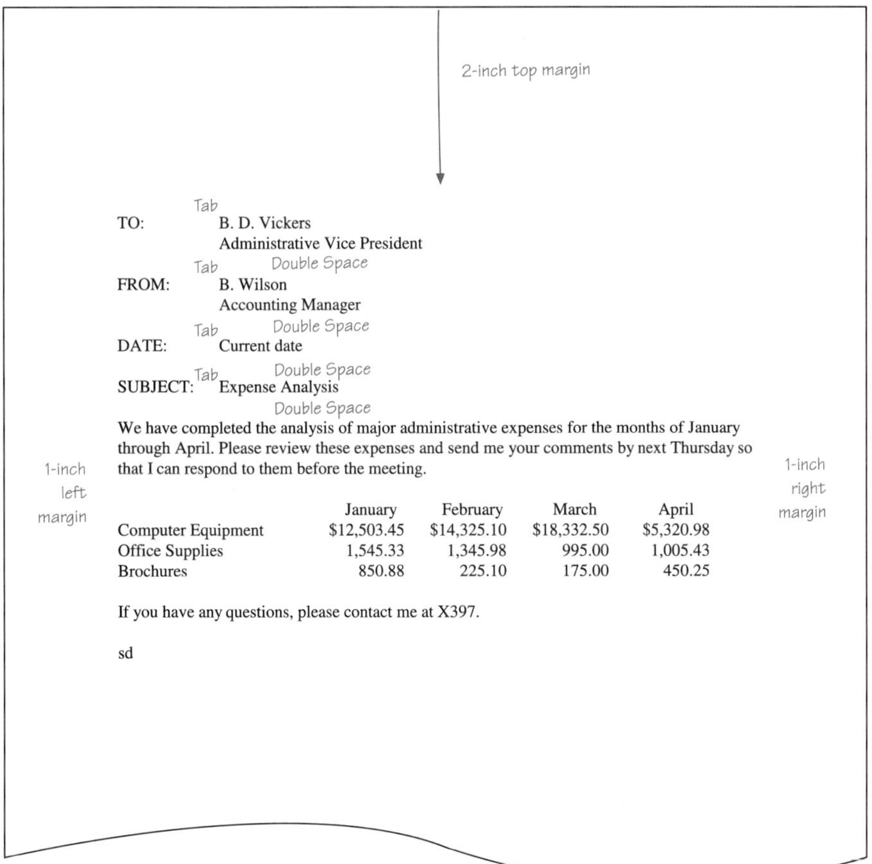

TO: B. D. Vickers
Administrative Vice President

FROM: B. Wilson
Accounting Manager

DATE: Current date

SUBJECT: Expense Analysis

We have completed the analysis of major administrative expenses for the months of January through April. Please review these expenses and send me your comments by next Thursday so that I can respond to them before the meeting.

	January	February	March	April
Computer Equipment	$12,503.45	$14,325.10	$18,332.50	$5,320.98
Office Supplies	1,545.33	1,345.98	995.00	1,005.43
Brochures	850.88	225.10	175.00	450.25

If you have any questions, please contact me at X397.

sd

FIGURE B-5
Interoffice Memorandum

appendix B

B.e Formatting Formal Outlines

Companies use outlines to organize data for a variety of purposes, such as reports, meeting agenda, and presentations. Word processing applications usually offer special features to help you create an outline. If you want to follow a formal outline format, you may need to add formatting to outlines created with these special features.

Margins for a short outline of two or three topics should be set at 1½ inches for the top margin and 2 inches for the left and right margins. For a longer outline, use a 2-inch top margin and 1-inch left and right margins.

The outline level-one text should be in uppercase characters. Second-level text should be treated like a title, with the first letter of the main words capitalized. Capitalize only the first letter of the first word at the third level. Double space before and after level one and single space the remaining levels.

Include at least two parts at each level. For example, you must have two level-one entries in an outline (at least I. and II.). If there is a second level following a level-one entry, it must contain at least two entries (at least A. and B.). All numbers must be aligned at the period and all subsequent levels must begin under the text of the preceding level, not under the number.[4]

Figure B-6 shows a formal outline prepared using the Word Outline Numbered list feature with additional formatting to follow a formal outline.

B.f Using Style Guides

A **style guide** provides a set of rules for punctuating and formatting text. There are a number of style guides used by writers, editors, business document proofreaders, and publishers. You can purchase style guides at a commercial bookstore, an online bookstore, or a college bookstore. Your local library likely has copies of different style guides and your instructor may have copies of several style guides for reference. Some popular style guides are *The Chicago Manual of Style* (The University of Chicago Press), *The Professional Secretary's Handbook* (Barron's), *The Holt Handbook* (Harcourt Brace College Publishers), and the *MLA Style Manual and Guide to Scholarly Publishing* (The Modern Language Association of America).

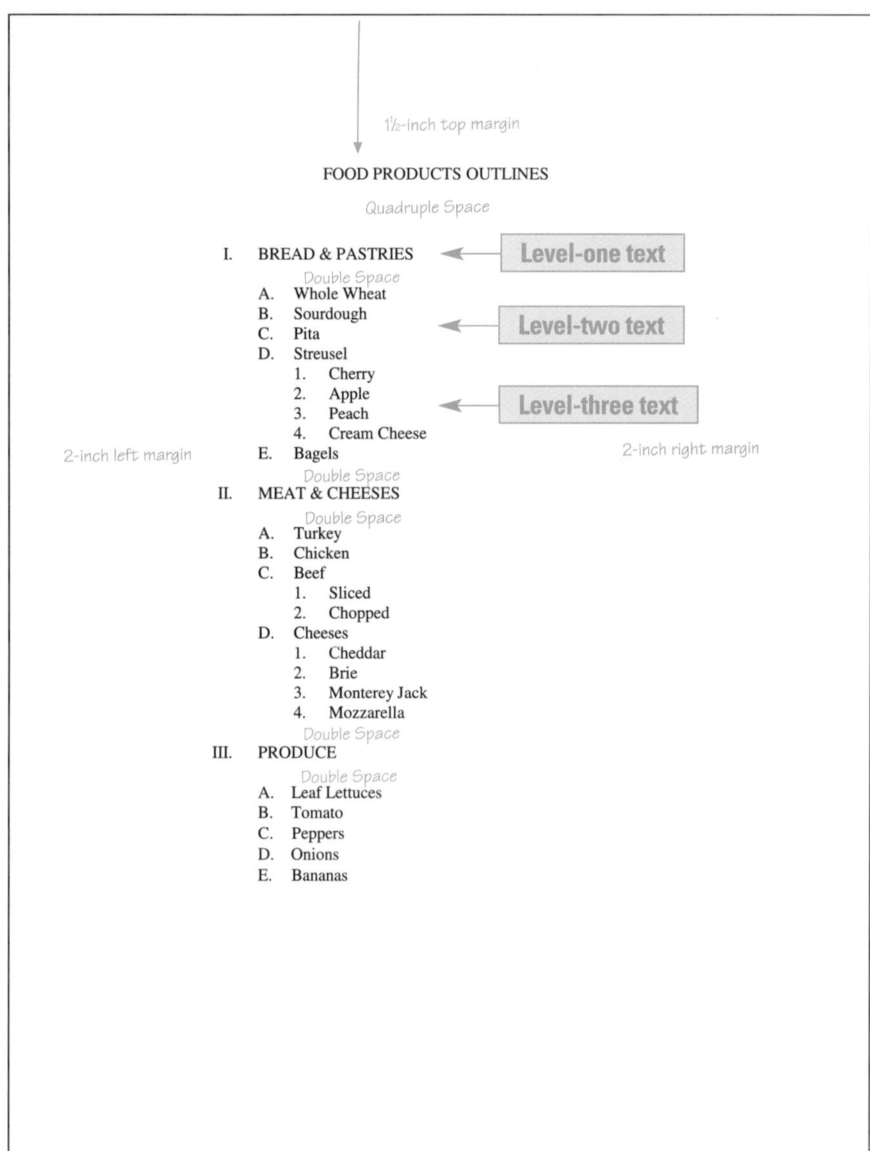

FOOD PRODUCTS OUTLINES

I. BREAD & PASTRIES
   A. Whole Wheat
   B. Sourdough
   C. Pita
   D. Streusel
      1. Cherry
      2. Apple
      3. Peach
      4. Cream Cheese
   E. Bagels

II. MEAT & CHEESES
   A. Turkey
   B. Chicken
   C. Beef
      1. Sliced
      2. Chopped
   D. Cheeses
      1. Cheddar
      2. Brie
      3. Monterey Jack
      4. Mozzarella

III. PRODUCE
   A. Leaf Lettuces
   B. Tomato
   C. Peppers
   D. Onions
   E. Bananas

FIGURE B-6
Formal Outline

B.g Using Proofreader's Marks

Standard proofreader's marks enable an editor or proofreader to make corrections or change notations in a document that can be recognized by anyone familiar with the marks. The following list illustrates standard proofreader's marks.

Defined		Examples
Paragraph	¶	¶ Begin a new paragraph at this
Insert a character	^	point. Insrt a letter here.
Delete	ℓ	Delete these words. Disregard
Do not change	stet or . . .	the previous correction. To
Transpose	tr	transpose is to around turn.
Move to the left	[	[Move this copy to the left.
Move to the right	]	]Move this copy to the right.
No paragraph	No ¶	No ¶ Do not begin a new paragraph
Delete and close up		here. Delete the hyphen from pre-empt and close up the space.
Set in caps	Caps or ≡	a sentence begins with a capital
Set in lower case	lc or /	letter. This Word should not
Insert a period	⊙	be capitalized. Insert a period⊙
Quotation marks	" "	"Quotation marks and a comma
Comma	^,	should be placed here, he said.
Insert space	#	Space between thesewords. An
Apostrophe	'	apostrophe is whats needed here.
Hyphen	=	Add a hyphen to Kilowatthour. Close
Close up	⁀	up the extra spa ce.
Use superior figure	∨	Footnote this sentence. Set
Set in italic	Ital. or ___	the words, sine qua non, in italics.
Move up		This word is too low. That word is
Move down		too high.

Endnotes

[1] Jerry W. Robinson et al., *Keyboarding and Information Processing* (Cincinnati: South-Western Educational Publishing, 1997).

[2] Ibid.

[3] Ibid.

[4] Ibid.

Appendix

Using Office XP Speech Recognition

Appendix Overview

You are familiar with using the keyboard and the mouse to key text and select commands. With Office XP, you also can use your voice to perform these same activities. Speech recognition enables you to use your voice to perform keyboard and mouse actions without ever lifting a hand. In this appendix, you learn how to set up Speech Recognition software and train the software to recognize your voice. You learn how to control menus, navigate dialog boxes, and open, save, and close a document. You then learn how to dictate text, including lines and punctuation, correct errors, and format text. Finally, you learn how to turn off and on Speech Recognition.

Learning Objectives

- Train your speech software
- Use voice commands
- Dictate, edit, and format by voice
- Turn Microsoft Speech Recognition on and off

C.a Training Your Speech Software

Speech recognition is an exciting new technology that Microsoft has integrated into its XP generation of products. Microsoft has been working on speech recognition for well over a decade. The state-of-the-art is advancing. If you haven't tried it before, this is a great time for you to experience this futuristic technology.

Voice recognition has important benefits:

- Microsoft's natural speech technologies can make your computer experience more enjoyable.
- Speech technology can increase your writing productivity.
- Voice recognition software can greatly reduce your risk for keyboard- and mouse-related injuries.

In the following activities, you learn to use your voice like a mouse and to write without the aid of the keyboard.

Connecting and Positioning Your Microphone

Start your speech recognition experience by setting up your microphone. There are several microphone styles used for speech recognition. The most common headset microphone connects to your computer's sound card, as shown in Figure C-1. Connect the microphone end to your computer's microphone audio input port. Connect the speaker end into your speech output port.

FIGURE C-1
Standard Sound Card Headset (Courtesy Plantronics Inc.)

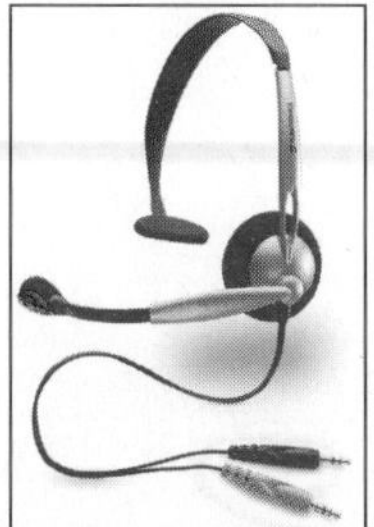

USB speech microphones, such as the one shown in Figure C-2, are becoming very popular because they normally increase performance and accuracy. USB is short for Universal Serial Bus. USB microphones bypass the sound card and input speech with less distortion into your system.

USB microphones are plugged into the USB port found in the back of most computers. Windows automatically installs the necessary USB drivers after you start your computer with the USB microphone plugged into its slot.

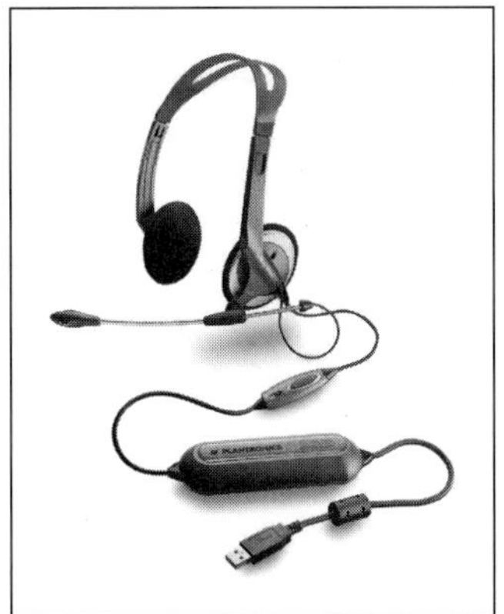

FIGURE C-2
A USB Headset (Courtesy Plantronics Inc.)

After your headset has been installed, put on your headset and position it comfortably. Remember these two important tips:

- Place the speaking side of your microphone about a thumb's width away from the side of your mouth, as shown in Figure C-3.
- Keep your microphone in the same position every time you speak. Changing your microphone's position can decrease your accuracy.

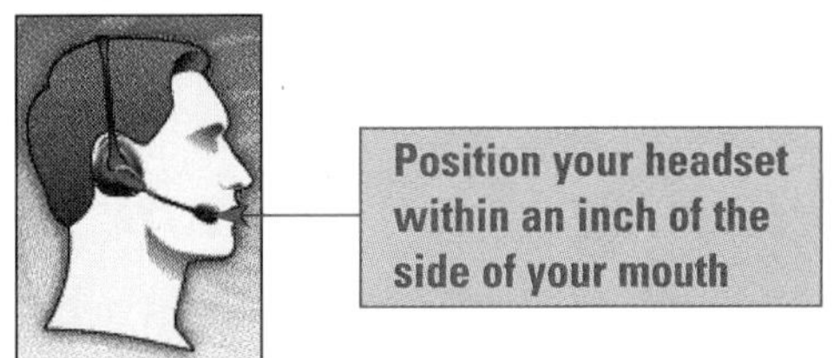
Position your headset within an inch of the side of your mouth

FIGURE C-3
Proper Headset Position

> **CAUTION TIP**
>
> If you see additional buttons on the Language Bar than shown in Figure C-4, click the Microphone button to hide them.

Installing Microsoft Speech Recognition

Open Microsoft Word and see if your speech software has already been installed. As Word opens, you should see either the floating Language Bar, shown in Figure C-4, or the Language Bar icon in the Windows Taskbar tray, as shown in Figure C-5.

Correction | Microphone | Tools | Write | Lined Paper | ?

FIGURE C-4
Floating Language Bar

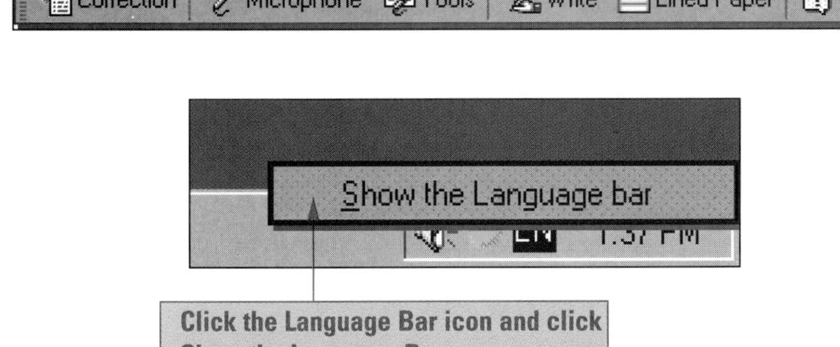
Show the Language bar
Click the Language Bar icon and click Show the Language Bar

FIGURE C-5
Language Bar Icon

appendix C

If you can open and see the Language Bar, jump to Step-by-Step C.2. However, if this essential tool is missing, proceed with Step-by-Step C.1.

Step-by-Step C.1

Step 1 To install Microsoft speech recognition, open Microsoft Word by clicking **Start**, **Programs**, **Microsoft Word**.

Step 2 Click **Tools**, **Speech** from the Word menu bar, as shown in Figure C-6.

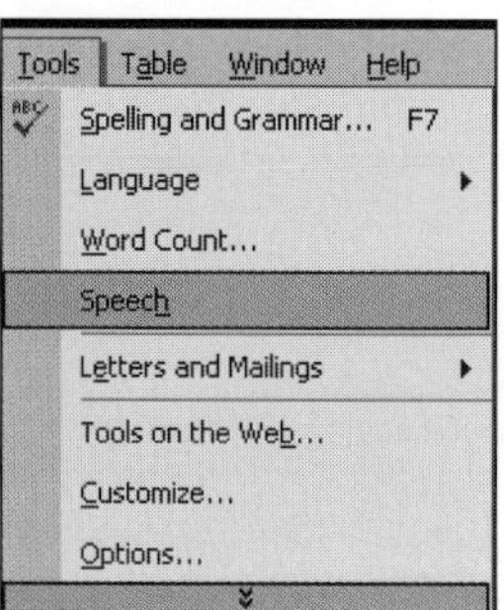

FIGURE C-6
Click Speech from the Tools menu

Step 3 You are prompted through the installation procedure. The process is a simple one. Follow the onscreen instructions.

Training Your System

Microsoft speech recognition can accommodate many different voices on the same computer. In order to work properly, your Microsoft Office Speech Recognition software must create a user **profile** for each voice it hears—including your voice.

If you are the first user and have just installed your speech software, chances are the system is already prompting you through the training steps. Skip to Step 3 in Step-by-Step C.2 for hints and help as you continue. However, if you are the second or later user of the system, you need to create a new profile by starting with Step 1.

Step-by-Step C.2

Step 1 To create your own personal speech profile, click the **Tools** button on the Language Bar and click **Options**, as shown in Figure C-7. This opens the Speech Properties dialog box.

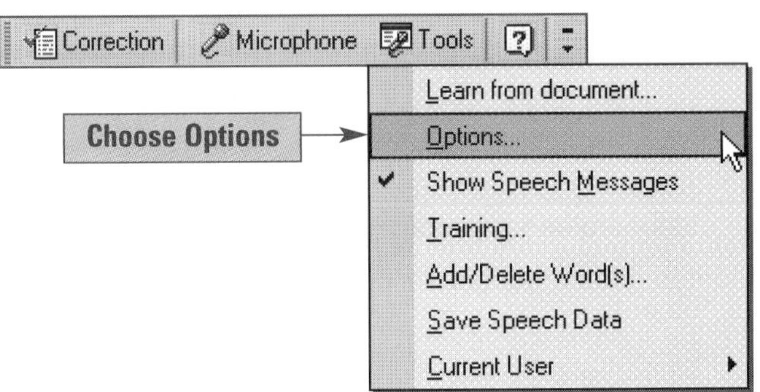

FIGURE C-7
Language Bar's Tools Menu

Step 2 In the Speech Properties dialog box, click **New**, as indicated in Figure C-8.

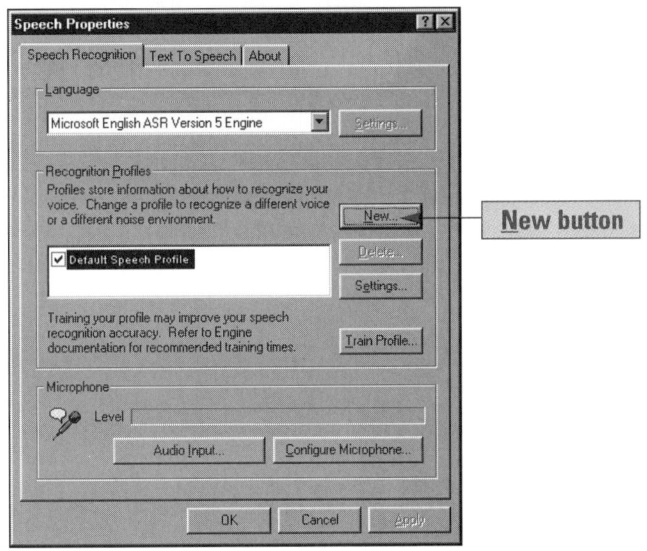

FIGURE C-8
Speech Properties Dialog Box

Step 3 Enter your name in the Profile Wizard, as shown in Figure C-9, and click **Next>** to continue. (*Note:* If you accidently click Finish instead of Next>, you must still train your profile by clicking Train Profile in the Speech Properties dialog box.)

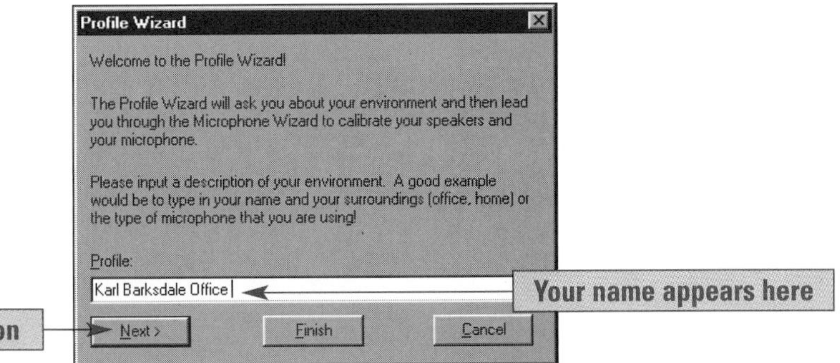

FIGURE C-9
New Profile Dialog Box

Step 4 Adjust your microphone, as explained on the Microphone Wizard Welcome dialog box, as shown in Figure C-10. Click **Next>** to begin adjusting your microphone.

FIGURE C-10
Correctly Position Your Microphone

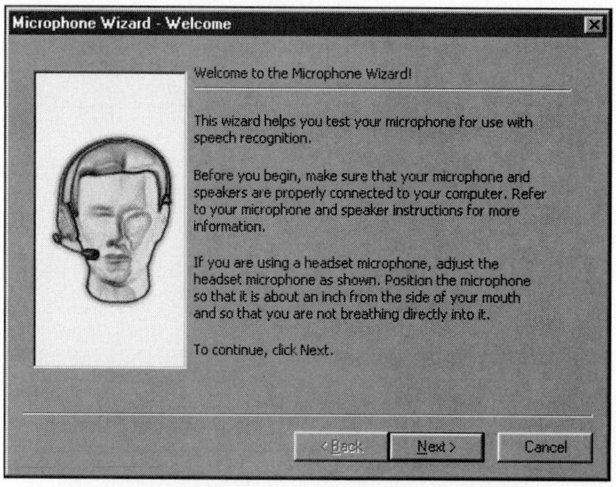

Microphone Wizard - Welcome

Welcome to the Microphone Wizard!

This wizard helps you test your microphone for use with speech recognition.

Before you begin, make sure that your microphone and speakers are properly connected to your computer. Refer to your microphone and speaker instructions for more information.

If you are using a headset microphone, adjust the headset microphone as shown. Position the microphone so that it is about an inch from the side of your mouth and so that you are not breathing directly into it.

To continue, click Next.

< Back | Next > | Cancel

Step 5 Read the test sentence indicated in Figure C-11 until the volume adjustment settings appear consistently in the green portion of the volume adjustment meter. Your volume settings are adjusted automatically as you speak. Click **Next>** to continue.

FIGURE C-11
Read Aloud to Adjust Your Microphone Volume

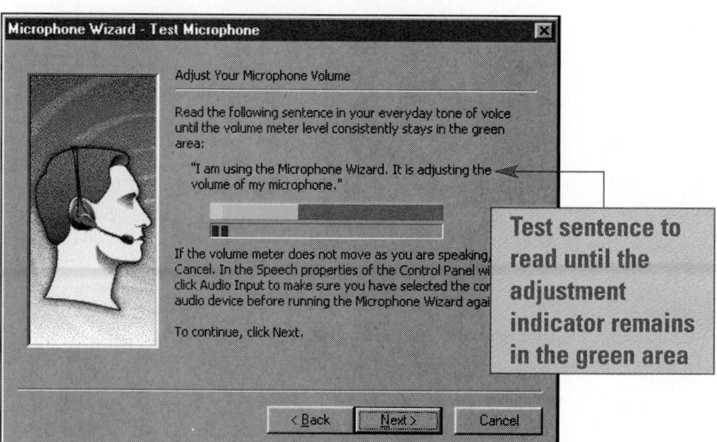

QUICK TIP

Microsoft Office Speech Recognition tells you if your microphone is not adequate for good speech recognition. You may need to try a higher quality microphone, install a compatible sound card, or switch to a USB microphone. Check the Microsoft Windows Help files for assistance with microphone problems.

Step 6 The next audio check tests the output of your speakers. Read the test sentence indicated in Figure C-12 and then listen. If you can hear your voice, your speakers are connected properly. Click **Finish** and continue.

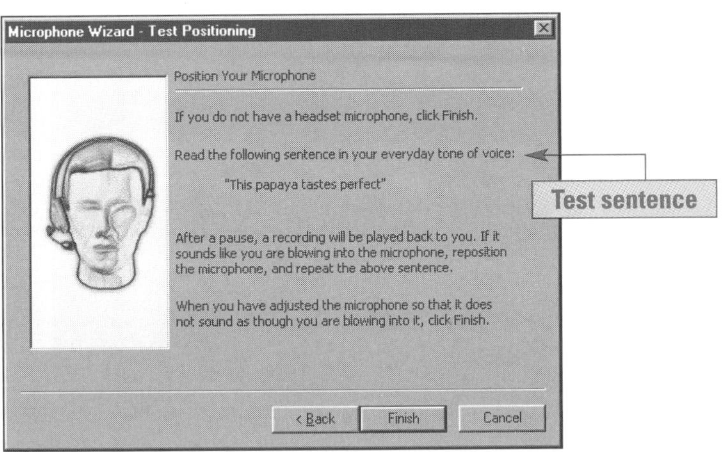

FIGURE C-12
Read Aloud to Test Your Sound Output

> **QUICK TIP**
>
> Your user file will remember your microphone settings from session to session. However, if others use the system before you, you may need to readjust the audio settings by clicking **Tools**, **Options**, **Configure Microphone**.

Training Your Software

Next, you are asked to train your software. During the training session, you read a training script or story for about 10 to 15 minutes. As you read, your software gathers samples of your speech. These samples help the speech software customize your speech recognition profile to your way of speaking. As you read, remember to:

- Read clearly.
- Use a normal, relaxed reading voice. Don't shout, but don't whisper softly either.
- Read at your normal reading pace. Do not read slowly and do not rush.

> **CAUTION TIP**
>
> Never touch any part of your headset or microphone while speaking. Holding or touching the microphone creates errors.

Step-by-Step C.3

Step 1 Microsoft Office Speech Recognition prepares you to read a story or script. Read the instruction screen shown in Figure C-13 and click **Next>** to continue.

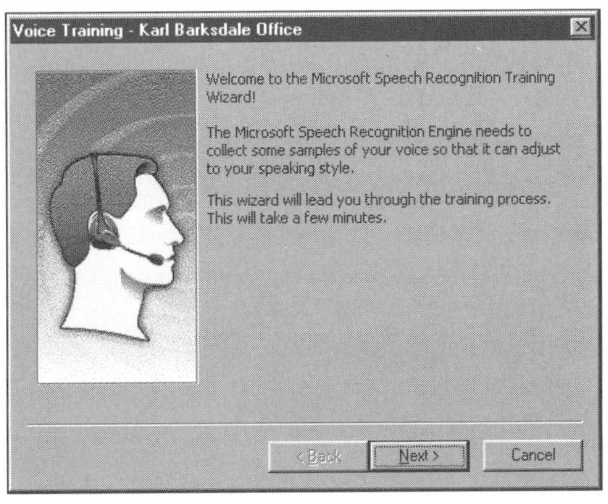

FIGURE C-13
Read the Onscreen Instructions Carefully

Step 2 Enter your gender and age information (see Figure C-14) to help the system calibrate its settings to your voice. Click **Next>** to continue.

FIGURE C-14
Enter Your Gender and Age Information

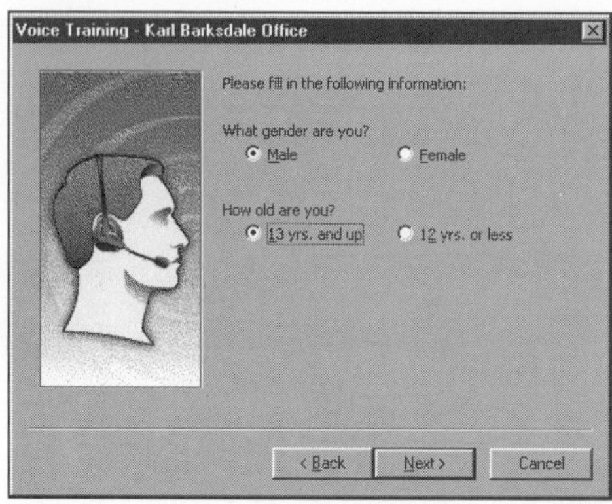

Step 3 Click **Sample** and listen to a short example of how to speak clearly to a computer. See Figure C-15. After the recording, click **Next>** to review the tips for the training session, and then click **Next>** to continue.

FIGURE C-15
Listen to the Speech Sample

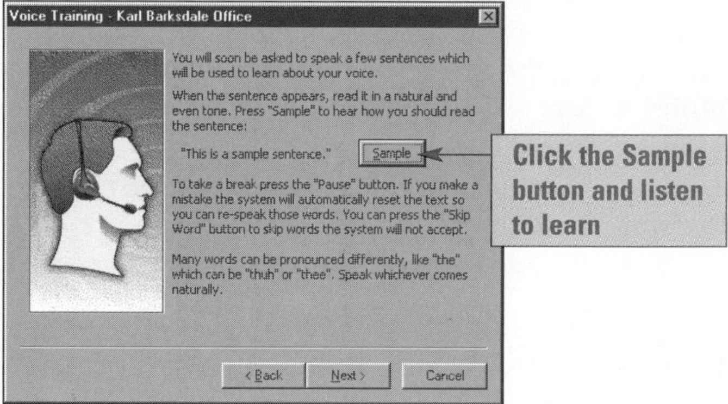

Step 4 Begin reading the training session paragraphs, as shown in Figure C-16. Text you have read is highlighted. The Training Progress bar lets you know how much reading is left. If you get stuck on a word, click **Skip Word** to move past the problem spot.

FIGURE C-16
Software Tracks Your Progress

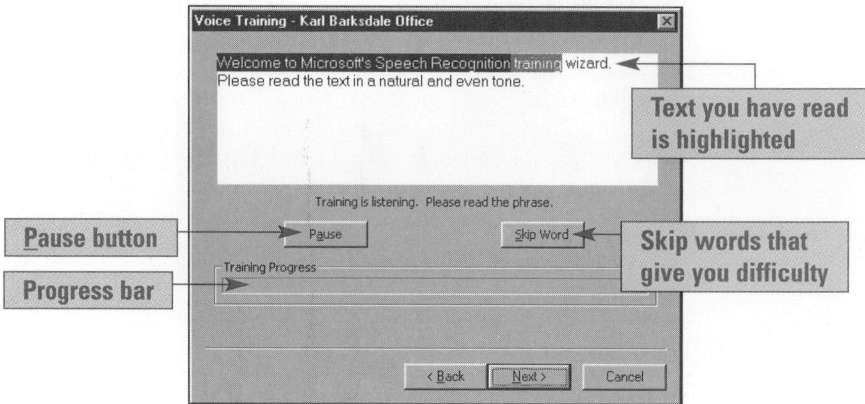

Step 5 The screen shown in Figure C-17 appears after you have finished reading the entire first story or training session script. You now have a couple of choices. Click **More Training**, click **Next>**, and continue reading additional scripts as explained in Step 6 (or you can click Finish and quit for the day).

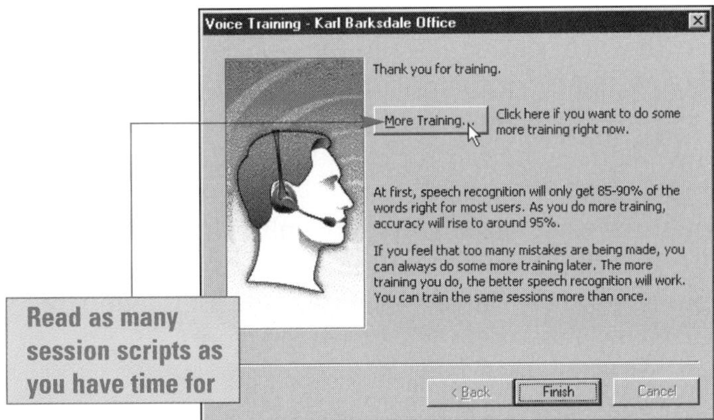

FIGURE C-17
First Training Script Completed

Step 6 Choose another training session story or script from the list, as shown in Figure C-18, and then click **Next>**.

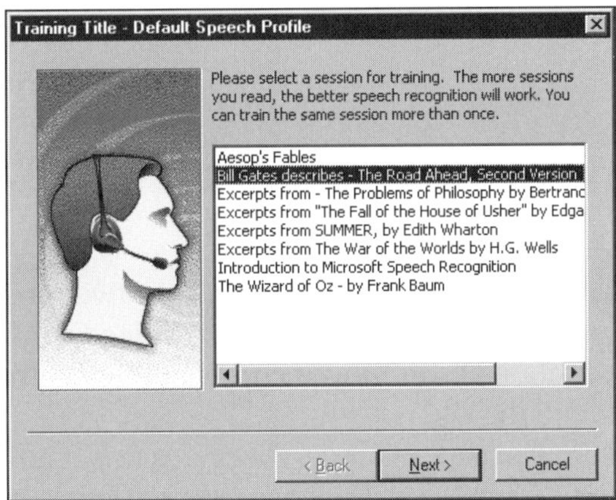

FIGURE C-18
Choose Another Story or Training Script to Read

Step 7 At the end of the training process, Microsoft Office Speech Recognition shows you a multimedia training tutorial (you may need to install Macromedia Flash to view the tutorial). Enjoy the tutorial before continuing.

QUICK TIP

The more stories you read, the better. Users with thick accents, or accuracy below 90 percent, must read additional stories. You can read additional training session scripts at any time by clicking **Tools**, **Training** on the Language Bar.

CAUTION TIP

You must read until Microsoft Office Speech Recognition has a large enough sample of your voice to process and adjust to your unique way of speaking. Click **Pause** to take a break. However, it is best to read the entire session training script in one sitting.

C.b Using Voice Commands

Microsoft makes it easy to replace mouse clicks with voice commands. The voice commands are very intuitive. In most cases, you simply say what you see. For example, to open the File menu, you can simply say **File**.

Microsoft Office XP voice commands allow you to control dialog boxes and menu bars, and to format documents by speaking. You can give your hands a rest by speaking commands instead of clicking them. This can help reduce your risk for carpal tunnel syndrome and other serious injuries.

Before you begin using voice commands, remember that if more than one person is using speech recognition on the same computer, you must select your user profile from the Current Users list. The list is found by clicking the Language Bar Tools menu, as shown in Figure C-19.

FIGURE C-19
Current Users List

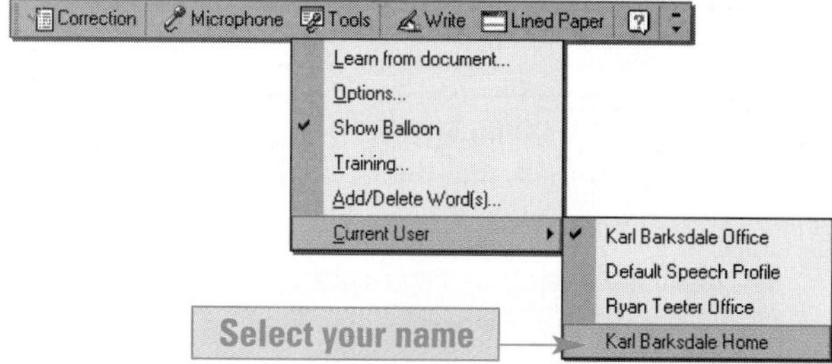

MENU TIP

After you have selected your user profile, you may wish to refresh your audio settings by clicking **Tools**, **Options**, **Configure Microphone**. This will help adjust the audio settings to the noise conditions in your current dictation environment.

Switching Modes and Moving the Language Bar

Microsoft Office Speech Recognition works in two modes. The first is called **Dictation mode**. The second is called **Voice Command mode**. Voice Command mode allows you to control menus, give commands, and format documents.

When using Voice Command mode, simply *say what you see on the screen or in dialog boxes*. You see how this works in the next few exercises. In Step-by-Step C.4, you learn how to switch between the two modes.

Step-by-Step C.4

Step 1 Open **Microsoft Word** and the **Language Bar**, if necessary.

Step 2 The Language Bar can appear collapsed (see Figure C-20) or expanded (see Figure C-21). You can switch between the two options by clicking the **Microphone** button.

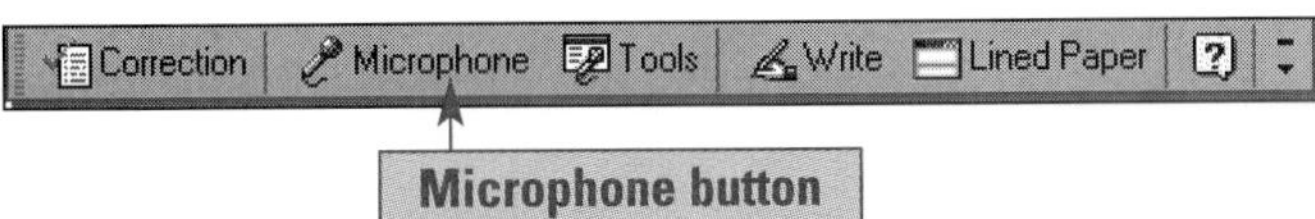

FIGURE C-20
Collapsed Language Bar

Clicking the Microphone button with your mouse turns on the microphone and expands the Language Bar.

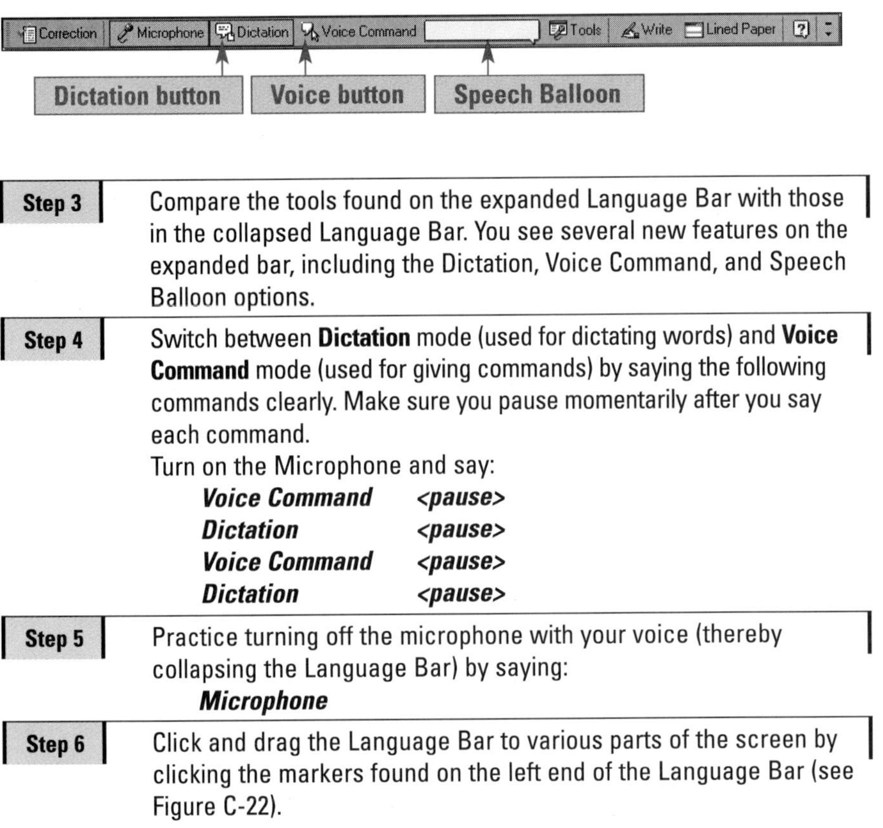

FIGURE C-21
Expanded Language Bar

Step 3 Compare the tools found on the expanded Language Bar with those in the collapsed Language Bar. You see several new features on the expanded bar, including the Dictation, Voice Command, and Speech Balloon options.

Step 4 Switch between **Dictation** mode (used for dictating words) and **Voice Command** mode (used for giving commands) by saying the following commands clearly. Make sure you pause momentarily after you say each command.
Turn on the Microphone and say:

Voice Command ***<pause>***
Dictation ***<pause>***
Voice Command ***<pause>***
Dictation ***<pause>***

Step 5 Practice turning off the microphone with your voice (thereby collapsing the Language Bar) by saying:
Microphone

Step 6 Click and drag the Language Bar to various parts of the screen by clicking the markers found on the left end of the Language Bar (see Figure C-22).

QUICK TIP

The Language Bar can float anywhere on the screen. Move the Language Bar to a spot that is convenient and out of the way. Most users position the Language Bar in the title bar or status bar when using speech with Microsoft Word.

Correction | Microphone | Tools | Write | Lined Paper

Click and drag the Language Bar marker

FIGURE C-22
Move the Language Bar to a Convenient Spot

Giving Menu Commands

When you use Microsoft Office Voice Commands, your word will be obeyed. Before you begin issuing commands, take a few seconds and analyze Figure C-23. The toolbars you will be working with in the next few activities are identified in the figure.

FIGURE C-23
Customize Microsoft Word with Your Voice

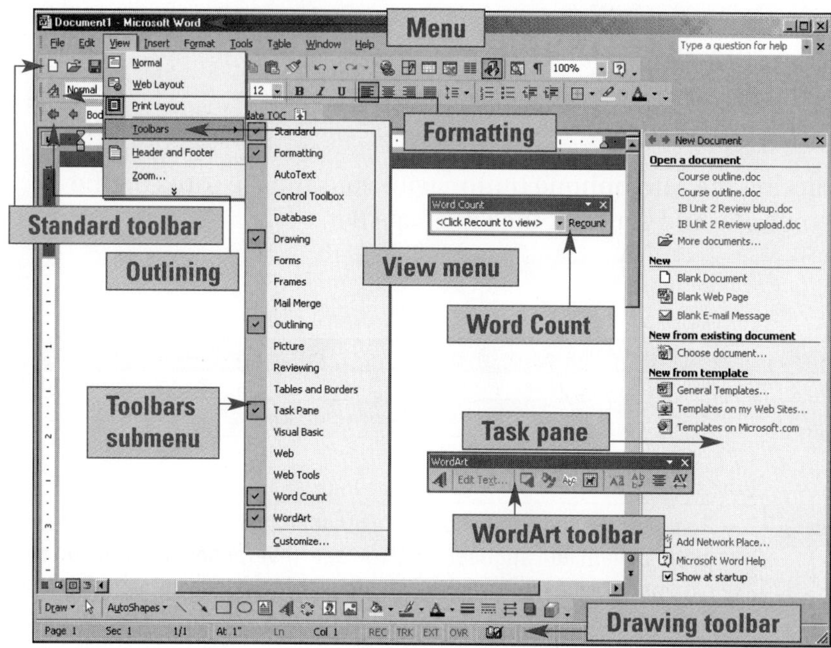

> **QUICK TIP**
>
> In Voice Command mode, you can say almost any command you would click with your mouse, and achieve the same result. For the most part, simply say what you see on the screen. Voice Commands are very easy to learn.

> **QUICK TIP**
>
> The Escape and Cancel commands are like pressing the ESC key on the keyboard. These commands cancel whatever menu you have voice-selected.

Step-by-Step C.5

Step 1 Switch on the **Microphone** from the Language Bar.

Step 2 Switch to Voice Command mode by saying:
Voice Command

Step 3 Open and close several menus by saying:
File *(Pause briefly between commands)*
Escape
Edit
Cancel
View
Escape

Step 4 Close or display a few of the popular toolbars found in Microsoft Word by saying the following commands:
View
Toolbars
Standard
View
Toolbars
Formatting
View
Toolbars
Drawing

Step 5 Close or redisplay the toolbars by saying the following commands:
View
Toolbars
Drawing
View
Toolbars
Formatting
View
Toolbars
Standard

Step 6 Practice giving voice commands by adding and removing the Task Pane and WordArt toolbar. Try some other options. When you are through experimenting, turn off the microphone and collapse the Language Bar by saying:
Microphone

Navigating Dialog Boxes

Opening files is one thing you do nearly every time you use Microsoft Office. To open files, you need to manipulate the Open dialog box (Figure C-24). A dialog box allows you to make decisions and execute voice commands. For example, in the Open dialog box you can switch folders and open files by voice.

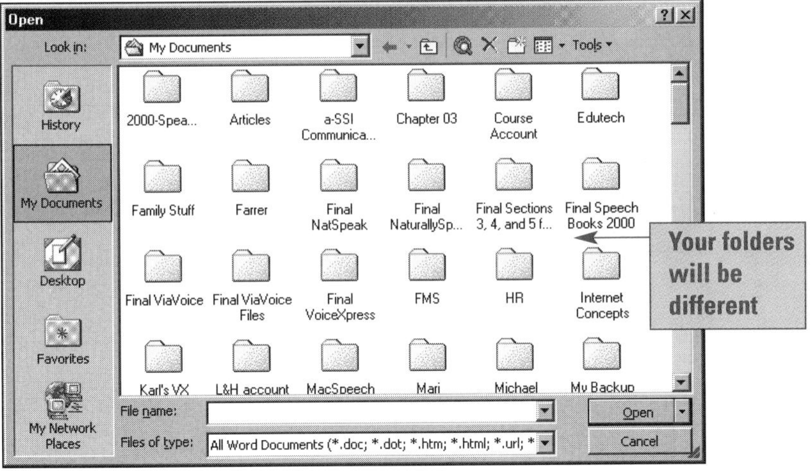

FIGURE C-24
Open Dialog Box

Step-by-Step C.6

Step 1 Turn on the **Microphone**, switch to Voice Command mode, and access the Open dialog box, as shown in Figure C-25, using the following commands:
Voice Command
File
Open

FIGURE C-25
Say File, Open

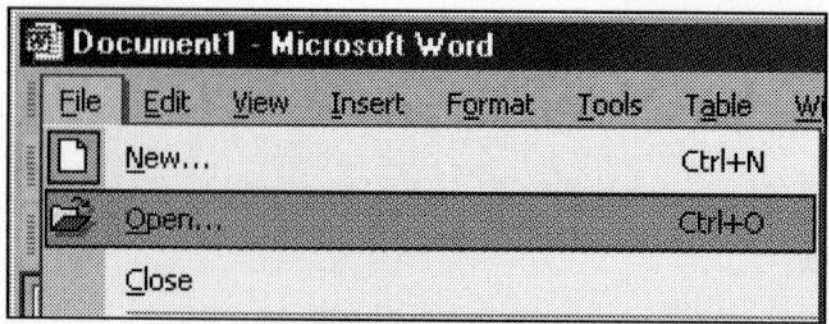

Step 2 Switch between various folder locations with your voice. In this case, you're going to switch between the Desktop, My Documents, and other folders located on the side of the Open dialog box, as shown in Figure C-26. Say the following voice commands to switch between folder locations. Pause slightly after saying each command:
Desktop
My Documents
History
Desktop
Favorites
My Documents

FIGURE C-26
Switch Between Various Folder Locations

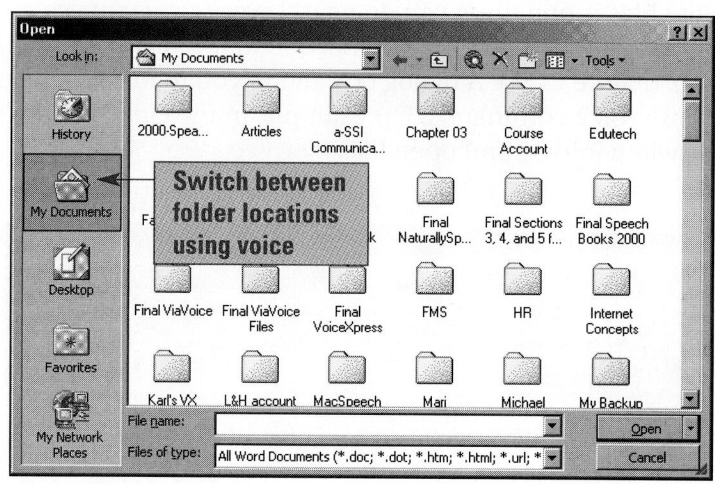

QUICK TIP

Any time a button in a dialog box appears dark around the edges, the button is active. You can access active buttons at any time by saying the name of the button or by saying **Enter**. You can also move around dialog boxes using the **Tab** or **Shift Tab** voice commands, or move between folders and files by saying **Up Arrow**, **Down Arrow**, **Left Arrow**, and **Right Arrow**. When selecting files, you'll probably find it much easier to use your mouse instead of your voice.

Step 3 You can change how your folders and files look in the Open dialog box by manipulating the Views menu, as shown in Figure C-27. Say the following voice commands to change the look of your folders and files:
Views
Small Icons
Views
List
Views
Details
Views
Thumbnails
Views
Large icons
Views
List

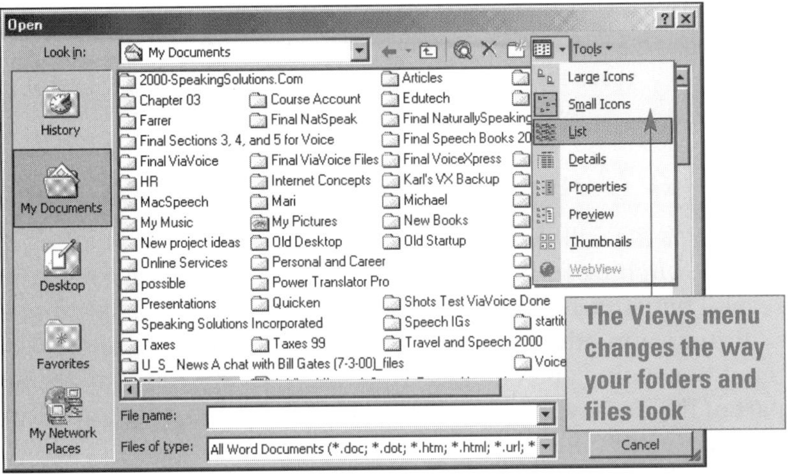

FIGURE C-27
Change the Look of Folders with the Views Menu

Step 4	Close the Open dialog box by using the Cancel command. Say: ***Cancel***

Open and Count a Document

In Step-by-Step C.7, you combine your traditional mouse skills with voice skills to accomplish tasks more conveniently. Use your skills to open a file. Then, use your menu selecting technique to open the Word Count toolbar and count the number of words in a document.

Step-by-Step C.7

Step 1	Using your voice, say ***File***, ***Open*** and select the **My Documents** folder (or the location of your Data Disk). View the folders and files in **List** view. (Review Step-by-Step C.6 if you have forgotten how to make these changes in the Open dialog box.)
Step 2	Scroll through the list of files with your mouse until you see the file called ***Prevent Injury***. To open the file, select it with your mouse and say: ***Open*** (or you also may say ***Enter***)
Step 3	As the file opens, notice that the document title is PREVENT INJURY WITH SPEECH. Speech recognition can help you avoid serious keyboarding and mouse injuries. Count the words in the article. Open the Word Count toolbar by saying the following: ***View*** ***Toolbars*** ***Word Count***
Step 4	With the Word Count toolbar open, say the following command to count the words: ***Recount***

QUICK TIP

To complete Step-by-Step C.7, the *Prevent Injury* document should be moved from the Data Disk to the My Documents folder on your computer.

appendix C

Step 5	How many words are contained in the article?
Step 6	Leave the *Prevent Injury* document open for the next activity.

Save a Document and Exit Word

Saving a file will give you a chance to practice manipulating dialog boxes. Switching from the keyboard and mouse to your voice has several benefits. For example, have you heard of carpal tunnel syndrome and other computer keyboard-related injuries caused by repetitive typing and clicking? By using your speech software even part of the time, you can reduce your risk for these long-term and debilitating nerve injuries.

In Step-by-Step C.8, you change the filename *Prevent Injury* to *My prevent injury file* using the Save As dialog box.

Step-by-Step C.8

Step 1	Make sure the ***Prevent Injury*** document appears on your screen. If you closed the document, repeat Step-by-Step C.7.
Step 2	Open the **Save As** dialog box. Notice that it is a lot like the Open dialog box. Try the following commands: ***Voice Command*** *(if necessary)* ***File*** ***Save as***
Step 3	Switch to the **My Documents** folder and display the folder in **List** view as you learned to do in Step-by-Step C.7.
Step 4	Click your mouse in the **File name:** text box and type the filename or switch to Dictation mode and name the file with your voice by saying: ***Dictation*** ***My prevent injury file***
Step 5	Save your document and close the Save As the box by saying: ***Voice Command*** ***Save***
Step 6	Close the **Word Count** toolbar using the steps you learned earlier.
Step 7	Close Microsoft Word and collapse the Language Bar with the following commands: (When asked whether to save other open documents, say ***No***.) ***File*** ***Close*** ***Microphone***

C.c Dictating, Editing, and Formatting by Voice

If you have always dreamed of the day when you could sit back, relax, and write the next great American novel by speaking into a microphone, well, that day has arrived. It is possible to write that novel, a report, or even a simple e-mail message at speeds of 130–160 words per minute. However, it takes practice to achieve an acceptable level of accuracy. This section is designed to help you build accuracy.

Microsoft Office Speech Recognition is not made for complete handsfree use. You still need to use your keyboard and mouse much of the time. But, if you're willing to put in some effort, you can improve your speaking accuracy to the point that you can dramatically improve your output.

Dictating

Microsoft Speech Recognition allows you to work in **Dictation** mode when voice writing words into your documents. Switching from Voice Command mode to Dictation mode is as easy as saying ***Dictation***.

In Dictation mode, don't stop speaking in the middle of a sentence—even if your words don't appear immediately. The software needs a few seconds to process what you're saying. Microsoft Office Speech Recognition lets you know it is working by placing a highlighted bar with dots in your document, as shown in Figure C-28. A few seconds later, your words appear.

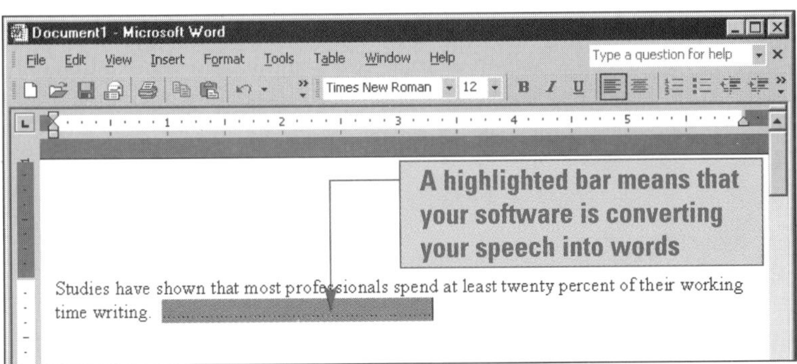

FIGURE C-28
Continue Talking Even If Your Words Don't Appear Instantly

QUICK TIP

The best way to improve dictation accuracy is to read additional training session stories to your computer. You should read at least three to five stories. Do this by clicking **Tools**, **Current User**, and double-checking to see if your user profile name has a check mark by it. Then, click **Tools**, **Training** from the Language Bar and follow the onscreen instructions.

appendix C

QUICK TIP

Think about the following as you begin voice writing:

- Speak naturally, without stopping in the middle of your sentences.
- Don't speak abnormally fast or slow.
- Say each word clearly. Don't slur your words or leave out sounds.

QUICK TIP

You'll need to dictate punctuation marks. Say the word ***Period*** to create a (.), say ***Comma*** to create a (,), say ***Question Mark*** for a (?), and ***Exclamation Mark/Point*** for (!).

During the next steps, don't be overly concerned about making mistakes. You learn some powerful ways to correct mistakes in the next few exercises. For now, experiment and see what happens.

Step-by-Step C.9

Step 1	Open **Microsoft Word** and the **Language Bar**, if necessary. Don't forget to select your user profile.
Step 2	Turn on the **Microphone**, switch to **Dictation mode**, and read this short selection into Microsoft Word. ***Dictation*** ***Studies have shown that most professionals spend at least twenty percent of their working time writing <period> You can use speech recognition software to help you in any career you choose <period> Microsoft speech can be used in the medical <comma> legal <comma> financial <comma> and educational professions <period>*** ***Microphone***
Step 3	Examine your paragraph. How well did you do? Count the mistakes or word errors. How many errors did you make?
Step 4	Now delete all the text on your screen. Start by turning on the **Microphone** and then switching to **Voice Command** mode by saying (remember to pause briefly after each command): ***Voice Command*** ***Edit*** ***Select All*** ***Backspace***
Step 5	Repeat the selection from Step 2. This time, say any word that gave you difficulty a little more clearly. See if your computer understands more of what you say this time around.
Step 6	Did you improve? Yes/No
Step 7	Delete all the text on your screen again before you continue, using the ***Voice Command, Edit, Select All, Backspace*** commands.

Using the New Line and New Paragraph Commands

In this next set of exercises, you have a chance to use the New Line and New Paragraph commands to organize text. These essential commands allow you to control the look and feel of your documents. (See Figure C-29.) It helps to pause briefly before and after you say each command.

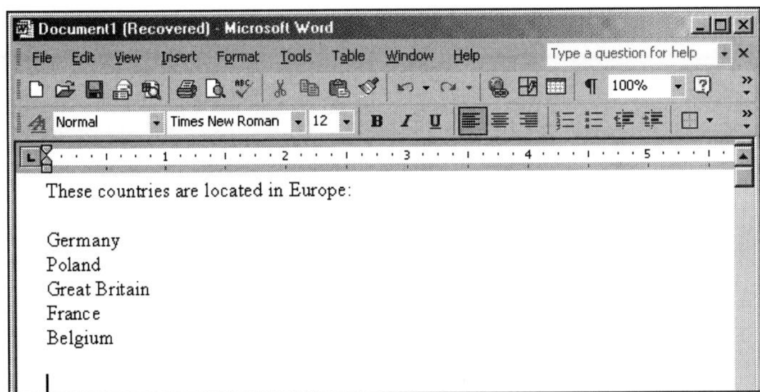

FIGURE C-29
New Line and New Paragraph Commands Organize Text

Step-by-Step C.10

Step 1 The New Line and New Paragraph commands help organize lists of information. Dictate the following list of European countries. Turn on the **Microphone**, if necessary, and say:

Dictation

These countries are located in Europe ***<colon>*** ***<New Paragraph>***

Germany	***<New Line>***
Poland	***<New Line>***
Great Britain	***<New Line>***
France	***<New Line>***
Belgium	***<New Paragraph>***

Step 2 Save the file in the Save As dialog box with the ***Voice Command, File, Save As*** commands.

Step 3 Click your mouse in the **File name:** text box and enter ***Countries of Europe*** as the filename. (*Note:* If you speak the filename, remember to switch to Dictation mode.)

Step 4 Close the Save As dialog box with the ***Voice Command, Save*** commands, and then clear your screen by saying ***Edit, Select All, Backspace.***

QUICK TIP

Say the word ***Colon*** to create a (:).

QUICK TIP

When dictating words in a list, it helps to pause slightly before and after saying the commands, as in ***<pause> New Line <pause>*** and ***<pause> New Paragraph <pause>***.

Using Undo

Microsoft Office Speech Recognition offers powerful ways to make corrections and train the software to recognize difficult words, so they appear correctly when you say them again. For example, erasing mistakes is easy with the Undo command. That's the first trick you learn in this section.

The Undo command works like pressing the Undo button or clicking Edit, Undo with your mouse. You can quickly erase the problem when you misspeak. All you need to do is switch to Voice Command mode and say ***Undo***.

CAUTION TIP

A common speech mistake occurs when speakers break words into syllables. For example, they may say **speak keen clear lee** instead of **speaking clearly.**

QUICK TIP

A key to great accuracy in speech recognition is to speak in complete phrases and sentences. Complete sentences and phrases make it easier for the software to understand what you're trying to say. The software makes adjustments based on the context of the words that commonly appear together. The more words you say as a group or phrase, the more information your software has to work with.

Step-by-Step C.11

Step 1 In this step, say the name of the academic subject, then erase it immediately with the Undo command and replace it with the next subject in the list. Erase the subject regardless of whether it is correct. Switch to Voice Command mode before saying Undo.

Dictation

Biology	***Voice Command***	***Undo***	***Dictation***
French	***Voice Command***	***Undo***	***Dictation***
American history	***Voice Command***	***Undo***	***Dictation***

Step 2 The Undo command deletes the last continuous phrase you have spoken. Say each of the following phrases, then use Undo to erase them.

To infinity and beyond	***Voice Command***	***Undo***	***Dictation***
The check is in the mail	***Voice Command***	***Undo***	***Dictation***
Money isn't everything	***Voice Command***	***Undo***	

Microphone

Correcting Errors

Correcting mistakes is obviously important. There are several ways to make corrections effectively.

Because speech recognition software recognizes phrases better than individual words, one of the best ways to correct a mistake is to use your mouse to select the phrase where the mistake occurs and then repeat the phrase. For example, in the sentence below the software has keyed the word ***share*** instead of the word ***sure***. Select the phrase (like the boldface example) with your mouse, then say the phrase again:

What you should select:	You sound **very share of yourself**.
What you would repeat:	**very sure of yourself**

If you still make a mistake, select the misspoken word with your mouse and take advantage of the power of the **Correction** button on the Language Bar. Carefully read through these steps and then practice what you learned in Step 5.

Step-by-Step C.12

Step 1 If you make an error, select the mistake, as shown in Figure C-30.

Step 2 With your microphone on, say ***Correction*** or click the Correction button with your mouse.

Step 3 If the correct alternative appears in the correction list, click the correct alternative with your mouse.

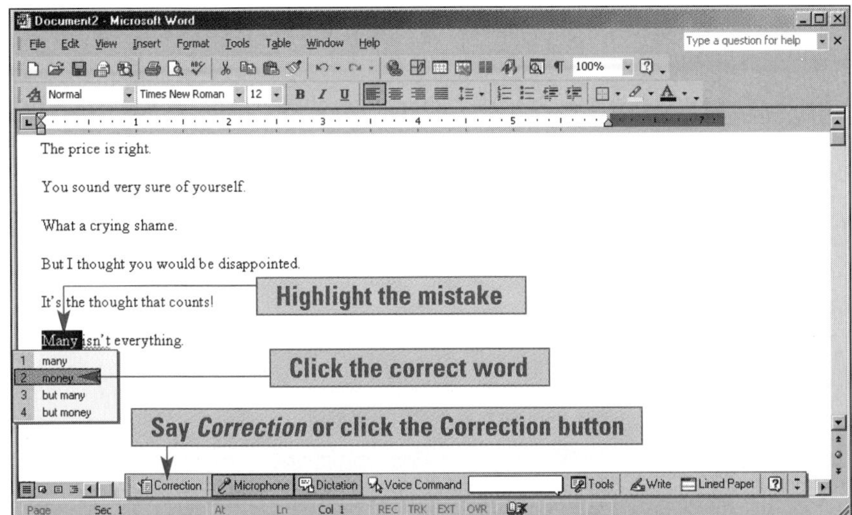

FIGURE C-30
Select the Mistake and Say *Correction*

Step 4 If the correct word does not appear, as in Figure C-31, key the correct response with your keyboard.

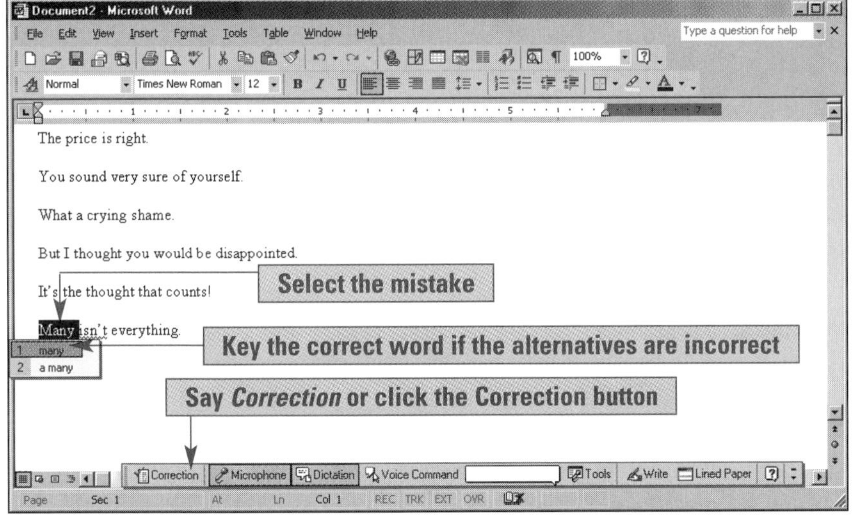

FIGURE C-31
If the Correct Word Doesn't Appear, Key the Word

Step 5 Now give it a try. Speak the following sentences. (*Hint:* Say the complete sentence before you make any corrections.) Try to correct the error first by repeating the phrase. Then, select individual word errors and use the Correction button to help you fix any remaining mistakes:

The price is right.
You sound very sure of yourself.
What a crying shame.
But, I thought you would be disappointed.
It's the thought that counts!
Money isn't everything.

Formatting Sentences

After you dictate text, you can format it, copy it, paste it, and manipulate it just like you would with a mouse. In this exercise, you dictate a few sentences, and then you change the font styles and make a copy of the sentences. That is a lot to remember, so take a look at what you are about to accomplish. Review Figure C-32 to get a sneak preview of this activity.

FIGURE C-32
Dictate, Format, and Copy and Paste These Lines

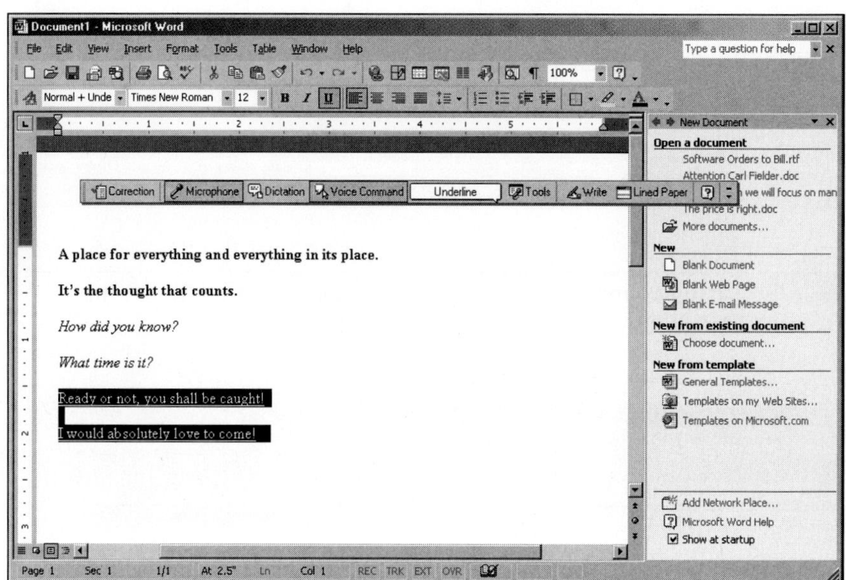

When you correct a mistake using the Correction button, Microsoft Office Speech Recognition plays back what you said and remembers any corrections that you make. This helps to ensure that the software won't make the same mistake the next time you say the same word or phrase. Use the Correction button as often as you can. This helps to improve your speech recognition accuracy.

A few quick reminders before you begin:

- Use your mouse and voice together to bold, italicize, and underline text.
- Say the basic punctuation marks, exclamation point/mark (!), period (.), comma (,), question mark (?), semicolon (;), colon (:).
- Start a new line with the New Paragraph command.

Step-by-Step C.13

Step 1 Speak the following sentences, using the New Paragraph command to space between each. Do not pause in the middle of any sentence. If you make mistakes, correct them using the Correction button, as explained in Step-by-Step C.12.

Dictation
A place for everything and everything in its place.
It's the thought that counts.
How did you know?
What time is it?
Ready or not, you shall be caught!
I would absolutely love to come!

Step 2 With your mouse, select the first two sentences and make them bold with the following commands:
Voice Command
Bold

Step 3 Select the two questions and italicize them by saying:
Italic

Step 4 Select the final two exclamatory sentences and underline them by saying:
Underline

Step 5 Copy all the text on your screen and paste a copy at the bottom of your document by saying:
Edit
Select All
Copy
Down Arrow
Paste

Step 6 Print your document with the following commands:
File
Print
OK

Step 7 Close your document without saving using the ***File, Close*** command and then say ***No*** when you are asked to save.

Step 8 Open a new document with your voice with the ***File, New, Blank Document*** commands and turn off your ***Microphone*** before you continue.

Adding and Training Names

Your speech software can remember what you teach it as long as you follow these simple steps. When you click Add/Delete Word(s) from the Tools menu, the Add/Delete Word(s) dialog box opens. This is a very powerful tool. It allows you to enter a name or any other word or phrase, click the **Record pronunciation** button, and record your pronunciation of the word or phrase.

Step-by-Step C.14

Step 1 Click **Tools, Add/Delete Word(s)** from the Language Bar, as shown in Figure C-33.

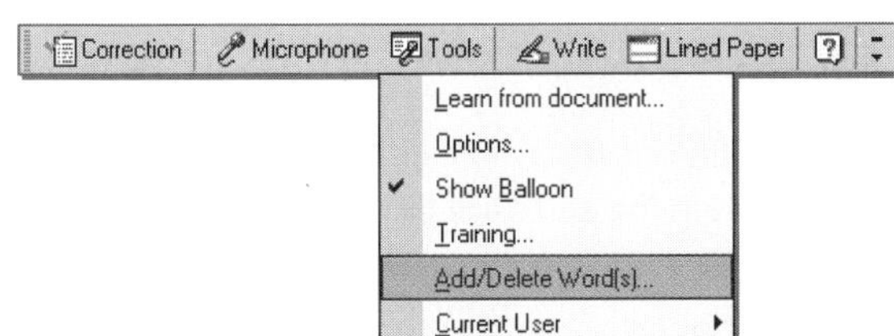

FIGURE C-33
Click the Add/Delete Word(s) Option

appendix C

Step 2 Enter your name into the **Word** text box as shown in Figure C-34.

FIGURE C-34
Enter Your Name in the Word Text Box

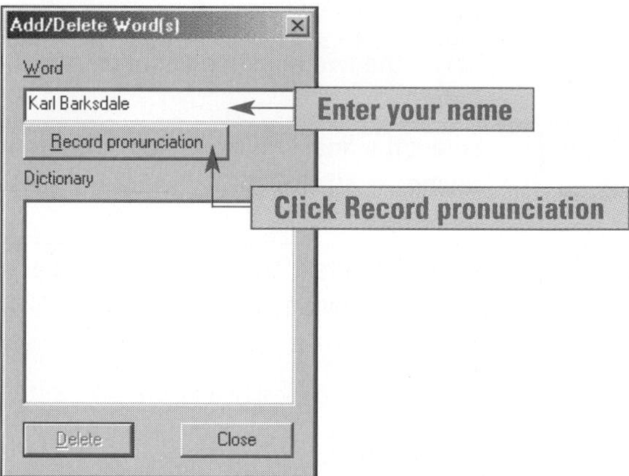

QUICK TIP

If your speech recognition software doesn't hear you properly, your name does not appear in the Dictionary. If this happens, try again. When the system has accepted your pronunciation of the word, the name appears in the Dictionary.

Step 3 Click the **Record pronunciation** button and say your name aloud.

Step 4 Your name appears in the Dictionary list. Double-click your name to hear a digitized voice repeat your name. (See Figure C-35.)

FIGURE C-35
Add/Delete Word(s) Dialog Box

CAUTION TIP

If your name doesn't appear properly when you say it, return to the Add/Delete Word(s) dialog box, select your name, then click the **Record pronunciation** button and re-record the correct pronunciation of your name.

Step 5 Close the Add/Delete Word(s) dialog box by clicking the **Close** button.

Step 6 Return to Microsoft Word, turn on your **Microphone**, switch to **Dictation** mode. Say your name several times and see if it appears correctly.

Step 7 To improve your accuracy, it's important to add troublesome words to your dictionary. Pick five words that have given you difficulty in the past. Train the software to recognize these words as explained in Steps 1 through 6. As you add and train for the pronunciation of those words, your accuracy improves bit by bit.

C.d Turning Microsoft Speech Recognition On and Off

Microsoft Office Speech Recognition isn't for everybody—at least not in its present form. It requires a powerful CPU and a lot of RAM. It also takes a quality headset. If you don't have the necessary hardware, chances are speech recognition isn't working very well for you.

Perhaps you are simply uncomfortable using speech software. You may be an expert typist with no sign of carpal tunnel syndrome or any other repetitive stress injury. Whatever your reason for choosing not to use Microsoft speech software, it is important to know how to disable the feature.

There are two ways to turn off your speech software. You can minimize the toolbar and place it aside temporarily, or you can turn it off entirely. If you decide you want to use speech recognition at a later time, you can always turn it back on again.

Turning Off Speech Recognition

Microsoft Speech Recognition allows you to minimize the Language Bar, putting it aside temporarily. Minimizing places the Language Bar in the taskbar tray in the form of the Language Bar icon. After the Language Bar has been minimized, it is then possible to turn the system off altogether. To see how this is accomplished, follow Step-by-Step C.15.

Step-by-Step C.15

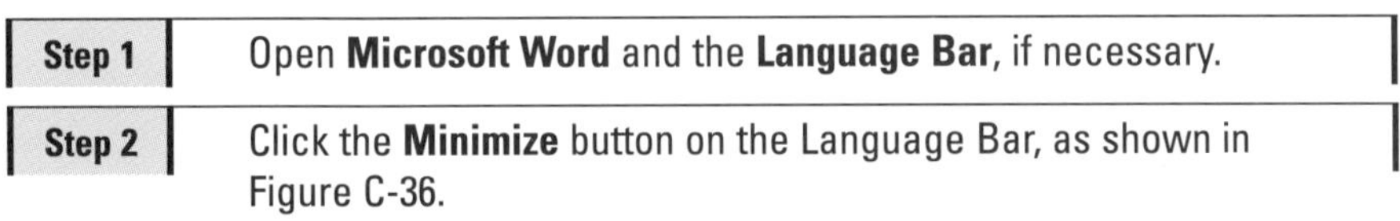

Step 1	Open **Microsoft Word** and the **Language Bar**, if necessary.
Step 2	Click the **Minimize** button on the Language Bar, as shown in Figure C-36.

FIGURE C-36
Click the Minimize Button on the Language Bar

appendix C

Step 3 When you minimize for the first time, a dialog box explains what is going to happen to your Language Bar, as shown in Figure C-37. Read this dialog box carefully, then click **OK**.

FIGURE C-37
Read This Information Carefully

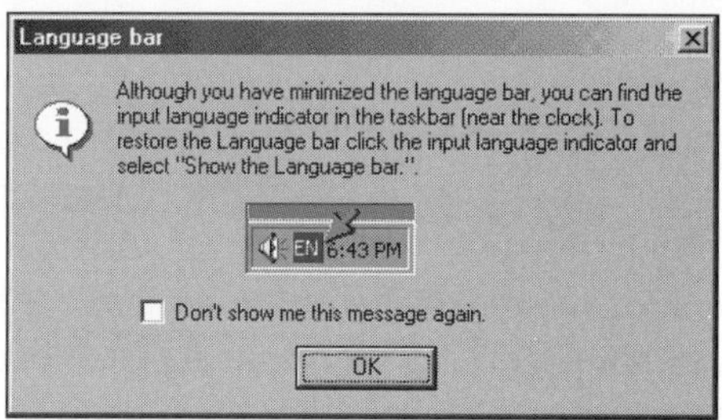

Step 4 Right-click the **Language Bar** icon in the taskbar. Several options appear, as shown in Figure C-38. Click **Close the Language Bar**.

FIGURE C-38
Right-Click the Language Bar Icon

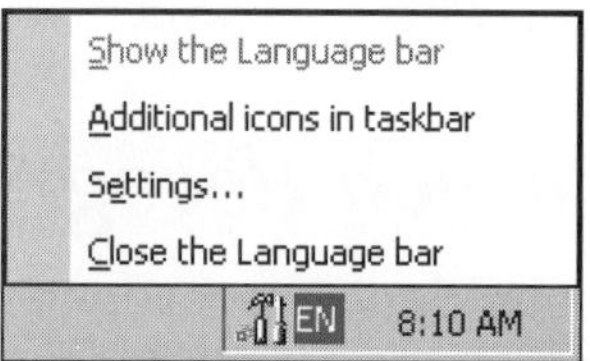

Step 5 Another dialog box opens to explain a process you can follow for restoring your speech operating system after you have turned it off. Click **OK**. The system is turned off and your language tools disappear, as shown in Figure C-39. Close Word. (*Note:* If you click **Cancel**, you return to normal and can continue using the speech recognition system by opening the Language Bar.)

FIGURE C-39
Click OK to Turn Off Speech Recognition

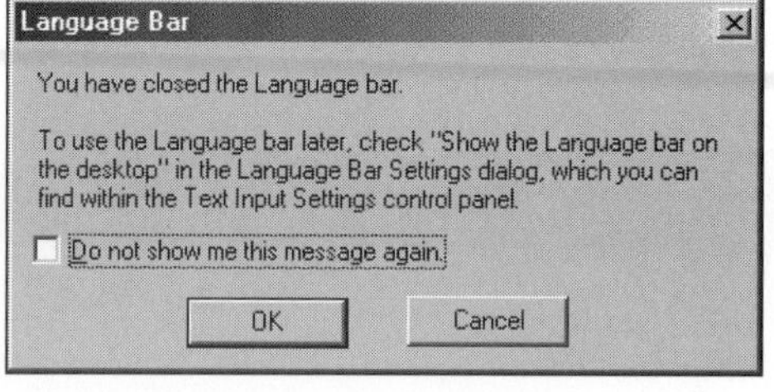

Turning On Speech Recognition

There are several ways to turn your speech recognition system back on. Follow Step-by-Step C.16.

Step-by-Step C.16

Step 1 Open **Microsoft Word** and click **Speech** on the **Tools** menu, as shown in Figure C-40. Your speech recognition software is restored and you can begin using it again.

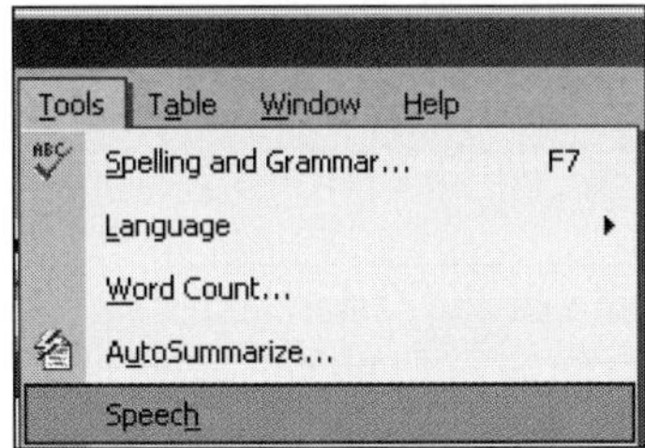

FIGURE C-40
Click Speech on the Tools Menu

If your speech software did not restore itself after Step 1, continue with Steps 2 through 5.

Step 2 Click the **Start** button, **Settings**, **Control Panel**. Then double-click the **Text Services** icon to open the Text Services dialog box, as shown in Figure C-41.

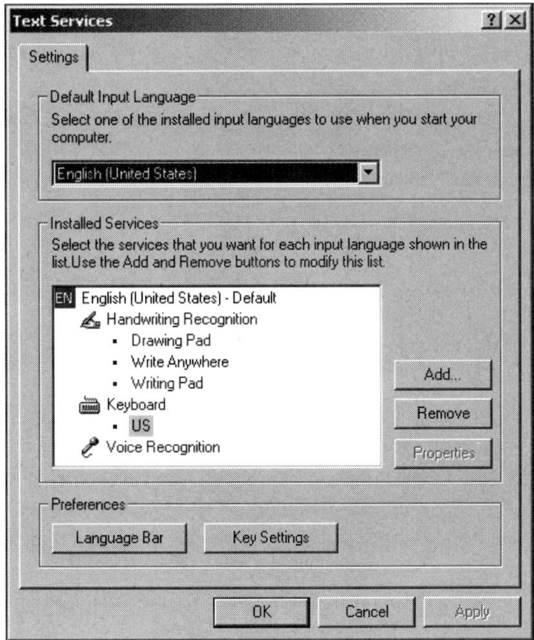

FIGURE C-41
Click Language Bar in the Text Input Settings Dialog Box

appendix C

Step 3 Click **Language Bar** in the Text Services dialog box.

Step 4 In the Language Bar Settings dialog box, click the **Show the Language bar on the desktop** check box to insert a check mark, as shown in Figure C-42.

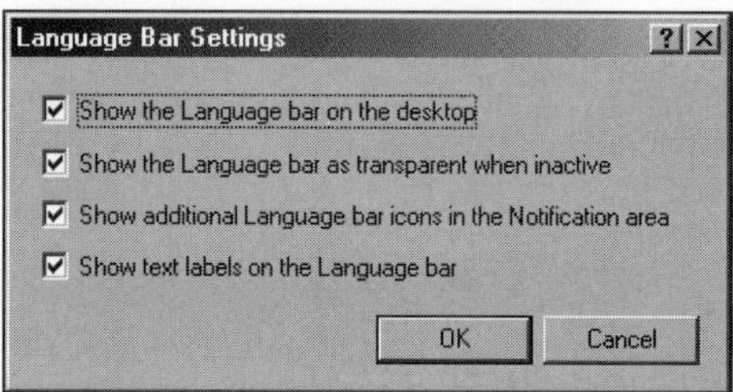

FIGURE C-42
Language Bar Settings Dialog Box

Step 5 Click **OK**, then exit and restart your computer. The speech software should be restored and you can begin speaking again. (*Note:* If the Language Bar is still missing after you launch Word, try selecting Tools, Speech one more time.)

Mastering and Using Microsoft Word 2002

APPROVED COURSEWARE

Core MOUS Objectives

Standardized Coding Number	Skill Sets and Skills Being Measured	Chapter Number	Chapter Pages	Exercise Pages	Exercises
W2002-1	***Inserting and Modifying Text***				
W2002-1-1	Insert, modify, and move text and symbols	1	WI 6, 7	WI 23–27	Skills Review 1–7, 9 Case Projects 1–8
		2	WI 34, 38	WI 50	Skills Review 5
		3	WI 59, 63, 68	WI 75–78	Skills Review 3–6, 8, 9 Case Projects 1–3, 5–8
		4 and throughout text	WI 96		
W2002-1-2	Apply and modify text formats	4 and throughout text	WI 81, 82, 83, 84, 86, 92	WI 101–104	Skills Review 1–8 Case Projects 1–8
W2002-1-3	Correct spelling and grammar usage	3	WI 55, 58	WI 74–78	Skills Review 1–3, 7, 8 Case Projects 1–3, 5-8
W2002-1-4	Apply font and text effects	4	WI 88, 90, 95	WI 102–104	Skills Review 6, 7 Case Projects 1, 2, 5
W2002-1-5	Enter and format date and time	2 and throughout text	WI 33	WI 48–53	Skills Review 1, 3, 5, 6, 7 Case Projects 1, 4–6, 8, 9
W2002-1-6	Apply character styles	4 and throughout text	WI 86	WI 101–104	Skills Review 1–5, 7, 8 Case Projects 1, 2, 4, 5, 7, 8

Standardized Coding Number	Skill Sets and Skills Being Measured	Chapter Number	Chapter Pages	Exercise Pages	Exercises
W2002-2	***Creating and Modifying Paragraphs***				
W2002-2-1	Modify paragraph formats	6 and throughout text	WI 125, 127, 129, 132	WI 151–155	Skills Review 1–8 Case Projects 1, 4, 6, 7
W2002-2-2	Set and modify tabs	5 and throughout text	WI 109, 111, 112, 113, 114	WI 118–122	Skills Review 1–8 Case Projects 1–6, 8
W2002-2-3	Apply bullet, outline, and numbering formats to paragraphs	6	WI 124, 142, 143	WI 151–155	Skills Review 1–3, 5, 7, 8 Case Project 8
W2002-2-4	Apply paragraph styles	6 and throughout text	WI 140	WI 152–155	Skills Review 4, 5 Case Project 4
W2002-3	***Formatting Documents***				
W2002-3-1	Create and modify a header and footer	6	WI 139	WI 151–154	Skills Review 1, 5, 6, 7
W2002-3-2	Apply and modify column settings	9	WI 191, 192, 193	WI 209–212	Skills Review 1, 3, 5, 6, 7 Case Projects 1, 2, 3, 7
W2002-3-3	Modify document layout and Page Setup options	2	WI 30, 32	WI 48–53	Skills Review 1, 3, 6, 7 Case Projects 1, 4–6, 8, 9
		6 and throughout text	WI 136, 137	WI 151–154	Skills Review 1–7
W2002-3-4	Create and modify tables	10	WI 214, 219, 222, 224	WI 228–233	Skills Review 1–8 Case Projects 1–8
W2002-3-5	Preview and print documents, envelopes, and labels	1	WI 10	WI 23–27	Skills Review 1–7, 9 Case Projects 1–8
		2		WI 48–53	Skills Review 1–8 Case Projects 1, 2, 4–6, 8, 9
		7	WI 157, 162	WI 169–172	Skills Review 1–8 Case Projects 1–8
		8 and throughout text	WI 174, 180	WI 186–189	Skills Review 1–8 Case Projects 1–5

Standardized Coding Number	Skill Sets and Skills Being Measured	Chapter Number	Chapter Pages	Exercise Pages	Exercises
W2002-4	***Managing Documents***				
W2002-4-1	Manage files and folders for documents	1	WI 18	WI 25	Skills Review 9
W2002-4-2	Create documents using templates	1 11 and throughout text	WI 18 WI 235	WI 23–27 WI 244–247	Skills Review 1, 3, 5, 7, 9 Case Projects 1–8 Skills Review 1–3, 5–8 Case Projects 1–8
W2002-4-3	Save documents using different names and file formats	1 and throughout text	WI 8, 17, 18	WI 23–27	Skills Review 1–7, 9 Case Projects 1–8
W2002-5	***Working with Graphics***				
W2002-5-1	Insert images and graphics	9	WI 194	WI 210, 212	Skills Review 3, 6 Case Projects 3, 5, 6, 7
W2002-5-2	Create and modify diagrams and charts	9	WI 198, 201	WI 209–212	Skills Review 2, 4, 7, 8 Case Projects 4, 8
W2002-6	***Workgroup Collaboration***				
W2002-6-1	Compare and merge documents	12	WI 254	WI 261–263	Skills Review 4, 7 Case Projects 1, 6
W2002-6-2	Insert, view, and edit comments	12	WI 253	WI 261–263	Skills Review 6 Case Project 7
W2002-6-3	Convert documents into Web pages	12	WI 255	WI 260–263	Skills Review 1, 5, 8 Case Project 4

Index

C

D

E

H

I

J

K

L

M

N

Q

R

S

U

V

W

X

Y

Z